PRIVACY AND
THE MEDIA

ASPEN SELECT SERIES

PRIVACY AND THE MEDIA

Fifth Edition

Daniel J. Solove
Eugene L. and Barbara A. Bernard Professor
of Intellectual Property and Technology Law
George Washington University Law School

Paul M. Schwartz
Jefferson E. Peyser Professor of Law
U.C. Berkeley School of Law
Faculty Director, Berkeley Center for Law & Technology

Cover image: Cocoon

To contact Customer Service, e-mail customer.service@aspenpublishing.com, call 1-800-950-5259, or mail correspondence to:

Aspen Publishing
Attn: Order Department
1 Wall Street
Burlington, MA 01803

Printed in the United States of America.

1 2 3 4 5 6 7 8 9 0

ISBN 979-8-8861-4339-3

SUSTAINABLE
FORESTRY
INITIATIVE

Certified Chain of Custody
Promoting Sustainable Forestry

www.sfiprogram.org

About Aspen Publishing

Aspen Publishing is a leading provider of educational content and digital learning solutions to law schools in the U.S. and around the world. Aspen provides best-in-class solutions for legal education through authoritative textbooks, written by renowned authors, and breakthrough products such as Connected eBooks, Connected Quizzing, and PracticePerfect.

The Aspen Casebook Series (famously known among law faculty and students as the "red and black" casebooks) encompasses hundreds of highly regarded textbooks in more than eighty disciplines, from large enrollment courses, such as Torts and Contracts, to emerging electives, such as Sustainability and the Law of Policing. Study aids such as the *Examples & Explanations* and the *Emanuel Law Outlines* series, both highly popular collections, help law students master complex subject matter.

Major products, programs, and initiatives include:

- **Connected eBooks** are enhanced digital textbooks and study aids that come with a suite of online content and learning tools designed to maximize student success. Designed in collaboration with hundreds of faculty and students, the Connected eBook is a significant leap forward in the legal education learning tools available to students.

- **Connected Quizzing** is an easy-to-use formative assessment tool that tests law students' understanding and provides timely feedback to improve learning outcomes. Delivered through CasebookConnect.com, the learning platform already used by students to access their Aspen casebooks, Connected Quizzing is simple to implement and integrates seamlessly with law school course curricula.

- **PracticePerfect** is a visually engaging, interactive study aid to explain commonly encountered legal doctrines through easy-to-understand animated videos, illustrative examples, and numerous practice questions. Developed by a team of experts, PracticePerfect is the ideal study companion for today's law students.

- The **Aspen Learning Library** enables law schools to provide their students with access to the most popular study aids on the market across all of their courses. Available through an annual subscription, the online library consists of study aids in e-book, audio, and video formats with full text search, note-taking, and highlighting capabilities.

- Aspen's **Digital Bookshelf** is an institutional-level online education bookshelf, consolidating everything students and professors need to ensure success. This program ensures that every student has access to affordable course materials from day one.

- **Leading Edge** is a community centered on thinking differently about legal education and putting those thoughts into actionable strategies. At the core of the program is the Leading Edge Conference, an annual gathering of legal education thought leaders looking to pool ideas and identify promising directions of exploration.

To my parents and grandparents—DJS

To Steffie, Clara, and Leo—PMS

SUMMARY OF CONTENTS

CONTENTS

PREFACE

    This text aims to provide a comprehensive and accessible introduction to the legal, social, and political issues involving information privacy and the media. The book contains three chapters. Chapter 1 provides a basic introduction to the issues and range of laws that address information privacy. Chapter 2 explores the definition, meaning, and value of privacy. Chapter 3 examines the complex relationship between privacy and the media.

    In this text, we focus extensively on tort law and the First Amendment. The defamation and privacy torts have an important impact on media dissemination of personal information. In addition, the First Amendment has a complex relationship to privacy. In many instances, the First Amendment and privacy prove to be mutually reinforcing. For example, privacy is often essential to freedom of assembly. But privacy can also come into conflict with the First Amendment. Protecting privacy can restrict freedom of the press and freedom of speech. It can restrict the media's ability to gather and disclose information. We explore topics such as anti-paparazzi laws, gossip and rumor on blogs and social network websites, and the use of people's names or photographs for commercial purposes, among many other issues.

    As the reference above to blogs indicates, we have incorporated material about the new media landscape in this casebook. For example, the Internet presents interesting problems for the application of defamation law and the privacy torts. Previously, it was primarily the mainstream news media that communicated libelous or private information to the public. Today, anybody can disseminate information around the world over the Internet. Rumor and gossip are increasingly spreading through blogs and social network sites. These new forms of media are giving rise to many difficult new problems, which we cover in depth.

    We have also included extensive notes and commentary, and we have integrated cases and statutes with theoretical and policy perspectives. To facilitate discussion and debate, we have included excerpts from commentators with a wide range of viewpoints. Technical terms are clearly explained. When selecting cases, we have included the leading cases as well as endeavored to provide a solid historical background and a timely and fresh perspective. We have strived to make this text a lively, thorough, and insightful introduction to the issues of privacy and the media that is accessible to those studying law, journalism, philosophy, and other fields.

A Note on the Casebook Website. We strive to keep the book up to date between editions, and we maintain a web page for the book with downloadable updates and other useful information. We invite you to visit the website:

https://informationprivacylaw.com

A Note on the Editing. We have deleted many citations and footnotes from the cases to facilitate readability. The footnotes that have been retained in the cases have been renumbered.

Daniel J. Solove
Paul M. Schwartz

November 2023

ACKNOWLEDGMENTS

Daniel J. Solove: I would like to thank Danielle Citron, Carl Coleman, Scott Forbes, Susan Freiwald, Tomás Gómez-Arostegui, Stephen Gottlieb, Marcia Hofmann, Chris Hoofnagle, John Jacobi, Orin Kerr, Raymond Ku, Peter Raven-Hansen, Joel Reidenberg, Neil Richards, Michael Risinger, Alicia Solow-Niederman, Lior Strahilevitz, Peter Swire, William Thompson, and Peter Winn for helpful comments and suggestions. Charlie Sullivan and Jake Barnes provided indispensable advice about how to bring this project to fruition. Special thanks to Richard Mixter at Aspen Publishing for his encouragement and faith in this project. Thanks as well to the other folks at Aspen who have contributed greatly to the editing and development of this book: John Devins, Christine Hannan, Carmen Reid, Jessica Barmack, John Burdeaux, and Sandra Doherty. I would like to thank my research assistants Jasmine Arooni, Allison Chesky, Peter Choy, Monica Contreras, Carly Grey, Kaitlyn Milinic, Maeve Miller, James Murphy, Poornima Ravishankar, Vladimir Semendyai, JP Schnabel, Sheerin Shahinpoor, Mingli Shi, John Spaccarotella, Tiffany Stedman, Shannon Sylvester, Lourdes Turrecha, Eli Weiss, and Kate Yannitte. I would also like to thank Dean Dayna Matthew for providing the resources I needed. And thanks to my wife Pamela Solove and son Griffin Solove, who kept me in good cheer throughout this project.

Paul M. Schwartz: For their suggestions, encouragement, and insights into information privacy law, I would like to thank Ken Bamberger, Fred Cate, Anupam Chander, Malcolm Crompton, Christopher Gulotta, Andrew Guzman, Chris Hoofnagle, Ted Janger, Jürgen Kühling, Ronald D. Lee, Lance Liebman, Viktor Mayer-Schönberger, Karl-Nikolaus Peifer, Robert Post, Joel Reidenberg, Ira Rubinstein, Indra Spieker genannt Döhmann, Lior Strahilevitz, Peter Swire, William M. Treanor, and Peter Winn.

I benefited as well from the help of my talented research assistants: Cesar Alvarez, Henry Becker, Benedikt Burger, Ryan Campbell, Sarah Chai, Kai-Dieter Classen, Leah Duranti, David Fang, Robert Fairbanks, Saabhir Gill, Sarah Haji, Kiana Harkema, Natalie Heim, Anne Hilby, Thaddeus Houston, Joey Kingerski, Jesse Koehler, Leo Koepp, Meet Mehta, Leah Mekhneche, Devon Mongeluzzi, Joseph Mornin, Emman Neukrug, Alpa Patel, Amelie Raepple, Karl Saddlemire, Brian St. John, Malvika Sinha, Laura Sullivan, Sophia Wallach, Kevin Yang, Andrea Zachrich, and Sebastian Zimmeck. Many thanks to my co-author, Daniel Solove. Many thanks as well to my mother, Nancy Schwartz, and to Laura

Schwartz and Ed Holden; David Schwartz; and Daniel Schwartz.

A profound debt is owed Spiros Simitis, a founder of European data protection law, who passed away in 2023. My interest in the subject of information privacy began in 1985 with his suggestion that I visit his office of the Hessian Data Protection Commissioner in Wiesbaden and sit in on meetings there. Through his scholarship, example, and friendship, Professor Simitis provided essential guidance to me during the many decades since that initial trip to Wiesbaden. His loss is an immeasurable one to the world of international data privacy.

In April 2020, privacy law lost another giant: my dear friend Joel Reidenberg. Professor Reidenberg's insights helped shaped our field, and his loss is deeply felt by so many of us. The privacy community benefited from his contributions, his warmth, and his friendship.

My portion of the book is dedicated to Steffie, Clara, and Leo, with my gratitude and love.

We are grateful to the following sources for their permission to reprint excerpts of their scholarship:

Anita L. Allen, *Dismantling the "Black Opticon": Privacy, Race, Equity, and Online Data-Protection Reform*, Yale Law Journal, Vol. 131 (2021-2022). The Yale Law Journal Company, Inc. Copyright © 2022.

American Law Institute. *Restatement (Second) of Torts*. Copyright © 1977 by the American Law Institute. Reproduced with permission. All rights reserved.

American Law Institute. *Restatement (Third) of the Law of Unfair Competition*. Copyright © 1995 by the American Law Institute. Reproduced with permission. All rights reserved.

Alvaro M. Bedoya, *Privacy as Civil Right*, New Mexico Law Review, Vol. 50, No. 3 (2020). University of New Mexico School of Law. Copyright © 2020.

Khiara M. Bridges, *Privacy Rights and Public Families*, Harvard Journal of Law and Gender, Vol. 34 (2011). Harvard Law School. Reprinted with permission.

Fred H. Cate, *Principles of Internet Privacy*, Connecticut Law Review, Vol. 32 (2000). University of Connecticut School of Law. Reprinted with permission.

Danielle Keats Citron, *Cyber Civil Rights*, Boston University Law Review, Vol. 89 (2009). Boston University School of Law. Reprinted with permission.

Danielle Keats Citron, *Sexual Privacy*, Yale Law Journal, Vol. 128 (2019). Yale Law School. Reprinted with permission.

Julie E. Cohen, *Examined Lives: Informational Privacy*, Stanford Law Review, Vol. 52 (2000). Stanford Law School. Reprinted with permission.

Richard A. Posner, *The Right of Privacy*, Georgia Law Review, Vol. 12 (1978). University of Georgia School of Law. Copyright © 1978.

Neil M. Richards, *The Puzzle of Brandeis, Privacy and Speech*, Vanderbilt Law Review, Vol. 63, No. 5 (2010). Vanderbilt University Law School. Reprinted with permission.

Paul M. Schwartz, *Privacy and Democracy in Cyberspace*, Vanderbilt Law Review, Vol. 52 (1999). Vanderbilt University Law School. Reprinted with permission.

Reva B. Siegel, *The Rule of Love: Wife Beating as Prerogative of Privacy*, Yale Law Journal, Vol. 105 (1996). Yale Law School. Copyright © 1996.

Spiros Simitis, *Reviewing Privacy in an Informational Society*, University of Pennsylvania Law Review, Vol. 135 (1987). University of Pennsylvania Law School. Copyright © 1987.

Daniel J. Solove, *Conceptualizing Privacy*, California Law Review, Vol. 90 (2002). University of California, Berkeley, School of Law. Copyright © 2002.

Daniel J. Solove, *The Virtues of Knowing Less: Justifying Privacy Protections Against Disclosure*, Duke Law Journal, Vol. 53 (2003). Duke University School of Law. Copyright © 2003.

PRIVACY AND THE MEDIA

CHAPTER 1

INTRODUCTION

CHAPTER OUTLINE

A. INFORMATION PRIVACY, TECHNOLOGY, AND THE LAW

We live in a world shaped by technology and fueled by information. Technological devices — such as mobile phones, video and audio recording devices, computers, and the Internet — have revolutionized our ability to capture information about the world and to communicate with each other. Information is the lifeblood of today's society. Increasingly, our everyday activities involve the transfer and recording of information. The government collects vast quantities of personal information in records pertaining to an individual's birth, marriage, divorce, property, court proceedings, motor vehicles, voting activities, criminal transgressions, professional licensing, and other activities. Private sector entities also amass gigantic databases of personal information for marketing purposes or to prepare credit histories. Wherever we go, whatever we do, we could easily leave behind a trail of data that is recorded and gathered together.

These new technologies, coupled with the increasing use of personal information by business and government, pose new challenges for the protection of privacy. This book is about the law's response to new challenges to privacy. A significant amount of law regulates information privacy in the United States and around the world. Is this law responsive to the present and future dangers to privacy? Can information privacy itself endanger other important values? What duties and responsibilities must corporations, government agencies, and other private and public sector entities have with regard to personal data? What rights do individuals have to prevent and redress invasions to their privacy? When and how should privacy rights be limited? Does the war on terrorism require less privacy and more sharing of information? How should the law respond to an age of rapid technological change? Has the meaning of privacy changed in the age of social media and powerful search engines? How does privacy change when refrigerators, automobiles, thermostats, and many other devices generate information about their users? These are some of the questions that this text will address.

This book's topic is information privacy law. Information privacy concerns the collection, use, and disclosure of personal information. Information privacy is often contrasted with "decisional privacy," which concerns the freedom to make decisions about one's body and family. Decisional privacy involves matters such as contraception, procreation, abortion, and child rearing, and is at the center of a series of Supreme Court cases often referred to as "substantive due process" or "the constitutional right to privacy." But information privacy increasingly incorporates elements of decisional privacy as the use of data both expands and limits individual autonomy.

Information privacy law is an interrelated web of tort law, federal and state constitutional law, federal and state statutory law, evidentiary privileges, property law, contract law, and criminal law. Information privacy law is relatively new, although its roots reach far back. It is developing coherence as privacy doctrines in one area are being used to inform and structure legal responses in other areas. Information privacy law raises a related set of political, policy, and philosophical questions: What is privacy? Why is privacy important? What is the impact of technology on privacy? How does privacy affect the efforts of law enforcement and national security agencies to protect the public? What is the role of the courts, the legislatures, and the law in safeguarding, or in placing limits on, privacy?

Furthermore, one might wonder: Why study information privacy law? There are a number of answers to this question. First, in today's Information Age, privacy is an issue of paramount significance for freedom, democracy, and security. One of the central issues of information privacy concerns the power of commercial and government entities over individual autonomy and decision making. Privacy also concerns the drawing of rules that may limit this autonomy and decision making by necessarily permitting commercial and government entities access to personal information. Understood broadly, information privacy plays an important role in the society we are constructing in today's Information Age.

Second, information privacy is an issue of growing public concern. Information privacy has become a priority on the legislative agenda of Congress and many state legislatures. Information privacy problems are also timely, frequently in the news, and often the subject of litigation.

Third, there are many new laws and legal developments regarding information privacy. It is a growth area in the law. Increased litigation, legislation, regulation, as well as public concern over privacy are spurring corporations in a variety of businesses to address privacy. Lawyers are drafting privacy policies, litigating privacy issues, and developing ways for dot-com companies, corporations, hospitals, insurers, and banks to conform to privacy regulations. A new position, the Chief Privacy Officer, is a mainstay at most corporations. The leading organization of these officers, the International Association of Privacy Professionals (IAPP), boasts thousands of members. Attorneys increasingly are grappling with privacy issues — either through litigation of privacy violations or through measures to comply with privacy regulations and to prevent litigation. All of these developments demand lawyers who are well-versed in the grand scheme and subtle nuances of information privacy law.

Fourth, information privacy law is an engaging and fascinating topic. The issues are controversial, complex, relevant, and current. Few areas of law are more closely intertwined with our world of rapid technological innovation. Moreover, concerns regarding information privacy play an important role in debates regarding security in post-9/11 America. The study of privacy law also helps us understand how our legal institutions respond to change and may help prepare us for other challenges ahead.

SIDIS V. F-R PUBLISHING CORP.

113 F.2d 806 (2d Cir. 1940)

[William James Sidis (1898–1944) was perhaps the most famous child prodigy of his day. According to Amy Wallace's biography of Sidis, *The Prodigy*, he was able to read the *New York Times* at the age of 18 months.[1] By the time he was three, William had learned to operate a typewriter and used it to compose a letter to Macy's to order toys. At that age, he also learned Latin "as a birthday present for his father." That year, after his father taught him the Greek alphabet, he taught himself to read Homer with the aid of a Greek primer. By the time he started elementary school, at the age of six, he could speak and read at least eight languages. At the age of five, he had already devised a method for calculating the day of the week on which any given date occurred, and when he was seven years old, he wrote a book about calendars. At that time, he had already prepared manuscripts about anatomy, astronomy, grammar, linguistics, and mathematics. At the age of eight, he created a new table of logarithms, which used a base of 12 instead of the conventional ten. From early childhood on, Sidis was also passionately interested in politics and world events. According to Wallace, Sidis was one of the few child prodigies in world history whose talents were not limited to a single field.

In 1909, Harvard University permitted Sidis to enroll in it; he was 11 years old and the youngest student in the history of Harvard. Sidis also made the front pages

---

[1] Amy Wallace, *The Prodigy* (1986).

of newspapers around the nation when on January 5, 1910, he delivered a two-hour lecture to the Harvard Mathematics Club. The *New York Times* featured Sidis on its front page of October 11, 1909, as "Harvard's Child Prodigy."[2]

Boris Sidis, William's father, was a distinguished physician, early pioneer of American psychology (and opponent of Sigmund Freud), and prolific author. In 1911, Boris published a book about his educational theories and his virulent opposition to the educational institutions of the day. At the time of the publication of this book, *Philistine and Genius*, William was 13, and in Wallace's description, "teetering on the edge of his endurance to public exposure." Although the book did not mention his son by name, it did discuss him and his accomplishments, which brought William additional publicity. Sarah Sidis, William's mother and herself a physician, had a domineering and deeply troubled relationship with her son. Neither she nor Boris did anything to shelter William from the great publicity that followed him from an early age and the tremendous stress that it created in his life.

When he graduated from Harvard at age 16, William told reporters: "I want to live the perfect life. The only way to live the perfect life is to live it in seclusion. I have always hated crowds." After graduating from college, Sidis accepted a teaching position at the Rice University in Houston. After a difficult eight months as a professor of mathematics there, William returned to Boston and enrolled in Harvard Law School in 1916. He left the law school in his last semester there without taking a degree.

From 1918 until a *New Yorker* article about him in 1937, Sidis engaged in socialist and other radical politics, published numerous newsletters, lived an active social life, addressed a monthly study group, wrote a treatise about the classification of streetcar transfers, and financed his life through a series of modest clerical jobs and sales of his patented "perpetual calendar." During this period, in 1925, Sidis also published *The Animate and the Inanimate*. In Wallace's view, this book is the first work on the subject of "black holes" in space as well as an extraordinary work in the field of cosmogony, or the study of the origins of the universe. The book did not receive a single review at the time and was ignored by academia.

Before 1937, Sidis had done an excellent job of avoiding publicity for a decade. In that year, however, a local paper, the *Boston Sunday Advertiser*, published an article about him. This was followed by the August 14, 1937, issue of the *New Yorker*, which contained a brief biographical sketch about Sidis, his life following his graduation from Harvard, and the subsequent decades during which he lived in obscurity.[3] The article was part of a regular feature of the magazine called "Where Are They Now?," which provided brief updates on the lives of famous figures of the past. The article was printed under the subtitle *April Fool*, a reference to the fact that Sidis was born on April Fool's Day. The article recounted the history of Sidis's life and his current whereabouts: "William James Sidis lives today, at the age of thirty-nine, in a hall bedroom of Boston's shabby south end." The article also contained numerous errors about Sidis's life.

---

[2] *Harvard's Child Prodigy: All Amazed at Mathematical Grasp of Youngest Matriculate, Aged 13 Years*, N.Y. Times, Oct. 10, 1909, at A1.

[3] J.L. Manley, *Where Are They Now?: April Fool!*, New Yorker 22 (Aug. 14, 1937).

A mystery still exists regarding the interview at the basis of this article. According to Wallace, Sidis's contemporary biographer, a member of the monthly study group, whom she refers to only as "John," had brought along a friend to one meeting. Several members of this group suspected that this woman, who was the daughter of a publisher at a large company, served as the basis for the *New Yorker*'s report. Yet, the mystery remains as this individual did not interview Sidis at the time of the monthly meeting. Wallace writes: "William always maintained that the entire article was a combination of imagination and old stories about him, and no strangers had gained access to his room." Another possibility is that Sidis spoke to someone without knowing that she was a reporter, which seems unlikely due to his aversion to publicity.

The *New Yorker* article described Sidis's famous childhood and then recounted his subsequent career as an insignificant clerk: "He seems to get a great and ironic enjoyment out of leading a life of wandering irresponsibility after a childhood of scrupulous regimentation." Sidis never remained at one job for too long because "his employers or fellow-workers [would] soon find out that he is the famous boy wonder, and he can't tolerate a position after that." According to Sidis: "The very sight of a mathematical formula makes me physically ill. . . . All I want to do is run an adding machine, but they won't let me alone." The article also described Sidis's dwelling, a small bedroom in a poor part of Boston and his personal activities, interests, and habits.

In his legal action against the *Boston Sunday Advertiser*, Sidis won a settlement of $375. Sidis also sued F-R Publishing Corporation, the publisher of the *New Yorker*. Among his claims were a violation of his privacy rights under §§ 50-51 of the N.Y. Civil Rights Law.]

CLARK, C.J. . . . It is not contended that any of the matter printed is untrue. Nor is the manner of the author unfriendly; Sidis today is described as having "a certain childlike charm." But the article is merciless in its dissection of intimate details of its subject's personal life, and this in company with elaborate accounts of Sidis' passion for privacy and the pitiable lengths to which he has gone in order to avoid public scrutiny. The work possesses great reader interest, for it is both amusing and instructive; but it may be fairly described as a ruthless exposure of a once public character, who has since sought and has now been deprived of the seclusion of private life.

The article of December 25, 1937, was a biographical sketch of another former child prodigy, in the course of which William James Sidis and the recent account of him were mentioned. The advertisement published in the New York World-Telegram of August 13, 1937, read: "Out Today. Harvard Prodigy. Biography of the man who astonished Harvard at age 11. Where are they now? by J.L. Manley. Page 22. The New Yorker."

The complaint contains a general allegation, repeated for all the claims, of publication by the defendant of *The New Yorker*, "a weekly magazine of wide circulation throughout the United States." Then each separate "cause" contains an allegation that the defendant publicly circulated the articles or caused them to be circulated in the particular states upon whose law that cause is assumed to be founded. Circulation of the New York World-Telegram advertisement is, however, alleged only with respect to the second "cause," for asserted violation of New York law.

Under the first "cause of action" we are asked to declare that this exposure transgresses upon plaintiff's right of privacy, as recognized in California, Georgia, Kansas, Kentucky, and Missouri. Each of these states except California grants to the individual a common law right, and California a constitutional right, to be let alone to a certain extent. The decisions have been carefully analyzed by the court below, and we need not examine them further. None of the cited rulings goes so far as to prevent a newspaper or magazine from publishing the truth about a person, however intimate, revealing, or harmful the truth may be. Nor are there any decided cases that confer such a privilege upon the press. . . .

It must be conceded that under the strict standards suggested by [Warren and Brandeis in their article, *The Right to Privacy*] plaintiff's right of privacy has been invaded. Sidis today is neither politician, public administrator, nor statesman. Even if he were, some of the personal details revealed were of the sort that Warren and Brandeis believed "all men alike are entitled to keep from popular curiosity."

But despite eminent opinion to the contrary, we are not yet disposed to afford to all of the intimate details of private life an absolute immunity from the prying of the press. Everyone will agree that at some point the public interest in obtaining information becomes dominant over the individual's desire for privacy. Warren and Brandeis were willing to lift the veil somewhat in the case of public officers. We would go further, though we are not yet prepared to say how far. At least we would permit limited scrutiny of the "private" life of any person who has achieved, or has had thrust upon him, the questionable and indefinable status of a "public figure."

William James Sidis was once a public figure. As a child prodigy, he excited both admiration and curiosity. Of him great deeds were expected. In 1910, he was a person about whom the newspapers might display a legitimate intellectual interest, in the sense meant by Warren and Brandeis, as distinguished from a trivial and unseemly curiosity. But the precise motives of the press we regard as unimportant. And even if Sidis had loathed public attention at that time, we think his uncommon achievements and personality would have made the attention permissible. Since then Sidis has cloaked himself in obscurity, but his subsequent history, containing as it did the answer to the question of whether or not he had fulfilled his early promise, was still a matter of public concern. The article in *The New Yorker* sketched the life of an unusual personality, and it possessed considerable popular news interest.

We express no comment on whether or not the newsworthiness of the matter printed will always constitute a complete defense. Revelations may be so intimate and so unwarranted in view of the victim's position as to outrage the community's notions of decency. But when focused upon public characters, truthful comments upon dress, speech, habits, and the ordinary aspects of personality will usually not transgress this line. Regrettably or not, the misfortunes and frailties of neighbors and "public figures" are subjects of considerable interest and discussion to the rest of the population. And when such are the mores of the community, it would be unwise for a court to bar their expression in the newspapers, books, and magazines of the day.

Plaintiff in his first "cause of action" charged actual malice in the publication, and now claims that an order of dismissal was improper in the face of such an allegation. We cannot agree. If plaintiff's right of privacy was not invaded by the article, the existence of actual malice in its publication would not change that result. Unless made so by statute, a truthful and therefore non-libelous statement will not become libelous when uttered maliciously. A similar rule should prevail on invasions of the right of privacy. "Personal ill-will is not an ingredient of the offence, any more than in an ordinary case of trespass to person or to property." Warren and Brandeis, supra at page 218. Nor does the malice give rise to an independent wrong based on an intentional invasion of the plaintiff's interest in mental and emotional tranquility.

If the article appearing in the issue of August 14, 1937, does not furnish grounds for action, then it is clear that the brief and incidental reference to it contained in the article of December 25, 1937, is not actionable. . . .

[The court concluded that the second cause of action under N.Y. Civil Rights Law was properly dismissed as well. The second cause of action charged invasion of the rights conferred on plaintiff by §§ 50 and 51 of the N.Y. Civil Rights Law. Section 50 states: "A person, firm or corporation that uses for advertising purposes, or for the purposes of trade, the name, portrait or picture of any living person without having first obtained the written consent of such person, or if a minor of his or her parent or guardian, is guilty of a misdemeanor." Section 51 gives the injured person an injunction remedy and damages. The court found: "Though a publisher sells a commodity, and expects to profit from the sale of his product, he is immune from the interdict of Secs. 50 and 51 so long as he confines himself to the unembroidered dissemination of facts. . . . *The New Yorker* articles limit themselves to the unvarnished, unfictionalized truth."]

NOTES & QUESTIONS

1. *Involuntary Public Figures.* After losing his privacy suit against the *New Yorker*, Sidis sued it for libel for the false information in the story. Among his charges, he claimed that a reader of the article would think that he was a reprehensible character, disloyal to his country, a loathsome and filthy person in personal habits, suffered a mental breakdown, and was a fool, who lived in misery and poverty. The *New Yorker* settled this case out of court for a small amount of money, which Wallace estimates in her biography of Sidis at between $500 and $600.

   Sidis suffered from high blood pressure, and, approximately three months after receiving the settlement from the *New Yorker*, on July 17, 1944, he died from a cerebral hemorrhage and pneumonia. He was 46 years old and had $652.81 in his bank account.

   The life of William Sidis illustrates a man profoundly disturbed by being thrust by his parents into the limelight as a child and by the media hounding him. He tried to spend his adult life fleeing from being the focus of any public attention. If he had been an involuntary public figure in the past, should this affect whether he should be able to retreat from the public eye in the future?

Does it matter that he became a public figure as a child, that is, that he did not voluntarily choose this status as an adult?

The *Sidis* case suggests the principle that once one is a public figure, one is always a public figure. Can people who were once famous ever retreat into obscurity?

2. ***Who Was J.L. Manley? What Did He Try to Convey in His Article?*** The Sidis article was written by a "J.L. Manley." In a biography of James Thurber, the famous American humorist, Burton Bernstein reveals that Thurber used Jared L. Manley as a pseudonym.[4] Under this signature, Thurber wrote 24 profiles of onetime celebrities, including the Sidis piece. All pieces were based on the research of other reporters at the *New Yorker*, including the unnamed reporter who actually interviewed Sidis.

In Thurber's own account of his time at the *New Yorker*, he faulted the *Sidis* court on one matter: "[N]owhere was there any indication of what I thought had stood out all through my story, implicit though it was — my feeling that the piece would help to curb the great American thrusting of talented children into the glare of fame or notoriety, a procedure in so many cases disastrous to the later career and happiness of the exploited youngsters."[5]

3. ***J.D. Salinger's Letters.*** In 1998, Joyce Maynard wrote an autobiography, *At Home in the World*, that describes her romance with J.D. Salinger in the 1970s. J.D. Salinger, an acclaimed author who wrote *The Catcher in the Rye*, had long ago completely retreated from public life and adopted a highly secluded existence in New Hampshire. In 1999, Maynard auctioned the letters J.D. Salinger wrote to her. She received $156,500 for the letters from the auction at Sotheby's. CNN reported at that time, "California philanthropist Peter Norton, who bought the letters, said he plans to return them to Salinger." Should Salinger have a right to privacy in the disclosure of the letters? Copyright law does create a copyright interest in unpublished letters — which prevents not only the publication of the entire contents of the letters, but a paraphrase of the letters that is too close to the actual text of the letters. *See Salinger v. Random House, Inc.*, 811 F.2d 90 (2d Cir. 1987). Should privacy law provide Salinger with the right to sue over the writing of Maynard's book?

4. ***Girls Gone Wild.*** A company markets videotapes of young college women at spring break or Mardi Gras flashing and undressing. The women, often intoxicated, reveal their nudity in public and give their permission to use the video footage on the company's videotapes, which are called "Girls Gone Wild." Later on, when sober, some of the women regret their decision to be in

---

[4] *See* Burton Bernstein, *Thurber* 261 (1975). Bernstein writes:

> For all the distractions of city life and his sleepless schedule, Thurber was getting a lot of good work done. In early 1936, he began to write (really rewrite, since some of the New Yorker's best reporters, like Eugene Kinkead, were doing the research) a number of short, retrospective Profiles. His nonfiction craft rose to a new high in these excellent pieces, which lent themselves to his human approach.

Id. Bernstein also reveals that Jared L. Manley was a name that Thurber cobbled together when writing his first piece about an old boxer based on the initials of the boxer John L. Sullivan and "Manley" based on "the manly art of self-defense."

[5] James Thurber, *My Years with Ross* (1959).

the video. Have they waived all privacy rights to their nude images on the video if they sign a consent form? Or should they be entitled to have some time to reconsider? Should they not be able to sign away these rights even when sober? Others have sued claiming that they were just filmed in public without signing a consent form. Do they have a valid privacy claim even when they exposed themselves in public?

5. *Privacy Inalienability.* Do we care whether or not Sidis knew he was talking to a reporter as opposed to a new neighbor? Can we assume that anyone who talks to a reporter has abandoned a privacy interest in the information that she shares with the journalist? More broadly, to what extent should privacy interests be tradable, waivable, or otherwise alienable?[6]

6. *Googleization.* The Internet makes the preservation and dissemination of information much easier. Information about a person can be easily discovered by "Googling" them. Google will pull up dozens, sometimes hundreds of thousands, of information fragments about a person. It is becoming increasingly difficult for people to hide their personal information, which once would fade into obscurity but is now preserved forever on the Internet. Youthful indiscretions become permanent baggage. Consider the plight of one Michael, who was briefly imprisoned as a minor. The information comes up on a Google search, and Michael finds that it is inhibiting his ability to date, since many of the women he dates inquire about his time in prison. They have obviously Googled him:

> "When you meet someone," Michael says, "you don't say, 'I had an affair one time,' or 'I was arrested for DUI once,' or 'I cheated on my taxes in 1984.' "... [W]hat Michael finds most disturbing are the sudden silences. "Instead of thinking, 'Was I curt last week?' or 'Did I insult this political party or that belief?' I have to think about what happened when I was 17."[7]

Is Sidis's claim to privacy quaint by today's standards? How do we protect privacy in a post-Google world?

B. INFORMATION PRIVACY LAW: ORIGINS AND TYPES

Information privacy law is a wide-ranging body of law, encompassing common law, constitutional law, statutory law, and international law. This section will provide a brief introduction to the various strands of information privacy law that will be covered throughout this book. It begins by looking in detail at the most important article ever written about privacy.

---

[6] Paul M. Schwartz, *Property, Privacy, and Personal Data*, 117 Harv. L. Rev. 2055, 2074 (2004).

[7] Neil Swidey, *A Nation of Voyeurs: How the Internet Search Engine Google Is Changing What We Can Find Out About Each Other and Raising Questions About Whether We Should*, Boston Globe Mag., Feb. 2, 2003, at 10.

1. COMMON LAW

(a) The Warren and Brandeis Article

The common law's development of tort remedies to protect privacy is one of the most significant chapters in the history of privacy law. In the late nineteenth century, considerable concerns about privacy captured the public's attention, ultimately resulting in the 1890 publication of Samuel Warren and Louis Brandeis's pathbreaking article, *The Right to Privacy*.[8] According to Roscoe Pound, the article did "nothing less than add a chapter to our law."[9] Harry Kalven even hailed it as the "most influential law review article of all."[10] The clearest indication of the article's ongoing vitality can be found in the Supreme Court's decision *Kyllo v. United States*, 533 U.S. 27 (2001). The Brandeis and Warren article is cited by the majority, those in concurrence, and even those in dissent.

Several developments in the late nineteenth century created a growing interest in privacy. First, the press became increasingly sensationalistic. Prior to the Civil War, wide-circulation newspapers were rare. However, the development of a new form of sensationalistic journalism, known as "yellow journalism," made newspapers wildly successful. In 1833, Benjamin Day began publishing a newspaper called *The Sun* patterned after the "penny presses" in London (so named because they sold for a penny). The *Sun* contained news of scandals, such as family squabbles, public drunkenness, and petty crimes. In about four months, the *Sun* had a circulation of 4,000, almost the same as the existing New York daily papers. Just two months later, the *Sun* was reaching 8,000 in circulation. Other penny press papers soon followed. In reporting on his travels in America, Charles Dickens observed that New York newspapers were "pulling off the roofs of private houses."[11] In his great novel of 1844, *The Life and Adventures of Martin Chuzzlewit*, he listed (imaginary) New York newspapers called *The Sewer, The Stabber, The Family Spy, The Private Listener, The Peeper, The Plunderer*, and *The Keyhole Reporter*.[12]

Between 1850 and 1890, newspaper circulation increased about 1,000 percent — from 100 papers with 800,000 readers to 900 papers with more than 8 million readers. Joseph Pulitzer and William Randolph Hearst became the leading rivals in the newspaper business, each amassing newspaper empires. Their highly sensationalistic journalism became the paradigm for yellow journalism.[13]

Second, technological developments caused great alarm for privacy. In their article, Warren and Brandeis pointed to the invention of "instantaneous photography" as a new challenge to privacy. Photography had been around for many years before Warren and Brandeis penned their article. However, the

---

[8] Samuel Warren & Louis Brandeis, *The Right to Privacy*, 4 Harv. L. Rev. 193 (1890).

[9] Quoted in Alpheus Mason, *Brandeis: A Free Man's Life* 70 (1946).

[10] Harry Kalven, Jr., *Privacy in Tort Law — Were Warren and Brandeis Wrong?*, 31 Law & Contemp. Probs. 326, 327 (1966).

[11] Charles Dickens, *American Notes* (1842).

[12] Charles Dickens, *The Life and Adventures of Martin Chuzzlewit* (1844).

[13] For more information about yellow journalism, *see generally* Gini Graham Scott, *Mind Your Own Business: The Battle for Personal Privacy* 37-38 (1995); Robert Ellis Smith, *Ben Franklin's Web Site: Privacy and Curiosity from Plymouth Rock to the Internet* 102-20 (2000).

equipment was expensive, cumbersome, and complicated to use. In 1884, the Eastman Kodak Company introduced the "snap camera," a handheld camera that was small and cheap enough for use by the general public. The snap camera allowed people to take candid photographs in public places for the first time. In the late nineteenth century, few daily newspapers even printed drawings, let alone photographs. Warren and Brandeis, however, astutely recognized the potential for the new technology of cameras to be used by the sensationalistic press.

The question of the origin of Warren and Brandeis's article has led to considerable debate. Some scholars suggest that Warren and Brandeis were strongly influenced by an article written in 1890 by E.L. Godkin, a famous social commentator in his day.[14] In the article, Godkin observed:

> . . . Privacy is a distinctly modern product, one of the luxuries of civilization, which is not only unsought for but unknown in primitive or barbarous societies. . . .
>
> The chief enemy of privacy in modern life is that interest in other people and their affairs known as curiosity, which in the days before newspapers created personal gossip. . . . [A]s long as gossip was oral, it spread, as regarded any one individual, over a very small area, and was confined to the immediate circle of his acquaintants. It did not reach, or but rarely reached, those who knew nothing of him. It did not make his name, or his walk, or his conversation familiar to strangers. . . . [G]ossip about private individuals is now printed, and makes its victim, with all his imperfections on his head, known to hundreds or thousands miles away from his place of abode. . . .[15]

Warren and Brandeis referred to Godkin's essay, and their article does bear some similarities to his work. Godkin was cynical about the possibility of a solution, expressing only the hope that attitudes would change to be more respectful of privacy. Warren and Brandeis had a different view. In their judgment, the law could and should provide protection for privacy.

Another theory suggests that incursions by journalists into the privacy of Samuel Warren inspired the article. Warren, a wealthy and powerful attorney in Boston, practiced law with Louis Brandeis, who later went on to become a U.S. Supreme Court Justice. In 1883, Samuel Warren married Mabel Bayard, the daughter of a prominent senator from Delaware, and set up house in Boston's Back Bay. The Warrens were among the Boston elite and were frequently reported on in the *Saturday Evening Gazette*, "which specialized in 'blue blood items,' " and "reported their activities in lurid detail."[16]

According to William Prosser, Warren was motivated to write the article because reporters intruded upon his daughter's wedding. However, this certainly could not have been the reason because in 1890, Warren's oldest daughter was not even ten years old![17] Another theory suggests that the impetus for writing the

[14] *See* Elbridge L. Adams, *The Right to Privacy and Its Relation to the Law of Libel*, 39 Am. L. Rev. 37 (1905); Dorothy J. Glancy, *The Invention of the Right to Privacy*, 21 Ariz. L. Rev. 1 (1979).

[15] E.L. Godkin, *The Rights of the Citizen: To His Own Reputation*, Scribner's Mag. (1890); *see also* E.L. Godkin, *The Right to Privacy*, The Nation (Dec. 25, 1890).

[16] Mason, *Brandeis, supra*, at 46.

[17] *See* James H. Barron, *Warren and Brandeis*, The Right to Privacy, 4 Harv. L. Rev. 193 (1890): *Demystifying a Landmark Citation*, 13 Suffolk L. Rev. 875 (1979).

article was Warren's displeasure about a number of stories in the *Gazette* about his dinner parties.[18]

A final account of the impetus for this famous article looks to the relationship between Samuel Warren and his younger brother Edward (Ned). According to Charles Colman, the "origin story" of *The Right to Privacy* is tied to Warren's concern about the risk posed by potential gossip and press intrusions on Ned, who was engaged in building "an increasingly visible gay life" for himself in the years leading up to the article's publication.[19] This period was also marked by increased criminal prosecutions of gay men. In Colman's reading, Warren, as "self-appointed guardian" for Ned and his other siblings, was seeking to develop a legal interest to protect Ned from "anyone with a personal, political, or financial axe to grind." The new right to privacy would also stop potential invasions on familial honor, which would also protect Warren himself, his other siblings, his wife, and their children.

Whatever inspired them to write, Warren and Brandeis published an article that profoundly shaped the development of the law of privacy.

SAMUEL D. WARREN AND LOUIS D. BRANDEIS, *THE RIGHT TO PRIVACY*
4 Harv. L. Rev. 193 (1890)

It could be done only on principles of private justice, moral fitness, and public convenience, which, when applied to a new subject, make common law without a precedent; much more when received and approved by usage.

— Willes, J., in *Millar v. Taylor,* 4 Burr. 2303, 2312

That the individual shall have full protection in person and in property is a principle as old as the common law; but it has been found necessary from time to time to define anew the exact nature and extent of such protection. Political, social, and economic changes entail the recognition of new rights, and the common law, in its eternal youth, grows to meet the demands of society. Thus, in very early times, the law gave a remedy only for physical interference with life and property, for trespasses *vi et armis*.[20] Then the "right to life" served only to protect the subject from battery in its various forms; liberty meant freedom from actual restraint; and the right to property secured to the individual his lands and his cattle. Later, there came a recognition of man's spiritual nature, of his feelings and his intellect. Gradually the scope of these legal rights broadened; and now the right to life has come to mean the right to enjoy life, — the right to be let alone; the right to liberty secures the exercise of extensive civil privileges; and the term "property" has grown to comprise every form of possession — intangible, as well as tangible.

---

[18] *See* Smith, *Ben Franklin's Web Site, supra,* at 118-19. For further discussion of the circumstances surrounding the publication of the article, see Martin Burgess Green, *The Mount Vernon Street Warrens: A Boston Story, 1860–1910* (1989); Morris L. Ernst & Alan U. Schwartz, *Privacy: The Right to Be Let Alone* 45-46 (1962); Philippa Strum, *Brandeis: Beyond Progressivism* (1993); Lewis J. Paper, *Brandeis* (1983); Irwin R. Kramer, *The Birth of Privacy Law: A Century Since Warren and Brandeis*, 39 Cath. U. L. Rev. 703 (1990); Dorothy Glancy, *The Invention of the Right to Privacy*, 21 Ariz. L. Rev. 1, 25-27 (1979); Symposium, *The Right to Privacy One Hundred Years Later*, 41 Case W. Res. L. Rev. 643-928 (1991).

[19] Charles E. Colman, *About Ned*, 129 Harv. L. F. 128 (2016).

[20] Editors' Note: Latin — By or with force and arms.

Thus, with the recognition of the legal value of sensations, the protection against actual bodily injury was extended to prohibit mere attempts to do such injury; that is, the putting another in fear of such injury. From the action of battery grew that of assault. Much later there came a qualified protection of the individual against offensive noises and odors, against dust and smoke, and excessive vibration. The law of nuisance was developed. So regard for human emotions soon extended the scope of personal immunity beyond the body of the individual. His reputation, the standing among his fellow-men, was considered, and the law of slander and libel arose. Man's family relations became a part of the legal conception of his life, and the alienation of a wife's affections was held remediable. Occasionally the law halted, — as in its refusal to recognize the intrusion by seduction upon the honor of the family. But even here the demands of society were met. A mean fiction, the action *per quod servitium amisit,*[21] was resorted to, and by allowing damages for injury to the parents' feelings, an adequate remedy was ordinarily afforded. Similar to the expansion of the right to life was the growth of the legal conception of property. From corporeal property arose the incorporeal rights issuing out of it; and then there opened the wide realm of intangible property, in the products and processes of the mind, as works of literature and art, goodwill, trade secrets, and trademarks.

This development of the law was inevitable. The intense intellectual and emotional life, and the heightening of sensations which came with the advance of civilization, made it clear to men that only a part of the pain, pleasure, and profit of life lay in physical things. Thoughts, emotions, and sensations demanded legal recognition, and the beautiful capacity for growth which characterizes the common law enabled the judges to afford the requisite protection, without the interposition of the legislature.

Recent inventions and business methods call attention to the next step which must be taken for the protection of the person, and for securing to the individual what Judge Cooley calls the right "to be let alone."[22] Instantaneous photographs and newspaper enterprise have invaded the sacred precincts of private and domestic life; and numerous mechanical devices threaten to make good the prediction that "what is whispered in the closet shall be proclaimed from the house-tops." For years there has been a feeling that the law must afford some remedy for the unauthorized circulation of portraits of private persons; and the evil of invasion of privacy by the newspapers, long keenly felt, has been but recently discussed by an able writer. The alleged facts of a somewhat notorious case brought before an inferior tribunal in New York a few months ago, directly involved the consideration of the right of circulating portraits; and the question whether our law will recognize and protect the right to privacy in this and in other respects must soon come before our courts for consideration.

Of the desirability — indeed of the necessity — of some such protection, there can, it is believed, be no doubt. The press is overstepping in every direction the obvious bounds of propriety and of decency. Gossip is no longer the resource of the idle and of the vicious, but has become a trade, which is pursued with industry as well as effrontery. To satisfy a prurient taste the details of sexual relations are

---

[21] Editors' Note: Latin — Whereby he lost the services (of his servant).

[22] Cooley on Torts, 2d ed., p. 29.

spread broadcast in the columns of the daily papers. To occupy the indolent, column upon column is filled with idle gossip, which can only be procured by intrusion upon the domestic circle. The intensity and complexity of life, attendant upon advancing civilization, have rendered necessary some retreat from the world, and man, under the refining influence of culture, has become more sensitive to publicity, so that solitude and privacy have become more essential to the individual; but modern enterprise and invention have, through invasions upon his privacy, subjected him to mental pain and distress, far greater than could be inflicted by mere bodily injury. Nor is the harm wrought by such invasions confined to the suffering of those who may be made the subjects of journalistic or other enterprise. In this, as in other branches of commerce, the supply creates the demand. Each crop of unseemly gossip, thus harvested, becomes the seed of more, and, in direct proportion to its circulation, results in a lowering of social standards and of morality. Even gossip apparently harmless, when widely and persistently circulated, is potent for evil. It both belittles and perverts. It belittles by inverting the relative importance of things, thus dwarfing the thoughts and aspirations of a people. When personal gossip attains the dignity of print, and crowds the space available for matters of real interest to the community, what wonder that the ignorant and thoughtless mistake its relative importance. Easy of comprehension, appealing to that weak side of human nature which is never wholly cast down by the misfortunes and frailties of our neighbors, no one can be surprised that it usurps the place of interest in brains capable of other things. Triviality destroys at once robustness of thought and delicacy of feeling. No enthusiasm can flourish, no generous impulse can survive under its blighting influence.

It is our purpose to consider whether the existing law affords a principle which can properly be invoked to protect the privacy of the individual; and, if it does, what the nature and extent of such protection is.

Owing to the nature of the instruments by which privacy is invaded, the injury inflicted bears a superficial resemblance to the wrongs dealt with by the law of slander and of libel, while a legal remedy for such injury seems to involve the treatment of mere wounded feelings, as a substantive cause of action. The principle on which the law of defamation rests, covers, however, a radically different class of effects from those for which attention is now asked. It deals only with damage to reputation, with the injury done to the individual in his external relations to the community, by lowering him in the estimation of his fellows. . . . In short, the wrongs and correlative rights recognized by the law of slander and libel are in their nature material rather than spiritual. That branch of the law simply extends the protection surrounding physical property to certain of the conditions necessary or helpful to worldly prosperity. On the other hand, our law recognizes no principle upon which compensation can be granted for mere injury to the feelings. . . . Injury of feelings may indeed be taken account of in ascertaining the amount of damages when attending what is recognized as a legal injury; but our system, unlike the Roman law, does not afford a remedy even for mental suffering which results from mere contumely and insult, from an intentional and unwarranted violation of the "honor" of another.

It is not however necessary, in order to sustain the view that the common law recognizes and upholds a principle applicable to cases of invasion of privacy, to invoke the analogy, which is but superficial, to injuries sustained, either by an attack upon reputation or by what the civilians called a violation of honor; for the legal doctrines relating to infractions of what is ordinarily termed the common-law right to intellectual and artistic property are, it is believed, but instances and applications of a general right to privacy, which properly understood afford a remedy for the evils under consideration.

The common law secures to each individual the right of determining, ordinarily, to what extent his thoughts, sentiments, and emotions shall be communicated to others. Under our system of government, he can never be compelled to express them (except when upon the witness-stand); and even if he has chosen to give them expression, he generally retains the power to fix the limits of the publicity which shall be given them. The existence of this right does not depend upon the particular method of expression adopted. It is immaterial whether it be by word or by signs, in painting, by sculpture, or in music. Neither does the existence of the right depend upon the nature or value of the thought or emotion, nor upon the excellence of the means of expression. The same protection is accorded to a casual letter or an entry in a diary and to the most valuable poem or essay, to a botch or daub and to a masterpiece. In every such case the individual is entitled to decide whether that which is his shall be given to the public. No other has the right to publish his productions in any form, without his consent. This right is wholly independent of the material on which, or the means by which, the thought, sentiment, or emotion is expressed. It may exist independently of any corporeal being, as in words spoken, a song sung, a drama acted. Or if expressed on any material, as in a poem in writing, the author may have parted with the paper, without forfeiting any proprietary right in the composition itself. The right is lost only when the author himself communicates his production to the public, — in other words, publishes it. It is entirely independent of the copyright laws, and their extension into the domain of art. The aim of those statutes is to secure to the author, composer, or artist the entire profits arising from publication; but the common-law protection enables him to control absolutely the act of publication, and in the exercise of his own discretion, to decide whether there shall be any publication at all. The statutory right is of no value, *unless* there is a publication; the common-law right is lost *as soon as* there is a publication.

What is the nature, the basis, of this right to prevent the publication of manuscripts or works of art? It is stated to be the enforcement of a right of property; and no difficulty arises in accepting this view, so long as we have only to deal with the reproduction of literary and artistic compositions. They certainly possess many of the attributes of ordinary property: they are transferable; they have a value; and publication or reproduction is a use by which that value is realized. But where the value of the production is found not in the right to take the profits arising from publication, but in the peace of mind or the relief afforded by the ability to prevent any publication at all, it is difficult to regard the right as one of property, in the common acceptation of that term. A man records in a letter to his son, or in his diary, that he did not dine with his wife on a certain day. No one into whose hands those papers fall could publish them to the world, even if possession of the documents had been obtained rightfully; and the prohibition would not be confined to the publication of a copy of the letter itself, or of the diary entry; the restraint extends also to a publication of the contents. What is the thing which is protected? Surely, not the intellectual act of recording the fact that the husband did not dine with his wife, but that fact itself. It is not the intellectual product, but the domestic occurrence. A man writes a dozen letters to different people. No person would be permitted to publish a list of the letters written. If the letters or the contents of the diary were protected as literary compositions, the scope of the protection afforded should be the same secured to a published writing under the copyright law. But the copyright law would not prevent an enumeration of the letters, or the publication of some of the facts contained therein. The copyright of a series of paintings or etchings would prevent a reproduction of the paintings as pictures; but it would not prevent a publication of list or even a description of them. Yet in the famous case of *Prince Albert v. Strange*, the court held that the common-law rule prohibited not merely the reproduction of the etchings which the plaintiff and Queen Victoria had made for their own pleasure, but also "the publishing (at least by printing or writing), though not by copy or resemblance, a description of them, whether more or less limited or summary, whether in the form of a catalogue or otherwise." Likewise, an unpublished collection of news possessing no element of a literary nature is protected from piracy.

That this protection cannot rest upon the right to literary or artistic property in any exact sense, appears the more clearly when the subject-matter for which protection is invoked is not even in the form of intellectual property, but has the attributes of ordinary tangible property. Suppose a man has a collection of gems or curiosities which he keeps private: it would hardly be contended that any person could publish a catalogue of them, and yet the articles enumerated are certainly not intellectual property in the legal sense, any more than a collection of stoves or of chairs.

The belief that the idea of property in its narrow sense was the basis of the protection of unpublished manuscripts led an able court to refuse, in several cases, injunctions against the publication of private letters, on the ground that "letters not possessing the attributes of literary compositions are not property entitled to protection;" and that it was "evident the plaintiff could not have considered the letters as of any value whatever as literary productions, for a letter cannot be considered of value to the author which he never would consent to have published." But those decisions have not been followed, and it may now be considered settled that the protection afforded by the common law to the author of any writing is entirely independent of its pecuniary value, its intrinsic merits, or of any intention to publish the same and, of course, also, wholly independent of the material, if any, upon which, or the mode in which, the thought or sentiment was expressed.

Although the courts have asserted that they rested their decisions on the narrow grounds of protection to property, yet there are recognitions of a more liberal doctrine. Thus in the case of *Prince Albert v. Strange*, already referred to, the opinions both of the Vice-Chancellor and of the Lord Chancellor, on appeal, show a more or less clearly defined perception of a principle broader than those which were mainly discussed, and on which they both placed their chief reliance. Vice-Chancellor Knight Bruce referred to publishing of a man that he had "written to particular persons or on particular subjects" as an instance of possibly injurious disclosures as to private matters, that the courts would in a proper case prevent; yet it is difficult to perceive how, in such a case, any right of privacy, in the narrow sense, would be drawn in question, or why, if such a publication would be restrained when it threatened to expose the victim not merely to sarcasm, but to ruin, it should not equally be enjoined, if it threatened to embitter his life. To deprive a man of the potential profits to be realized by publishing a catalogue of his gems cannot *per se* be a wrong to him. The possibility of future profits is not a right of property which the law ordinarily recognizes; it must, therefore, be an infraction of other rights which constitutes the wrongful act, and that infraction is equally wrongful, whether its results are to forestall the profits that the individual himself might secure by giving the matter a publicity obnoxious to him, or to gain an advantage at the expense of his mental pain and suffering. . . .

These considerations lead to the conclusion that the protection afforded to thoughts, sentiments, and emotions, expressed through the medium of writing or of the arts, so far as it consists in preventing publication, is merely an instance of the enforcement of the more general right of the individual to be let alone. It is like the right not [to] be assaulted or beaten, the right not [to] be imprisoned, the right not to be maliciously prosecuted, the right not to be defamed. In each of these rights, as indeed in all other rights recognized by the law, there inheres the quality of being owned or possessed — and (as that is the distinguishing attribute of property) there may be some propriety in speaking of those rights as property. But, obviously, they bear little resemblance to what is ordinarily comprehended under that term. The principle which protects personal writings and all other personal productions, not against theft and physical appropriation, but against publication in any form, is in reality not the principle of private property, but that of an inviolate personality.

If we are correct in this conclusion, the existing law affords a principle which may be invoked to protect the privacy of the individual from invasion either by the too enterprising press, the photographer, or the possessor of any other modern device for recording or reproducing scenes or sounds. . . .

It should be stated that, in some instances where protection has been afforded against wrongful publication, the jurisdiction has been asserted, not on the ground of property, or at least not wholly on that ground, but upon the ground of an alleged breach of an implied contract or of a trust or confidence. . . .

This process of implying a term in a contract, or of implying a trust (particularly where the contract is written, and where there is no established usage or custom), is nothing more nor less than a judicial declaration that public morality, private justice, and general convenience demand the recognition of such a rule, and that the publication under similar circumstances would be considered an intolerable abuse. So long as these circumstances happen to present a contract upon which such a term can be engrafted by the judicial mind, or to supply relations upon which a trust or confidence can be erected, there may be no objection to working out the desired protection through the doctrines of contract or of trust. But the court can hardly stop there. The narrower doctrine may have satisfied the demands of society at a time when the abuse to be guarded against could rarely have arisen without violating a contract or a special confidence; but now that modern devices afford abundant opportunities for the perpetration of such wrongs without any participation by the injured party, the protection granted by the law must be placed upon a broader foundation. While, for instance, the state of the photographic art was such that one's picture could seldom be taken without his consciously "sitting" for the purpose, the law of contract or of trust might afford the prudent man sufficient safeguards against the improper circulation of his portrait; but since the latest advances in photographic art have rendered it possible to take pictures surreptitiously, the doctrines of contract and of trust are inadequate to support the required protection, and the law of tort must be resorted to. The right of property in its widest sense, including all possession, including all rights and privileges, and hence embracing the right to an inviolate personality, affords alone that broad basis upon which the protection which the individual demands can be rested.

Thus, the courts, in searching for some principle upon which the publication of private letters could be enjoined, naturally came upon the ideas of a breach of confidence, and of an implied contract; but it required little consideration to discern that this doctrine could not afford all the protection required, since it would not support the court in granting a remedy against a stranger; and so the theory of property in the contents of letters was adopted. Indeed, it is difficult to conceive on what theory of the law the casual recipient of a letter, who proceeds to publish it, is guilty of a breach of contract, express or implied, or of any breach of trust, in the ordinary acceptation of that term. Suppose a letter has been addressed to him without his solicitation. He opens it, and reads. Surely, he has not made any contract; he has not accepted any trust. He cannot, by opening and reading the letter, have come under any obligation save what the law declares; and, however expressed, that obligation is simply to observe the legal right of the sender, whatever it may be, and whether it be called his right or property in the contents of the letter, or his right to privacy. . . .

We must therefore conclude that the rights, so protected, whatever their exact nature, are not rights arising from contract or from special trust, but are rights as against the world; and, as above stated, the principle which has been applied to protect these rights is in reality not the principle of private property, unless that word be used in an extended and unusual sense. The principle which protects personal writings and any other productions of the intellect of or the emotions, is the right to privacy, and the law has no new principle to formulate when it extends this protection to the personal appearance, sayings, acts, and to personal relation, domestic or otherwise.

If the invasion of privacy constitutes a legal *injuria*, the elements for demanding redress exist, since already the value of mental suffering, caused by an act wrongful in itself, is recognized as a basis for compensation.

The right of one who has remained a private individual, to prevent his public portraiture, presents the simplest case for such extension; the right to protect one's self from pen portraiture, from a discussion by the press of one's private affairs, would be a more important and far-reaching one. If casual and unimportant statements in a letter, if handiwork, however inartistic and valueless, if possessions of all sorts are protected not only against reproduction, but against description and enumeration, how much more should the acts and sayings of a man in his social and domestic relations be guarded from ruthless publicity. If you may not reproduce a woman's face photographically without her consent, how much less should be tolerated the reproduction of her face, her form, and her actions, by graphic descriptions colored to suit a gross and depraved imagination.

The right to privacy, limited as such right must necessarily be, has already found expression in the law of France.

It remains to consider what are the limitations of this right to privacy, and what remedies may be granted for the enforcement of the right. To determine in advance of experience the exact line at which the dignity and convenience of the individual must yield to the demands of the public welfare or of private justice would be a difficult task; but the more general rules are furnished by the legal analogies already developed in the law of slander and libel, and in the law of literary and artistic property.

1. The right to privacy does not prohibit any publication of matter which is of public or general interest. . . .

The design of the law must be to protect those persons with whose affairs the community has no legitimate concern, from being dragged into an undesirable and undesired publicity and to protect all persons, whatsoever; their position or station, from having matters which they may properly prefer to keep private, made public against their will. It is the unwarranted invasion of individual privacy which is reprehended, and to be, so far as possible, prevented. The distinction, however, noted in the above statement is obvious and fundamental. There are persons who may reasonably claim as a right, protection from the notoriety entailed by being made the victims of journalistic enterprise. There are others who, in varying degrees, have renounced the right to live their lives screened from public observation. Matters which men of the first class may justly contend, concern themselves alone, may in those of the second be the subject of legitimate interest to their fellow-citizens. Peculiarities of manner and person, which in the ordinary individual should be free from comment, may acquire a public importance, if found in a candidate for public office. Some further discrimination is necessary, therefore, than to class facts or deeds as public or private according to a standard to be applied to the fact or deed *per se*. To publish of a modest and retiring individual that he suffers from an impediment in his speech or that he cannot spell correctly, is an unwarranted, if not an unexampled, infringement of his rights, while to state and comment on the same characteristics found in a would-be congressman could not be regarded as beyond the pale of propriety. . . .

Any rule of liability adopted must have in it an elasticity which shall take account of the varying circumstances of each case, — a necessity which unfortunately renders such a doctrine not only more difficult of application, but also to a certain extent uncertain in its operation and easily rendered abortive. Besides, it is only the more flagrant breaches of decency and propriety that could in practice be reached, and it is not perhaps desirable even to attempt to repress everything which the nicest taste and keenest sense of the respect due to private life would condemn. . . .

2. The right to privacy does not prohibit the communication of any matter, though in its nature private, when the publication is made under circumstances which would render it a privileged communication according to the law of slander and libel.

Under this rule, the right to privacy is not invaded by any publication made in a court of justice, in legislative bodies, or the committees of those bodies; in municipal assemblies, or the committees of such assemblies, or practically by any communication made in any other public body, municipal or parochial, or in any body quasi public, like the large voluntary associations formed for almost every purpose of benevolence, business, or other general interest; and (at least in many jurisdictions) reports of any such proceedings would in some measure be accorded a like privilege. Nor would the rule prohibit any publication made by one in the discharge of some public or private duty, whether legal or moral, or in conduct of one's own affairs, in matters where his own interest is concerned.

3. The law would probably not grant any redress for the invasion of privacy by oral publication in the absence of special damage. . . .

The injury resulting from such oral communications would ordinarily be so trifling that the law might well, in the interest of free speech, disregard it altogether.

4. The right to privacy ceases upon the publication of the facts by the individual, or with his consent. . . .

5. The truth of the matter published does not afford a defence. Obviously this branch of the law should have no concern with the truth or falsehood of the matters published. It is not for injury to the individual's character that redress or prevention is sought, but for injury to the right of privacy. For the former, the law of slander and libel provides perhaps a sufficient safeguard. The latter implies the right not merely to prevent inaccurate portrayal of private life, but to prevent its being depicted at all.

6. The absence of "malice" in the publisher does not afford a defence.

Personal ill-will is not an ingredient of the offence, any more than in an ordinary case of trespass to person or to property. Such malice is never necessary to be shown in an action for libel or slander at common law, except in rebuttal of some defence, *e.g.*, that the occasion rendered the communication privileged, or, under the statutes in this State and elsewhere, that the statement complained of was true. The invasion of the privacy that is to be protected is equally complete and equally injurious, whether the motives by which the speaker or writer was actuated are, taken by themselves, culpable or not; just as the damage to character, and to some extent the tendency to provoke a breach of the peace, is equally the result of defamation without regard to the motives leading to its publication. Viewed as a wrong to the individual, this rule is the same pervading the whole law of torts, by which one is held responsible for his intentional acts, even though they are committed with no sinister intent; and viewed as a wrong to society, it is the same principle adopted in a large category of statutory offences.

The remedies for an invasion of the right of privacy are also suggested by those administered in the law of defamation, and in the law of literary and artistic property, namely: —

1. An action of tort for damages in all cases. Even in the absence of special damages, substantial compensation could be allowed for injury to feelings as in the action of slander and libel.

2. An injunction, in perhaps a very limited class of cases.

It would doubtless be desirable that the privacy of the individual should receive the added protection of the criminal law, but for this, legislation would be required. Perhaps it would be deemed proper to bring the criminal liability for such publication within narrower limits; but that the community has an interest in preventing such invasions of privacy, sufficiently strong to justify the introduction of such a remedy, cannot be doubted. Still, the protection of society must come mainly through a recognition of the rights of the individual. Each man is responsible for his own acts and omissions only. If he condones what he reprobates, with a weapon at hand equal to his defence, he is responsible for the results. If he resists, public opinion will rally to his support. Has he then such a weapon? It is believed that the common law provides him with one, forged in the slow fire of the centuries, and to-day fitly tempered to his hand. The common law has always recognized a man's house as his castle, impregnable, often, even to its own officers engaged in the execution of its command. Shall the courts thus close the front entrance to constituted authority, and open wide the back door to idle or prurient curiosity?

NOTES & QUESTIONS

1. *The Need for a New Right.* The article argued for the creation of a new right — the right to privacy. Why did the authors believe that other legal claims were inadequate? For example, why does the law of defamation or the law of contracts not provide a sufficient remedy for the harm described by the authors? Why do Warren and Brandeis reject property rights and copyright as tools to protect privacy?

2. *Deriving a Right to Privacy in the Common Law.* How do Warren and Brandeis derive a right to privacy from the common law? Under what principle do they locate this right? In a footnote in the article, Warren and Brandeis observe:

> The application of an existing principle to a new state of facts is not judicial legislation. To call it such is to assert that the existing body of law consists practically of the statutes and decided cases, and to deny that the principles (of which these cases are ordinarily said to be evidence) exist at all. It is not the application of an existing principle to new cases, but the introduction of a new principle, which is properly termed judicial legislation.
>
> But even the fact that a certain decision would involve judicial legislation should not be taken against the property of making it. This power has been commonly exercised by our judges, when applying to a new subject principles of private justice, moral fitness, and public convenience. Indeed, the elasticity of our law, its adaptability to new conditions, the capacity for growth, which has enabled it to meet the wants of an ever changing society and to apply immediate relief for every recognized wrong, have been its greatest boast. . . .

Why do they include this footnote? Do you agree with their argument?

3. *Inviolate Personality in the United States and Germany.* The authors describe privacy as not "the principle of private property but that of inviolate personality." What does that mean? James Whitman traces the idea of the personality right from Warren and Brandeis back to nineteenth-century German legal philosophy:

> . . . [N]ineteenth-century Germans often thought of "freedom" as opposed primarily to determinism. To be free was, in the first instance, not to be free from government control, nor to be free to engage in market transactions. Instead, to be free was to exercise free will, and the defining characteristic of creatures with free will was that they were unpredictably individual, creatures whom no science of mechanics or biology could ever capture in their full richness. For Germans who thought of things in this way, the purpose of

"freedom" was to allow each individual fully to realize his potential as an individual: to give full expression to his peculiar capacities and powers.[23]

Although the Warren and Brandeis article has been highly influential, their concept of a personality right has failed to gain traction in U.S. privacy law. Nonetheless, the idea of a personality right has formed the basis of modern German information privacy law. As Paul Schwartz and Karl-Nikolaus Peifer state, it is "a 'source right' that has proven a fertile source for the creation of a related series of legal rights" in Germany.[24] More specifically, they note that "the right has been used to protect honor and reputation, privacy in a spatial sense (a '*Privatsphäre*,' or a private area), individuality, and commercial uses of personality." Why do you think the concept of a "right of personality" has been unsuccessful as a legal concept for privacy in the United States?

4. ***"The Right to Be Let Alone."*** Warren and Brandeis refer to privacy as "the right to be let alone." This phrase was coined by Judge Thomas Cooley earlier in his famous treatise on torts.[25] Do Warren and Brandeis define what privacy is or elaborate upon what being "let alone" consists of? If so, what do they say privacy is? Is this a good account of what constitutes privacy?

5. ***The Scope of the Right to Privacy.*** Brandeis and Warren were careful not to describe privacy as an absolute right. They set out six limitations on the right to privacy. Consider the first limitation and the relationship between the right to privacy and the need for publication on matters of public concern. What conclusions do the authors reach about these competing claims? According to Warren and Brandeis, would the reporting that a public official engaged in illegal business practices be protected by a right to privacy? What about illicit sexual activity? Consider the holding of the *Sidis* court regarding a person who was once of public interest due to his great achievements. Do you think that Warren and Brandeis would agree with the conclusion of *Sidis*?

6. ***The Nature of the Injury Caused by Privacy Invasions.*** Warren and Brandeis argue that privacy invasions are more harmful than bodily injuries. Do you agree? Warren and Brandeis characterize the injury caused by the violation of privacy as an injury to the feelings. Do you agree? Or do you think that the injury extends beyond an injury to the feelings?

7. ***Remedies.*** Brandeis and Warren suggest two remedies for an invasion of privacy — an action in tort and injunction. These remedies are similar to those in defamation and copyright. What do the authors say about a criminal remedy?

8. ***Criticisms.*** Some have argued that the article is a defense of bourgeois values, i.e., the freedom of an elite group to avoid public scrutiny.[26] Which aspects of the article support this view? Do parts of the article suggest otherwise? Is privacy, as described in the Warren and Brandeis article, a class-based right?

---

[23] James Q. Whitman, *The Two Western Cultures of Privacy: Dignity Versus Liberty*, 113 Yale L.J. 1151, 1181 (2004).

[24] Paul M. Schwartz & Karl-Nikolaus Peifer, *Prosser's Privacy and the German Right of Personality*, 98 Cal. L. Rev. 1925, 1952 (2010).

[25] Thomas M. Cooley, *Law of Torts* 29 (2d ed. 1888).

[26] *See* Donald R. Pember, *Privacy and the Press* (1972).

9. *Did Brandeis Change His Mind?* Neil Richards argues that Brandeis's views about the importance of publicity and free speech eventually eclipsed the views he set forth in his article with Warren. According to Richards, the First Amendment views that Brandeis developed in the 1920s are "inconsistent with many aspects of the right to privacy that he called for in 1890." As a further matter, Richard contends that "to the extent [Brandeis] retained a belief in tort privacy to the end of his life, it was a narrow category subordinated to the interests of publicity and free speech." At a normative level, Richards builds on Brandeis to develop a "concept of intellectual privacy" — a more focused concept that views privacy as a paramount value when it "is relevant to the activities of thinking, reading, and discussing safeguarded by the First Amendment."[27]

(b) The Recognition of Warren and Brandeis's Privacy Torts

Warren and Brandeis's 1890 article suggested that the existing causes of action under the common law did not adequately protect privacy but that the legal concepts in the common law could be modified to achieve the task.

As early as 1903, courts and legislatures responded to the Warren and Brandeis article by creating a number of privacy torts to redress the harms that Warren and Brandeis had noted. In *Roberson v. Rochester Folding Box Co.*, 64 N.E. 442 (N.Y. 1902), the New York Court of Appeals refused to recognize a common law tort action for privacy invasions. Franklin Mills Flour displayed a lithograph of Abigail Roberson (a teenager) on 25,000 advertisement flyers without her consent. The lithograph printed her photograph with the advertising pun: "Flour of the Family." Roberson claimed that the use of her image on the flyer caused her great humiliation and resulted in illness requiring medical help. The court, however, concluded:

> . . . There is no precedent for such an action to be found in the decisions of this court. . . . Mention of such a right is not to be found in Blackstone, Kent, or any other of the great commentators upon the law; nor, so far as the learning of counsel or the courts in this case have been able to discover, does its existence seem to have been asserted prior to about the year 1890. . . .
>
> The legislative body could very well interfere and arbitrarily provide that no one should be permitted for his own selfish purpose to use the picture or the name of another for advertising purposes without his general consent. In such event no embarrassment would result to the general body of law, for the law would be applicable only to cases provided for by statute. The courts, however, being without authority to legislate, are required to decide cases upon principle, and so are necessarily embarrassed by precedents created by an extreme, and therefore unjustifiable, application of an old principle. . . . [W]hile justice in a given case may be worked out by a decision of the court according to the notions of right which govern the individual judge or body of judges comprising the court, the mischief which will finally result may be almost incalculable under our system, which makes a decision in one case a precedent for decisions in all future cases which are akin to it in the essential facts. . . .

---

[27] Neil Richards, *The Puzzle of Brandeis, Privacy, and Speech*, 63 Vand. L. Rev. 1295, 1312 (2010).

Shortly after the decision, a note in the *Yale Law Journal* criticized the *Roberson* decision because it enabled the press "to pry into and grossly display before the public matters of the most private and personal concern."[28] One of the judges in the majority defended the opinion in the *Columbia Law Review*.[29]

In 1903, the New York legislature responded to the explicit invitation in *Roberson* to legislate by creating a privacy tort action by statute. *See* N.Y. Civ. Rights Act § 51. This statute is still in use today. As you will see again later in this text, courts are frequently engaged in a dialogue with legislatures about the scope of privacy rights.

In the 1905 case *Pavesich v. New England Life Insurance Co.*, 50 S.E. 68 (Ga. 1905), Georgia became the first state to recognize a common law tort action for privacy invasions. There, a newspaper published a life insurance advertisement with a photograph of the plaintiff without the plaintiff's consent. The court held:

> . . . The right of privacy has its foundation in the instincts of nature. It is recognized intuitively, consciousness being the witness that can be called to establish its existence. Any person whose intellect is in a normal condition recognizes at once that as to each individual member of society there are matters private, and there are matters public so far as the individual is concerned. Each individual as instinctively resents any encroachment by the public upon his rights which are of a private nature as he does the withdrawal of those of his rights which are of a public nature. A right of privacy in matters purely private is therefore derived from natural law. . . .
>
> All will admit that the individual who desires to live a life of seclusion cannot be compelled against his consent, to exhibit his person in any public place, unless such exhibition is demanded by the law of the land. He may be required to come from his place of seclusion to perform public duties — to serve as a juror and to testify as a witness and the like; but, when the public duty is once performed, if he exercises his liberty to go again into seclusion, no one can deny him the right. One who desires to live a life of partial seclusion has a right to choose the times, places, and manner in which and at which he will submit himself to the public gaze. Subject to the limitation above referred to, the body of a person cannot be put on exhibition at any time or at any place without his consent. . . .
>
> It therefore follows from what has been said that a violation of the right of privacy is a direct invasion of a legal right of the individual. . . .

In 1960, Dean William Prosser wrote his famous article, *Privacy*, examining the over 300 privacy tort cases decided in the 70 years since the Warren and Brandeis article.

---

[28] *An Actionable Right to Privacy?*, 12 Yale L.J. 34 (1902).

[29] Denis O'Brien, *The Right to Privacy*, 2 Colum. L. Rev. 486 (1902).

WILLIAM PROSSER, *PRIVACY*

48 Cal. L. Rev. 383 (1960)

. . . The law of privacy comprises four distinct kinds of invasion of four different interests of the plaintiff, which are tied together by the common name, but otherwise have almost nothing in common except that each represents an interference with the right of the plaintiff, in the phrase coined by Judge Cooley, "to be let alone." Without any attempt at exact definition, these four torts may be described as follows:

1. Intrusion upon the plaintiff's seclusion or solitude, or into his private affairs.
2. Public disclosure of embarrassing private facts about the plaintiff.
3. Publicity which places the plaintiff in a false light in the public eye.
4. Appropriation, for the defendant's advantage, of the plaintiff's name or likeness. . . .

Judge Briggs has described the present state of the law of privacy as "still that of a haystack in a hurricane." Disarray there certainly is; but almost all of the confusion is due to a failure to separate and distinguish these four forms of invasion and to realize that they call for different things. . . .

Taking them in order — intrusion, disclosure, false light, and appropriation — the first and second require the invasion of something secret, secluded or private pertaining to the plaintiff; the third and fourth do not. The second and third depend upon publicity, while the first does not, nor does the fourth, although it usually involves it. The third requires falsity or fiction; the other three do not. The fourth involves a use for the defendant's advantage, which is not true of the rest. Obviously this is an area in which one must tread warily and be on the lookout for bogs. Nor is the difficulty decreased by the fact that quite often two or more of these forms of invasion may be found in the same case, and quite conceivably in all four.

There has nevertheless been a good deal of consistency in the rules that have been applied to the four disparate torts under the common name. As to any one of the four, it is agreed that the plaintiff's right is a personal one, which does not extend to the members of his family, unless, as is obviously possible, their own privacy is invaded along with his. The right is not assignable; and while the cause of action may or may not survive after his death, according to the survival rules of the particular state, there is no common law right of action for a publication concerning one who is already dead. . . .

At an early stage of its existence, the right of privacy came into head-on collision with the constitutional guaranty of freedom of the press. The result was the slow evolution of a compromise between the two. Much of the litigation over privacy has been concerned with this compromise, which has involved two closely related, special and limited privileges arising out of the rights of the press. One of these is the privilege of giving further publicity to already public figures. The other is that of giving publicity to news, and other matters of public interest. The one primarily concerns the person to whom publicity is given; the other the event, fact or other subject-matter. They are, however, obviously only different phases of the same thing.

NOTES & QUESTIONS

1. ***The Restatement of Torts.*** Prosser's analytical framework imposed order and clarity on the jumbled line of cases that followed the Warren and Brandeis article. The Restatement of Torts recognizes the four torts Prosser described in his article. These torts are known collectively as "invasion of privacy." The torts are: (1) intrusion upon seclusion, (2) public disclosure of private facts, (3) false light, and (4) appropriation.

2. ***The Interests Protected by the Privacy Torts.*** In response to Prosser's assertion that the privacy torts have almost "nothing in common," Edward Bloustein replied that "what provoked Warren and Brandeis to write their article was a fear that a rampant press feeding on the stuff of private life would destroy individual dignity and integrity and emasculate individual freedom and independence." This underlying principle is a protection of "human dignity" and "personality."[30]

   In contrast to Bloustein, Robert Post contends that the privacy torts do "not simply uphold the interests of individuals against the demands of the community, but instead safeguard[ ] rules of civility that in some significant measure constitute both individuals and community." Post argues that the torts establish boundaries between people, which when violated create strife. The privacy torts promote "forms of respect [for other people] by which we maintain a community."[31]

3. ***Prosser's Privacy at 50.*** In 2010, the *California Law Review* held a symposium at Berkeley Law School to celebrate the fiftieth anniversary of the publication of Prosser's *Privacy*. The verdict on the momentous article is mixed. Lior Strahilevitz advocates abandoning the Prosser categories and replacing them with a unitary tort for invasion of privacy. The key under the recast privacy tort would simply be whether "the gravity of the harm to the plaintiff's privacy interest [is] outweighed by a paramount public policy interest."[32]

   Along similar negative lines, Neil Richards and Daniel Solove concluded that Prosser's view of the privacy tort has been "rigid and ossifying." Dean Prosser "stunted [privacy law's] development in ways that have limited its ability to adapt to the problems of the Information Age." The authors conclude that tort law should look beyond the narrow categories Prosser proposed in order for it to "regain the creative spirit it once possessed." One way for tort law to do so, in their view, would be to adopt the English approach to the tort of confidentiality.[33]

---

[30] Edward J. Bloustein, *Privacy as an Aspect of Human Dignity: An Answer to Dean Prosser*, 39 N.Y.U. L. Rev. 962, 974, 1000-01 (1964).

[31] Robert C. Post, *The Social Foundations of Privacy: Community and Self in the Common Law Tort*, 77 Cal. L. Rev. 957 (1989).

[32] Lior Strahilevitz, *Reunifying Privacy Law*, 98 Cal. L. Rev. 2007 (2010).

[33] Neil Richards & Daniel Solove, *Prosser's Privacy Law: A Mixed Legacy*, 98 Cal. L. Rev. 1887, 1924 (2010).

In contrast, Paul Schwartz and Karl-Nikolaus Peifer praised Prosser: "Prosser pragmatically assessed the kind and amount of privacy that the American legal system was willing to accommodate." In their summary, "Prosser's contribution generated useful doctrinal categories where previously had been unclassified cases and a lingering air of skepticism towards the tort."[34]

Would it be useful to extend the four privacy torts as Richards and Solove propose? Or would a better approach be to replace Prosser's four torts with pure balancing as Strahilevitz advocates? Or do Prosser's categories adequately capture the various privacy interests that should be addressed by tort law?

LAKE V. WAL-MART STORES, INC.

582 N.W.2d 231 (Minn. 1998)

BLATZ, C.J. . . . Elli Lake and Melissa Weber appeal from a dismissal of their complaint for failure to state a claim upon which relief may be granted. The district court and court of appeals held that Lake and Weber's complaint alleging intrusion upon seclusion, appropriation, publication of private facts, and false light publicity could not proceed because Minnesota does not recognize a common law tort action for invasion of privacy. We reverse as to the claims of intrusion upon seclusion, appropriation, and publication of private facts, but affirm as to false light publicity.

Nineteen-year-old Elli Lake and 20-year-old Melissa Weber vacationed in Mexico in March 1995 with Weber's sister. During the vacation, Weber's sister took a photograph of Lake and Weber naked in the shower together. After their vacation, Lake and Weber brought five rolls of film to the Dilworth, Minnesota Wal-Mart store and photo lab. When they received their developed photographs along with the negatives, an enclosed written notice stated that one or more of the photographs had not been printed because of their "nature."

In July 1995, an acquaintance of Lake and Weber alluded to the photograph and questioned their sexual orientation. Again, in December 1995, another friend told Lake and Weber that a Wal-Mart employee had shown her a copy of the photograph. By February 1996, Lake was informed that one or more copies of the photograph were circulating in the community.

Lake and Weber filed a complaint against Wal-Mart Stores, Inc. and one or more as-yet unidentified Wal-Mart employees on February 23, 1996, alleging the four traditional invasion of privacy torts — intrusion upon seclusion, appropriation, publication of private facts, and false light publicity. . . . The district court granted Wal-Mart's motion to dismiss, explaining that Minnesota has not recognized any of the four invasion of privacy torts. The court of appeals affirmed.

Whether Minnesota should recognize any or all of the invasion of privacy causes of action is a question of first impression in Minnesota. . . .

This court has the power to recognize and abolish common law doctrines. The common law is not composed of firmly fixed rules. Rather, as we have long recognized, the common law:

---

[34] Paul M. Schwartz & Karl-Nikolaus Peifer, *Prosser's Privacy and the German Right of Personality*, 98 Cal. L. Rev. 1925, 1982 (2010).

is the embodiment of broad and comprehensive unwritten principles, inspired by natural reason, an innate sense of justice, adopted by common consent for the regulation and government of the affairs of men. It is the growth of ages, and an examination of many of its principles, as enunciated and discussed in the books, discloses a constant improvement and development in keeping with advancing civilization and new conditions of society. Its guiding star has always been the rule of right and wrong, and in this country its principles demonstrate that there is in fact, as well as in theory, a remedy for all wrongs.

As society changes over time, the common law must also evolve:

It must be remembered that the common law is the result of growth, and that its development has been determined by the social needs of the community which it governs. It is the resultant of conflicting social forces, and those forces which are for the time dominant leave their impress upon the law. It is of judicial origin, and seeks to establish doctrines and rules for the determination, protection, and enforcement of legal rights. Manifestly it must change as society changes and new rights are recognized. To be an efficient instrument, and not a mere abstraction, it must gradually adapt itself to changed conditions.

To determine the common law, we look to other states as well as to England.

The tort of invasion of privacy is rooted in a common law right to privacy first described in an 1890 law review article by Samuel Warren and Louis Brandeis. The article posited that the common law has always protected an individual's person and property, with the extent and nature of that protection changing over time. The fundamental right to privacy is both reflected in those protections and grows out of them:

Thus, in the very early times, the law gave a remedy only for physical interference with life and property, for trespass vi et armis. Then the "right to life" served only to protect the subject from battery in its various forms; liberty meant freedom from actual restraint; and the right to property secured to the individual his lands and his cattle. Later, there came a recognition of a man's spiritual nature, of his feelings and his intellect. Gradually the scope of these legal rights broadened; and now the right to life has come to mean the right to enjoy life, — the right to be let alone; the right to liberty secures the exercise of extensive civil privileges; and the term "property" has grown to comprise every form of possession — intangible, as well as tangible.

Although no English cases explicitly articulated a "right to privacy," several cases decided under theories of property, contract, or breach of confidence also included invasion of privacy as a basis for protecting personal violations. The article encouraged recognition of the common law right to privacy, as the strength of our legal system lies in its elasticity, adaptability, capacity for growth, and ability "to meet the wants of an ever changing society and to apply immediate relief for every recognized wrong.". . .

Today, the vast majority of jurisdictions now recognize some form of the right to privacy. Only Minnesota, North Dakota, and Wyoming have not yet recognized any of the four privacy torts. Although New York and Nebraska courts have declined to recognize a common law basis for the right to privacy and instead provide statutory protection, we reject the proposition that only the legislature may establish new causes of action. The right to privacy is inherent in the English protections of individual property and contract rights and the "right to be let alone" is recognized as part of the common law across this country. Thus, it is within the province of the judiciary to establish privacy torts in this jurisdiction.

Today we join the majority of jurisdictions and recognize the tort of invasion of privacy. The right to privacy is an integral part of our humanity; one has a public persona, exposed and active, and a private persona, guarded and preserved. The heart of our liberty is choosing which parts of our lives shall become public and which parts we shall hold close. . . .

We decline to recognize the tort of false light publicity at this time. We are concerned that claims under false light are similar to claims of defamation, and to the extent that false light is more expansive than defamation, tension between this tort and the First Amendment is increased.

False light is the most widely criticized of the four privacy torts and has been rejected by several jurisdictions. . . .

Thus we recognize a right to privacy present in the common law of Minnesota, including causes of action in tort for intrusion upon seclusion, appropriation, and publication of private facts, but we decline to recognize the tort of false light publicity. . . .

TOMLJANOVICH, J. dissenting. I would not recognize a cause of action for intrusion upon seclusion, appropriation or publication of private facts. . . .

An action for an invasion of the right to privacy is not rooted in the Constitution. "[T]he Fourth Amendment cannot be translated into a general constitutional 'right to privacy.' " *Katz v. United States*, 389 U.S. 347, 350 (1967). Those privacy rights that have their origin in the Constitution are much more fundamental rights of privacy — marriage and reproduction. *See Griswold v. Connecticut*, 381 U.S. 479, 485 (1965) (penumbral rights of privacy and repose protect notions of privacy surrounding the marriage relationship and reproduction).

We have become a much more litigious society since 1975 when we acknowledged that we have never recognized a cause of action for invasion of privacy. We should be even more reluctant now to recognize a new tort.

In the absence of a constitutional basis, I would leave to the legislature the decision to create a new tort for invasion of privacy.

NOTES & QUESTIONS

1. *Other Remedies?* If the Minnesota Supreme Court had rejected the privacy tort, what other legal remedies might be available to Elli Lake?
2. *Postscript.* What happened in *Lake* after the Minnesota Supreme Court's decision? In response to a query from the casebook authors, the lead attorney for the *Lake* plaintiff, Keith L. Miller of Miller, Norman & Associates, Ltd., explained that his client lost at the trial that followed the remand. He writes: "The jury found that an invasion of Ms. Lake's privacy had occurred, but that it did not happen 'in the course and scope' of a Wal-Mart worker's employment." In other words, tort notions of agency were found to apply, and a privacy tort violation could be attributed to Wal-Mart only if the employee had carried out the tort in the course and scope of employment. Miller added:

"Our proof was problematic because, expectedly, no employee could specifically be identified as the culprit. It was all circumstantial." Finally, he summarized his experience litigating this case: "Gratifying? Certainly. Remunerative? Not so much."

3. ***Legislatures vs. Courts.*** The dissent in *Lake* contends, in a similar way as *Roberson*, that it should be the legislature, not the courts, that recognizes new tort actions to protect privacy. In New York, the statute passed in response to *Roberson* remains the state's source for privacy tort remedies. Like New York, some states have recognized the privacy torts legislatively; other states, like Georgia in *Pavesich* and Minnesota in *Lake*, have recognized them judicially. Which means of recognizing the torts do you believe to be most justifiable? Why? Does the legislature have expertise that courts lack? Are courts more or less sensitive to civil rights issues, such as privacy?

(c) Privacy Protection in Tort Law

The Privacy Torts. Prosser's classification of these torts survives to this day. The Restatement (Second) of Torts recognizes four privacy torts:

(1) *Public Disclosure of Private Facts.* This tort creates a cause of action for one who publicly discloses a private matter that is "highly offensive to a reasonable person" and "is not of legitimate concern to the public." Restatement (Second) of Torts § 652D (1977).

(2) *Intrusion upon Seclusion.* This tort provides a remedy when one intrudes "upon the solitude or seclusion of another or his private affairs or concerns" if the intrusion is "highly offensive to a reasonable person." Restatement (Second) of Torts § 652B (1977).

(3) *False Light.* This tort creates a cause of action when one publicly discloses a matter that places a person "in a false light" that is "highly offensive to a reasonable person." Restatement (Second) of Torts § 652E (1977).

(4) *Appropriation.* Under this tort, a plaintiff has a remedy against one "who appropriates to his own use or benefit the name or likeness" of the plaintiff. Restatement (Second) of Torts § 652C (1977).

Today, most states recognize some or all of these torts.

Breach of Confidentiality. The tort of breach of confidentiality provides a remedy when a professional (i.e., doctor, lawyer, banker) divulges a patient's or client's confidential information.

Defamation. The law of defamation existed long before Warren and Brandeis's article. Defamation law, consisting of the torts of libel and slander, creates liability when one makes a false statement about a person that harms the person's reputation. The Supreme Court has held that the First Amendment places certain limits on defamation law.

Infliction of Emotional Distress. The tort of intentional infliction of emotional distress can also serve as a remedy for certain privacy invasions. This tort provides a remedy when one "by extreme and outrageous conduct intentionally or recklessly causes severe emotional distress to another." Restatement (Second) of Torts § 46 (1977). Since privacy invasions can often result in severe emotional distress, this tort may provide a remedy. However, it is limited by the requirement of "extreme and outrageous conduct."

(d) Privacy Protection in Evidence Law

The law of evidence has long recognized privacy as an important goal that can override the truth-seeking function of the trial. Under the common law, certain communications are privileged, and hence cannot be inquired into during a legal proceeding. The law of evidence has recognized the importance of protecting the privacy of communications between attorney and client, priest and penitent, husband and wife, physician and patient, and psychotherapist and patient.

(e) Privacy Protection via Property Rights

Property Rights. Although there are few property laws specifically governing privacy, these laws often implicate privacy. The appropriation tort is akin to a property right, and some commentators suggest that personal information should be viewed as a form of property.[35] If personal information is understood as a form of property, the tort of conversion might apply to those who collect and use a person's private data. Recall, however, that Warren and Brandeis rejected property as an adequate protection for privacy. What kind of market structures might be needed if personal data is to be traded or sold?

Trespass. The law of trespass, which provides tort remedies and criminal penalties for the unauthorized entry onto another's land, can protect privacy. There is some overlap between the torts of intrusion and trespass, as many forms of intrusion involve a trespass as well.

(f) Privacy Protection in Contract Law

Sometimes specific contractual provisions protect against the collection, use, or disclosure of personal information. In certain contexts, courts have entertained actions for breach of implied contract or tort actions based on implicit duties once certain relationships are established, such as physician-patient relationships, which have been analogized to fiduciary relationships. Privacy policies as well as terms of service containing privacy provisions can sometimes be analogized to a contract.

Contract can also function as a way of sidestepping state and federal privacy laws. Many employers make employees consent to drug testing as well as e-mail and workplace surveillance in their employment contracts.

---

[35] *See, e.g.,* Alan Westin, *Privacy and Freedom* 324 (1967); *see also* Richard S. Murphy, *Property Rights in Personal Information: An Economic Defense of Privacy*, 84 Geo. L.J. 2381 (1996); Richard A. Posner, *The Economics of Justice* (1981); Lawrence Lessig, *Code and Other Laws of Cyberspace* 154-62 (1999); Paul M. Schwartz, *Property, Privacy, and Personal Data*, 117 Harv. L. Rev. 2055 (2004).

(g) Privacy Protection in Criminal Law

Warren and Brandeis noted that under certain circumstances, criminal law would be appropriate to protect privacy. The criminal law protects bodily invasions, such as assault, battery, and rape. The privacy of one's home is also protected by criminal sanctions for trespass. Stalking and harassing can give rise to criminal culpability. The crime of blackmail prohibits coercing an individual by threatening to expose her personal secrets. Many of the statutes protecting privacy also contain criminal penalties, such as the statutes pertaining to wiretapping and identity theft.

2. CONSTITUTIONAL LAW

Federal Constitutional Law. Although the U.S. Constitution does not specifically mention privacy, it has a number of provisions that protect privacy, and it has been interpreted as providing a right to privacy. In some instances the First Amendment serves to safeguard privacy. For example, the First Amendment protects the right to speak anonymously. *See McIntyre v. Ohio Election Comm'n*, 514 U.S. 334 (1995). The First Amendment's Freedom of Association Clause protects individuals from being compelled to disclose the groups to which they belong or contribute. Under the First Amendment "Congress shall make no law . . . abridging . . . the right of the people peaceably to assemble. . . ." For example, the Court has struck down the compulsory disclosure of the names and addresses of an organization's members, *see NAACP v. Alabama*, 357 U.S. 449 (1958), as well as a law requiring public teachers to list all organizations to which they belong or contribute. *See Shelton v. Tucker*, 364 U.S. 479 (1960).

The Third Amendment protects the privacy of the home by preventing the government from requiring soldiers to reside in people's homes: "No Soldier shall, in time of peace be quartered in any house, without the consent of the Owner, nor in time of war, but in a manner to be prescribed by law."

The Fourth Amendment provides that people have the right "to be secure in their persons, houses, papers, and effects, against unreasonable searches and seizures. . . ." Almost 40 years after writing *The Right to Privacy*, Brandeis, then a Supreme Court Justice, wrote a dissent that has had a significant influence on Fourth Amendment law. The case was *Olmstead v. United States*, 277 U.S. 438 (1928), where the Court held that wiretapping was not an invasion of privacy under the Fourth Amendment because it was not a physical trespass into the home. Justice Brandeis dissented, contending that the central interest protected by the Fourth Amendment was not property but the "right to be let alone":

> The protection guaranteed by the amendments is much broader in scope. The makers of our Constitution undertook to secure conditions favorable to the pursuit of happiness. They recognized the significance of man's spiritual nature, of his feelings and of his intellect. They knew that only a part of the pain, pleasure and satisfactions of life are to be found in material things. They sought to protect Americans in their beliefs, their thoughts, their emotions and their sensations. They conferred, as against the government, the right to be let alone — the most comprehensive of rights and the right most valued by civilized men. To protect that right, every unjustifiable intrusion by the government upon the privacy of the

individual, whatever the means employed, must be deemed a violation of the Fourth Amendment.

Brandeis's dissent demonstrated that the "right to be let alone" did not merely have common law roots (as he had argued in *The Right to Privacy*) but also had constitutional roots as well in the Fourth Amendment.

Modern Fourth Amendment law incorporates much of Brandeis's view. In *Katz v. United States*, 389 U.S. 347 (1967), the Court held that the Fourth Amendment "protects people, not places" and said that the police must obtain a warrant when a search takes place in a public pay phone on a public street. The Court currently determines a person's right to privacy by the "reasonable expectations of privacy" test, a standard articulated in Justice Harlan's concurrence to *Katz*. First, a person must "have exhibited an actual (subjective) expectation of privacy" and, second, "the expectation [must] be one that society is prepared to recognize as 'reasonable.'"

The Fifth Amendment guarantees that: "No person . . . shall be compelled in any criminal case to be a witness against himself. . . ." This right, commonly referred to as the "privilege against self-incrimination," protects privacy by restricting the ability of the government to force individuals to divulge certain information about themselves.

In the landmark 1965 case *Griswold v. Connecticut*, 318 U.S. 479 (1965), the Court declared that an individual has a constitutional right to privacy. The Court located this right within the "penumbras" or "zones" of freedom created by an expansive interpretation of the Bill of Rights. Subsequently, the Court has handed down a line of cases protecting certain fundamental life choices such as abortion and aspects of one's intimate sexual life.

In *Whalen v. Roe*, 429 U.S. 589 (1977), the Court extended its substantive due process privacy protection to information privacy, holding that the "zone of privacy" protected by the Constitution encompasses the "individual interest in avoiding disclosure of personal matters." This offshoot of the right to privacy has become known as the "constitutional right to information privacy."

State Constitutional Law. A number of states have directly provided for the protection of privacy in their constitutions. For example, the Alaska Constitution provides: "The right of the people to privacy is recognized and shall not be infringed." Alaska Const. art. I, § 22. According to the California Constitution: "All people are by their nature free and independent and have inalienable rights. Among these are enjoying and defending life and liberty, acquiring, possessing, and protecting property, and pursuing and obtaining safety, happiness, and privacy." Cal. Const. art. I, § 1. Unlike most state constitutional provisions, the California constitutional right to privacy applies not only to state actors but also to private parties. *See, e.g., Hill v. NCAA*, 865 P.2d 638 (Cal. 1994). The Florida Constitution provides: "Every natural person has the right to be let alone and free from governmental intrusion into his private life except as otherwise provided herein." Fla. Const. art. I, § 23.[36]

---

[36] For more examples, see Ariz. Const. art. II, § 8; Mont. Const. art. II, § 10; Haw. Const. art. I, § 6; Ill. Const. art. I, §§ 6, 12; La. Const. art. I, § 5; S.C. Const. art. I, § 10; Wash. Const. art. I, § 7. For a further discussion of state constitutional protections of privacy, see Timothy O. Lenz, *"Rights*

3. STATUTORY LAW

Federal Statutory Law. From the mid-1960s to the mid-1970s, privacy emerged as a central political and social concern. In tune with the heightened attention to privacy, philosophers, legal scholars, and others turned their focus on privacy, raising public awareness about the growing threats to privacy from technology.[37]

In the mid-1960s, electronic eavesdropping erupted into a substantial public issue, spawning numerous television news documentaries as well as receiving significant attention in major newspapers. A proposal for a National Data Center in 1965 triggered public protest and congressional hearings. At this time, the computer was a new and unexplored technological tool that raised risks of unprecedented data collection about individuals, with potentially devastating effects on privacy. Indeed, toward the end of the 1960s, the issue of the collection of personal information in databases had become one of the defining social issues of American society.

During this time the Supreme Court announced landmark decisions regarding the right to privacy, including *Griswold v. Connecticut* in 1965 and *Roe v. Wade* in 1973, which were landmark decisions regarding the right to decisional/reproductive privacy and autonomy. The famous reasonable expectations of privacy test in Fourth Amendment jurisprudence emerged in 1967 with *Katz v. United States.*

Due to growing fears about the ability of computers to store and search personal information, Congress devoted increasing attention to the issue of privacy. As Priscilla Regan observes:

> In 1965, a new problem was placed on the congressional agenda by subcommittee chairs in both the House and the Senate. The problem was defined as the invasion of privacy by computers and evoked images of *1984*, the "Computerized Man," and a dossier society. Press interest was high, public concern was generated and resulted in numerous letters being sent to members of Congress, and almost thirty days of congressional hearings were held in the late 1960s and early 1970s.[38]

In 1973, in a highly influential report, the U.S. Department of Health, Education, and Welfare (HEW) undertook an extensive review of data processing in the United States. Among many recommendations, the HEW report proposed that a Code of Fair Information Practices be established. The Fair Information Practices consist of a number of basic information privacy principles that allocate rights and responsibilities in the collection and use of personal information:

Talk" About Privacy in State Courts, 60 Alb. L. Rev. 1613 (1997); Mark Silverstein, Note, *Privacy Rights in State Constitutions: Models for Illinois?*, 1989 U. Ill. L. Rev. 215.

[37] *See, e.g.,* Vance Packard, *The Naked Society* (1964); Myron Brenton, *The Privacy Invaders* (1964); Alan Westin, *Privacy and Freedom* (1967); Arthur Miller, *The Assault on Privacy* (1971); *Nomos XII: Privacy* (J. Ronald Pennock & J.W. Chapman eds., 1971); Alan Westin & Michael A. Baker, *Databanks in a Free Society: Computers, Record-Keeping and Privacy* (1972); Aryeh Neier, *The Secret Files They Keep on You* (1975); Kenneth L. Karst, *"The Files": Legal Controls over the Accuracy and Accessibility of Stored Personal Data*, 31 Law & Contemp. Probs. 342 (1966); Symposium, *Computers, Data Banks, and Individual Privacy*, 53 Minn. L. Rev. 211-45 (1968); Symposium, *Privacy*, 31 Law & Contemp. Probs. 251-435 (1966).

[38] Priscilla M. Regan, *Legislating Privacy: Technology, Social Values, and Public Policy* 82 (1995).

- There must be no personal-data record-keeping systems whose very existence is secret.

- There must be a way for an individual to find out what information about him is in a record and how it is used.

- There must be a way for an individual to prevent information about him obtained for one purpose from being used or made available for other purposes without his consent.

- There must be a way for an individual to correct or amend a record of identifiable information about him.

- Any organization creating, maintaining, using, or disseminating records of identifiable personal data must ensure the reliability of the data for their intended use and must take reasonable precautions to prevent misuse of the data.[39]

As Marc Rotenberg observes, the Fair Information Practices have "played a significant role in framing privacy laws in the United States."[40]

Beginning in the 1970s, Congress has passed a number of laws protecting privacy in various sectors of the information economy:

- Fair Credit Reporting Act of 1970, Pub. L. No. 90-32, 15 U.S.C. §§ 1681 et seq. — provides citizens with rights regarding the use and disclosure of their personal information by credit reporting agencies.

- Privacy Act of 1974, Pub. L. No. 93-579, 5 U.S.C. § 552a — provides individuals with a number of rights concerning their personal information maintained in government record systems, such as the right to see one's records and to ensure that the information in them is accurate.

- Family Educational Rights and Privacy Act of 1974, Pub. L. No. 93-380, 20 U.S.C. §§ 1221 note, 1232g — protects the privacy of school records.

- Right to Financial Privacy Act of 1978, Pub. L. No. 95-630, 12 U.S.C. §§ 3401–3422 — requires a subpoena or search warrant for law enforcement officials to obtain financial records.

- Foreign Intelligence Surveillance Act of 1978, Pub. L. No. 95-511, 15 U.S.C. §§ 1801-1811 — regulates foreign intelligence gathering within the U.S.

- Privacy Protection Act of 1980, Pub. L. No. 96-440, 42 U.S.C. § 2000aa — restricts the government's ability to search and seize the work product of the press and the media.

- Cable Communications Policy Act of 1984, Pub. L. No. 98-549, 47 U.S.C. § 551 — mandates privacy protection for records maintained by cable companies.

---

[39] *See* U.S. Dep't of Health, Education, and Welfare, *Secretary's Advisory Committee on Automated Personal Data Systems, Records, Computers, and Rights of Citizens* viii (1973).

[40] Marc Rotenberg, *Fair Information Practices and the Architecture of Privacy (What Larry Doesn't Get)*, Stan. Tech. L. Rev. 1, 44 (2001).

- Electronic Communications Privacy Act of 1986, Pub. L. No. 99-508 and Pub. L. No. 103-414, 18 U.S.C §§ 2510–2522, 2701–2709 — updates federal electronic surveillance law to respond to the new developments in technology.

- Computer Matching and Privacy Protection Act of 1988, Pub. L. No. 100-503, 5 U.S.C. §§ 552a — regulates automated investigations conducted by government agencies comparing computer files.

- Employee Polygraph Protection Act of 1988, Pub. L. No. 100-347, 29 U.S.C. §§ 2001–2009 — governs the use of polygraphs by employers.

- Video Privacy Protection Act of 1988, Pub. L. No. 100-618, 18 U.S.C. §§ 2710–2711 — protects the privacy of videotape rental information.

- Telephone Consumer Protection Act of 1991, Pub. L. No. 102-243, 47 U.S.C. § 227 — provides certain remedies from repeat telephone calls by telemarketers.

- Driver's Privacy Protection Act of 1994, Pub. L. No. 103-322, 18 U.S.C. §§ 2721–2725 — restricts the states from disclosing or selling personal information in their motor vehicle records.

- Health Insurance Portability and Accountability Act of 1996, Pub. L. No. 104-191 — gives the Department of Health and Human Services (HHS) the authority to promulgate regulations governing the privacy of medical records.

- Identity Theft and Assumption Deterrence Act of 1998, Pub. L. No. 105-318, 18 U.S.C. § 1028 — criminalizes the transfer or use of fraudulent identification with the intent to commit unlawful activity.

- Children's Online Privacy Protection Act of 1998, Pub. L. No. 106-170, 15 U.S.C. §§ 6501–6506 — restricts the use of information gathered from children under age 13 by Internet websites.

- Gramm-Leach-Bliley Act of 1999, Pub. L. No. 106-102, 15 U.S.C. §§ 6801–6809 — requires privacy notices and provides opt-out rights when financial institutions seek to disclose personal data to other companies.

- CAN-SPAM Act of 2003, Pub. L. No. 108-187 — provides penalties for the transmission of unsolicited e-mail.

- Fair and Accurate Credit Transactions Act of 2003, Pub. L. No. 108-159 — amends and updates the Fair Credit Reporting Act, providing (among other things) additional protections against identity theft.

- Video Voyeurism Prevention Act of 2004, Pub. L. No. 108-495, 18 U.S.C. § 1801 — criminalizes the capturing of nude images of people (when on federal property) under circumstances where they have a reasonable expectation of privacy.

- Health Information Technology for Economic and Clinical Health Act (HITECH Act) of 2009, Pub. L. No. 111-5 — expands HIPAA's coverage, strengthens penalties for HIPAA violations, and provides for data breach notification under HIPAA.

Not all of Congress's legislation regarding privacy has been protective of privacy. A number of statutes have mandated the government collection of sensitive personal data or facilitated government investigation techniques, such as the Bank Secrecy Act of 1970, the Communications Assistance for Law Enforcement Act of 1994, and the USA-PATRIOT Act of 2001.

State Statutory Law. The states have passed statutes protecting privacy in many contexts, regulating both the public and private sectors. These laws cover a wide range of subjects, from employment records and medical records to library records and student records.

States have led the way in the area of breach notification. Following California's enactment of such a statute, every state has now enacted breach notification statutes. These laws differ in many of their requirements, including when notification of breach is required. Many states also have enacted data disposal statutes, and an increasing number of state statutes are setting substantive requirements for data security.

A recent important trend at the state level has been the enactment of biometric privacy laws. Illinois has one of the most important of these statutes. There has been significant litigation pursuant to this law with major court decisions and negotiated settlements.

Finally, California enacted a far-reaching privacy law in 2018. The California Consumer Privacy Act (CCPA) contains far-reaching consumer privacy protections and rights. Other states have followed by passing similar types of laws. States enacting such consumer privacy laws include Colorado, Connecticut, Indiana, Iowa, Montana, Tennessee, Texas, Utah, and Virginia.

4. INTERNATIONAL LAW

Privacy is a global concern. International law and, more precisely, the privacy laws of other countries and international privacy norms, implicate privacy interests in the United States. For example, commercial firms in the United States must comply with the various standards for global commerce. The Organization of Economic Cooperation and Development (OECD) developed privacy guidelines in 1980 that formed the basis for privacy laws around the world.

In 1995, the European Union issued the *European Community Directive on Data Protection*, which outlined the basic principles for privacy legislation for European Union member countries.[41] The Directive became effective on October 25, 1998. The Directive was replaced by the sweeping General Data Protection Regulation (GDPR) on May 25, 2018. The GDPR became immediately binding law in all EU Member States on that date.[42]

More than 160 countries have enacted a comprehensive privacy laws. The United States still lacks a comprehensive federal privacy law; it has a sectoral approach, with many different laws regulating privacy in different economic sectors or industries.

---

[41] *See* Directive of the European Parliament and the Council of Europe on the Protection of Individuals with Regard to the Processing of Personal Data and on the Free Movement of Such Data (1996).

[42] European Commission, Regulation 2016/670 of the European Parliament and of the Council of 27 April 2016 on the protection of individuals with regard to the processing of personal data and on the free movement of such data, and repealing Directive 95/46/EC, O.J. L119, 1 (May 4, 2016).

CHAPTER 2

PERSPECTIVES ON PRIVACY

CHAPTER OUTLINE

A. THE PHILOSOPHICAL DISCOURSE ABOUT PRIVACY

1. THE CONCEPT OF PRIVACY AND THE RIGHT TO PRIVACY

At the outset, it is important to distinguish between the concept of privacy and the right of privacy. As Hyman Gross observed, "[t]he law does not determine what privacy is, but only what situations of privacy will be afforded legal protection."[1] Privacy as a concept involves what privacy entails and how it is to be valued. Privacy as a right involves the extent to which privacy is (and should be) legally protected.

While instructive and illuminative, law cannot be the exclusive material for constructing a concept of privacy. Law is the product of the weighing of competing values, and it sometimes embodies difficult trade-offs. In order to determine what the law *should* protect, we cannot merely look to what the law *does* protect.

---

[1] Hyman Gross, *The Concept of Privacy*, 42 N.Y.U. L. Rev. 34, 36 (1967).

2. THE PUBLIC AND PRIVATE SPHERES

A long-standing distinction in philosophical discourse is between the public and private spheres. Some form of boundary between public and private has been maintained throughout the history of Western civilization.[2]

Generally, the public sphere is the realm of life experienced in the open, in the community, and in the world of politics. The private sphere is the realm of life where one retreats to isolation or to one's family. At its core is the world of the home. The private sphere, observes Edward Shils, is a realm where the individual "is not bound by the rules that govern public life. . . . The 'private life' is a secluded life, a life separated from the compelling burdens of public authority."[3]

According to Hannah Arendt, both spheres are essential dimensions of human life:

> . . . In ancient feeling, the privative trait of privacy, indicated in the word itself, was all-important; it meant literally a state of being deprived of something, and even of the highest and most human of man's capacities. A man who lived only a private life, who like the slave was not permitted to enter the public realm, or like the barbarian had chosen not to establish such a realm, was not fully human. We no longer think primarily of deprivation when we use the word "privacy," and this is partly due to the enormous enrichment of the private sphere through modern individualism. . . .
>
> To live an entirely private life means above all to be deprived of things essential to a truly human life: to be deprived of the reality that comes from being seen and heard by others, to be deprived of an "objective" relationship with them that comes from being related to and separated from them through the intermediary of a common world of things, to be deprived of the possibility of achieving something more permanent than life itself. . . .
>
> . . . [T]he four walls of one's private property offer the only reliable hiding place from the common public world, not only from everything that goes on in it but also from its very publicity, from being seen and being heard. A life spent entirely in public, in the presence of others, becomes, as we would say, shallow. While it retains visibility, it loses the quality of rising into sight from some darker ground which must remain hidden if it is not to lose its depth in a very real, non-subjective sense. . . . [4]

John Stuart Mill relied upon a notion of the public/private dichotomy to determine when society should regulate individual conduct. Mill contended that there was a realm where people had social responsibilities and where society could properly restrain people from acting or punish them for their deeds. This realm consisted in acts that were hurtful to others or to which people "may rightfully be compelled to perform; such as to give evidence in a court of justice; to bear his fair share in the common defence, or in any other joint work necessary to the interest of the society of which he enjoys the protection." However, "there is a sphere of action in which society, as distinguished from the individual, has, if any, only an

---

[2] *See* Georges Duby, *Foreword*, in *A History of the Private Life I: From Pagan Rome to Byzantium* viii (Paul Veyne ed. & Arthur Goldhammer trans., 1987); *see also* Jürgen Habermas, *The Structural Transformation of the Public Sphere* (Thomas Burger trans., 1991).

[3] Edward Shils, *Privacy: Its Constitution and Vicissitudes*, 31 Law & Contemp. Probs. 281, 283 (1966).

[4] Hannah Arendt, *The Human Condition* (1958).

indirect interest; comprehending all that portion of a person's life and conduct which affects only himself, or if it also affects others, only with their free, voluntary, and undeceived consent and participation." Conduct within this sphere consists of "self-regarding" acts, and society should not interfere with such acts. As Mill further elaborated:

> . . . I fully admit that the mischief which a person does to himself may seriously affect, both through their sympathies and their interests, those nearly connected with him and, in a minor degree, society at large. When, by conduct of this sort, a person is led to violate a distinct and assignable obligation to any other person or persons, the case is taken out of the self-regarding class, and becomes amenable to moral disapprobation in the proper sense of the term. . . . Whenever, in short, there is a definite damage, or a definite risk of damage, either to an individual or to the public, the case is taken out of the province of liberty, and placed in that of morality or law.
>
> But with regard to the merely contingent, or, as it may be called, constructive injury which a person causes to society, by conduct which neither violates any specific duty to the public, nor occasions perceptible hurt to any assignable individual except himself; the inconvenience is one which society can afford to bear, for the sake of the greater good of human freedom. . . . [5]

B. THE DEFINITION AND THE VALUE OF PRIVACY

The following excerpts explore the definition and value of privacy. Those who attempt to define privacy seek to describe what privacy constitutes. Over the past four decades, academics have defined privacy as a right of personhood, intimacy, secrecy, limited access to the self, and control over information. However, defining privacy has proven to be quite complicated, and many commentators have expressed great difficulty in defining precisely what privacy is. In the words of one commentator, "even the most strenuous advocate of a right to privacy must confess that there are serious problems of defining the essence and scope of this right."[6] According to Robert Post, "[p]rivacy is a value so complex, so entangled in competing and contradictory dimensions, so engorged with various and distinct meanings, that I sometimes despair whether it can be usefully addressed at all."[7]

Conceptualizing privacy not only involves defining privacy but articulating the value of privacy. The value of privacy concerns its importance — how privacy is to be weighed relative to other interests and values. The excerpts that follow attempt to grapple with the complicated task of defining privacy and explaining why privacy is worth protecting.

---

[5] John Stuart Mill, *On Liberty* 12, 13, 74-75 (1859).

[6] William M. Beaney, *The Right to Privacy and American Law*, 31 Law & Contemp. Probs. 253, 255 (1966).

[7] Robert C. Post, *Three Concepts of Privacy*, 89 Geo. L.J. 2087, 2087 (2001).

DANIEL J. SOLOVE, *CONCEPTUALIZING PRIVACY*
90 Cal. L. Rev. 1087 (2002)

Despite what appears to be a welter of different conceptions of privacy, I argue that they can be dealt with under six general headings, which capture the recurrent ideas in the discourse. These headings include: (1) the right to be let alone — Samuel Warren and Louis Brandeis's famous formulation for the right to privacy; (2) limited access to the self — the ability to shield oneself from unwanted access by others; (3) secrecy — the concealment of certain matters from others; (4) control over personal information — the ability to exercise control over information about oneself; (5) personhood — the protection of one's personality, individuality, and dignity; and (6) intimacy — control over, or limited access to, one's intimate relationships or aspects of life. Some of the conceptions concentrate on means to achieve privacy; others focus on the ends or goals of privacy. Further, there is overlap between conceptions, and the conceptions discussed under different headings are by no means independent from each other. For example, control over personal information can be seen as a subset of limited access to the self, which in turn bears significant similarities to the right to be let alone. . . .

The most prevalent problem with the conceptions is that they are either too narrow or too broad. The conceptions are often too narrow because they fail to include the aspects of life that we typically view as private, and are often too broad because they fail to exclude matters that we do not deem private. Often, the same conceptions can suffer from being both too narrow and too broad. I contend that these problems stem from the way that the discourse goes about the task of conceptualizing privacy. . . .

Most attempts to conceptualize privacy thus far have followed the traditional method of conceptualizing. The majority of theorists conceptualize privacy by defining it *per genus et differentiam*. In other words, theorists look for a common set of necessary and sufficient elements that single out privacy as unique from other conceptions. . . .

[Philosopher Ludwig] Wittgenstein suggests that certain concepts might not share one common characteristic; rather they draw from a common pool of similar characteristics, "a complicated network of similarities overlapping and criss-crossing: sometimes overall similarities, sometimes similarities of detail." . . . Wittgenstein uses the term "family resemblances," analogizing to the overlapping and crisscrossing characteristics that exist between members of a family, such as "build, features, colour of eyes, gait, temperament, etc." For example, in a family, each child has certain features similar to each parent; and the children share similar features with each other; but they may not all resemble each other in the same way. Nevertheless, they all bear a resemblance to each other. . . .

When we state that we are protecting "privacy," we are claiming to guard against disruptions to certain practices. Privacy invasions disrupt and sometimes completely annihilate certain practices. Practices can be disrupted in certain ways, such as interference with peace of mind and tranquility, invasion of solitude, breach of confidentiality, loss of control over facts about oneself, searches of one's person and property, threats to or violations of personal security, destruction of reputation, surveillance, and so on.

There are certain similarities in particular types of disruptions as well as in the practices that they disrupt; but there are differences as well. We should conceptualize privacy by focusing on the specific types of disruption and the specific practices disrupted rather than looking for the common denominator that links all of them. If privacy is conceptualized as a web of interconnected types of disruption of specific practices, then the act of conceptualizing privacy should consist of mapping the typography of the web. . . .

It is reductive to carve the world of social practices into two spheres, public and private, and then attempt to determine what matters belong in each sphere. First, the matters we consider private change over time. While some form of dichotomy between public and private has been maintained throughout the history of Western civilization, the matters that have been considered public and private have metamorphosed throughout history due to changing attitudes, institutions, living conditions, and technology. The matters we consider to be private are shaped by culture and history, and have differed across cultures and historical epochs.

Second, although certain matters have moved from being public to being private and vice versa, the change often has been more subtle than a complete transformation from public to private. Particular matters have long remained private but in different ways; they have been understood as private but because of different attributes; or they have been regarded as private for some people or groups but not for others. In other words, to say simply that something is public or private is to make a rather general claim; what it means for something to be private is the central question. We consider our Social Security number, our sexual behavior, our diary, and our home private, but we do not consider them private in the same way. A number of aspects of life have commonly been viewed as private: the family, body, and home to name a few. To say simply that these things are private is imprecise because what it means for them to be private is different today than it was in the past. . . .

. . . [P]rivacy is not simply an empirical and historical question that measures the collective sense in any given society of what is and has long been considered to be private. Without a normative component, a conception of privacy can only provide a status report on existing privacy norms rather than guide us toward shaping privacy law and policy in the future. If we focus simply on people's current expectations of privacy, our conception of privacy would continually shrink given the increasing surveillance in the modern world. Similarly, the government could gradually condition people to accept wiretapping or other privacy incursions, thus altering society's expectations of privacy. On the other hand, if we merely seek to preserve those activities and matters that have historically been considered private, then we fail to adapt to the changing realities of the modern world. . . .

NOTES & QUESTIONS

1. *Core Characteristics vs. Family Resemblances.* Is there a core characteristic common in all the things we understand as being "private"? If so, what do you think it is? Can privacy be more adequately conceptualized by shifting away from the quest to find the common core characteristics of privacy?

2. *Context.* Solove contends that the meaning of privacy depends upon context, that there is no common denominator to all things we refer to as "privacy." Does this make privacy too amorphous a concept?

Consider Helen Nissenbaum:

> Specifically, whether a particular action is determined a violation of privacy is a function of several variables, including the nature of the situation, or context; the nature of the information in relation to that context; the roles of agents receiving information; their relationships to information subjects; on what terms the information is shared by the subject; and the terms of further dissemination.
> . . .
> [N]orms of privacy in fact vary considerably from place to place, culture to culture, period to period; this theory not only incorporates this reality but systematically pinpoints the sources of variation. A second consequence is that, because questions about whether particular restrictions on flow are acceptable call for investigation into the relevant contextual details, protecting privacy will be a messy task, requiring a grasp of concepts and social institutions as well as knowledge of facts of the matter.[8]

3. *Privacy as Control over Information.* A number of theorists conceive of privacy as a form of control over personal information.[9] Consider Charles Fried's definition of privacy:

> At first approximation, privacy seems to be related to secrecy, to limiting the knowledge of others about oneself. This notion must be refined. It is not true, for instance, that the less that is known about us the more privacy we have. Privacy is not simply an absence of information about what is in the minds of others; rather it is the *control* we have over information about ourselves.
> To refer for instance to the privacy of a lonely man on a desert island would be to engage in irony. The person who enjoys privacy is able to grant or deny access to others. . . .
> Privacy, thus, is control over knowledge about oneself. But it is not simply control over the quantity of information abroad; there are modulations in the quality of the knowledge as well. We may not mind that a person knows a general fact about us, and yet feel our privacy invaded if he knows the details.[10]

Is this a compelling definition of privacy?

In contrast to privacy-as-control, Christena Nippert-Eng, a sociologist, talks about the managerial dimension of privacy. Based on her wide-reaching field interviews, Nippert-Eng concludes that "participants find it incumbent upon themselves to create their own pockets of uninterruptible time and space, or take make decisions without letting anyone else unduly pressure them into a

---

[8] Helen Nissenbaum, *Privacy as Contextual Integrity*, 79 Wash. L. Rev. 119, 155-56 (2004). For a more complete account of Nissenbaum's theory, see Helen Nissenbaum, *Privacy in Context: Technology, Policy, and the Integrity of Social Life* (2010).

[9] *See* Adam Carlyle Breckenridge, *The Right to Privacy* 1 (1970); Randall P. Bezanson, *The Right to Privacy Revisited: Privacy, News, and Social Change, 1810–1990*, 80 Cal. L. Rev. 1133 (1992). For a critique of privacy as control, see Anita L. Allen, *Privacy as Data Control: Conceptual, Practical, and Moral Limits of the Paradigm*, 32 Conn. L. Rev. 861 (2000).

[10] Charles Fried, *Privacy*, 77 Yale L.J. 475 (1968).

particular choice."[11] She adds that "a need to *manage* one's privacy" runs through all the definitions of privacy offered by her interview participants.

4. ***Privacy as Limited Access to the Self.*** Another group of theorists view privacy as a form of limited access to the self. Consider Ruth Gavison:

> . . . Our interest in privacy . . . is related to our concern over our accessibility to others: the extent to which we are known to others, the extent to which others have physical access to us, and the extent to which we are the subject of others' attention. This concept of privacy as concern for limited accessibility enables us to identify when losses of privacy occur. Furthermore, the reasons for which we claim privacy in different situations are similar. They are related to the functions privacy has in our lives: the promotion of liberty, autonomy, selfhood, and human relations, and furthering the existence of a free   society. . . .
>
> The concept of privacy suggested here is a complex of these three independent and irreducible elements: secrecy, anonymity, and solitude. Each is independent in the sense that a loss of privacy may occur through a change in any one of the three, without a necessary loss in either of the other two. The concept is nevertheless coherent because the three elements are all part of the same notion of accessibility, and are related in many important ways.[12]

How does this theory of privacy differ from the notion of privacy as "the right to be let alone"? How does it differ from privacy as control over information? How much control should individuals have over access to themselves? Should the decision depend upon each particular person's desires? Or should there be an objective standard — a reasonable degree of control over access?

5. ***Privacy as Intimacy.*** A number of theorists argue that "intimacy" appropriately defines what information or matters are private. For example, Julie Inness argues that "intimacy" is the common denominator in all the matters that people claim to be private. Privacy is "the state of the agent having control over decisions concerning matters that draw their meaning and value from the agent's love, caring, or liking. These decisions cover choices on the agent's part about access to herself, the dissemination of information about herself, and her actions."[13]

Jeffrey Rosen adopts a similar view when he writes:

> . . . Privacy protects us from being misdefined and judged out of context in a world of short attention spans, a world in which information can easily be

---

[11] Christena Nippert-Eng, *Islands of Privacy* 7 (2010).

[12] Ruth Gavison, *Privacy and the Limits of Law*, 89 Yale L.J. 421 (1980); *see also* Edward Shils, *Privacy: Its Constitution and Vicissitudes*, 31 Law & Contemp. Probs. 281, 281 (1996); Sissela Bok, *Secrets: On the Ethics of Concealment and Revelation* 10-11 (1982); Ernest Van Den Haag, *On Privacy*, in *Nomos XII: Privacy* 149 (J. Ronald Pennock & J.W. Chapman eds., 1971); Sidney M. Jourard, *Some Psychological Aspects of Privacy*, 31 L. & Contemp. Probs. 307, 307 (1966); David O'Brien, *Privacy, Law, and Public Policy* 16 (1979); Hyman Gross, *The Concept of Privacy*, 42 N.Y.U. L. Rev. 34 (1967).

[13] Julie C. Inness, *Privacy, Intimacy, and Isolation* 56, 58, 63, 64, 67 (1992). For other proponents of privacy as intimacy, see Robert S. Gerstein, *Intimacy and Privacy*, in *Philosophical Dimensions of Privacy: An Anthology* 265, 265 (Ferdinand David Schoeman ed., 1984); James Rachels, *Why Privacy Is Important*, in *Philosophical Dimensions of Privacy: An Anthology* 290, 292 (Ferdinand David Schoeman ed., 1984); Tom Gerety, *Redefining Privacy*, 12 Harv. C.R.-C.L. L. Rev. 233 (1977).

confused with knowledge. True knowledge of another person is the culmination of a slow process of mutual revelation. It requires the gradual setting aside of social masks, the incremental building of trust, which leads to the exchange of personal disclosures. It cannot be rushed; this is why, after intemperate self-revelation in the heat of passion, one may feel something close to self-betrayal. True knowledge of another person, in all of his or her complexity, can be achieved only with a handful of friends, lovers, or family members. In order to flourish, the intimate relationships on which true knowledge of another person depends need space as well as time: sanctuaries from the gaze of the crowd in which slow mutual self-disclosure is possible.

When intimate personal information circulates among a small group of people who know us well, its significance can be weighed against other aspects of our personality and character. By contrast, when intimate information is removed from its original context and revealed to strangers, we are vulnerable to being misjudged on the basis of our most embarrassing, and therefore most memorable, tastes and preferences. . . . In a world in which citizens are bombarded with information, people form impressions quickly, based on sound bites, and these impressions are likely to oversimplify and misrepresent our complicated and often contradictory characters.[14]

Does "intimacy" adequately separate private matters from public ones? Can something be private but not intimate? Can something be intimate but not private?

In reaction to Rosen's views on privacy, Lawrence Lessig restates the problem of short attention spans in this fashion: "Privacy, the argument goes, would remedy such a problem by concealing those things that would not be understood with the given attention span. Privacy's function . . . is not to protect the presumptively innocent from true but damaging information, but rather to protect the actually innocent from damaging conclusions drawn from misunderstood information."[15] Lessig notes his skepticism regarding this approach: privacy will not alone solve the problem with the information market. Moreover, there "are possible solutions to this problem of attention span. But what should be clear is that there is no guarantee that a particular problem of attention span will have any solution at all."

6. ***Alan Westin's Four States of Privacy.*** Alan Westin views privacy as having four basic states – solitude, intimacy, anonymity, and reserve. *Solitude* involves the individual being "separated from the group and freed from the observation of other persons." According to Westin, "solitude is the most complete state of privacy that individuals can achieve." *Intimacy* involves "acting as part of a small unit that claims and is allowed to exercise corporate seclusion so that it may achieve a close, relaxed, and frank relationship between two or more individuals." *Anonymity* "occurs when the individual is in public places or performing public acts but still seeks, and finds, freedom from identification and surveillance." Finally, *reserve* involves "the creation of a psychological barrier against unwanted intrusion; this occurs when the individual's need to limit communication about himself is protected by the willing discretion of

---

[14] Jeffrey Rosen, *The Unwanted Gaze: The Destruction of Privacy in America* 8-9 (2000).
[15] Lawrence Lessig, *Privacy and Attention Span*, 89 Geo. L.J. 2063, 2065 (2001).

those surrounding him."[16]

7. ***Revising the Prosser Taxonomy.*** Daniel Solove contends that the taxonomy of four privacy interests identified by William Prosser, *supra,* must be revised as well as expanded beyond tort law. Solove identifies 16 different kinds of activity that create privacy harms or problems:

> The first group of activities that affect privacy involve information collection. *Surveillance* is the watching, listening to, or recording of an individual's activities. *Interrogation* consists of various forms of questioning or probing for information.
>
> A second group of activities involves the way information is stored, mani-pulated, and used — what I refer to collectively as "information processing." *Aggregation* involves the combination of various pieces of data about a person. *Identification* is linking information to particular individuals. *Insecurity* involves carelessness in protecting stored information from being leaked or improperly accessed. *Secondary use* is the use of information collected for one purpose for a different purpose without a person's consent. *Exclusion* concerns the failure to allow people to know about the data that others have about them and participate in its handling and use. These activities do not involve the gathering of data, since it has already been collected. Instead, these activities involve the way data is maintained and used.
>
> The third group of activities involves the dissemination of information. *Breach of confidentiality* is breaking the promise to keep a person's information confidential. *Disclosure* involves the revelation of truthful information about a person which impacts the way others judge that person's character. *Exposure* involves revealing another's nudity, grief, or bodily functions. *Increased accessibility* is amplifying the accessibility of information. *Blackmail* is the threat to disclose personal information. *Appropriation* involves the use of another's identity to serve the aims and interests of another. *Distortion* consists of the dissemination of false or misleading information about individuals. Information dissemination activities all involve the spreading or transfer of personal data — or the threat to do so.
>
> The fourth and final group of activities involves invasions into people's private affairs. Invasion, unlike the other groupings, need not involve personal information (although in numerous instances, it does). *Intrusion* concerns invasive acts that disturb one's tranquility or solitude. *Decisional interference* involves the government's incursion into people's decisions regarding their private affairs.[17]

8. ***Reductionists.*** Some theorists, referred to as "reductionists," assert that privacy can be reduced to other concepts and rights. For example, Judith Jarvis Thomson contends that there is nothing particularly distinctive about privacy and to talk about things as violating the "right to privacy" is not all that useful. Privacy is really a cluster of other rights, such as the right to liberty, property rights, and the right not to be injured: "[T]he right to privacy is everywhere overlapped by other rights."[18] Is there something distinctive about privacy? Or

---

[16] Alan Westin, *Privacy and Freedom* (1967).

[17] Daniel J. Solove, *A Taxonomy of Privacy,* 154 U. Pa. L. Rev. 477 (2006). For a more complete account of Solove's theory, see Daniel J. Solove, *Understanding Privacy* (2008).

[18] Judith Jarvis Thomson, *The Right to Privacy,* 4 Phil. & Pub. Aff. 295 (1975).

can privacy be explained in terms of other, more primary rights and interests? What does privacy capture that these other rights and interests (autonomy, property, liberty, etc.) do not?

JULIE E. COHEN, *EXAMINED LIVES: INFORMATIONAL PRIVACY AND THE SUBJECT AS OBJECT*

52 Stan. L. Rev. 1373 (2000)

Prevailing market-based approaches to data privacy policy — including "solutions" in the form of tradable privacy rights or heightened disclosure requirements before consent — treat preferences for informational privacy as a matter of individual taste, entitled to no more (and often much less) weight than preferences for black shoes over brown or red wine over white. But the values of informational privacy are far more fundamental. A degree of freedom from scrutiny and categorization by others promotes important noninstrumental values and serves vital individual and collective ends.

First, informational autonomy comports with important values concerning the fair and just treatment of individuals within society. From Kant to Rawls, a central strand of Western philosophical tradition emphasizes respect for the fundamental dignity of persons, and a concomitant commitment to egalitarianism in both principle and practice. Advocates of strong data privacy protection argue that these principles have clear and very specific implications for the treatment of personally-identified data: They require that we forbid data-processing practices that treat individuals as mere conglomerations of transactional data, or that rank people as prospective customers, tenants, neighbors, employees, or insureds based on their financial or genetic desirability. . . .

Autonomous individuals do not spring full-blown from the womb. We must learn to process information and to draw our own conclusions about the world around us. We must learn to choose, and must learn something before we can choose anything. Here, though, information theory suggests a paradox: "Autonomy" connotes an essential independence of critical faculty and an imperviousness to influence. But to the extent that information shapes behavior, autonomy is radically contingent upon environment and circumstance. . . . Autonomy in a contingent world requires a zone of relative insulation from outside scrutiny and interference — a field of operation within which to engage in the conscious construction of self. The solution to the paradox of contingent autonomy, in other words, lies in a second paradox: To exist in fact as well as in theory, autonomy must be nurtured.

A realm of autonomous, unmonitored choice, in turn, promotes a vital diversity of speech and behavior. The recognition that anonymity shelters constitutionally-protected decisions about speech, belief, and political and intellectual association — decisions that otherwise might be chilled by unpopularity or simple difference — is part of our constitutional tradition. . . .

The benefits of informational privacy are related to, but distinct from, those afforded by seclusion from visual monitoring. It is well-recognized that respite from visual scrutiny affords individuals an important measure of psychological repose. Within our society, at least, we are accustomed to physical spaces within which we can be unobserved, and intrusion into those spaces is experienced as violating the boundaries of self. But the scrutiny, and the repose, can be informational as well as visual, and this does not depend entirely on whether the behavior takes place "in private." The injury, here, does not lie in the exposure of formerly private behaviors to public view, but in the dissolution of the boundaries that insulate different spheres of behavior from one another. The universe of all information about all record-generating behaviors generates a "picture" that, in some respects, is more detailed and intimate than that produced by visual observation, and that picture is accessible, in theory and often in reality, to just about anyone who wants to see it. In such a world, we all may be more cautious.

The point is not that people will not learn under conditions of no-privacy, but that they will learn differently, and that the experience of being watched will constrain, ex ante, the acceptable spectrum of belief and behavior. Pervasive monitoring of every first move or false start will, at the margin, incline choices toward the bland and the mainstream. The result will be a subtle yet fundamental shift in the content of our character, a blunting and blurring of rough edges and sharp lines. . . . The condition of no-privacy threatens not only to chill the expression of eccentric individuality, but also, gradually, to dampen the force of our aspirations to it. . . .

. . . [T]he insulation provided by informational privacy also plays a subtler, more conservative role in reinforcing the existing social fabric. Sociologist Erving Goffman demonstrated that the construction of social facades to mediate between self and community is both instinctive and expected. Alan Westin describes this social dimension of privacy as "reserve." This characterization, though, seems incomplete. On Goffman's account, the construction of social personae isn't just about withholding information that we don't want others to have. It is about defining the parameters of social interaction in ways that maximize social ease, and thus is about collective as well as individual comfort. We do not need, or even want, to know each other that well. Less information makes routine interactions easier; we are then free to choose, consensually and without embarrassment, the interactions that we wish to treat as less routine. Informational privacy, in short, is a constitutive element of a civil society in the broadest sense of that term. . . .

NOTES & QUESTIONS

1. *Privacy as a Social Value.* Cohen argues that privacy not only protects individuals but also broader societal values. In another work, she elaborates that privacy involves "boundary management" which is necessary for "human flourishing" — an essential component for a robust civil society.[19] Consider the following argument from Priscilla Regan:

   . . . [The] emphasis of privacy as an individual right or an individual interest provides a weak basis for formulating policy to protect privacy. When privacy is defined as an individual right, policy formulation entails a balancing of the individual right to privacy against a competing interest or right. In general, the competing interest is recognized as a social interest. . . . As a result, privacy has

---

[19] Julie E. *Cohen, Configuring the Networked Self: Law, Code, and the Play of Everyday Practice* (2012).

been on the defensive, with those alleging a privacy invasion bearing the burden of proving that a certain activity does indeed invade privacy and that the "social" benefit to be gained from the privacy invasion is less important than the individual harm incurred. . . .

Privacy is a *common value* in that all individuals value some degree of privacy and have some common perceptions about privacy. Privacy is also a *public value* in that it has value not just to the individual as an individual or to all individuals in common but also to the democratic political system. . . .

A public value of privacy derives not only from its protection of the individual as an individual but also from its usefulness as a restraint on the government or on the use of power. . . .[20]

2. *Coercing Privacy.* Anita Allen contends that people regularly surrender their privacy and that we should "coerce" privacy in some cases. In other words, privacy must be seen as an inalienable right, one that people cannot give away.

To speak of "coercing" privacy is to call attention to privacy as a foundation, a precondition of a liberal egalitarian society. Privacy is not an optional good, like a second home or an investment account. . . .

A hard task seems to lay before us — namely, deciding which forms of privacy are so critical that they should become matters of coercion. . . .

As liberals, we should not want people to sell all their freedom, and, as liberals, we should not want people to sell all their privacy and capacities for private choices. This is, in part, because the liberal conceptions of private choice as freedom from governmental and other outside interference with decision-making closely link privacy and freedom. The liberal conception of privacy as freedom from unwanted disclosures, publicity, and loss of control of personality also closely links privacy to freedom. . . .

Government will have to intervene in private lives for the sake of privacy and values associated with it. . . . The threat to liberalism is not that individuals sometimes expose their naked bodies in public places, display affection with same-sex partners in public, or broadcast personal information on national television. The threat to liberalism is that in an increasing variety of ways our lives are being emptied of privacy on a daily basis, especially physical and informational privacy.[21]

What if a person wants to live in the spotlight or to give away her personal information? Why shouldn't she be allowed to do so? Recall those who defined privacy as control over information. One aspect of control is that an individual can decide for herself how much privacy she desires. What would Allen say about such a definition of privacy?

---

[20] Priscilla M. Regan, *Legislating Privacy: Technology, Social Values, and Public Policy* 213, 225 (1995).

[21] Anita L. Allen, *Coercing Privacy,* 40 Wm. & Mary L. Rev. 723 (1999)

PAUL M. SCHWARTZ, *PRIVACY AND DEMOCRACY IN CYBERSPACE*

52 Vand. L. Rev. 1609 (1999)

. . . Self-determination is a capacity that is embodied and developed through social forms and practices. The threat to this quality arises when private or government action interferes with a person's control of her reasoning process. . . . [P]erfected surveillance of naked thought's digital expression short-circuits the individual's own process of decisionmaking. . . .

The maintenance of a democratic order requires both deliberative democracy and an individual capacity for self-determination. . . . [T]he emerging pattern of information use in cyberspace poses a risk to these two essential values. Our task now is to develop privacy standards that are capable of structuring the right kind of information use. . . .

Most scholars, and much of the law in this area, work around a liberal paradigm that we can term "privacy-control." From the age of computer mainframes in the 1960s to the current reign of the Internet's decentralized networks, academics and the law have gravitated towards the idea of privacy as a personal right to control the use of one's data. . . .

. . . [One flaw with the "privacy-control" paradigm is the "autonomy trap."] [T]he organization of information privacy through individual control of personal data rests on a view of autonomy as a given, preexisting quality. . . .

As a policy cornerstone, however, the idea of privacy-control falls straight into the "autonomy trap." The difficulty with privacy-control in the Information Age is that individual self-determination is itself shaped by the processing of personal data. . . .

To give an example of an autonomy trap in cyberspace, the act of clicking through a "consent" screen on a Web site may be considered by some observers to be an exercise of self-reliant choice. Yet, this screen can contain boilerplate language that permits all further processing and transmission of one's personal data. Even without a consent screen, some Web sites place consent boilerplate within a "privacy statement" on their home page or elsewhere on their site. For example, the online version of one New York newspaper states, "By using this site, you agree to the Privacy Policy of the New York Post." This language presents the conditions for data processing on a take-it-or-leave-it basis. It seeks to create the legal fiction that all who visit this Web site have expressed informed consent to its data processing practices. An even more extreme manifestation of the "consent trap" is a belief that an initial decision to surf the Web itself is a self-reliant choice to accept all further use of one's personal data generated by this activity. . . .

The liberal ideal views autonomous individuals as able to interact freely and equally so long as the government or public does not interfere. The reality is, however, that individuals can be trapped when such glorification of freedom of action neglects the actual conditions of choice. Here, another problem arises with self-governance through information-control: the "data seclusion deception." The idea of privacy as data seclusion is easy to explain: unless the individual wishes to surrender her personal information, she is to be free to use her privacy right as a trump to keep it confidential or to subject its release to conditions that she alone wishes to set. The individual is to be at the center of shaping data anonymity. Yet, this right to keep data isolated quickly proves illusory because of the demands of the Information Age. . . .

NOTES & QUESTIONS

1. ***Privacy and Personhood.*** Like Schwartz, a number of theorists argue that privacy is essential for self-development. According to Jeffrey Reiman, privacy "protects the individual's interest in becoming, being, and remaining a person."[22] The notion that privacy protects personhood or identity is captured in Warren and Brandeis's notion of "inviolate personality." How does privacy promote self-development?

   Consider the following: "Every acceptance of a public role entails the repression, channelizing, and deflection of 'private' or personal attention, motives, and demands upon the self in order to address oneself to the expectations of others."[23] Can we really be ourselves in the public sphere? Is our "public self" any less part of our persona than our "private self"?

2. ***Privacy and Democracy.*** Schwartz views privacy as essential for a democratic society. Why is privacy important for political participation?

3. ***Privacy and Role Playing.*** Alan Westin observes:

   > Each person is aware of the gap between what he wants to be and what he actually is, between what the world sees of him and what he knows to be his much more complex reality. In addition, there are aspects of himself that the individual does not fully understand but is slowly exploring and shaping as he develops. Every individual lives behind a mask in this manner; indeed, the first etymological meaning of the word "person" was "mask," indicating both the conscious and expressive presentation of the self to a social audience. If this mask is torn off and the individual's real self bared to a world in which everyone else still wears his mask and believes in masked performances, the individual can be seared by the hot light of selective, forced exposure.[24]

   Is there a "true" or "core" or "authentic" self? Or do we perform many roles and perhaps have multiple selves? Is there a self beneath the roles that we play?

   Daniel Solove contends that "[s]ociety accepts that public reputations will be groomed to some degree. . . . Society protects privacy because it wants to provide individuals with some degree of influence over how they are judged in the public arena."[25] To what extent should the law allow people to promote a polished public image and hide the dirt in private?

4. ***Individual Autonomy, Democratic Order, and Data Trade.*** In a later article, Schwartz argues from the premise that "[p]ersonal information is an important currency in the new millennium."[26] He rejects arguments that opposed

---

[22] Jeffrey H. Reiman, *Privacy, Intimacy, and Personhood*, in *Philosophical Dimensions of Privacy: An Anthology* 300, 308 (Ferdinand David Schoeman ed., 1984).

[23] Joseph Bensman & Robert Lilienfeld, *Between Public and Private: Lost Boundaries of the Self* 174 (1979).

[24] Alan Westin, *Privacy and Freedom* (1967).

[25] Daniel J. Solove, *The Virtues of Knowing Less: Justifying Privacy Protections Against Disclosure,* 53 Duke L.J. 957 (2003).

[26] Paul M. Schwartz, *Property, Privacy, and Personal Data*, 117 Harv. L. Rev. 2055 (2004).

propertization of personal data, and develops a model to permit data trade consistent with individual autonomy and the maintenance of a democratic order. A key concept in this model is that of the "privacy commons," where privacy is viewed "as a social and not merely an individual good." As a result, Schwartz states, "If sound rules for the use of personal data are not established and enforced, society as a whole will suffer because people will decline to engage in a range of different social interactions due to concerns about use of personal information. A public good — the privacy commons — will be degraded." Do you think that property is a sound concept for building a public goods approach to information privacy?

5. *Privacy Law and Information Flow.* Generally, one would assume that greater information flow facilitates democracy — it enables more expression, more political discourse, more information about the workings of government. Spiros Simitis, however, contends that privacy is "necessary to secure the individual's ability to communicate and participate."[27] How are these two notions about information flow to be reconciled? Consider Joel Reidenberg:

> Data privacy rules are often cast as a balance between two basic liberties: fundamental human rights on one side and the free flow of information on the other side. Yet, because societies differ on how and when personal information should be available for private and public sector needs, the treatment and interaction of these liberties will express a specific delineation between the state, civil society, and the citizen.[28]

Privacy, according to Reidenberg, involves establishing a balance between protecting the rights of individuals and enabling information flow. Do you think these interests always exist in opposition? Consider financial services, communications networks, and medical care. Does privacy impair or enable information flow?[29]

C. CRITICS OF PRIVACY

RICHARD A. POSNER, *THE RIGHT OF PRIVACY*
12 Ga. L. Rev. 393 (1978)

People invariably possess information, including facts about themselves and contents of communications, that they will incur costs to conceal. Sometimes such

---

[27] Spiros Simitis, *Reviewing Privacy in an Information Society,* 135 U. Pa. L. Rev. 707 (1987).

[28] Joel R. Reidenberg, *Resolving Conflicting International Data Privacy Rules in Cyberspace,* 52 Stan. L. Rev. 1315 (2000).

[29] For additional reading about philosophical theories of privacy, see Judith W. DeCew, *In Pursuit of Privacy: Law, Ethics, and the Rise of Technology* (1997) (surveying and critiquing various theories of privacy); Anita L. Allen, *Uneasy Access: Privacy for Women in a Free Society* (1988) (same); Ferdinand David Schoeman, ed., *Philosophical Dimensions of Privacy* (1984) (anthology of articles about the concept of privacy).

information is of value to others: that is, others will incur costs to discover it. Thus we have two economic goods, "privacy" and "prying." . . .

[M]uch of the casual prying (a term used here without any pejorative connotation) into the private lives of friends and colleagues that is so common a feature of social life is also motivated, to a greater extent than we may realize, by rational considerations of self-interest. Prying enables one to form a more accurate picture of a friend or colleague, and the knowledge gained is useful in one's social or professional dealings with him. For example, in choosing a friend one legitimately wants to know whether he will be discreet or indiscreet, selfish or generous, and these qualities are not always apparent on initial acquaintance. Even a pure altruist needs to know the (approximate) wealth of any prospective beneficiary of his altruism in order to be able to gauge the value of a transfer to him.

The other side of the coin is that social, like business, dealings present opportunities for exploitation through misrepresentation. Psychologists and sociologists have pointed out that even in every day life people try to manipulate by misrepresentation other people's opinion of them. As one psychologist has written, the "wish for privacy expresses a desire . . . to control others' perceptions and beliefs vis-à-vis the self-concealing person." Even the strongest defenders of privacy describe the individual's right to privacy as the right to "control the flow of information about him." A seldom remarked corollary to a right to misrepresent one's character is that others have a legitimate interest in unmasking the deception.

Yet some of the demand for private information about other people is not self-protection in the foregoing sense but seems mysteriously disinterested — for example, that of the readers of newspaper gossip columns, whose "idle curiosity" Warren and Brandeis deplored, groundlessly in my opinion. Gossip columns recount the personal lives of wealthy and successful people whose tastes and habits offer models — that is, yield information — to the ordinary person in making consumption, career, and other decisions. . . . Gossip columns open people's eyes to opportunities and dangers; they are genuinely informational. . . .

Warren and Brandeis attributed the rise of curiosity about people's lives to the excesses of the press. The economist does not believe, however, that supply creates demand. A more persuasive explanation for the rise of the gossip column is the secular increase in personal incomes. There is apparently very little privacy in poor societies, where, consequently, people can easily observe at first hand the intimate lives of others. Personal surveillance is costlier in wealthier societies both because people live in conditions that give them greater privacy from such observation and because the value (and hence opportunity cost) of time is greater—too great to make a generous allotment of time to watching neighbors worthwhile. People in wealthier societies sought an alternative method of informing themselves about how others live and the press provided it. A legitimate and important function of the press is to provide specialization in prying in societies where the costs of obtaining information have become too great for the Nosey Parker. . . .

Transaction-cost considerations may also militate against the assignment of a property right to the possessor of a secret. . . . Consider, for example, . . . whether the law should allow a magazine to sell its subscriber list to another magazine without obtaining the subscribers' consent. . . . [T]he costs of obtaining subscriber approval would be high relative to the value of the list. If, therefore, we believe that these lists are generally worth more to the purchasers than being shielded from possible unwanted solicitations is worth to the subscribers, we should assign the property right to the magazine; and the law does this. . . .

Much of the demand for privacy . . . concerns discreditable information, often information concerning past or present criminal activity or moral conduct at variance with a person's professed moral standards. And often the motive for concealment is, as suggested earlier, to mislead those with whom he transacts. Other private information that people wish to conceal, while not strictly discreditable, would if revealed correct misapprehensions that the individual is trying to exploit, as when a worker conceals a serious health problem from his employer or a prospective husband conceals his sterility from his fiancée. It is not clear why society should assign the property right in such information to the individual to whom it pertains; and the common law, as we shall see, generally does not. . . .

We think it wrong (and inefficient) that the law should permit a seller in hawking his wares to make false or incomplete representations as to their quality. But people "sell" themselves as well as their goods. They profess high standards of behavior in order to induce others to engage in social or business dealings with them from which they derive an advantage but at the same time they conceal some of the facts that these acquaintances would find useful in forming an accurate picture of their character. There are practical reasons for not imposing a general legal duty of full and frank disclosure of one's material. . . .

. . . [E]veryone should be allowed to protect himself from disadvantageous transactions by ferreting out concealed facts about individuals which are material to the representations (implicit or explicit) that those individuals make concerning their moral qualities.

It is no answer that such individuals have "the right to be let alone." Very few people want to be let alone. They want to manipulate the world around them by selective disclosure of facts about themselves. Why should others be asked to take their self-serving claims at face value and be prevented from obtaining the information necessary to verify or disprove these claims?

NOTES & QUESTIONS

1. *Posner's Conception of Privacy.* What is Posner's definition of privacy? How does Posner determine the value of privacy (i.e., how it should be weighed relative to other interests and values)? In what circumstances is Posner likely to defend a privacy claim?
2. *Irrational Judgments.* One economic argument for privacy is that sometimes people form irrational judgments based upon learning certain information about others. For example, an employer may not hire certain people based on their political views or associations, sexual orientation, mental illness, and prior criminal convictions — even though these facts may have no relevance to a potential employee's abilities to do the job. These judgments decrease efficiency. In *The Economics of Justice*, Posner offers a response:

   This objection overlooks the opportunity costs of shunning people for stupid reasons, or, stated otherwise, the gains from dealing with someone whom others shun irrationally. If ex-convicts are good workers but most employers do not know this, employers who do know will be able to hire them at a below-average wage because of their depressed job opportunities and will thereby obtain a competitive advantage over the bigots. In a diverse, decentralized, and competitive society, irrational shunning will be weeded out over time. . . [30]

Will the market be able to eradicate irrational judgments?

3. *Information Dissemination and Economic Efficiency.* Does economic theory necessarily lead to the conclusion that more personal information is generally preferable? Consider Richard Murphy's critique of Posner:

> [D]emarcating a relatively large sphere for the private self creates an opportunity for discovery or actualization of a "true" nature, which may have a value beyond the utility of satisfying preferences. . . . As Roger Rosenblatt put it, "Out of our private gropings and self-inspections grow our imaginative values — private language, imagery, memory. In the caves of the mind one bats about to discover a light entirely of one's own which, though it should turn out to be dim, is still worth a life." Unless a person can investigate without risk of reproach what his own preferences are, he will not be able to maximize his own happiness.[31]

When can the circulation of less personal information be more economically efficient than greater information flow?

4. *The Privacy Paradox: Why Don't Individuals Protect Their Privacy?* Empirical studies frequently report on growing privacy concerns across the United States. Yet, individuals seem willing to exchange privacy for services or small rewards and generally fail to adopt technologies and techniques that would protect their privacy. If people are willing to sell their privacy for very little in return, isn't this evidence that they do not really value privacy as much as they say they do?

Alessandro Acqusiti and Jens Grossklags have pointed to a number of reasons for this divergence between stated privacy preferences and actual behavior:

> First, incomplete information affects privacy decision making because of externalities (when third parties share personal information about an individual, they might affect that individual without his being part of the transaction between those parties), information asymmetries (information relevant to the privacy decision process — for example, how personal information will be used — might be known only to a subset of the parties making decisions), risk (most privacy related payoffs are not deterministic), and uncertainties (payoffs might not only be stochastic, but dependent on unknown random distributions). Benefits and costs associated with privacy intrusions and protection are complex, multifaceted, and context-specific. They are frequently bundled with other products and services (for example, a search engine query can prompt the desired result but can also give observers information about the searcher's

---

[30] Richard A. Posner, *The Economics of Justice* (1981). Posner further develops his theories about privacy in Richard A. Posner, *Overcoming Law* 531-51 (1995). Posner first set out his views on privacy in Richard A. Posner, *An Economic Theory of Privacy*, Regulations (May/June 1978).

[31] Richard S. Murphy, *Property Rights in Personal Information: An Economic Defense of Privacy*, 84 Geo. L.J. 2381 (1996).

interests), and they are often recognized only after privacy violations have taken place. They can be monetary but also immaterial and, thus, difficult to quantify.

Second, even if individuals had access to complete information, they would be unable to process and act optimally on vast amounts of data. Especially in the presence of complex, ramified consequences associated with the protection or release of personal information, our innate bounded rationality limits our ability to acquire, memorize and process all relevant information, and it makes us rely on simplified mental models, approximate strategies, and heuristics. . . .

Third, even if individuals had access to complete information and could successfully calculate optimization strategies for their privacy sensitive decisions, they might still deviate from the rational strategy. A vast body of economic and psychological literature has revealed several forms of systematic psychological deviations from rationality that affect individual decision making. . . . Research in psychology . . . documents how individuals mispredict their own future preferences or draw inaccurate conclusions from past choices. In addition, individuals often suffer from self-control problems — in particular, the tendency to trade off costs and benefits in ways that damage their future utility in favor of immediate gratification. Individuals' behavior can also be guided by social preferences or norms, such as fairness or altruism. Many of these deviations apply naturally to privacy-sensitive scenarios.[32]

The phenomenon that people say they value privacy yet fail to take steps to protect it is known as the "privacy paradox." Daniel Solove, however, argues that the privacy paradox is a myth:

Attitudes and behavior only appear to be in conflict; they actually involve different things. The behavior in the privacy paradox involves people making decisions about risk in very specific contexts. In contrast, people's attitudes about their privacy concerns or how much they value privacy are much more general in nature. . . .

Individual risk decisions in particular contexts indicate little about how people value their own privacy, which is distinct from how people value privacy in general. Further, the value of privacy cannot be determined empirically by examining individual valuations of privacy and cannot be reduced to a monetary figure based on specific transactions. Privacy's value is as a constitutive element in society, not a bartered good in the marketplace.[33]

FRED H. CATE, *PRINCIPLES OF INTERNET PRIVACY*

32 Conn. L. Rev. 877 (2000)

Perhaps the most important consideration when balancing restrictions on information is the historical importance of the free flow of information. The free flow concept is one that is not only enshrined in the First Amendment, but frankly in any form of democratic or market economy. In the United States, we have placed extraordinary importance on the open flow of information. As the Federal Reserve Board noted in its report to Congress on data protection in financial institutions, "it is the freedom to speak, supported by the availability of information and the

---

[32] Alessandro Acquisti & Jens Grossklags, *Privacy and Rationality in Decision Making*, IEEE, Security and Privacy 24 (2005).

[33] Daniel J. Solove, *The Myth of the Privacy Paradox*, 89 Geo. Wash. L. Rev. 1, 4-5 (2021).

free-flow of data, that is the cornerstone of a democratic society and market economy."

The significance of open data flows is reflected in the constitutional provisions not only for freedom of expression, but for copyrights — to promote the creation and dissemination of expression, and for a post office — to deliver the mail and the news. Federal regulations demonstrate a sweeping preference for openness, reflected in the Freedom of Information Act, Government in the Sunshine Act, and dozens of other laws applicable to the government. There are even more laws requiring disclosure by private industry, such as the regulatory disclosures required by securities and commodities laws, banking and insurance laws, and many others. This is a very basic tenet of the society in which we live. Laws that restrict that free flow almost always conflict with this basic principle. That does not mean that such laws are never upheld, but merely that they face a considerable constitutional hurdle.

This is done with good reason. Open information flows are not only essential to self-governance; they have also generated significant, practical benefits. The ready availability of personal information helps businesses "deliver the right products and services to the right customers, at the right time, more effectively and at lower cost," Fred Smith, founder and President of the Competitive Enterprise Institute, has written. Federal Reserve Board Governor Edward Gramlich testified before Congress in July 1999 that "[i]nformation about individuals' needs and preferences is the cornerstone of any system that allocates goods and services within an economy." The more such information is available, he continued, "the more accurately and efficiently will the economy meet those needs and preferences." . . .

Perhaps most importantly, widely accessible personal information has helped to create a democratization of opportunity in the United States. Anyone can go almost anywhere, make purchases from vendors they will never see, maintain accounts with banks they will never visit, and obtain credit far from home all because of open information flows. Americans can take advantage of opportunities based on their records, on what they have done rather than who they know, because access to consumer information makes it possible for distant companies and creditors to make rational decisions about doing business with individuals. The open flow of information gives consumers real choice. This is what the open flow of information principle reflects, not just the constitutional importance of information flows, but their significant economic and social benefits as well.

NOTES & QUESTIONS

1. ***The Pros and Cons of the Free Flow of Information.*** In a striking passage, Cate points out that free flows of information create a "democratization of opportunity in the United States." With this phrase, he reminds us that part of the equality at the basis of American life concerns economic opportunity, and that, in his view, a certain kind of flow of personal information will contribute to this goal. While privacy can be problematic, can open access to information also raise difficulties? How should one establish a baseline for open access or restricted access to personal information?

2. ***The Costs of Privacy.*** Can you think of some of the other important values with which privacy might conflict and the costs that privacy can impose? What should be the baseline in measuring costs?

3. ***The Benefits of Information Collection and Use.*** Consider Kent Walker:

> Having some information about yourself out there in the world offers real convenience that goes beyond dollars and cents. Many people benefit from warehousing information — billing and shipping addresses, credit card numbers, individual preferences, and the like — with trustworthy third parties. Such storage of information can dramatically simplify the purchasing experience, ensure that you get a nonsmoking room, or automate the task of ordering a kiddie meal every time your child boards a plane. Likewise, most people prefer to use a credit card rather than a debit card, trading confidentiality of purchases for the convenience of deferred payment.[34]

Is there a tradeoff between privacy and convenience? Does privacy impede efficiency in the modern world?

D. THE FEMINIST PERSPECTIVE ON PRIVACY

REVA B. SIEGEL, *"THE RULE OF LOVE": WIFE BEATING AS PREROGATIVE AND PRIVACY*

105 Yale L.J. 2117 (1996)

. . . The Anglo-American common law originally provided that a husband, as master of his household, could subject his wife to corporal punishment or "chastisement" so long as he did not inflict permanent injury upon her. During the nineteenth century, an era of feminist agitation for reform of marriage law, authorities in England and the United States declared that a husband no longer had the right to chastise his wife. Yet, for a century after courts repudiated the right of chastisement, the American legal system continued to treat wife beating differently from other cases of assault and battery. While authorities denied that a husband had the right to beat his wife, they intervened only intermittently in cases of marital violence: Men who assaulted their wives were often granted formal and informal immunities from prosecution, in order to protect the privacy of the family and to promote "domestic harmony." In the late 1970s, the feminist movement began to challenge the concept of family privacy that shielded wife abuse, and since then, it has secured many reforms designed to protect women from marital violence. . .

.

Until the late nineteenth century, Anglo-American common law structured marriage to give a husband superiority over his wife in most aspects of the relationship. By law, a husband acquired rights to his wife's person, the value of her paid and unpaid labor, and most property she brought into the marriage. A wife

---

[34] Kent Walker, *Where Everybody Knows Your Name: A Pragmatic Look at the Costs of Privacy and the Benefits of Information Exchange,* 2000 Stan. Tech. L. Rev. 2, 39, 46, 48 (2000).

was obliged to obey and serve her husband, and the husband was subject to a reciprocal duty to support his wife and represent her within the legal system. . . .

As master of the household, a husband could command his wife's obedience, and subject her to corporal punishment or "chastisement" if she defied his authority. In his treatise on the English common law, Blackstone explained that a husband could "give his wife moderate correction." . . .

During the 1850s, woman's rights advocates organized numerous conventions throughout the Northeast and Midwest, published newspapers, and conducted petition campaigns seeking for women the right to vote and demanding various reforms of marriage law. And in time the movement did elicit a response. Legislatures and courts began to modify the common law of marital status — first giving wives the right to hold property in marriage, and then the right to their earnings and the rudiments of legal agency: the right to file suit in their own names and to claim contract and tort damages. . . .

. . . By the 1880s, prominent members of the American Bar Association advocated punishing wife beaters at the whipping post, and campaigned vigorously for legislation authorizing the penalty. Between 1876 and 1906, twelve states and the District of Columbia considered enacting legislation that provided for the punishment of wife beaters at the whipping post. The bills were enacted in Maryland (1882), Delaware (1901), and Oregon (1906). . . .

We are left with a striking portrait of legal change. Jurists and lawmakers emphatically repudiated the doctrine of marital chastisement, yet responded to marital violence erratically — often condoning it, and condemning it in circumstances suggesting little interest in the plight of battered wives. Given this record, how are we to make sense of chastisement's demise? . . .

A key concept in the doctrinal regime that emerged from chastisement's demise was the notion of marital privacy. During the antebellum era, courts began to invoke marital privacy as a supplementary rationale for chastisement, in order to justify the common law doctrine within the discourse of companionate marriage, when rationales rooted in authority-based discourses of marriage had begun to lose their persuasive power. . . .

. . . By now it should be clear enough how privacy talk was deployed in the domestic violence context to enforce and preserve authority relations between man and wife. . . .

. . . By the early twentieth century, numerous state supreme courts had barred wives from suing their husbands for intentional torts — typically on the grounds that "the tranquility of family relations" would be "disturb[ed]." . . .

It was not until the late 1970s that the contemporary women's rights movement mounted an effective challenge to this regime. Today, after numerous protest activities and law suits, there are shelters for battered women and their children, new arrest procedures for police departments across the country, and even federal legislation making gender-motivated assaults a civil rights violation. . . .

There is remarkably little scholarship on the social history of privacy discourses; consequently, we know very little about the ways in which conceptions of privacy shaped popular understandings of marriage, or marital violence, in the nineteenth century. But there is no reason to assume that, before demise of the chastisement prerogative, married persons understood a traditional prerogative of marriage, rooted in notions of a husband's authority as master and head of his household, in a framework of "privacy" and "domestic harmony." It seems just as likely that legal elites devised the story linking "privacy" and "domestic harmony" to wife beating in the wake of chastisement's demise (or in anticipation of it). . . .

NOTES & QUESTIONS

1. *Privacy and Gender.* As the *Rhodes* court stated in 1868: "We will not interfere with family government in trifling cases. We will no more interfere where the husband whips the wife, than where the wife whips the husband; and yet we would hardly be supposed to hold, that a wife has a *right* to whip her husband." Is this decision really a neutral one? Does the right to privacy described by Warren and Brandeis apply equally to men and women?[35]

2. *The Uses of the Public/Private Distinction.* Catharine MacKinnon writes:

> The liberal ideal of the private holds that, as long as the public does not interfere, autonomous individuals interact freely and equally. Privacy is the ultimate value of the negative state. Conceptually, this private is hermetic. It means that which is inaccessible to, unaccountable to, unconstructed by, anything beyond itself. By definition, it is not part of or conditioned by anything systematic outside it. It is personal, intimate, autonomous, particular, individual, the original source and final outpost of the self, gender neutral. It is defined by everything that feminism reveals women have never been allowed to be or to have, and by everything that women have been equated with and defined in terms of men's ability to have. . . . This right to privacy is a right of men "to be let alone" to oppress women one at a time. . . .

According to MacKinnon, "For women the measure of the intimacy has been the measure of oppression. This is why feminism has seen the personal as the political." She notes that "the legal concept of privacy can and has shielded the place of battery, marital rape, and women's exploited domestic labor. It has preserved the central institutions whereby women are deprived of identity, autonomy, control, and self-definition. It has protected a primary activity through which male supremacy is expressed and enforced."[36]

Is MacKinnon's negative response to the public/private distinction justifiable given the prior uses of this distinction?

Consider Anita Allen:

> Critiques of privacy such as MacKinnon's go wrong at the point where the historic unequal treatment of women and the misuse of the private household to further women's domination is taken as grounds for rejecting either the condition of privacy itself or the long-overdue legal rights to effective decision-making that promote and protect that condition. Privacy, here broadly defined as the inaccessibility of persons, their mental states, or information about them to the senses and surveillance devices of others . . . does not pose an inherent threat to women. Nor do sex, love, marriage, and children any longer presume the total abrogation of the forms of privacy a woman might otherwise enjoy. On the contrary, women today are finally in a position to expect, experience, and

---

[35] For a feminist critique of the Warren and Brandeis article, see Anita L. Allen & Erin Mack, *How Privacy Got Its Gender*, 10 N. Ill. U. L. Rev. 441 (1990).

[36] Catherine A. MacKinnon, *Toward a Feminist Theory of the State* (1989).

exploit real privacy within the home and within heterosexual relationships. The women's movement, education, access to affordable birth control, liberalized divorce laws, and the larger role for women in politics, government, and the economy have expanded women's opinions and contributed to the erosion of oppressively nonegalitarian styles of home life. These advances have enhanced the capacity of American men and women, but especially and for the first time women, to secure conditions of adequate and meaningful privacy at home paramount to moral personhood and responsible participation in families and larger segments of society. Instead of rejecting privacy as "male ideology" and subjugation, women can and ought to embrace opportunities for privacy and the exercise of reproductive liberty in their private lives.[37]

Do you agree with Anita Allen that privacy should not be abandoned as a value despite its checkered past?[38]

3. *To What Extent Can Law Change Social Practices?* According to Frances Olsen, "The notion of noninterference in the family depends upon some shared conception of proper family roles, and 'neutrality' [of the State] can be understood only with reference to such roles."[39] This idea suggests that privacy, within or without the family, might also depend on shared views as to proper social roles. Do you agree?

Olsen also notes: "The theory of the private family, like free market theory, includes the assertion that particularized adjustments of seemingly unfair or inhumane results will not actually serve anybody's long run interests." Specifically, "it is claimed that state intervention to protect the weaker family members from abuse by the stronger is ineffective because powerful, underlying 'real' relations between family members will inevitably reassert themselves." This argument, which one might term the argument from futility, was rejected in the course of the twentieth century by the powerful social movement to stop spousal abuse and mistreatment of children. Are similar arguments from futility being made today about the "inevitable" erosion of privacy?

DANIELLE KEATS CITRON, *SEXUAL PRIVACY*
128 Yale L.J. 1870 (2019)

The barriers that protect information about our intimate lives are under assault. Networked technologies are exploited to surveil and expose individuals' naked bodies and intimate activities. Home devices are used to spy on intimates and ex-intimates. Hidden cameras film people in bedrooms and restrooms, and "up their skirts" without permission. People are coerced into sharing nude images and

---

[37] Anita L. Allen, *Uneasy Access: Privacy for Women in a Free Society* (1988).

[38] For an overview of the feminist critique of privacy, see generally Judith W. DeCew, *In Pursuit of Privacy: Law, Ethics, and the Rise of Technology* 81-94 (1997); Patricia Boling, *Privacy and the Politics of Intimate Life* (1996); Frances Olsen, *Constitutional Law: Feminist Critiques of the Public/Private Distinction*, 10 Const. Commentary 327 (1993); Ruth Gavison, *Feminism and the Public/Private Distinction*, 45 Stan. L. Rev. 21 (1992).

[39] Frances Olsen, *The Family and the Market: A Study of Ideology and Legal Reform*, 96 Harv. L. Rev. 1497, 1506 (1983).

making sex videos under threat of public disclosure. Sexually explicit images are posted online without their subjects' permission. Technology enables the creation of hyper-realistic "deep fake" sex videos that insert people's faces into pornography.

At the heart of each of these abuses is an invasion of sexual privacy--the social norms (behaviors, expectations, and decisions) that govern access to, and information about, individuals' intimate lives. Sexual privacy concerns the concealment of naked bodies and intimate activities including, but not limited to, sexual intercourse. It involves personal decisions about intimate life, such as whether to entrust others with information about one's sexuality or gender, or whether to expose one's body to others. As I am using the term, sexual privacy is both descriptive and normative. It concerns how the social norms surrounding individuals' intimate lives are currently experienced and how they should be experienced.

Sexual privacy sits at the apex of privacy values because of its importance to sexual agency, intimacy, and equality. We are free only insofar as we can manage the boundaries around our bodies and intimate activities. With sexual privacy, we can experiment with our bodies, our sexuality, and our gender. We can author our intimate lives and be seen as whole human beings rather than as just our intimate parts or innermost sexual fantasies.

Without sexual privacy, we have difficulty forming intimate relationships. We develop relationships of love and caring through a process of mutual self-disclosure and vulnerability. Partners reveal their innermost selves to one other with the expectation that they will protect each other's intimate information. When a partner's confidence is betrayed, it can be difficult to trust others in the future.

Equal opportunity is on the line as well. Women and individuals from marginalized communities shoulder the brunt of the abuse. They suffer stigmatization in the wake of sexual-privacy invasions. They lose their jobs and have difficulty finding new ones. They feel humiliated and ashamed. Sexual-privacy violations deny them the ability to enjoy life's crucial opportunities.

Despite sexual privacy's importance, reforms have proceeded slowly. This is partly because we lack a clear conception of what sexual privacy is and the harms wrought by its invasion. Policy makers and companies have addressed particular abuses only in isolation. One day, the discussion centers on nonconsensual pornography; the next, it centers on sextortion; and so on. Because the full breadth of the harm is not in view, policy makers fail to realize the costs of these violations.

Social attitudes have also stymied reform efforts. Some contend that sexual privacy merits no attention because sexual-privacy invasions involve problems of victims' making. Others warn that efforts to protect sexual privacy reinforce outmoded views of sexual modesty and shame or that sexual privacy would simply hide the abuse of the vulnerable.

Yet sexual privacy need not work this way. A comprehensive account of sexual privacy would bring into view the full breadth of the harm inflicted by its invasion. It would allow us to appreciate the true nature of social attitudes dismissing sexual privacy as unimportant. Saying that victims "asked for it" is just another way that society has long trivialized harms suffered by people from marginalized communities. Far from re-inscribing shame, the identification and protection of sexual privacy would affirm people's ability to manage the boundaries of their intimate lives. It would convey respect for individuals' choices about whom they entrust with their bodies and intimate information.

But would the protection of sexual privacy inevitably conceal abuse of the vulnerable? Past need not be prologue. Courts once immunized male batterers from assault law in the name of "family privacy." Missing from this privacy calculus was the invasion of battered women's sexual privacy. In the home, battered women were subject to unwanted inspection, exhibition, and abuse. Their bodies were not their own—society protected male batterers' privacy interests at the expense of battered women's sexual privacy. Courts should have considered the sexual-privacy interests of all the parties involved—including women in the home. Today, law and society must take full account of all individuals' privacy interests, with a clear understanding of sexual privacy's distinct importance.

NOTES & QUESTIONS

1. *A Hierarchy of Privacy Interests*. Danielle Citron is concerned about invasions of sexual privacy, which she defines as "the social norms . . . that govern access to, and information about, individuals' intimate lives." In her view, sexual privacy sits among the foundational privacy values, along with intellectual privacy, health privacy, and children's privacy, among others. As she contends, "We are free only insofar as we can manage the boundaries around our bodies and intimate activities." How is the law to best evaluate competing claims of privacy relating to intimate activities? What examples of possible claims come to mind beyond those that Citron references involving battered women and male batterers?

2. *Extra Protection for Intimate Information*. In *A New Compact for Intimate Information*, Citron considers the way that people's intimate lives now are under constant surveillance.[40] She points to how people subscribe to dating apps or have highly sensitive information collected by "data brokers, cyber stalking apps, and sites devoted to nonconsensual pornography." Citron also analyzes the implications of "femtech," which are "apps and services that collect information about women's period cycles, fertility, pregnancies, menopause, and sexual and reproductive histories," as well as adult sites that track people's searches and video views and sell them to advertisers and marketers.

   Her response to these kinds of surveillance is to propose "a new compact for the protection of intimate information," including limits on collection, use restrictions, and, perhaps most interestingly, a "data death penalty," which would allow courts to permanently prohibit a party from processing intimate information. Does the "data death penalty" raise problematic issues regarding the free flow of data? Is the concept of "manipulation" one that the law can define? Should "femtech" be regulated with a sectoral privacy law, in the fashion, for example, that U.S. law regulates financial institutions (through the Gramm-Leach-Bliley Act) and credit reporting agencies (through the Fair Credit Reporting Act)?

---

[40] Danielle Citron, *A New Compact for Intimate Information*, 61 Wm & Mary L. Rev 1763 (2020).

3. ***Feminist Surveillance Studies.*** Rachel Dubrofsky and Shoshana Amielle Magnet have called for a feminist perspective on surveillance studies. In their view, a feminist analysis can reveal "the ways in which supposedly 'neutral' technologies" lead to disenfranchisement.[41] They write, "although whole-body imaging technologies are specifically marketed to emphasize that they do not profile individuals based on the color of their skin, these technologies nevertheless, in directly targeting particular communities . . . serve to intensify existing inequalities." In their example, "backscatter x-rays continue the direct attack on the civil rights of transgender folks." Are there other areas in which a feminist perspective will expand and deepen our understanding of privacy?

4. ***Information Privacy Post-*Dobbs.** In its decision in *Dobbs v. Jackson Women's Health Organization* (2022), the Supreme Court overruled *Roe v. Wade* (1973), which had protected a constitutional right to abortion. Azi Huq and Rebecca Wexler have warned that reproductive choice and its limitation now will "turn upon information."[42] They observe that criminal and civil restrictors of reproductive choice depend on information, just as access to reproductive choice and to counseling turns on digital communications. In response, Huq and Wexler predict that there will be four distinct digital "quarters" in which coming abortion wars will take place. "(1) technology firms' decisions to collect and retain data; (2) technology firms' responses to regulators' demands for information; (3) technological infrastructure that empowers individual users to access information privately and securely; and (4) state and federal data privacy and evidentiary privilege regulation or legislation." How is information privacy law best to protect those digital activities in which pregnant persons act in search for reproductive choice?

E. THE CIVIL RIGHTS PERSPECTIVE ON PRIVACY

Contemporary patterns of surveillance increasingly affect everyone. At the same time, the kind of surveillance directed towards marginalized populations differs from that faced by more privileged parties. The resulting impact of surveillance on these groups is also different. This section explores the civil rights perspective on privacy.

The following article is by Federal Trade Commissioner Alvaro Bedoya, and was written while he served as founding director of the Center on Privacy & Technology at Georgetown University Law Center. In it, Bedoya talks about his earlier work as chief counsel at the Senate Judiciary Subcommittee on Privacy, Technology, and the Law. Commissioner Bedoya was sworn in at the FTC in May 16, 2022 for a term that expires in September 2026.

---

[41] Rachel E. Dubrofsky & Shoshana Amielle Magnet, *Introduction*, 1, 5 *in Feminist Surveillance Studies* (Rachel E. Dubrofsky & Shoshana Amielle Magnet eds., 2015).

[42] Aziz Z. Huq & Rebecca Wexler, *Digital Privacy for Reproductive Choice in the Post-*Roe *Era*, 98 N.Y.U. L. Rev. 555 (2023).

After the Bedoya article, there is an excerpt from an article by Anita Allen on "the Black Opticon." In it, Allen identifies three categories of bias and discrimination that African Americans face due to the collection of personal data online.

ALVARO M. BEDOYA, *PRIVACY AS CIVIL RIGHT*

50 N. Mexico L. Rev. 301 (2020)

Yes, privacy is a civil liberty. I am here to tell you that privacy is also a civil right. When we talk about privacy only as a civil liberty, we erase those patterns of harm, that color of surveillance. And when we talk about privacy only as a civil liberty, we also ignore the benefits of privacy: Surveillance threatens vulnerable people fighting for equality. Privacy is what protects them and makes it possible. . . .

When we talk about the disparate impact of surveillance, we have to be careful. We must not reinforce the idea that the targets of surveillance are helpless victims. Often, in fact, the "other" is being watched precisely because they are fighting back. And sometimes, they win—and that watching fails and is utterly useless. . . .

The FBI surveilled César Chávez for roughly a decade. . . . The FBI followed César Chávez nearly everywhere he went. Farmworkers picket grape growers in Delano. The FBI is there. Farmworkers march through the San Joaquin Valley to Sacramento. The FBI is on the route. Farmworkers start to organize in the Rio Grande Valley. The FBI follows.

The final FBI file on César Chávez was fifteen hundred pages long. It listed Chávez's daily routine, what he ate for breakfast. The specific songs that Joan Baez sang at his rallies. His relatives, where they worked, where they lived. It was a minutely detailed portrait of César Chávez's life that has actually proven quite useful for historians of the farmworker rights movement.

What won't you find in those fifteen hundred pages? A single incriminating detail.

César Chávez was not a communist. His associates were not communists. He was faithful to his wife. He did not misuse union funds. And when the farmworkers demonstrated, when they used their bodies to affect change, they were not violent. They turned the other cheek. There are actually FBI telegrams on farmworker protests that say in all caps "EXTREMELY ORDERLY." And there is a note of frustration to them. Because the FBI never "caught" César Chávez in anything.

Unfortunately, César Chávez's story is uncommon: The man was a saint; the rest of us are human.

Marcus Garvey was human. J. Edgar Hoover followed him, also. His agents would literally peer into the windows of his hotel rooms. But Hoover hadn't caught Garvey on anything.

Then the government got a hold of a marketing brochure for stock in the Black Star Line, which Garvey founded and ran. The brochure showed a handsome steamship named for Phyllis Wheatley, the famous African American poet.

But Garvey had moved too quickly. He was negotiating for that ship, but he didn't own it yet. In fact, the sale fell through. And so the government learned that and used it to charge and convict Garvey of mail fraud. They sent him to prison, and deported him in 1927. . . .

The Rev. Martin Luther King, Jr. was human. Hoover's FBI followed him, wiretapped him, and bugged his hotels. Senior FBI officials compiled a recording of his extramarital affairs and sent it to his office, along with a note threatening blackmail and implying that Dr. King should kill himself.

The package was forwarded to the King family home. It was Coretta Scott King who found it and opened it. "They are out to break me," Dr. King told a friend. "They are out to get me, harass me, and break my spirit." . . . .

It is easy to focus on J. Edgar Hoover, but these patterns predated him and continued long after his passing. Let's talk about how they continue today. . . .

Since last summer, ICE has publicly reserved the right to use information from scared, detained kids, and the families who want to care for them, to find, arrest, and deport their families. And it has happened to one hundred and seventy people, including at least three in New Mexico.

There's a detail here that I think is haunting. Last fall, when a coalition of NGOs wrote a letter to DHS and HHS denouncing what was happening, there was an unusual number of Japanese American organizations who signed on: The Japanese Americans Citizens League, the Japanese American Service Committee, the Fred T. Korematsu Center for Law and Equality. There were many other civil rights groups, but no other national origin group was represented like that.

Why? Well, it turns out that in the 1940s, when our government ordered Americans of Japanese descent into internment camps, they had help from the Census. In 1940, Japanese American families had been surveyed, and were promised that their information would remain confidential. But Congress then waived those rules, and used that confidential census data to find and incarcerate them in internment camps like the ones that were here in Lordsburg and Santa Fe.

On May 12, 1950, when Senator Chávez said "we are a nation of dissenters," when he said that "your ancestors and my ancestors left [their homes] because they were dissenters," because "[they] were not satisfied with the things as they were," he wasn't just talking about the Pilgrims. He was talking about immigrants, activists. He was talking about vulnerable people who dare to want more.

Surveillance is a tool that the powerful use to stop that. . . .

On June 6, 2013, I was sitting down for dinner at Bertucci's Pizza on Connecticut Avenue in Washington, D.C. and my Blackberry started lighting up.

So I opened it up. Edward Snowden had just revealed that the NSA was tracking the calls of not one, not some, but rather millions of Verizon customers. That first leak ushered in the most intense and important surveillance debate in a generation.

At that time, I was the chief counsel to the Senate Judiciary Subcommittee on Privacy, Technology, and the Law. It was my job to run one of the key subcommittees tasked with finding out what the NSA was doing and then writing legislation to rein them in.

So, you know, no more pizza. The next year was a blur of hearings and negotiations. . . .

But we made some progress; we passed an NSA reform bill with many strengths and yes, many weaknesses. Yet, even then, in that haze of activity, I remember thinking to myself during those negotiations, but particularly in the hearings, "When are we going to talk about the history of surveillance, and the people it affects? We're calling business groups to testify, civil liberties groups— why aren't we calling civil rights groups?"

Once I left the Senate and came to Georgetown Law, I had time to re-read the transcripts and all of the news stories in that period. And it was worse than I had thought. Because it turns out that three months after Edward Snowden went public, the NSA itself disclosed that it hadn't just been the FBI that had wiretapped Dr. King. The NSA wiretapped him, also, along with Mohammad Ali and Whitney Young of the National Urban League. This was a part of an operation aimed at finding out if U.S. political activists were working with the Soviet Union (They were not.). . . . In 2013 and 2014, the threat of surveillance to civil rights was not some obscure, abstract thing. It was staring us in the face. You would expect senators to debate that.

They did not. . . . [S]enators never discussed, in depth, any aspect of how surveillance can be and has been used to target and harm racial and religious minorities. The senators talked about how the revelations hurt our relationships with our allies. They quantified the billions of dollars in predicted losses to American cloud computing companies and other businesses. They called three separate industry witnesses to talk about it. The senators even spoke about how the leaks harmed military morale and reputation.

But when it came time to talk about how NSA spying was affecting people— not nations or institutions—that granularity was gone. Instead, it was a high-level discussion about our right to privacy, free speech, and chilling effects. It was about how the spying had infringed on the liberties of "millions of Americans," "the American public," or "the American people." It was the same story of "everyone is watched."

Let me acknowledge that I'm just as guilty as anyone else for all of this. I organized one of those hearings. I suggested that my boss call an industry witness when we could have called a witness from the civil rights community. And I staffed my boss at numerous other hearings, floor speeches, and public events. I was a part of the problem.

What I want to stress to you, though, is that what happened during NSA reform is the rule, not the exception. When Congress meets to talk about surveillance, be it police surveillance and particularly NSA surveillance, it is the exceptional member of Congress who sees this pattern of disparate impact, and who acts to reverse it.

In the last two to three years, this has started to change. In particular, Chairman Elijah Cummings, Chairman Bennie Thompson, Cedric Richmond of the Congressional Black Caucus, and others, are starting to ask questions. Questions about racial bias in face recognition technology; about how ICE planned to scan the social media of all immigrants to target deportations; questions underscoring the fact that surveillance isn't just a threat to liberty—it is a threat to equality also.
. . .

When there is that moral lag, that gap between what is legal and what is right, privacy is the shield that allows the unpopular and persecuted to survive and thrive. It is what allows them to labor "in a private way," far beyond the government's eyes.

And so, as we build a world of pervasive surveillance, we have to ask ourselves: Are we building a world without underground railroads? Are we building a world where that kind of dissent is impossible?

ANITA L. ALLEN, *DISMANTLING THE "BLACK OPTICON"*
131 Yale L.J. Forum 301 (Feb. 20, 2022)

In pursuit of equitable data privacy, American lawmakers should focus on the experiences of marginalized populations no less than privileged populations. For Black Americans, those experiences feature three compounding vulnerabilities: (1) multiple forms of excessive and discriminatory surveillance; (2) targeted exclusion through differential access to online opportunities; and (3) exploitative online financial fraud and deception. Digital-privacy and data-protection law proposals fashioned to promote equitable governance online must be responsive to calls for improved online governance made by and on behalf of African Americans relating to these forms of pervasive and persistent disadvantage. . . .

African Americans dwell under the attentive eye of a Black Opticon, a threefold system of societal disadvantage comprised of discriminatory oversurveillance (the panopticon), exclusion (the ban-opticon), and predation (the con-opticon). This disadvantage—propelled by algorithms and machine-learning technologies that are potentially unfair and perpetuate group bias—is inimical to data privacy and an ideal of data processing that respects the data subject's claim to human dignity and equality. Structural racism renders African Americans especially vulnerable to disparities and disadvantages online. Highlighting the problem of algorithmic bias, Dominique Harrison asserted that "Black and Brown people are stripped of equitable opportunities in housing, schools, loans, and employment because of biased data." As Harrison's observations attest, my Black Opticon metaphor—denoting the ways Black people and their data can be visually observed and otherwise paid attention to online—encapsulates literal aspects of the urgent privacy and data-protection problem facing African Americans. . . .

The Black Opticon exists—and has long existed—inasmuch as wrongful discrimination and bias persistently focus panoptic surveillance on African Americans, leading to oversurveillance. Location tracking, the related use of facial-recognition tools, and targeted surveillance of groups and protestors exercising their fundamental rights and freedoms are paramount data-privacy practices disproportionally impacting African Americans. . . .

I now turn to another feature of the Black Opticon, namely, targeting Black people for exclusion from beneficial opportunities on the basis of race. Discriminatory exclusion requires obtaining information identifying a person as African American. . . .

Discriminatory practices (i.e., those that rely on racialized sorting by humans and machines that reinforce racism and deny equal access to services and opportunities) thrive on online platforms. Platforms have come under attack for targeted advertising that discriminates against consumers of color with respect to housing, credit, and services, for hosting racially biased advertisements, and for facilitating unequal and discriminatory access to ridesharing and vacation rentals. . . .

Personal data of people of color are also gathered and used to induce purchases and contracts through con jobs, scams, lies, and trickery. Discriminatory predation describes the use of communities of color's data to lure them into making exploitative agreements and purchases. This feature of the Black Opticon searches out and targets vulnerable African Americans online and offline for con-job inclusion. Predatory surveillance is the flip side of the exclusionary-surveillance coin. . . .

The Black Opticon pays the wrong kinds of attention to African Americans, using the resources of internet platforms and other digital technologies to gather, process, and share data about who we are, where we are, and to what we are vulnerable.

NOTES & QUESTIONS

1. *Disproportionate Effects of Surveillance.* Commissioner Bedoya's lecture honors the first U.S.-born Hispanic senator, Senator Dennis Chávez of New Mexico and his legacy of advocacy for civil rights and civil liberties. Bedoya is concerned that a commonly accepted notion regarding the ubiquitous nature of surveillance ignores how throughout American history the burdens of surveillance have fallen overwhelmingly on the shoulders of immigrants, heretics, people of color, the poor, and anyone else considered "other." In his view, privacy is to be understood as a civil right: "A shield that allows the unpopular and persecuted to survive and thrive."

   In 2016, Bedoya talked about how past patterns of surveillance continue to this date. He writes:

   > There is a myth in this country that in a world where everyone is watched, everyone is watched equally. It's as if an old and racist J. Edgar Hoover has been replaced by the race-blind magic of computers, mathematicians, and Big Data. The truth is more uncomfortable. Across our history and to this day, people of color have been the disproportionate victims of unjust surveillance; Hoover was no aberration. And while racism has played its ugly part, the justification for this monitoring was the same we hear today: national security.[43]

2. *Understanding Privacy as a Civil Right.* Why does it matter whether privacy is understood as a civil right? Consider Tiffany Li:

   > [A]s a classical civil liberty, privacy protects the rights of assembly and speech for political dissidents and community advocates. However, conceptualizing privacy as only a civil liberty ignores the fact that these privacy rights, including the core rights to speech and assembly, have never been awarded equally to all Americans. If nothing else, a civil rights gloss on privacy rights can help us understand privacy in a way that might one day match protection for civil liberties.

---

[43] Alvaro Bedoya, *The Color of Surveillance*, Slate (Jan. 18. 2016), at https://slate.com/technology/2016/01/what-the-fbis-surveillance-of-martin-luther-king-says-about-modern-spying.html. For historical background about surveillance's disproportionate focus and effects on African-Americans, see Simone Browne, *Dark Matters: On the Surveillance of Blackness* (2015)

Framing privacy primarily as a consumer protection right does not go nearly far enough to address the power imbalance between corporations and consumers and does not address the ways in which consumer privacy rights and violations of those rights can shape laws and norms outside of the consumer context.[44]

Scott Skinner-Thompson observes:

[E]xisting *legal* theories of privacy have, by and large, given inadequate attention to the amplified importance of privacy to marginalized communities and been unable to connect those privacy harms to doctrinal solutions. Instead, in various legal contexts, privacy continues to be conceptualized and framed as a broad, amorphous, universalist value – something akin to autonomy, dignity, or personhood – that fails to capture the discrete, particular, and *material* harms that directly result from privacy violations.[45]

3. ***The Panoptic Sort.*** In *The Panoptic Sort,* a highly influential early book about information privacy, Oscar Gandy sees parallels in our digital data-driven world and Jeremy Bentham's Panopticon, a prison architected with cells encircling a central observation tower. Michel Foucault later noted that modern society, with its burgeoning surveillance technology, was becoming a Panopticon – a way to control and oppress people, achieving obedience at a cost of stifling difference, deviance, and individuality. Gandy writes:

I see the panoptic sort as a kind of high-tech, cybernetic triage through which individuals and groups of people are being sorted according to their presumed economic or political value. The poor, especially poor people of color, are increasingly being treated as broken material or damaged goods to be discarded or sold at bargain prices to scavengers in the marketplace.[46]

In an afterward to the book, written nearly thirty years later, Gandy notes that while it is important to focus on the bias embedded in data used to train algorithms, it is even more important to examine the "biases that are inherent in the societal processes that generate the data in the first place."[47]

4. ***Dismantling the Black Opticon.*** In the final part of her essay, Anita Allen calls for development of a race-conscious African American Online Equity Agenda that is designed to help dismantle the Black Opticon. In her view, all of the digital economy should be regulated in the interests of nondiscrimination, antiracism, and anti-subordination. In the context of information privacy, she calls for new resources for the Federal Trade Commission and creation of a new federal data-protection agency. Allen also critiques Virginia's state privacy bill, and faults it for exempting nonprofits and state government entities, including the police, jails, and prisons. Among the other weaknesses that she identifies in the statute is its lack of a private right of action. In your opinion, what are the most important steps for a privacy law to take in order to stop discriminatory

---

[44] Tiffany C. Li, *Privacy as/and Civil Rights,* 36 Berkeley Tech L.J. 1265 (2021).

[45] Scott Skinner-Thompson, *Privacy at the Margins* (2021).

[46] Oscar H. Gandy, Jr., *The Panoptic Sort: A Political Economy of Personal Information* (2d ed. 2021) (originally published in 1993).

[47] *Id.* at 275.

oversurveillance, exclusion, and fraud?

5. ***Disproportionate Privacy Invasions on Gay People.*** Ari Waldman notes that "quantitative and qualitative data show that gay and bisexual men who use geosocial dating apps are more likely than the general population and other sexual minorities to have their intimate images taken and shared without their consent."[48] In his view, however, it would be neither fair nor persuasive to blame victims. He writes, "Victims of nonconsensual image sharing are not asking to have their privacy invaded; they are merely engaging in an important facet of modern social life that is governed, organically and by design, by powerful norms of disclosure." How should the law address the problem of privacy violations having a greater impact on certain groups more than other groups?

6. ***The Questionable Neutrality of Big Data and Algorithms.*** Andrew Ferguson argues that far too often, technologies that appear neutral as to race are used in ways that have a disparate impact on people of color:

> While race would never be included as part of the algorithm, many of the variables (police contacts, prior arrests, gang affiliations) directly correlate with racially discriminatory law enforcement practices. If the data is colored black, it means that the predictive policing system (using that data) could generate biased results.

Algorithms themselves might not directly involve race, Ferguson argues, but if the algorithms are fed data that has racial bias, the algorithm's results will reflect the biases in the data: "[I]f input data is infected with racial bias, how can the resulting algorithmic output be trusted?" As data-driven policing increases, it "reifies many of the systemic inequalities of traditional policing. . . . Targeting high-risk blocks because of the number of returning citizens or people on probation living there encodes the prior decisions of a criminal justice system that disproportionately punishes people of color."[49] Suspect-based predictive policing is also based on data that is skewed based on unequal police targeting of people of color.

Technologies of data analysis can thus amplify problematic disproportionate impacts of policing and can don a cloak of neutrality. How should the law regulate these technologies in light of these problems?

Safiya Noble has demonstrated how search engine algorithms reflect racism. When she did searches for "black girls," for example, the results were "filled with porn." Similar searches for whites did not produce these disturbing results. Algorithms draw from society's underlying racism and sexism and do not merely reflect it back; they reify, systematize, increase, and legitimize these troubling dimensions of society. "How do we reconcile the fact that ethnic and cultural communities have little to no control over being indexed in ways that

---

[48] Ari Ezra Waldman, *Law, Privacy, and Online Dating: "Revenge Porn" in Gay Online Communities*, 44 Law & Social Inquiry 987 (2019).

[49] Andrew Gunthrie Ferguson, *The Rise of Big Data Policing: Surveillance, Race, and the Future of Law Enforcement* 47, 132 (2017).

they may not want?" Noble asks. "How does a group resolve the ways that the public engaged with Google as if it is the arbiter of truth?"[50]

Algorithms, which are what form the working engine of AI, are being used make important decisions about people, such as determinations about pretrial detention, sentencing, policing, lending, hiring, education, and more. Because these algorithms involve gathering and processing massive quantities of personal data and have profound effects on people, they involve privacy issues. But the algorithms also raise problems beyond privacy, such as racism and discrimination. To what extent is privacy the appropriate lens to think about these issues? In a number of circumstances, privacy is interwoven with other issues. Privacy law can be a useful tool but it could also come up short if it is the only tool used.

F. PRIVACY, POVERTY, AND SOCIAL CLASS

The following article draws on ethnographic fieldwork research by Khiara Bridges in a large public hospital in Manhattan, which the author calls "Alpha Hospital." As Bridges notes, "The overwhelming majority of pregnant patients receiving prenatal care from the Alpha obstetrics clinic are poor, and almost all rely upon Medicaid, specifically the Prenatal Care Assistance Program, to cover the costs of their prenatal healthcare expenses."

KHIARA M. BRIDGES, *PRIVACY RIGHTS AND PUBLIC FAMILIES*
34 Harv. J. L. & Gender 113 (2011)

. . . We are asked to understand the disquietude generated by this felt tension as the quixotic longing for the persistence of the poor woman's privacy rights/liberty interests. We are told to surrender our notions of the inalienability of rights like the right to privacy. And we are expected to realize that the conflict exists only when we insist upon the continuance of the woman's privacy right/liberty interests; indeed, when we allow that the woman has bartered her rights in exchange for government assistance, the tension resolves and in its place remains a "legitimate," unfettered state presence in women's private lives.

This begs the question: what does it reveal about the nature of rights in our particular sociopolitical location when a right—once imagined as fundamental among jurists and legal scholars, as well as among those who believe themselves to be in possession of it—is so easily bartered away? Perhaps we misspeak when we assert that poor women's rights have been exchanged for state assistance. And perhaps we dissemble the actual nature of rights within our political economy when we claim that the state violates the "right" of the pregnant woman seeking Medicaid coverage of her prenatal care expenses. Perhaps nothing has been bartered, nothing has been violated.

---

[50] Safiya Umoja Noble, *Algorithms of Oppression: How Search Engines Reinforce Racism* (2018).

That is, perhaps "rights" are always already a function of class, such that the poor do not have any rights about which to speak. The Medicaid-mandated apparatus within the Alpha obstetrics clinic does not violate the rights of the pregnant patients because their socioeconomic status precludes their possession of any "rights" that the state is bound to respect. Many scholars have intimated towards this conclusion without decisively arriving at it. . . . It is not that . . . patients, because of their poverty, do not have presumptions of privacy; rather, their privacy is presumed altogether nonexistent. So framed, it does not appear that wealth helps to buy the presumption of privacy, but rather wealth is the condition of possibility for privacy. Class is the salient characteristic within Alpha because it enables an exit from the Medicaid device that demands the evacuation of the pregnant woman's rights. . . .

[T]he ease with which the poor barter their rights suggests that it may be more accurate to describe the poor as never having rights to begin with. Indeed, a more honest description may entail admitting that, in our particular sociopolitical location, wealth is a condition of possibility for rights. . . .

It deserves underscoring that my argument is not about the impoverishment of rights discourse. My claim is not that, at this time, rights are formulated as rights against government interference when what is needed are rights to some conception of liberty. While a reformulation of rights as imposing an affirmative duty on the state, rather than an interdiction upon state action—that is, a conversion of rights to "rights to" rather than "rights against"—would be a dramatic improvement to the present state of rights within the U.S., this transformation within rights discourse may not adequately resolve the dilemma at hand. That is, even if rights were conceptualized and enforced as rights to some conception of liberty, the poor may still find themselves without these new rights to positive government action. Is there reason to believe that "rights to" would not still remain a function of class? There is a danger that the poor would, in spite of a revolutionary reformulation of rights, find themselves in the same predicament in which they now find themselves: possessing "rights" without substance, meaning, or effect.

NOTES & QUESTIONS

1. *Wealth as a Precondition for Privacy.* In her article, Khiara Bridges draws on her field research at Alpha Hospital regarding acceptance of governmental assistance for prenatal care, through Medicaid. Her conclusion from her interviews is that wealth functions as a precondition for privacy. Participation in the Prenatal Care Assistance Program mandates "compelled consultations [that] function as a gross and substantial intrusion by the government into poor, pregnant women's private lives." Bridges argues, "Indeed, the families that these women seek to create or expand are made 'public' inasmuch as the state insists upon expunging the highly-idealized line that is thought to protect the 'private family' from state involvement in order to maintain a supervisory, regulatory, and occasionally punitive presence in poor women's families." Are there other contexts in which "wealth is the condition of possibility for privacy"?

2. ***The Poverty of Privacy Rights.*** In her book, *The Poverty of Privacy Rights,* Khiara Bridges notes that theories of privacy's value to society often rest upon the assumption that privacy will be put to good uses (at least most of the time). However, "if the individual enjoying privacy rights will not put them to good uses, her enjoyment of these rights will not produce the value that otherwise justifies their provision." Bridges then argues that "due to the moral construction of poverty, there is a presumption that poor mothers will not put privacy rights to good uses. Indeed, the moral construction of poverty asserts that the poor are behaviorally and/or ethically flawed. . . . [P]oor mothers are not given privacy rights because society, and thus the law, presumes that their enjoyment of privacy will realize no value or negative value."[51]

One possible way to address this problem is to rethink the flawed "moral construction of poverty" that Bridges critiques. As Bridges contends, until assumptions about poor women—that "if they are left to their own devices, they will not lead a moral life"—are changed, then "poor women and mothers will continue to be deprived of privacy rights."[52]

Another possible way to address the problem is to forbid the alienability of privacy rights. In this way, the government could be restricted from making poor women trade away their privacy rights. Would this type of solution work?

3. ***The Surveillance of the Administrative Surveillance State.*** In his book, *Overseers of the Poor,* sociologist John Gilliom documents the extensive surveillance regime imposed upon low-income welfare mothers. In particular, he focuses on the language and stories of the women subjected to the surveillance. He notes how many women do not speak in terms of privacy rights. This is understandable, he explains, because "they have been stripped of formal privacy rights claims by signing an encompassing waiver in the 'consent' form that was part of their multi-page [welfare] application. Further, federal court decisions and congressional action in the 1970s and early 1980s removed almost any limits on state surveillance in administering welfare programs." Welfare mothers "live in a context defined by understandable confusion and ignorance about basic regulations, by fear of the welfare agency and its enforcement of those regulations, and by profound need for the support that the welfare system provides." The mothers do not assert rights or demand rights because "the structural, institutional, and social pressures that push against an assertion of rights in this setting."[53]

Should there be greater limits on the surveillance powers of the administrative agencies? With welfare, the argument in support of government surveillance is that the overseeing is necessary to police against fraud, that those that bestow benefits can define the terms to receive them, and that the welfare recipients consent to the tradeoff. Do these arguments justify heightened surveillance?

---

[51] Khiara M. Bridges, *The Poverty of Privacy Rights* 12 (2017).

[52] Id. at 205.

[53] John Gilliom, *Overseers of the Poor: Surveillance, Resistance, and the Limits of Privacy* 71, 91 (2001).

4. ***The Privacy of People on Parole, Probation, or Community Supervision.*** Kate Weisburd notes that there is "increasingly invasive and largely unregulated electronic surveillance of those on community supervision." Weisburd notes that a common justification for this extensive surveillance is that people consent to it because it is a preferable alternative to prison. Weisburd critiques this argument:

> [E]ven though the defendant has not explicitly consented to the conditions of supervision, courts will often impose or uphold supervision terms as implicitly consensual in the sense that the defendant has acquiesced to a sentence that includes a term of supervision. Furthermore, the term of supervised release is on top of a period of incarceration and does not replace the prison sentence. In this way, supervised release is not an alternative to prison. And yet, the very term "search condition" linguistically reflects an assumption that community supervision is always a privilege because the alternative would be jail—even if the reality is that a defendant has no actual choice.[54]

As with the heightened surveillance system imposed on welfare recipients, consent is the common justification. Is consent in these contexts too coercive? Weisburd also points out that consent is not adequately informed because "few meaningful opportunities exist for defendants to gain the necessary information before waiving procedural rights as part of a plea or offer of a more lenient sentence."[55] When should privacy rights be waivable based on consent? In some contexts, should privacy rights be nonwaivable?

5. ***Democratic Privacy***. For Mary Anne Franks, the "contemporary pro-privacy anti-surveillance movement" is deeply flawed.[56] She argues: "The [modern privacy] movement is not primarily concerned with the harms imposed on the most vulnerable members of society, but rather with threats to mainstream and elite interests." This movement will at best lead only to "privacy reform that will protect, or at least not harm, the most powerful groups."

Franks calls for a "democratization of privacy, by structuring it around the needs and interests of those who suffer the most." Rather than an "anemic defense of anemic privacy rights that will have little chance of weathering the next great threat to expression and autonomy," the need is understand "the very long and destructive history of the surveillance of marginalized bodies, in particular black bodies, poor bodies, and female bodies." As an example of the required focus, Franks draws on the work of David Sklansky to look to a concept of "privacy as refuge"—to focus on harms flowing from physical searches of homes and bodies.[57] She argues that many commentators focus too heavily on new technologies, such as online surveillance via Google and other companies. These commentators often miss the fact that "[f]or the less privileged members of society, surveillance does not simply mean inhibited

---

[54] Kate Weisburd, *Sentenced to Surveillance: Fourth Amendment Limits on Electronic Monitoring*, 98 N.C.L Rev. 717, 720, 741 (2020).

[55] *Id.* at 742.

[56] Mary Anne Franks, *Democratic Surveillance*, 30 Harv. J. Law & Tech. 426 (2017).

[57] *Id.* For more on the concept of "privacy as refuge," see David Alan Sklansky, *Too Much Information: How Not to Think about Privacy and the Fourth Amendment*, 102 Cal. L. Rev. 1069 (2014).

Internet searches or decreased willingness to make online purchases; it can mean an entire existence under scrutiny, with every personal choice carrying a risk of bodily harm."

In short, Franks warns against a trivialization of violations of information privacy compared to "violations of physical and decisional privacy." Rather, the law is to develop "truly inclusive privacy protections." If privacy is democratized in this fashion, what kinds of protections should be created for informational privacy?

CHAPTER **3**

PRIVACY AND THE MEDIA

CHAPTER OUTLINE

D. APPROPRIATION OF NAME OR LIKENESS

E. PRIVACY PROTECTIONS FOR ANONYMITY AND RECEIPT OF IDEAS

In 1890, Samuel Warren and Louis Brandeis wrote about the increasing prolife-ration of gossip in newspapers.[1] Today, the problems Warren and Brandeis were concerned about are dramatically magnified by the vast expansion of the media. In addition to newspapers, there are magazines, movies, television, and the Internet. From marketers to moviemakers, from tabloids to 24-hour news channels, from talk shows to reality TV, we are witnessing an explosion in the demand for images, video, and stories about the personal lives of individuals, both famous and obscure. Further, anybody with a website can now disseminate information instantly around the world.

Warren and Brandeis were also concerned with photography, a new technol-ogy that had the potential to greatly facilitate information gathering by the media. Today, technologies of gathering data are significantly more sophisticated. Video cameras are in widespread use and exist in miniature forms for easy concealment; high-powered telephoto lenses can enable one to film or photograph from large distances. Moreover, almost every cell phone now contains a small built-in camera.

This chapter focuses on legal remedies for the gathering and dissemination of personal information by media entities. "Media" is understood broadly in this chapter to include people and businesses that gather and disseminate information to inform, advertise, or entertain. The chapter then explores four general types of privacy incursion by the media: (1) intrusions and harassment in the course of gathering information; (2) the disclosure of truthful information, (3) the dissemi-nation of misleading or false information; and (4) the appropriation of name or likeness. The principal remedies for media incursions into privacy are the four privacy torts inspired by Warren and Brandeis's article. The privacy torts are not the only remedies for privacy invasions. The tort of defamation, discussed at length in this chapter, is an older remedy for a particular type of privacy intrusion — the dissemination of false information. Another remedy is the tort of infliction of emotional distress, which is discussed briefly in section C. Additionally, a number of states have enacted statutes that protect against particular forms of disclosure.

---

[1] Samuel D. Warren & Louis D. Brandeis, *The Right to Privacy,* 4 Harv. L. Rev. 193 (1890).

A. INFORMATION GATHERING

In order to report the news, journalists must gather information. This task often involves being nosy, inquisitive, and aggressive. Given the vast proliferation of media and the tremendous competition to get breaking information and live video or photographs, there is great potential for media information gathering to become intrusive and harassing, especially when a person becomes the subject of a prominent story. In response to such intrusions by information gatherers, an injured party has available a number of remedies.

1. INTRUSION UPON SECLUSION

INTRUSION UPON SECLUSION

Restatement (Second) of Torts § 652B

One who intentionally intrudes, physically or otherwise, upon the solitude or seclusion of another or his private affairs or concerns, is subject to liability to the other for invasion of his privacy, if the intrusion would be highly offensive to a reasonable person.

NOTES & QUESTIONS

1. ***Intrusion upon Seclusion vs. Public Disclosure of Private Facts.*** The tort of intrusion concerns the way that the information is obtained. In contrast, for the tort of public disclosure of private facts, liability does not depend upon how the information is obtained. Consider the following commentary to the Restatement:

   Comment (a): Intrusion "does not depend upon any publicity given to the person whose interest is invaded or to his affairs."
   Comment (b): "The intrusion itself makes the defendant subject to liability, even though there is no publication or other use of any kind of the photograph or information outlined."

NADER V. GENERAL MOTORS CORP.

255 N.E.2d 765 (N.Y. Ct. App. 1970)

FULD, C.J. . . . The plaintiff [Ralph Nader], an author and lecturer on automotive safety, has, for some years, been an articulate and severe critic of General Motors' products from the standpoint of safety and design. According to the complaint — which, for present purposes, we must assume to be true — the appellant [General Motors Corporation], having learned of the imminent publication of the plaintiff's book "Unsafe at Any Speed," decided to conduct a campaign of intimidation against him in order to "suppress plaintiff's criticism of and prevent his disclosure of information" about its products. To that end, the appellant authorized and directed the other defendants to engage in a series of activities which, the plaintiff claims in his first two causes of action, violated his right to privacy.

Specifically, the plaintiff alleges that the appellant's agents (1) conducted a series of interviews with acquaintances of the plaintiff, "questioning them about, and casting aspersions upon (his) political . . . racial and religious views. . . ; his integrity; his sexual proclivities and inclinations; and his personal habits"; (2) kept him under surveillance in public places for an unreasonable length of time; (3) caused him to be accosted by girls for the purpose of entrapping him into illicit relationships; (4) made threatening, harassing and obnoxious telephone calls to him; (5) tapped his telephone and eavesdropped, by means of mechanical and electronic equipment, on his private conversations with others; and (6) conducted a "continuing" and harassing investigation of him. [Nader's complaint, among other things, contained a cause of action for intrusion.]

. . . It should be emphasized that the mere gathering of information about a particular individual does not give rise to a cause of action under [the intrusion tort]. Privacy is invaded only if the information sought is of a confidential nature and the defendant's conduct was unreasonably intrusive. Just as a common-law copyright is lost when material is published, so, too, there can be no invasion of privacy where the information sought is open to public view or has been voluntarily revealed to others. In order to sustain a cause of action for invasion of privacy, therefore, the plaintiff must show that the appellant's conduct was truly "intrusive" and that it was designed to elicit information which would not be available through normal inquiry or observation. . . .

. . . At most, only two of the activities charged to the appellant are, in our view, actionable as invasions of privacy under the law of the District of Columbia. . . .

Turning, then, to the particular acts charged in the complaint, we cannot find any basis for a claim of invasion of privacy, under District of Columbia law, in the allegations that the appellant, through its agents or employees, interviewed many persons who knew the plaintiff, asking questions about him and casting aspersions on his character. Although those inquiries may have uncovered information of a personal nature, it is difficult to see how they may be said to have invaded the plaintiff's privacy. Information about the plaintiff which was already known to others could hardly be regarded as private to the plaintiff. Presumably, the plaintiff had previously revealed the information to such other persons, and he would necessarily assume the risk that a friend or acquaintance in whom he had confided might breach the confidence. If, as alleged, the questions tended to disparage the plaintiff's character, his remedy would seem to be by way of an action for defamation, not for breach of his right to privacy.

Nor can we find any actionable invasion of privacy in the allegations that the appellant caused the plaintiff to be accosted by girls with illicit proposals, or that it was responsible for the making of a large number of threatening and harassing telephone calls to the plaintiff's home at odd hours. Neither of these activities, howsoever offensive and disturbing, involved intrusion for the purpose of gathering information of a private and confidential nature. . . .

Apart, however, from the foregoing allegations which we find inadequate to spell out a cause of action for invasion of privacy under District of Columbia law, the complaint contains allegations concerning other activities by the appellant or its agents which do satisfy the requirements for such a cause of action. The one which most clearly meets those requirements is the charge that the appellant and its codefendants engaged in unauthorized wiretapping and eavesdropping by mechanical and electronic means. . . .

There are additional allegations that the appellant hired people to shadow the plaintiff and keep him under surveillance. In particular, he claims that, on one occasion, one of its agents followed him into a bank, getting sufficiently close to him to see the denomination of the bills he was withdrawing from his account. From what we have already said, it is manifest that the mere observation of the plaintiff in a public place does not amount to an invasion of his privacy. But, under certain circumstances, surveillance may be so "overzealous" as to render it actionable. Whether or not the surveillance in the present case falls into this latter category will depend on the nature of the proof. A person does not automatically make public everything he does merely by being in a public place, and the mere fact that Nader was in a bank did not give anyone the right to try to discover the amount of money he was withdrawing. On the other hand, if the plaintiff acted in such a way as to reveal that fact to any casual observer, then, it may not be said that the appellant intruded into his private sphere. In any event, though, it is enough for present purposes to say that the surveillance allegation is not insufficient as a matter of law. . . .

BRIETEL, J. concurring in the result. . . . [S]cholars, in trying to define the elusive concept of the right of privacy, have, as of the present, subdivided the common law right into separate classifications, most significantly distinguishing between unreasonable intrusion and unreasonable publicity. This does not mean, however, that the classifications are either frozen or exhausted, or that several of the classifications may not overlap.

Concretely applied to this case, it is suggested, for example, that it is premature to hold that the attempted entrapment of plaintiff in a public place by seemingly promiscuous ladies is no invasion of any of the categories of the right to privacy and is restricted to a much more limited cause of action for intentional infliction of mental distress. Moreover, it does not strain credulity or imagination to conceive of the systematic "public" surveillance of another as being the implementation of a plan to intrude on the privacy of another. Although acts performed in "public," especially if taken singly or in small numbers, may not be confidential, at least arguably a right to privacy may nevertheless be invaded through extensive or exhaustive monitoring and cataloguing of acts normally disconnected and anonymous.

These are but illustrations of the problems raised in attempting to determine issues of relevancy and allocability of evidence in advance of a trial record. The other allegations so treated involve harassing telephone calls, and investigatory interviews. It is just as important that while allegations treated singly may not constitute a cause of action, they may do so in combination, or serve to enhance other violations of the right to privacy.

It is not unimportant that plaintiff contends that a giant corporation had allegedly sought by surreptitious and unusual methods to silence an unusually effective critic. If there was such a plan, and only a trial would show that, it is unduly restrictive of the future trial to allocate the evidence beforehand based only on a pleader's specification of overt acts on the bold assumption that they are not connected causally or do not bear on intent and motive.

It should be observed, too, that the right to privacy, even as thus far developed, does not always refer to that which is not known to the public or is confidential. Indeed, the statutory right of privacy in this State and perhaps the most traditional right of privacy in the "common law sense" relates to the commercialized publicity of one's face or name, perhaps the two most public aspects of an individual. . . .

Accordingly, because of the prematurity of ruling on any other question but the sufficiency of the causes of action, I concur in result only.

NOTES & QUESTIONS

1. *Postscript.* General Motors eventually settled the case with Nader for $425,000. It also made a public apology to Nader.[2]
2. *Betrayal of Confidentiality.* The *Nader* court finds that interviewing friends and family members is not an actionable intrusion because "the plaintiff had previously revealed the information to such other persons, and he would necessarily assume the risk that a friend or acquaintance in whom he had confided might breach the confidence." The general rule in the United States is that a person must accept the risk of betrayal when sharing information with others, except with professionals such as lawyers or doctors who have duties to maintain confidentiality. In contrast, in England, a duty of confidentiality extends to friends and family. Should there be such a duty in the United States?
3. *Surveillance in Public Places.* The Restatement of Torts adopts a similar approach to the majority in *Nader*:

   > The defendant is subject to liability under the rule stated in this Section only when he has intruded into a private place, or has otherwise invaded a private seclusion that the plaintiff has thrown about his person or affairs. Thus there is no liability for the examination of a public record concerning the plaintiff, or of documents that the plaintiff is required to keep and make available for public inspection. Nor is there liability for observing him or even taking his photograph while he is walking on the public highway, since he is not then in seclusion, and his appearance is public and open to the public eye. Even in a public place, however, there may be some matters about the plaintiff, such as his underwear or lack of it, that are not exhibited to the public gaze; and there may still be invasion of privacy when there is intrusion upon these matters. Restatement (Second) of Torts § 652B comment (c).

   Judge Breitel's concurrence goes even further than the majority: "Although acts performed in 'public,' especially if taken singly or in small numbers, may not be confidential, at least arguably a right to privacy may nevertheless be invaded through extensive or exhaustive monitoring and cataloguing of acts normally disconnected and anonymous." How does Breitel's approach differ from the majority's approach and that of the Restatement?
4. *Harassing Phone Calls.* *Nader* holds that there is no actionable invasion of privacy caused by a "large number of threatening and harassing telephone calls

---

[2] For more background about case, see Stuart M. Speiser, *Lawsuit* (1980).

. . . at odd hours." The Restatement of Torts (Second) takes a different view. It first concedes that "there is no liability for knocking at the plaintiff's door, or calling him to the telephone on one occasion or even two or three, to demand payment of a debt." But the Restatement then states: "It is only when the telephone calls are repeated with such persistence and frequency as to amount to a course of hounding the plaintiff, that becomes a substantial burden to his existence, that his privacy is invaded." Restatement (Second) of Torts § 652B comment (d).

Courts have also found that harassing a person by telephone can support a tort privacy claim. In *Donnel v. Lara*, 703 S.W.2d 257 (Tex. App. 1985), the court held that excessive telephone harassment "by placing repeated phone calls to [a person's] residence at unreasonable hours" can be actionable. In *Harms v. Miami Daily News, Inc.*, 127 So. 2d 715 (Fla. App. 1961), the defendant published in the newspaper the following statement: "Wanna hear a sexy telephone voice? Call [number] and ask for Louise." As a result, the plaintiff was "flooded with hundreds of telephone calls by various and sundry persons." The court concluded that the plaintiff had an actionable claim against the defendant, and that there was sufficient evidence for the jury to decide whether it was highly offensive.

5. ***Wiretapping and Electronic Surveillance.*** In *Hamberger v. Eastman*, 206 A.2d 239 (N.H. 1964), a husband and wife brought an intrusion action against their landlord for installing a secret recording device in their bedroom. The device had wires going into the landlord's residence. The court sided with the plaintiffs:

> The defendant contends that the right of privacy should not be recognized on the facts of the present case as they appear in the pleadings because there are no allegations that anyone listened or overheard any sounds or voices originating from the plaintiffs' bedroom. The tort of intrusion on the plaintiffs' solitude or seclusion does not require publicity and communication to third persons although this would affect the amount of damages, as Prosser makes clear. The defendant also contends that the right of privacy is not violated unless something has been published, written or printed and that oral publicity is not sufficient. Recent cases make it clear that this is not a requirement.
>
> If the peeping Tom, the big ear and the electronic eavesdropper (whether ingenious or ingenuous) have a place in the hierarchy of social values, it ought not to be at the expense of a married couple minding their own business in the seclusion of their bedroom who have never asked for or by their conduct deserved a potential projection of their private conversations and actions to their landlord or to others.

6. ***The Highly Offensive Requirement.*** What intrusions are "highly offensive to a reasonable person" as required by the tort? Courts have held that trespasses into places where people have reasonable expectations of privacy are actionable, as are unjustified searches. *See, e.g., Gerard v. Parish of Jefferson*, 424 So. 2d 440 (La. App. 1982) (dog catcher entered plaintiff's property without authorization); *K-Mart Corp. v. Trotti*, 677 S.W.2d 632 (Tex. App. 1984) (unauthorized search of employee's personal locker). In *Klebanoff v. McMongale*, 552 A.2d 677 (Pa. Super. 1988), about 20 to 30 pro-life

demonstrators picketed noisily on the public street directly outside of an abortion doctor's home. This had a "devastating effect . . . on the [doctor and his family's] quiet enjoyment of their home," and the family was "figuratively, and perhaps literally, trapped within the home, and held captive." The court held that the protestors could be enjoined.

As illustrated by *Hamberger* and *Nader,* non-physical activities such as wiretapping and overzealous surveillance can amount to highly offensive intrusions. Peering into a person's home windows can be actionable according to the court in *Pinkerton Nat'l Detective Agency, Inc. v. Stevens,* 132 S.E.2d 119 (Ga. App. 1963). In *Pulla v. Amoco Oil Co.*, 882 F. Supp. 836 (S.D. Iowa 1994), the court held that it was actionable when the defendant illegally accessed the plaintiff's credit card records to determine if he abused his sick leave at work.

DIETEMANN V. TIME, INC.

449 F.2d 245 (9th Cir. 1971)

HUFSTEDLER, C.J. . . . Plaintiff, a disabled veteran with little education, was engaged in the practice of healing with clay, minerals, and herbs — as practiced, simple quackery.

Defendant, Time, Incorporated, a New York corporation, publishes Life Magazine. Its November 1, 1963 edition carried an article entitled "Crackdown on Quackery." The article depicted plaintiff as a quack and included two pictures of him. One picture was taken at plaintiff's home on September 20, 1963, previous to his arrest on a charge of practicing medicine without a license, and the other taken at the time of his arrest.

Life Magazine entered into an arrangement with the District Attorney's Office of Los Angeles County whereby Life's employees would visit plaintiff and obtain facts and pictures concerning his activities. Two employees of Life, Mrs. Jackie Metcalf and Mr. William Ray, went to plaintiff's home on September 20, 1963. When they arrived at a locked gate, they rang a bell and plaintiff came out of his house and was told by Mrs. Metcalf and Ray that they had been sent there by a friend, a Mr. Johnson. The use of Johnson's name was a ruse to gain entrance. Plaintiff admitted them and all three went into the house and into plaintiff's den.

The plaintiff had some equipment which could at best be described as gadgets, not equipment which had anything to do with the practice of medicine. Plaintiff, while examining Mrs. Metcalf, was photographed by Ray with a hidden camera without the consent of plaintiff. One of the pictures taken by him appeared in Life Magazine showing plaintiff with his hand on the upper portion of Mrs. Metcalf's breast while he was looking at some gadgets and holding what appeared to be a wand in his right hand. Mrs. Metcalf had told plaintiff that she had a lump in her breast. Plaintiff concluded that she had eaten some rancid butter 11 years, 9 months, and 7 days prior to that time. Other persons were seated in the room during this time.

The conversation between Mrs. Metcalf and plaintiff was transmitted by radio transmitter hidden in Mrs. Metcalf's purse to a tape recorder in a parked automobile occupied by Joseph Bride, Life employee, John Miner of the District

Attorney's Office, and Grant Leake, an investigator of the State Department of Public Health. While the recorded conversation was not quoted in the article in Life, it was mentioned that Life correspondent Bride was making notes of what was being received via the radio transmitter, and such information was at least referred to in the article.

The foregoing events were photographed and recorded by an arrangement among Miner of the District Attorney's Office, Leake of the State Department of Public Health, and Bride, a representative of Life. It had been agreed that Life would obtain pictures and information for use as evidence, and later could be used by Life for publication. . . .

Plaintiff, although a journeyman plumber, claims to be a scientist. Plaintiff had no listings and his home had no sign of any kind. He did not advertise, nor did he have a telephone. He made no charges when he attempted to diagnose or to prescribe herbs and minerals. He did accept contributions.

[The plaintiff was arrested at his home on a charge of practicing medicine without a license. After the plaintiff entered a plea of nolo contendere to the charges, Life's article was published. The plaintiff sued Life in federal district court. The district court concluded that the defendant had invaded the plaintiff's privacy and awarded $1,000 in damages.]

. . . In jurisdictions other than California in which a common law tort for invasion of privacy is recognized, it has been consistently held that surreptitious electronic recording of a plaintiff's conversation causing him emotional distress is actionable. Despite some variations in the description and the labels applied to the tort, there is agreement that publication is not a necessary element of the tort, that the existence of a technical trespass is immaterial, and that proof of special damages is not required. . . .[3]

. . . [W]e have little difficulty in concluding that clandestine photography of the plaintiff in his den and the recordation and transmission of his conversation without his consent resulting in his emotional distress warrants recovery for invasion of privacy in California. . . .

Plaintiff's den was a sphere from which he could reasonably expect to exclude eavesdropping newsmen. He invited two of defendant's employees to the den. One who invites another to his home or office takes a risk that the visitor may not be what he seems, and that the visitor may repeat all he hears and observes when he leaves. But he does not and should not be required to take the risk that what is heard and seen will be transmitted by photograph or recording, or in our modern world, in full living color and hi-fi to the public at large or to any segment of it that the visitor may select. A different rule could have a most pernicious effect upon the dignity of man and it would surely lead to guarded conversations and conduct where candor is most valued, e.g., in the case of doctors and lawyers.

The defendant claims that the First Amendment immunizes it from liability for invading plaintiff's den with a hidden camera and its concealed electronic instruments because its employees were gathering news and its instrumentalities "are indispensable tools of investigative reporting." We agree that newsgathering

---

[3] Editors' Note: Special damages, or "consequential" damages, are damages that follow from the initial harm. They include lost profits and other diminishments of the plaintiff's income, such as increased expenses.

is an integral part of news dissemination. We strongly disagree, however, that the hidden mechanical contrivances are "indispensable tools" of newsgathering. Investigative reporting is an ancient art; its successful practice long antecedes the invention of miniature cameras and electronic devices. The First Amendment has never been construed to accord newsmen immunity from torts or crimes committed during the course of newsgathering. The First Amendment is not a license to trespass, to steal, or to intrude by electronic means into the precincts of another's home or office. It does not become such a license simply because the person subjected to the intrusion is reasonably suspected of committing a crime.

Defendant relies upon the line of cases commencing with *New York Times Co. v. Sullivan* and extending through *Rosenbloom v. Metromedia, Inc.* to sustain its contentions that (1) publication of news, however tortiously gathered, insulates defendant from liability for the antecedent tort, and (2) even if it is not thus shielded from liability, those cases prevent consideration of publication as an element in computing damages. . . .

No interest protected by the First Amendment is adversely affected by permitting damages for intrusion to be enhanced by the fact of later publication of the information that the publisher improperly acquired. Assessing damages for the additional emotional distress suffered by a plaintiff when the wrongfully acquired data are purveyed to the multitude chills intrusive acts. It does not chill freedom of expression guaranteed by the First Amendment. A rule forbidding the use of publication as an ingredient of damages would deny to the injured plaintiff recovery for real harm done to him without any countervailing benefit to the legitimate interest of the public in being informed. The same rule would encourage conduct by news media that grossly offends ordinary men. . . .

DESNICK V. AMERICAN BROADCASTING CO., INC.

44 F.3d 1345 (7th Cir. 1995)

[Dr. Desnick owned an ophthalmic clinic known as the Desnick Eye Center. The Eye Center had 25 offices in four states and performed over 10,000 cataract operations each year, mainly on elderly persons under Medicare. In 1993, Entine, the producer of ABC's news program *Primetime Live*, telephoned Dr. Desnick and told him that the show wanted to do a segment on cataract practices. Entine told Desnick that the segment would be "fair and balanced" and that it would not include undercover surveillance. Desnick permitted an ABC crew to videotape the Eye Center's Chicago office, to film a cataract operation, and to interview doctors and patients. However, unknown to Desnick, Entine sent seven people with concealed cameras to the Eye Center's Wisconsin and Indiana offices. These seven people posed as patients and requested eye operations. Glazer and Simon are among the employees who were secretly videotaped examining these "test patients."

When the program aired, it was introduced by Sam Donaldson, who began by stating: "We begin tonight with the story of a so-called 'big cutter,' Dr. James Desnick. . . . [I]n our undercover investigation of the big cutter you'll meet tonight, we turned up evidence that he may also be a big charger, doing unnecessary cataract surgery for the money." As part of the segment, brief interviews with four patients of the Desnick Eye Center were shown. While one of the patients was satisfied ("I was blessed"), the other three were not. Indeed, one of them commented, "If you got three eyes, he'll get three eyes." Donaldson then reported on the experiences of the seven test patients. The two who were under 65 and therefore ineligible for Medicare reimbursement were found by the clinic not to need cataract surgery. The Desnick eye clinic told four of the other five that they did need this operation.

Donaldson told the viewer that *Primetime Live* hired a professor of ophthalmology to examine the test patients who had been told they needed cataract surgery. The professor not only said that these patients did not need it, but with regard to one, he stated, "I think it would be near malpractice to do surgery on him." Later in the segment he denies that this could just be an honest difference of opinion between professionals. The show also mentioned that the Illinois Medical Board had charged Dr. Desnick with malpractice and deception. Additionally, the show contained an "ambush interview" of Dr. Desnick while he was at an airport, with Donaldson shouting out allegations of fraud to Desnick.

Among a number of causes of action raised by the plaintiffs, who included the Desnick Eye Clinic, and Simon and Glazer as individual plaintiffs, is an action for intrusion upon seclusion.]

POSNER, C.J. . . . To enter upon another's land without consent is a trespass. The force of this rule has, it is true, been diluted somewhat by concepts of privilege and of implied consent. But there is no journalists' privilege to trespass. And there can be no implied consent in any nonfictitious sense of the term when express consent is procured by a misrepresentation or a misleading omission. The Desnick Eye Center would not have agreed to the entry of the test patients into its offices had it known they wanted eye examinations only in order to gather material for a television expose of the Center and that they were going to make secret videotapes of the examinations. Yet some cases . . . deem consent effective even though it was procured by fraud. There must be *something* to this surprising result. Without it a restaurant critic could not conceal his identity when he ordered a meal, or a browser pretend to be interested in merchandise that he could not afford to buy. Dinner guests would be trespassers if they were false friends who never would have been invited had the host known their true character, and a consumer who in an effort to bargain down an automobile dealer falsely claimed to be able to buy the same car elsewhere at a lower price would be a trespasser in the dealer's showroom. Some of these might be classified as privileged trespasses, designed to promote competition. Others might be thought justified by some kind of implied consent — the restaurant critic for example might point by way of analogy to the use of the "fair use" defense by book reviewers charged with copyright infringement and argue that the restaurant industry as a whole would be injured if restaurants could exclude critics. But most such efforts at rationalization would be little better than evasions. The fact is that consent to an entry is often given legal effect even though the entrant has intentions that if known to the owner of the property would cause him for perfectly understandable and generally ethical or at least lawful reasons to revoke his consent.

The law's willingness to give effect to consent procured by fraud is not limited to the tort of trespass. The *Restatement* gives the example of a man who obtains consent to sexual intercourse by promising a woman $100, yet (unbeknownst to her, of course) he pays her with a counterfeit bill and intended to do so from the start. The man is not guilty of battery, even though unconsented-to sexual intercourse is a battery. Yet we know that to conceal the fact that one has a venereal disease transforms "consensual" intercourse into battery. Seduction, standardly effected by false promises of love, is not rape; intercourse under the pretense of rendering medical or psychiatric treatment is, at least in most states. It certainly is battery. Trespass presents close parallels. If a homeowner opens his door to a purported meter reader who is in fact nothing of the sort — just a busybody curious about the interior of the home — the homeowner's consent to his entry is not a defense to a suit for trespass. And likewise if a competitor gained entry to a business firm's premises posing as a customer but in fact hoping to steal the firm's trade secrets.

How to distinguish the two classes of case — the seducer from the medical impersonator, the restaurant critic from the meter-reader impersonator? The answer can have nothing to do with fraud; there is fraud in all the cases. It has to do with the interest that the torts in question, battery and trespass, protect. The one protects the inviolability of the person, the other the inviolability of the person's property. The woman who is seduced wants to have sex with her seducer, and the restaurant owner wants to have customers. The woman who is victimized by the medical impersonator has no desire to have sex with her doctor; she wants medical treatment. And the homeowner victimized by the phony meter reader does not want strangers in his house unless they have authorized service functions. The dealer's objection to the customer who claims falsely to have a lower price from a competing dealer is not to the physical presence of the customer, but to the fraud that he is trying to perpetuate. The lines are not bright — they are not even inevitable. They are the traces of the old forms of action, which have resulted in a multitude of artificial distinctions in modern law. But that is nothing new.

There was no invasion in the present case of any of the specific interests that the tort of trespass seeks to protect. The test patients entered offices that were open to anyone expressing a desire for ophthalmic services and videotaped physicians engaged in professional, not personal, communications with strangers (the testers themselves). The activities of the offices were not disrupted. . . . Nor was there any "inva[sion of] a person's private space," as in our hypothetical meter-reader case, as in the famous case of *De May v. Roberts*, 9 N.W. 146 (Mich. 1881) (where a doctor, called to the plaintiff's home to deliver her baby, brought along with him a friend who was curious to see a birth but was not a medical doctor, and represented the friend to be his medical assistant), as in one of its numerous modern counterparts, . . . and as in *Dietemann v. Time, Inc.*, 449 F.2d 245 (9th Cir. 1971), on which the plaintiffs in our case rely. *Dietemann* involved a home. True, the portion invaded was an office, where the plaintiff performed quack healing of nonexistent ailments. The parallel to this case is plain enough, but there is a difference. Dietemann was not in business, and did not advertise his services or charge for them. His quackery was private.

No embarrassingly intimate details of anybody's life were publicized in the present case. There was no eavesdropping on a private conversation; the testers recorded their own conversations with the Desnick Eye Center's physicians. There was no violation of the doctor-patient privilege. There was no theft, or intent to steal, trade secrets; no disruption of decorum, of peace and quiet; no noisy or distracting demonstrations. Had the testers been undercover FBI agents, there would have been no violation of the Fourth Amendment, because there would have been no invasion of a legally protected interest in property or privacy. . . .

What we have said largely disposes of [the claim of] infringement of the right of privacy. . . . The right of privacy embraces several distinct interests, but the only ones conceivably involved here are the closely related interests in concealing intimate personal facts and in preventing intrusion into legitimately private activities, such as phone conversations. As we have said already, no intimate personal facts concerning the two individual plaintiffs . . . were revealed; and the only conversations that were recorded were conversations with the testers themselves.

NOTES & QUESTIONS

1. *Investigative Reporting.* As is illustrated by *Dietemann* and *Desnick*, investigative reporting often depends upon deception. Those cases are split on the issue of whether such investigative techniques can give rise to intrusion. Recall the *Dietemann* court's statement that the "First Amendment is not a license to trespass, to steal, or to intrude by electronic means into the precincts of another's home or office."

Investigative reporting has served an important function throughout history. In 1887, a reporter named Nellie Bly pretended to be mentally ill to gain access to a mental asylum. Her portrayal of the brutal conditions led to significant reforms. Upton Sinclair went undercover as a meatpacker to expose conditions in slaughterhouses for his book *The Jungle* in 1904. C. Thomas Dienes argues that the media functions "as the eyes and ears of the people." He argues that "when the government fails in its responsibility to protect the public against fraudulent and unethical business and professional practices, whether because of lack of resources or unwillingness, media exposure of such practices can and often does provide the spur forcing government action."[4]

2. *Posner's Analogies in* **Desnick.** Judge Posner draws an analogy between (1) seduction with false promises of love in order to have sexual intercourse and (2) the deceitful trespass in *Desnick.* Are these situations really analogous?

3. *Trespass: The* **Food Lion Case.** The tort of trespass is related to the tort of intrusion. To commit a trespass, one must enter upon another's land without consent. To what extent does trespass overlap with intrusion? In many respects, it has fewer requirements — no requirement that solitude or seclusion be invaded, that a private matter be involved, or that the invasion be highly offensive. On the other hand, intrusion can be committed without entering upon another's land.

Can one trespass if one obtains consent through deception? And can a person trespass if she is present upon another's land with consent but secretly engages

---

[4] C. Thomas Dienes, *Protecting Investigative Journalism*, 67 Geo. Wash. L. Rev. 1139, 1141, 1143 (1999). For further background about investigative journalism and the use of deception, see Bernard W. Bell, *Secrets and Lies: News Media and Law Enforcement Use of Deception as an Investigative Tool*, 60 U. Pitt. L. Rev. 745 (1999).

in activities that the landowner would likely not authorize? Consider *Food Lion, Inc. v. ABC*, 194 F.3d 505 (4th Cir. 2001). ABC reporters investigated allegations of unsanitary food-handling practices at supermarkets operated by Food Lion, Inc. Two reporters submitted fake resumes to obtain jobs at Food Lion supermarkets. The reporters secretly videotaped the food-handling practices at the stores. The video was broadcast on the show *Primetime Live*. "The broadcast included, for example, videotape that appeared to show Food Lion employees repackaging and redating fish that had passed the expiration date, grinding expired beef with fresh beef, and applying barbeque sauce to chicken past its expiration date in order to mask the smell and sell it as fresh in the gourmet food section." Food Lion sued for fraud, breach of duty of loyalty, trespass, and unfair trade practices. Food Lion won at trial — $1,400 on the fraud claim, $1 each for the duty of loyalty and trespass claims, and $1,500 on the unfair trade practices claim. The jury awarded approximately $5.5 million in punitive damages on the fraud claim, which the court reduced to $315,000.

On appeal, the court dismissed the fraud and unfair trade practices claims but affirmed the duty of loyalty and trespass claims.

Regarding the trespass claim, the court reasoned:

> [I]t is a trespass to enter upon another's land without consent. Accordingly, consent is a defense to a claim of trespass. Even consent gained by misrepresentation is sometimes sufficient. *See Desnick v. American Broad. Cos.,* 44 F.3d 1345 (7th Cir. 1995). The consent to enter is canceled out, however, "if a wrongful act is done in excess of and in abuse of authorized entry." . . .
>
> Although Food Lion consented to Dale's entry to do her job, she exceeded that consent when she videotaped in non-public areas of the store. . . .

The court only affirmed the duty of loyalty and trespass claims. As a result, Food Lion could only collect $2 in damages because the punitive damages were based on the fraud claim. Although *Food Lion* did not involve the tort of intrusion, to what extent is its holding regarding the tort of trespass applicable to intrusion cases? Is its holding consistent with *Dietemann* and *Desnick*?

4. *Intrusion Liability for the Receipt of Data Obtained by Intrusion.* In *Pearson v. Dodd*, 410 F.2d 701 (D.C. Cir. 1969), two former employees of Senator Thomas Dodd of Connecticut, with the assistance of two of Dodd's active staff members, entered Dodd's office without authorization and surreptitiously made copies of many documents in his files. These documents related to Dodd's relationship to lobbyists for foreign interests. Newspaper columnists Drew Pearson and Jack Anderson published articles containing information from these documents. Pearson and Anderson did not participate in or order the illegal copying; they only received copies of the documents knowing that they had been copied without authorization. Dodd sued Pearson and Anderson for invasion of privacy. The court held that intrusion could not extend to those who merely received the information:

> If we were to hold appellants liable for invasion of privacy on these facts, we would establish the proposition that one who receives information from an intruder, knowing it has been obtained by improper intrusion, is guilty of a tort.

In an untried and developing area of tort law, we are not prepared to go so far. A person approached by an eavesdropper with an offer to share in the information gathered through the eavesdropping would perhaps play the nobler part should he spurn the offer and shut his ears. However, it seems to us that at this point it would place too great a strain on human weakness to hold one liable in damages who merely succumbs to temptation and listens.

SHULMAN V. GROUP W PRODUCTIONS, INC.

955 P.2d 469 (Cal. 1998)

WERDEGAR, J. . . . On June 24, 1990, plaintiffs Ruth and Wayne Shulman, mother and son, were injured when the car in which they and two other family members were riding on interstate 10 in Riverside County flew off the highway and tumbled down an embankment into a drainage ditch on state-owned property, coming to rest upside down. Ruth, the most seriously injured of the two, was pinned under the car. Ruth and Wayne both had to be cut free from the vehicle by the device known as "the jaws of life."

A rescue helicopter operated by Mercy Air was dispatched to the scene. The flight nurse, who would perform the medical care at the scene and on the way to the hospital, was Laura Carnahan. Also on board were the pilot, a medic and Joel Cooke, a video camera operator employed by defendants Group W Productions, Inc., and 4MN Productions. Cooke was recording the rescue operation for later broadcast.

Cooke roamed the accident scene, videotaping the rescue. Nurse Carnahan wore a wireless microphone that picked up her conversations with both Ruth and the other rescue personnel. Cooke's tape was edited into a piece approximately nine minutes long, which, with the addition of narrative voice-over, was broadcast on September 29, 1990, as a segment of *On Scene: Emergency Response*.

The segment begins with the Mercy Air helicopter shown on its way to the accident site. The narrator's voice is heard in the background, setting the scene and describing in general terms what has happened. . . .

The videotape shows only a glimpse of Wayne, and his voice is never heard. Ruth is shown several times, either by brief shots of a limb or her torso, or with her features blocked by others or obscured by an oxygen mask. She is also heard speaking several times. Carnahan calls her "Ruth" and her last name is not mentioned on the broadcast.

While Ruth is still trapped under the car, Carnahan asks Ruth's age. Ruth responds, "I'm old." On further questioning, Ruth reveals she is 47, and Carnahan observes that "it's all relative. You're not that old." During her extrication from the car, Ruth asks at least twice if she is dreaming. At one point she asks Carnahan, who has told her she will be taken to the hospital in a helicopter: "Are you teasing?" At another point she says: "This is terrible. Am I dreaming?" She also asks what happened and where the rest of her family is, repeating the questions even after being told she was in an accident and the other family members are being cared for. While being loaded into the helicopter on a stretcher, Ruth says: "I just want to die." Carnahan reassures her that she is "going to do real well," but Ruth repeats: "I just want to die. I don't want to go through this."

Ruth and Wayne are placed in the helicopter, and its door is closed. The narrator states: "Once airborne, Laura and [the flight medic] will update their patients' vital signs and establish communications with the waiting trauma teams at Loma Linda." Carnahan, speaking into what appears to be a radio microphone, transmits some of Ruth's vital signs and states that Ruth cannot move her feet and has no sensation. The video footage during the helicopter ride includes a few seconds of Ruth's face, covered by an oxygen mask. Wayne is neither shown nor heard.

The helicopter lands on the hospital roof. With the door open, Ruth states while being taken out: "My upper back hurts." Carnahan replies: "Your upper back hurts. That's what you were saying up there." Ruth states: "I don't feel that great." Carnahan responds: "You probably don't."

Finally, Ruth is shown being moved from the helicopter into the hospital. . . .

The accident left Ruth a paraplegic. When the segment was broadcast, Wayne phoned Ruth in her hospital room and told her to turn on the television because "Channel 4 is showing our accident now." Shortly afterward, several hospital workers came into the room to mention that a videotaped segment of her accident was being shown. Ruth was "shocked, so to speak, that this would be run and I would be exploited, have my privacy invaded, which is what I felt had happened." She did not know her rescue had been recorded in this manner and had never consented to the recording or broadcast. . . .

Ruth and Wayne sued the producers of *On Scene: Emergency Response*, as well as others. The first amended complaint included two causes of action for invasion of privacy, one based on defendants' unlawful intrusion by videotaping the rescue in the first instance and the other based on the public disclosure of private facts, i.e., the broadcast. . . .

We ask first whether defendants "intentionally intrude[d], physically or otherwise, upon the solitude or seclusion of another," that is, into a place or conversation private to Wayne or Ruth. . . .

Cameraman Cooke's mere presence at the accident scene and filming of the events occurring there cannot be deemed either a physical or sensory intrusion on plaintiffs' seclusion. Plaintiffs had no right of ownership or possession of the property where the rescue took place, nor any actual control of the premises. Nor could they have had a reasonable expectation that members of the media would be excluded or prevented from photographing the scene; for journalists to attend and record the scenes of accidents and rescues is in no way unusual or unexpected.

Two aspects of defendants' conduct, however, raise triable issues of intrusion on seclusion. First, a triable issue exists as to whether both plaintiffs had an objectively reasonable expectation of privacy in the interior of the rescue helicopter, which served as an ambulance. Although the attendance of reporters and photographers at the scene of an accident is to be expected, we are aware of no law or custom permitting the press to ride in ambulances or enter hospital rooms during treatment without the patient's consent. . . .

Second, Ruth was entitled to a degree of privacy in her conversations with Carnahan and other medical rescuers at the accident scene, and in Carnahan's conversations conveying medical information regarding Ruth to the hospital base. Cooke, perhaps, did not intrude into that zone of privacy merely by being present at a place where he could hear such conversations with unaided ears. But by placing a microphone on Carnahan's person, amplifying and recording what she said and heard, defendants may have listened in on conversations the parties could reasonably have expected to be private. . . .

We turn to the second element of the intrusion tort, offensiveness. . . .

On this summary judgment record, we believe a jury could find defendants' recording of Ruth's communications to Carnahan and other rescuers, and filming in the air ambulance, to be "'highly offensive to a reasonable person.'" With regard to the depth of the intrusion, a reasonable jury could find highly offensive the placement of a microphone on a medical rescuer in order to intercept what would otherwise be private conversations with an injured patient. In that setting, as defendants could and should have foreseen, the patient would not know her words were being recorded and would not have occasion to ask about, and object or consent to, recording. Defendants, it could reasonably be said, took calculated advantage of the patient's "vulnerability and confusion." Arguably, the last thing an injured accident victim should have to worry about while being pried from her wrecked car is that a television producer may be recording everything she says to medical personnel for the possible edification and entertainment of casual television viewers.

For much the same reason, a jury could reasonably regard entering and riding in an ambulance — whether on the ground or in the air — with two seriously injured patients to be an egregious intrusion on a place of expected seclusion. Again, the patients, at least in this case, were hardly in a position to keep careful watch on who was riding with them, or to inquire as to everyone's business and consent or object to their presence. A jury could reasonably believe that fundamental respect for human dignity requires the patients' anxious journey be taken only with those whose care is solely for them and out of sight of the prying eyes (or cameras) of others.

Nor can we say as a matter of law that defendants' motive — to gather usable material for a potentially newsworthy story — necessarily privileged their intrusive conduct as a matter of common law tort liability. A reasonable jury could conclude the producers' desire to get footage that would convey the "feel" of the event — the real sights and sounds of a difficult rescue — did not justify either placing a microphone on Nurse Carnahan or filming inside the rescue helicopter. Although defendants' purposes could scarcely be regarded as evil or malicious (in the colloquial sense), their behavior could, even in light of their motives, be thought to show a highly offensive lack of sensitivity and respect for plaintiffs' privacy. . . . A reasonable jury could find that defendants, in placing a microphone on an emergency treatment nurse and recording her conversation with a distressed, disoriented and severely injured patient, without the patient's knowledge or consent, acted with highly offensive disrespect for the patient's personal privacy. . . .

NOTES & QUESTIONS

1. ***The Restatement (Second) on "Offensiveness."*** The *Shulman* court found that, on summary judgment, it was possible to find the recording of Ruth's comments to rescuers and filming in the air ambulance to be "highly offensive." The behavior could be thought to show "a highly offensive lack of sensitivity and respect for plaintiff's privacy." The Restatement (Second) Torts provides further guidance on the types of behavior that can be said to meet this standard. In Comment d to § 652B, it states: "There is ... no liability unless the interference with the P's seclusion is a substantial one, of a kind that would be highly offensive to the ordinary reasonable man, as the result of conduct to which the reasonable man would strongly object."

The Restatement then offers four examples to demonstrate the dividing lines between unacceptable and acceptable conduct in this regard. Its first example involves "knocking at the plaintiff's door, or calling him on the telephone on one occasion or even two or three, to demand payment of a debt." The Restatement adds, "It is only when the telephone calls are repeated with such persistence and frequency as to amount to a course of hounding the p., that it becomes a substantial burden to his existence, that his privacy is invaded." Recall that in *Nader v. General Motors*, supra, the New York court had rejected Nader's claim based on "a large number of threatening and harassing telephone calls to the plaintiff's home at odd hours." Do you view this behavior as highly offensive?

Second, the Restatement offers an illustration regarding an impatient landlord. It states:

> A, a landlord, calls upon B, his tenant, at nine o'clock on Sunday morning, to demand payment of the rent, although he knows that B is not ready to pay it and that B objects to such a visit on Sunday. B is seriously annoyed. This is not an invasion of B's privacy.

The third and fourth examples from the Restatement provide gendered perspectives that view women and their privacy as objects of particular solicitude. One is reminded by these examples that the date of the Restatement's adoption, which was in 1976, means that it is now almost a half-century old and inevitably reflects a bygone era in at least certain ways. The third example concerns a woman in a hospital sickbed, and the fourth, a "lady of social prominence."

Here are these examples from the Restatement of invasions upon seclusion:

> A, a woman, is sick in the hospital with a rare disease that arouses public curiosity. B, a newspaper reporter, calls her on the telephone and asks for an interview, but she refuses to see him. B then goes to the hospital, enters A's room and over her objection takes her photograph. B has invaded A's privacy.

> A, a professional photographer, seeking to promote his business telephones B, a lady of social prominence, every day for a month, insisting that she come to his studio and be photographed. The calls are made at meal times, late at night and at other inconvenient times, and A ignores B's requests to desist. A has invaded B's privacy.

In considering these examples today, do you view all, or some of them, as "highly offensive" intrusions upon seclusion? Why or why not?

A more recent case found that "expression" will be protected as newsworthy unless "the means by which a person's privacy was invaded was truly outrageous." *Foster v. Svenson*, 128 A.D. 3d 150 (N.Y. App. Div. 2015). This court referenced a test requiring "*atrocious, indecent, and utterly despicable* conduct." Do you agree with this approach?

2. ***Intrusion in Public Places.*** Consider *Sanders v. ABC*, 978 P.2d 67 (Cal. 1999), decided by the same court one year after *Shulman*. In *Sanders*, a reporter obtained a job with a telephone psychics company that gave "readings" to callers for a fee. The psychics worked in a large room with rows of cubicles. The reporter secretly videotaped conversations of the plaintiff, an employee, with others at his cubicle or other cubicles. The plaintiff sued for intrusion upon seclusion. The defendants argued that the employee lacked a reasonable expectation of privacy in his conversations because they could be seen and overheard by co-workers. The court sided with the plaintiff:

> ... [W]e adhere to the view suggested in *Shulman*: privacy, for purposes of the intrusion tort, is not a binary, all-or-nothing characteristic. There are degrees and nuances to societal recognition of our expectations of privacy: the fact that the privacy one expects in a given setting is not complete or absolute does not render the expectation unreasonable as a matter of law. Although the intrusion tort is often defined in terms of "seclusion" the seclusion referred to need not be absolute. "Like 'privacy,' the concept of 'seclusion' is relative. The mere fact that a person can be seen by someone does not automatically mean that he or she can legally be forced to be subject to being seen by everyone."

2. ANTI-PAPARAZZI AND VIDEO VOYEURISM STATUTES

Paparazzi are aggressive photographers who often harass celebrities to take candid photographs to sell to newspapers, tabloids, and magazines. Fueling the behavior of the paparazzi are the exorbitant prices that photographs of celebrities command. For example, a photo of Princess Diana embracing Dodi Al-Fayed was sold for over $3 million. According to the *New York Times*, "A growing constellation of Web sites, magazines and television programs serve [gossip] up minute by minute, creating a river of cash for secrets of the stars, or near stars."[5] It estimated the revenue stream of the "new world of round-the-clock" gossip at $3 billion annually.

Paparazzi have a reputation for being very invasive into the privacy of celebrities. For example, paparazzi flew over Michael J. Fox's wedding in helicopters to take photographs. Disguised photographers took photographs of Paul Reiser's baby in the hospital. Paparazzi also camped outside Reiser's backyard taking photographs with telephoto lenses. Paparazzi chased Arnold Schwarzenegger and Maria Shriver off the road to take the first photos of him leaving the hospital after heart surgery. In 2005, paparazzi followed Lindsey Lohan as she drove onto a dead end street. When she tried to make a U-turn, one

---

[5] Jim Rutenberg, *The Gossip Machine, Churning Out Cash*, N.Y. Times, May 22, 2011.

photographer drove his automobile into her vehicle. Lohan suffered cuts and bruises from the accident. To what extent does the law of privacy restrict the behavior of paparazzi?

The Notorious Ron Galella. Ron Galella was perhaps the most famous of the paparazzi. During his long career, he took more than 3 million photos of celebrities. He was particularly aggressive and sparked the ire of many of his subjects. Marlon Brando once punched him and broke his jaw.

In *Galella v. Onassis*, 487 F.2d 986 (2d Cir. 1973), the infamous photographer Ron Galella sued Jacqueline Onassis, the widow of President John F. Kennedy, after she directed Secret Service agents to arrest him. He had been attempting to take photos of Onassis and her two children, John and Caroline, on many occasions. He "interrupted Caroline at tennis, and invaded the children's private schools. At one time he came uncomfortably close in a power boat to Mrs. Onassis swimming." The incident involving the arrest was triggered when Galella took pictures of John riding his bike in Central Park. "He jumped out into the boy's path, causing the agents concern for John's safety."

Onassis countersued for damages and injunctive relief, arguing in part that Galella invaded his privacy and engaged in harassment. The trial court dismissed Galella's claim and found for Onassis. The court noted that Gallella had "insinuated himself into the very fabric of Mrs. Onassis' life" and ordered injunctive relief preventing Galella from approaching Onassis and her children within 100 yards of their home and school, 75 yards of the children, and 50 yards of Onassis. Galella appealed. The U.S. Court of Appeals for the Second Circuit affirmed: "Galella's action went far beyond the reasonable bounds of news gathering. When weighed against the de minimis public importance of the daily activities of the defendant, Galella's constant surveillance, his obtrusive and intruding presence, was unwarranted and unreasonable." The court further reasoned: "Galella does not seriously dispute the court's finding of tortious conduct. Rather, he sets up the First Amendment as a wall of immunity protecting newsmen from any liability for their conduct while gathering news. There is no such scope to the First Amendment right. Crimes and torts committed in news gathering are not protected."

According to the *New Yorker*, Galella repeatedly violated the terms of the court order in the *Onassis* litigation, which led to a settlement in which he agreed to stop photographing Onassis.[6] Nonetheless, Galella lost little time in publishing a volume, *Jacqueline* (1978), containing his Onassis photographs. Galella published numerous other volumes of his candid photographs. He is considered as the father of the modern celebrity photography industry as well as a celebrity himself.

Galella passed away in May 2022 at the age of 91 years old. The headline on his prominent obituary in the *New York Times* called him a "Celebrity-Hounding Photographer."[7] The article noted that he was "brazen and relentless in chasing the famous, particularly Jacqueline Kennedy Onassis" before adding "[b]ut his

---

[6] Tad Friend, *No Pictures!*, 86 The New Yorker 24-25 (May 31, 2010). The article described the photographer as "a tireless stalker with an Elmer Fudd laugh."

[7] Paul Vitello, *Ron Galella, Celebrity-Hounding Photographer, Dies at 91*, N.Y. Times (May 5, 2022).

pictures also came to be admired." The *New York Times* also found that Galella "for better or worse helped define today's boundary-challenged culture of celebrity."

The California Anti-Paparazzi Act. Princess Diana's death in 1997 precipitated calls for anti-paparazzi legislation in the United States. On the evening of August 30, Princess Diana and Dodi Al-Fayed were being chauffeured in a Mercedes from the Ritz Hotel in Paris. Paparazzi followed the Mercedes on motorcycles and in cars. A chase developed, and according to eyewitnesses, the motorcycles were swarming around the Mercedes as it entered a tunnel. The Mercedes crashed in the tunnel, killing both Princess Diana and Dodi Al-Fayed. About 10 to 15 photographers gathered around the Mercedes after the crash and continued to take pictures at the scene of the accident.

In the United States, anti-paparazzi legislation was introduced in Congress but failed to be passed. In 1998, California became the first state to adopt anti-paparazzi legislation with the California Anti-Paparazzi Act, Cal. Civ. Code § 1708.8. In 2005, California amended the existing statute to add enhanced penalties for violations of the statute by paparazzi who engage in an "assault" to capture a photograph. Further amendments to the statute followed in 2009 and 2010. The latter law permits fines as well as imprisonment for up to a year for photographers who break traffic laws or interfere with the operation of their target's car while pursuing a photograph.

California's Anti-Paparazzi Act does not supplant the state's existing privacy torts. Rather, it provides rights and remedies "in addition to any other rights and remedies provided by law." § 1708.8(i).

The Act recognizes three forms of invasion of privacy. First, it defines liability for "physical invasion of privacy":

(a) A person is liable for physical invasion of privacy when the person knowingly enters onto the land or into the airspace above the land of another person without permission or otherwise commits a trespass in order to capture any type of visual image, sound recording, or other physical impression of the plaintiff engaging in a private, personal, or familial activity and the invasion occurs in a manner that is offensive to a reasonable person.

"Personal or familial activity" is defined as including but not limited to:

(A) Intimate details of the plaintiff's personal life under circumstances in which the plaintiff has a reasonable expectation of privacy.

(B) Interaction with the plaintiff's family or significant others under circumstances in which the plaintiff has a reasonable expectation of privacy. . .

(D) Any activity that occurs on a residential property under circumstances in which the plaintiff has a reasonable expectation of privacy.

(E) Other aspects of the plaintiff's private affairs or concerns under circumstances in which the plaintiff has a reasonable expectation of privacy. § 1708.8(l)(1).

Second, the Act defines liability for "constructive invasion of privacy":

(b) A person is liable for constructive invasion of privacy when the person attempts to capture, in a manner that is offensive to a reasonable person, any type of visual image, sound recording, or other physical impression of the plaintiff engaging in a private, personal, or familial activity, through the use of any device, regardless of whether there is a physical trespass, if this image, sound recording, or other physical impression could not have been achieved without a trespass unless the device was used.

Third, the Anti-Paparazzi law prohibits an "assault or false imprisonment committed with the intent to capture any type of visual image, sound recording, or other physical impression of the plaintiff."

The Act provides for increased damages for the three types of privacy violations defined above. This provision holds that a person who commits any of these three acts:

... is liable for up to three times the amount of any general and special damages that are proximately caused by the violation of this section. This person may also be liable for punitive damages . . . . If the plaintiff proves that the invasion of privacy was committed for a commercial purpose, the person shall also be subject to disgorgement to the plaintiff of any proceeds or other consideration obtained as a result of the violation of this section. A person who comes within the description of this subdivision is also subject to a civil fine of not less than five thousand dollars ($5,000) and not more than fifty thousand dollars ($50,000)..

§ 1708.8(d). The statute also has provisions for liability for a person "who directs, solicits, actually induces, or actually causes another person, regardless of whether there is an employer-employee relationship, to violate any provision of" the law. § 1708.8(e). However, the Act does not punish the sale or dissemination of images or recordings in violation of the Act unless "the person, in the first transaction following the taking or capture of the visual image, sound recording, or other physical impression" acted "with actual knowledge that it was taken or captured in violation" of the Anti-Paparazzi law. § 1708.8(f)(1).

Since the Act is aimed at limiting the intrusive activities of paparazzi, not merely the invasion of privacy caused by having one's photograph taken or voice recorded, the Act applies even if no image or recording is ever captured or sold. § 1708.8(j).

How does California's Anti-Paparazzi Act differ from the ordinary intrusion upon seclusion tort? Do you think it will prevent the intrusive activities that it seeks to limit?

Does California's Anti-Paparazzi Act violate the First Amendment to the U.S. Constitution? Erwin Chemerinsky contends that newsgathering, although currently not protected by the First Amendment, should be protected by intermediate scrutiny because the "very notion of a marketplace of ideas rests on the availability of information. Aggressive newsgathering, such as by undercover reporters, is often the key to gathering the information." However, Chemerinsky goes on to argue that the California Anti-Paparazzi Act would survive intermediate scrutiny "because it substantially advances the government's interest in safeguarding privacy in the home."[8] In contrast, C. Thomas Dienes contends:

[8] Erwin Chemerinsky, *Protect the Press: A First Amendment Standard for Safeguarding Aggressive Newsgathering*, 33 U. Rich. L. Rev. 1143, 1159, 1163-64 (2000).

the antipaparazzi legislation singles out press photography and sound recording for significant and discriminatory burdens. Even if such acts do not themselves constitute speech, they are protected means of newsgathering vital to press publication. If the photographs and sound recordings cannot be made, they cannot be published. As the Supreme Court said in *Arcara v. Cloud Books, Inc.*, laws are subject to heightened scrutiny "although directed at activity with no expressive component, [if they] impose a disproportionate burden upon those engaged in protected First Amendment activities." Because media speech-related activity is significantly and disproportionately burdened, the antipaparazzi laws should be treated as presumptively unconstitutional, subject to strict scrutiny review.[9]

Video Voyeurism Statutes. Video voyeurism involves the use of video or photography to capture people naked without their consent. Websites have been popping up with "upskirt" photos — pictures taken up women's skirts. Several states have passed video voyeurism laws, some with criminal penalties. *See, e.g.,* La. Rev. Stat. Ann. § 14:283; N.J. Stat. Ann. § 2C:18-3; N.Y. Penal Law § 250.45. For example, consider the law passed by Washington:

> [a] person commits the crime of voyeurism if, for the purpose of arousing or gratifying the sexual desire of any person, he or she knowingly views, photographs, or films another person, without that person's knowledge and consent, while the person being viewed, photographed, or filmed is in a place where he or she would have a reasonable expectation of privacy. RCW 9A.44.115

The statute defined the place where people have a reasonable expectation of privacy as:

> (i) A place where a reasonable person would believe that he or she could disrobe in privacy, without being concerned that his or her undressing was being photographed or filmed by another; *or*
> (ii) A place where one may reasonably expect to be safe from casual or hostile intrusion or surveillance. . . .

In *Washington v. Glas,* 54 P.3d 147 (Wash. 2002), Sean Glas was convicted under the statute for taking photos up women's skirts in a shopping mall without their consent. The court dismissed Glas's conviction because "although the Legislature may have intended to cover intrusions of privacy in public places, the plain language of the statute does not accomplish this goal." The court reasoned that "[c]asual surveillance frequently occurs in public. Therefore, public places could not logically constitute locations where a person could reasonably expect to be safe from casual or hostile intrusion or surveillance."

Shortly after this opinion, in 2003, Washington revised its statute to include "intimate areas of another person without that person's knowledge and consent and under circumstances where the person has a reasonable expectation of privacy, whether in a public or private place." RCW 9A.44.115.

In 2004, the U.S. Congress passed the Video Voyeurism Prevention Act, 18 U.S.C. § 1801, which prohibits knowingly capturing an image of an "individual's naked or undergarment clad genitals, pubic area, buttocks, or female breast . . . under circumstances in which that individual has a reasonable expectation of

---

[9] C. Thomas Dienes, *Protecting Investigative Journalism,* 67 Geo. Wash. L. Rev. 1139 (1999).

privacy regarding such body part or parts." The law only applies in the "special maritime and territorial jurisdiction of the United States."

B. DISCLOSURE OF TRUTHFUL INFORMATION

In certain circumstances, the law provides remedies for individuals who suffer harm as a result of the disclosure of their personal information. One of the primary remedies is the tort of public disclosure of private facts. Other remedies include statutes passed by states and the federal government that restrict the disclosure of specific information. For example, a number of states have laws prohibiting the disclosure of the identities of sexual offense victims. *See, e.g.*, N.Y. Civ. Rights L. § 50-b; 42 Pa. Comp. Stat. § 5988. States have also provided statutory remedies for the disclosure that a person has AIDS. *See, e.g.*, 410 Ill. Comp. Stat. 305/9; Fla. Stat. § 381.004. Federal wiretap law prohibits the disclosure of a communication that one has reason to know was obtained through an illegal wiretap. *See* 18 U.S.C. § 2511(1)(c). This provision of federal wiretap law is the subject of *Bartnicki v. Vopper*, discussed below. What types of disclosures of personal information can and should give rise to civil liability? How can liability for the disclosure of true information coexist with the First Amendment's protection of free speech?

1. PUBLIC DISCLOSURE OF PRIVATE FACTS

(a) Introduction

PUBLICITY GIVEN TO PRIVATE LIFE

Restatement (Second) of Torts § 652D

One who gives publicity to a matter concerning the private life of another is subject to liability to the other for invasion of his privacy, if the matter publicized is of a kind that
    (a) would be highly offensive to a reasonable person, and
    (b) is not of legitimate concern to the public

NOTES & QUESTIONS

1. *Publicity.* "Publicity" means that the matter is communicated to the "public at large" or "to so many persons that the matter must be regarded as substantially certain to become one of public knowledge." The Restatement (comment b) notes that communicating "a fact concerning the plaintiff's private life to a single person or even to a small group of persons" is not sufficient to establish publicity. The Restatement commentary goes on to explain:

> On the other hand, any publication in a newspaper or a magazine, even of small circulation, or in a handbill distributed to a large number of persons, or any broadcast over the radio, or statement made in an address to a large audience,

is sufficient to give publicity within the meaning of the term as it is used in this Section. The distinction, in other words, is one between private and public communication.

Most courts have followed the Restatement and concluded that disclosure to a small group of individuals does not constitute publicity. For example, in *Yoder v. Smith*, 112 N.W.2d 862 (Iowa 1962), the court held that the publicity element was not satisfied when the defendant disclosed the plaintiff's debts to the plaintiff's employer. In *Wells v. Thomas*, 569 F. Supp. 426 (E.D. Pa. 1983), the court held that disclosure to a plaintiff's co-workers at a hospital was not sufficient to establish the publicity element.

In contrast, posting information in public places constitutes sufficient publicity. In *Brents v. Morgan*, 299 S.W. 967 (Ky. 1927), the court held that there was sufficient publicity when the owner of an automobile garage posted a large sign on a show window of his garage stating that the plaintiff owed him a debt. In *Biederman's of Springfield, Inc. v. Wright*, 322 S.W.2d 892 (Mo. 1959), the court concluded that making loaded comments to a person "in a public restaurant with numerous customers present satisfies any reasonable requirement as to publicity."

However, consider *Miller v. Motorola, Inc.*, 560 N.E2d 900 (Ill. App. 1990). The plaintiff shared information that with her employer's nurse that she was undergoing a mastectomy and reconstructive surgeries. The information was disclosed to other employees. The court held that although the information was made to a small group, "in circumstances where a special relationship exists between the plaintiff and the 'public' to whom the information has been disclosed, the disclosure may be just as devastating to the person even though the disclosure was made to a limited number of people." The court in *Miller* followed an earlier case, *Beaumont v. Brown*, 257 N.W.2d 522 (Mich. 1977), which explained: "An invasion of a plaintiff's right to privacy is important if it exposes private facts to a public whose knowledge of those facts would be embarrassing to the plaintiff."

Which approach to publicity do you agree with? Consider Jonathan Mintz:

> A person loses some sense of privacy the moment a second person divulges a private fact to a third person, particularly when the third person is a member of the same community as the first person. Thus, the degree of publicity, and the corresponding degree of injury to a person's dignity, is a factor better addressed in damage calculations than in summary judgments or motions to dismiss.[10]

Why does the publicity requirement exist? As one court observed, the requirement of widespread publicity "singles out the print, film, and broadcast media for legal restraints that will not be applied to gossip-mongers in neighborhood taverns or card-parties, to letter writers or telephone tattlers." *Anderson v. Fisher Broadcasting Co.*, 712 P.2d 803, 805 (Or. 1986). A major function of the publicity requirement is to prevent lawsuits for a wide array of gossip, which often occurs between just a few people. The publicity

---

[10] Jonathan B. Mintz, *The Remains of Privacy's Disclosure Tort: An Exploration of the Private Domain*, 55 Md. L. Rev. 425, 438 (1996).

requirement attempts to exclude mere gossip from the tort. Would the public disclosure tort apply too widely without the publicity requirement?

2. *Highly Offensive.* The disclosure must be highly offensive. According to the Restatement (comment c):

> Complete privacy does not exist in this world except in a desert, and anyone who is not a hermit must expect and endure the ordinary incidents of the community life of which he is a part. Thus he must expect the more or less casual observation of his neighbors as to what he does, and that his comings and goings and his ordinary daily activities, will be described in the press as a matter of casual interest to others. The ordinary reasonable man does not take offense at a report in a newspaper that he has returned from a visit, gone camping in the woods or given a party at his house for his friends. Even minor and moderate annoyance, as for example through public disclosure of the fact that the plaintiff has clumsily fallen downstairs and broken his ankle, is not sufficient to give him a cause of action under the rule stated in this Section. It is only when the publicity given to him is such that a reasonable person would feel justified in feeling seriously aggrieved by it, that the cause of action arises.

Note the irony. The Restatement commentary suggests that the ordinary person does not take offense of a newspaper report that he has "given a party at his house for his friends." Indeed, it was such a newspaper report that some suggest inspired Samuel Warren to write the law review article with Louis Brandeis that gave rise to this very tort.

3. *Newsworthiness.* As stated by Restatement (comment f): "When the subject-matter of the publicity is of legitimate public concern, there is no invasion of privacy." Recall that the first exception to the right to privacy proposed by Brandeis and Warren was for "any publication of matter which is of general public interest."

4. *Recognition of the Tort by the States.* Most states recognize the public disclosure tort.[11] There are some states that have not recognized the tort: Nebraska, New York, North Carolina, North Dakota, Rhode Island, Utah, and Virginia.[12] As you read in *Lake v. Wal-Mart*, Minnesota, a long time holdout on recognizing the public disclosure tort, finally recognized the tort in 1998.

---

[11] For more background about the public disclosure tort, see Jonathan B. Mintz, *The Remains of Privacy's Disclosure Tort: An Exploration of the Private Domain,* 55 Md. L. Rev. 425 (1996); Robert C. Post, *The Social Foundations of Privacy: Community and Self in the Common Law Tort,* 77 Cal. L. Rev. 957 (1989); Peter L. Felcher & Edward L. Rubin, *Privacy, Publicity, and the Portrayal of Real People by the Media,* 88 Yale L.J. 1577 (1979); Dorsey D. Ellis, Jr., *Damages and the Privacy Tort: Sketching a "Legal Profile,"* 64 Iowa L. Rev. 1111 (1979); Randall Bezanson, *Public Disclosure as News: Injunctive Relief and Newsworthiness in Privacy Actions Involving the Press,* 64 Iowa L. Rev. 1061 (1979); John W. Wade, *Defamation and the Right to Privacy,* 15 Vand. L. Rev. 1093 (1962).

[12] *See* Geoff Dendy, Note, *The Newsworthiness Defense to the Public Disclosure Tort,* 85 Ky. L.J. 147, 158 (1997).

(b) Private Matters

GILL V. HEARST PUBLISHING CO.

253 P.2d 441 (Cal. 1953)

SPENCE, J. . . . [P]laintiffs, husband and wife, sought damages for an alleged invasion of their right of privacy. . . . Plaintiffs' original complaint was predicated solely on the charge that in the October, 1947, issue of Harper's Bazaar, a magazine published and distributed by the corporate defendants, there appeared an unauthorized photograph of plaintiffs taken by defendants' employee while plaintiffs were seated in an affectionate pose at their place of business, a confectionery and ice cream concession in the Farmers' Market in Los Angeles. This photograph was used to illustrate an article entitled "And So the World Goes Round," a short commentary reaffirming "the poet's conviction that the world could not revolve without love," despite "vulgarization" of the sentiment by some, and that ballads may still be written about everyday people in love. . . .

Plaintiffs . . . amended their complaint to allege that the same photograph was republished with defendants' consent in the May, 1949, issue of the Ladies' Home Journal, a monthly magazine published and distributed by the Curtis Publishing Company. . . . Specifically, it is here alleged that the "picture" was republished with the "knowledge, permission and consent" of defendants and that "credit" for the publication was given to and required by defendants; that the published photograph depicts plaintiffs in an "uncomplimentary" pose; that plaintiffs' right of privacy was thereby invaded and plaintiffs were subjected to humiliation and annoyance to their damage in the sum of $25,000. . . .

. . . [M]ere publication of the photograph standing alone does not constitute an actionable invasion of plaintiffs' right of privacy. The right "to be let alone" and to be protected from undesired publicity is not absolute but must be balanced against the public interest in the dissemination of news and information consistent with the democratic processes under the constitutional guaranties of freedom of speech and of the press. The right of privacy may not be extended to prohibit any publication of matter which may be of public or general interest. . . .

The picture allegedly was taken at plaintiffs' "place of business," a confectionery and ice cream concession in the Farmers' Market, Los Angeles. It shows plaintiffs, a young man and young woman, seated at a counter near a cash register, the young woman apparently in intent thought, with a notebook and pencil in her hands, which rest on the counter. Plaintiffs are dressed informally and are in a romantic pose, the young man having one arm about the young woman. There are at least five other persons plainly visible in the photograph in positions in close proximity to plaintiffs as the central figures. Apparently the picture has no particular news value but is designed to serve the function of entertainment as a matter of legitimate public interest. However, the constitution guaranties of freedom of expression apply with equal force to the publication whether it be a news report or an entertainment feature, and defendants' liability accrues only in the event that it can be said that there has been a wrongful invasion of plaintiffs' right of privacy.

In considering the nature of the picture in question, it is significant that it was not surreptitiously snapped on private grounds, but rather was taken of plaintiffs in a pose voluntarily assumed in a public market place. . . . Here plaintiffs, photographed at their concession allegedly "well known to persons and travelers throughout the world" as conducted for "many years" in the "world-famed" Farmers' Market, had voluntarily exposed themselves to public gaze in a pose open to the view of any persons who might then be at or near their place of business. By their own voluntary action plaintiffs waived their right of privacy so far as this particular public pose was assumed. . . . , for "There can be no privacy in that which is already public." *Melvin v. Reid*, 297 P. 91, 93. The photograph of plaintiffs merely permitted other members of the public, who were not at plaintiffs' place of business at the time it was taken, to see them as they had voluntarily exhibited themselves. Consistent which their own voluntary assumption of this particular pose in a public place, plaintiffs' right to privacy as to this photographed incident ceased and it in effect became a part of the public domain, as to which they could not later rescind their waiver in an attempt to assert a right of privacy. . . . In short, the photograph did not disclose anything which until then had been private, but rather only extended knowledge of the particular incident to a somewhat larger public then had actually witnessed it at the time of occurrence.

Nor does there appear to be anything "uncomplimentary" or discreditable in the photograph itself, so that its publication might be objectionable as going "beyond the limits of decency" and reasonably indicate defendants' conduct to be such that they "should have realized it would be offensive to persons of ordinary sensibilities." Here the picture of plaintiffs, sitting romantically close to one another, the man with his arm around the woman, depicts no more than a portrayal of an incident which may be seen almost daily in ordinary life couples in a sentimental mood on public park benches, in railroad depots or hotel lobbies, at public games, the beaches, the theatres. Such situation is readily distinguishable from cases where the right of privacy has been enforced with regard to the publication of a picture which was shocking, revolting or indecent in its portrayal of the human body. In fact, here the photograph may very well be said to be complimentary and pleasing in its pictorial representation of plaintiffs.

Plaintiffs have failed to cite, and independent research has failed to reveal, any case where the publication of a mere photograph under the circumstances here prevailing a picture (1) taken in a pose voluntarily assumed in a public place and (2) portraying nothing to shock the ordinary sense of decency or propriety has been held an actionable invasion of the right of privacy. To so hold would mean that plaintiffs "under all conceivable circumstances had an absolute legal right to (prevent publication of) any photograph of them taken without their permission. If every person has such a right, no (periodical) could lawfully publish a photograph of a parade or a street scene. We are not prepared to sustain the assertion of such a right." . . .

CARTER, J. dissenting. I dissent, however, from the holding that the publication of the photograph alone did not violate plaintiffs' right of privacy. . . .

[F]irst, it should be quite obvious that there is no news or educational value whatsoever in the photograph alone. It depicts two persons (plaintiffs) in an amorous pose. There is nothing to show whether they are or are not married. While some remote news significance might be attached to persons in such a pose on the theory that the public likes and is entitled to see persons in such a pose, there is no reason why the publisher need invade the privacy of John and Jane Doe for his purpose. He can employ models for that purpose and the portion of the public interested will never know the difference but its maudlin curiosity will be appeased.

For the same reasons the discussion in the majority opinion to the effect that plaintiffs consented to the publication because they assumed the pose in a public place is fallacious. But in addition, such a theory is completely at odds with the violation of the right of privacy. By plaintiffs doing what they did in view of a tiny fraction of the public, does not mean that they consented to observation by the millions of readers of the defendant's magazine. In effect, the majority holding means that anything anyone does outside of his own home is with consent to the publication thereof, because, under those circumstances he waives his right of privacy even though there is no news value in the event. If such were the case, the blameless exposure of a portion of the naked body of a man or woman in a public place as the result of inefficient buttons, hooks or other clothes-holding devices could be freely photographed and widely published with complete immunity. The majority opinion confuses the situation, as have some of the other cases, with the question of newsworthiness. It has been said that when a person is involved in either a public or private event, voluntarily or involuntarily, of news value, that he has waived his right of privacy. Plainly such is not the case where the event is involuntary such as the victim of a holdup. . . . There is no basis for the conclusion that the second a person leaves the portals of his home he consents to have his photograph taken under all circumstances thereafter. There being no legitimate public interest, there is no excuse for the publication.

The [argument] that the picture would not offend the senses of an ordinary person is equally untenable. It is alleged in plaintiffs' complaint, and admitted by the demurrer that it so offended them. It is then a matter of proof at the trial. Certainly reasonable men could view the picture as showing plaintiffs in a sultry or sensual pose. For this Court to say as a matter of law that such portrayal would not seriously offend the feelings of an ordinary man is to take an extreme view to say the least. The question is one for the trier of fact. If it is in part a question of law it is so only to the extent that the right does not extend to "supersensitiveness or agoraphobia." An examination of the photograph shows that it would offend the feelings of persons other than oversensitive ones. . . .

In announcing a rule of law defining the right of a private citizen to be left alone, and not have his photograph published to the four winds, especially when he is depicted in an uncomplimentary pose, courts should consider the effect of such publication upon the sensibility of the ordinary private citizen, and not upon the sensibility of those persons who seek and enjoy publicity and notoriety and seeing their pictures on public display, or those who are in the "public eye" such as public officials, clergymen, lecturers, actors and others whose professional career brings them in constant contact with the public and in whom the public or some segment thereof is interested. Obviously anything the latter group may do or say has news or educational value such cannot be said of the persons engaged in private business or employment who constitute more that 90% of our population. These private citizens, who desire to be left alone, should have and enjoy a right of privacy so long as they do nothing which can reasonably be said to have news value. Certainly this right is entitled to protection. It seems to me that the law should be so molded as to protect the right of the 90% who do not desire publicity or notoriety and who may be offended by publications such as that here involved. . . .

NOTES & QUESTIONS

1. *Privacy in Public.* Similar to *Gill,* many courts hold that matters cease to be "private" when occurring in public. Appearing in public "necessarily involves doffing the cloak of privacy which the law protects." *Cefalu v. Globe Newspaper Co.*, 391 N.E.2d 935, 939 (Mass. App. 1979). In *Penwell v. Taft Broadcasting*, 469 N.E.2d 1025 (Ohio App. 1984), a husband and wife were arrested in a bar, handcuffed, and taken to the police station, where it was discovered that they had been arrested due to mistaken identity. A television film crew that arrived at the bar with the police filmed the plaintiff's arrest and removal from the bar, and the footage was later broadcast by the television station. The court dismissed the plaintiff's public disclosure action because the arrest was filmed in public and was "left open to the public eye." Does appearing in public extinguish a person's claim to privacy?

2. *Google Street View.* Google Street View allows Web surfers to see images of each street at street level. In the United States, Google provides an opt-out option for individuals who do not wish to have an image of their residence included in the Street View database. The Borings, who live on a private road outside of Pittsburgh, sued Google for taking Street View pictures without their permission. In an unpublished opinion, the Third Circuit affirmed a lower court's granting of Google's motion to dismiss. *Boring v. Google*, 38 Media L. Rep. 1306 (2010). On the intrusion upon seclusion claim, the Third Circuit declared, "No person of ordinary sensibility would be shamed, humiliated, or have suffered mentally as a result of a vehicle entering into his or her ungated driveway and photographing the view from there." As for publicity given to private life, it also found that the Borings failed to establish that the publicity would be highly offensive to a reasonable person.

   As an international comparison, protests in 2010 Germany against Google's introduction of this same service led the company to permit individuals, including persons who live in apartment buildings, to opt out their residence from the database *before* it went live. Which version of opt-out is preferable?

   The result of the opt-out in Germany in 2010 proved dramatic. Many people opted out, and Street View was heavily blurred out. As one website explained the consequences, the service's "utility was minimal and, as a result, Google opted to cease updating its Street view imagery in the country despite continuing to do so around Europe."[13]

   Fast-forward to 2023. In June 2023, Google restarted its capturing of Street View imagery in Germany. It will continue to permit opting out by residents of

---

[13] Ben Schoon, *Google Maps Street View returns to Germany with first new captures since 2010,* 9to5 Google (June 9, 2023), at https://9to5google.com/2023/06/09/google-street-view-germany/.

their houses and apartment buildings and will delete older images. As it does elsewhere in the world, Google also has a process to automatically blur faces and automobile license plates that may be captured by its Street View automobiles. In its announcement of this re-launch of Street View, Google noted that a poll it commissioned showed more than 91% of German now have a positive or very positive opinion of Street View.[14] It also stated that it was working closely with the Hamburg Data Protection Commission, the relevant authority.

Do you think Street View is problematic or unproblematic on privacy grounds? Are there additional safeguards that you think Google should offer?

3. *Photography of Public Scenes.* Judge Carter, in dissent, argues that there is a difference between engaging in public displays of affection "in view of a tiny fraction of the public" and being observed by millions of magazine readers. Thus, the prior public exposure of the plaintiffs did not extinguish their privacy claim. How is the law to draw the appropriate line? At what point does the public exposure of the plaintiff's activities become too great to sustain a claim that the activities are private? Suppose, for example, a photographer is taking photos of people in the park. How is that photographer to know if she can publish the photos? Should she obtain the consent of everyone captured in the photos? According to the majority opinion, if Judge Carter's view were the law, this "would mean that plaintiffs under all conceivable circumstances had an absolute legal right to (prevent publication of) any photograph of them taken without their permission. If every person has such a right, no (periodical) could lawfully publish a photograph of a parade or a street scene." How would Judge Carter respond?

DAILY TIMES DEMOCRAT V. GRAHAM
162 So. 2d 474 (Ala. 1964)

HARWOOD, J. This is an appeal from a judgment in favor of the plaintiff in an action charging an invasion by the defendant of the plaintiff's right of privacy. Damages were assessed by the jury at $4,166.00. . . .

Appellee is a woman 44 years of age who has lived in Cullman County, Alabama her entire life. She is married and has two sons, ages 10 and 8. The family resides in a rural community where her husband is engaged in the business of raising chickens. . . .

On 9 October 1961, the Cullman County Fair was in progress. On that day the appellee took her two children to the Fair. After going on some of the rides, the boys expressed a wish to go through what is called in the record the "Fun House." The boys were afraid to enter alone so the appellee accompanied them. She testified she had never been through a Fun House before and had no knowledge

---

[14] Sven Trep, *Aktualisierung für Google Street View in Deutschland*, Google The Keyword Deutschland (June 8, 2023), at https://blog.google/intl/de-de/produkte/suchen-entdecken/google-street-view-aktualisierung-deutschland/

that there was a device that blew jets of air up from the platform of the Fun House upon which one exited therefrom.

The appellee entered the Fun House with her two boys and as she was leaving her dress was blown up by the air jets and her body was exposed from the waist down, with the exception of that portion covered by her "panties."

At this moment the appellant's photographer snapped a picture of the appellee in this situation. This was done without the appellee's knowledge or consent. Four days later the appellant published this picture on the front page of its newspaper.

The appellant publishes about five thousand newspapers daily which are delivered to homes, mailed to subscribers, and displayed on racks in various locations in the city of Cullman and elsewhere.

On the Sunday following the publication of the picture, the appellee went into the city of Cullman. There she saw the appellant's newspaper display with her picture on the front page in one of the appellant's newspaper racks, and she also saw copies of the said newspaper in other places.

While the appellee's back was largely towards the camera in the picture, her two sons are in the picture, and the photograph was recognized as being of her by other people with whom she was acquainted. The matter of her photograph was mentioned to the appellee by others on several occasions. Evidence offered by the appellee during the trial tended to show that the appellee, as a result of the publication of the picture, became embarrassed, self-conscious, upset and was known to cry on occasions. . . .

. . . Counsel contends that as a matter of law the publication of the photograph was a matter of legitimate news of interest to the public; that the publishing of the picture was in connection with a write-up of the Fair, which was a matter of legitimate news. If this be so, then of course the appellant would have been privileged to have published the picture. . . .

We can see nothing of legitimate news value in the photograph. Certainly it discloses nothing as to which the public is entitled to be informed. . . .

Not only was this photograph embarrassing to one of normal sensibilities, we think it could properly be classified as obscene, in that "obscene" means "offensive to modesty or decency"; or expressing to the mind or view something which delicacy, purity, or decency forbid to be expressed. . . .

Counsel further argues that the court erred in refusal of appellant's requested affirmative charges in that appellee's picture was taken at the time she was a part of a public scene, and the publication of the photograph could not therefore be deemed an invasion of her privacy as a matter of law.

The proposition for which appellant contends is probably best illustrated by the following quotation from *Forster v. Manchester*, 410 Pa. 192, 189 A.2d 147:

> On the public street, or in any other public place, the plaintiff has no right to be alone, and it is no invasion of his privacy to do no more than follow him about. Neither is it such an invasion to take his photograph in such a place, since this amounts to nothing more than making a record, not differing essentially from a full written description of a public sight which anyone present would be free to see.

Admittedly this principle is established by the cases. As well stated in *Hinish v. Meir & Frank Co., Inc.*, 113 P.2d 438:

When a legal principle is pushed to an absurdity, the principle is not abandoned, but the absurdity avoided.

In other words, a purely mechanical application of legal principles should not be permitted to create an illogical conclusion.

To hold that one who is involuntarily and instantaneously enmeshed in an embarrassing pose forfeits her right of privacy merely because she happened at the moment to be part of a public scene would be illogical, wrong, and unjust.

One who is a part of a public scene may be lawfully photographed as an incidental part of that scene in his ordinary status. Where the status he expects to occupy is changed without his volition to a status embarrassing to an ordinary person of reasonable sensitivity, then he should not be deemed to have forfeited his right to be protected from an indecent and vulgar intrusion of his right of privacy merely because misfortune overtakes him in a public place. . . .

NOTES & QUESTIONS

1. *Voluntary vs. Involuntary Exposure.* The court holds that although Graham was in public, the exposure of her body was involuntary, and hence a private matter. Does whether a matter is public or private depend upon voluntary or involuntary disclosure or upon one's expectation? Is *Graham* consistent with *Gill v. Hearst Publishing Co.*? Can these cases be reconciled?

   Also consider *McNamara v. Freedom Newspapers, Inc.*, 802 S.W.2d 901 (Tex. Ct. App. 1991). A newspaper published a photo of a high school soccer player's inadvertently exposed genitalia while running on a soccer field. The plaintiff, McNamara, relied on *Daily Times Democrat v. Graham*, but the court found *Graham* unpersuasive and concluded:

   > The uncontroverted facts in this case establish that the photograph of McNamara was taken by a newspaper photographer for media purposes. The picture accurately depicted a public event and was published as part of a newspaper article describing the game. At the time the photograph was taken, McNamara was voluntarily participating in a spectator sport at a public place. None of the persons involved in the publishing procedure actually noticed that McNamara's genitals were exposed.

   Can *McNamara* be reconciled with *Graham*?

2. *Privacy and Communication to Other People.* Generally, a fact widely known about a person is not considered private; however, certain limited disclosures of information do not destroy its private nature. In *Times Mirror Co. v. Superior Court*, 244 Cal. Rptr. 556 (Cal. Ct. App. 1988), the plaintiff (Doe) discovered the murdered body of her roommate lying on the floor of her apartment and saw the perpetrator before she fled the apartment. Doe's identity was withheld from the public by the police to protect her safety (since the murderer was still at large), but her identity was leaked to a reporter and published in a newspaper article about the incident. Doe sued for public disclosure, and the newspaper argued that the matter was not private because Doe revealed it to certain neighbors, friends, family members, and investigating officials. The court, however, concluded that Doe had not "rendered otherwise private information

public by cooperating in the criminal investigation and seeking solace from friends and relatives."

How many people must a person tell a secret to before it ceases to become private? In *Y.G. v. Jewish Hospital,* 795 S.W.2d 488 (Mo. Ct. App. 1990), a couple used in vitro fertilization at a hospital to become pregnant. While people at the hospital knew about their use of in vitro fertilization, the couple kept this hidden from others because it was against the teachings of their church. At a party in this hospital for in vitro couples, a camera crew from a television station filmed the plaintiffs (despite their making reasonable efforts to not be filmed). The court held that the plaintiffs retained an expectation of privacy because "attending this limited gathering . . . did not waive their right to keep their condition and the process of in vitro private, in respect to the general public." In *Multimedia WMAZ, Inc. v. Kubach,* 443 S.E.2d 491 (Ga. 1994), an HIV-positive plaintiff disclosed that he had the disease to about 60 people — family, friends, doctors, and members of an HIV support group. The plaintiff agreed to appear on a television show with his face obscured, but the obscuring process was botched, and the plaintiff was identifiable. He sued, and the court concluded that his telling his HIV-positive status to 60 people did not extinguish his privacy interest because these people "cared about him . . . or because they also had AIDS."

In contrast, consider *Duran v. Detroit News, Inc.,* 504 N.W.2d 715 (Mich. Ct. App. 1993). A Colombian judge, who indicted the violent drug lord Pablo Escobar, fled to Detroit after receiving death threats. She told a few people about her identity. Reporters, however, revealed her address and discussed the million-dollar bounty on her head. The court rejected Duran's public disclosure claim because she had exposed her identity "to the public eye." In *Fisher v. Ohio Dep't of Rehabilitation and Correction,* 578 N.E.2d 901 (Ohio Ct. Cl. 1988), the plaintiff told just four co-workers about encounters with her child that had "sexual overtones." The court concluded that the information was no longer private because the plaintiff "publicly and openly" told it to her co-workers.

Can you articulate a coherent approach to guide courts when analyzing how sharing information with other people affects the privacy of that information?

3. ***Social Networks and Boundaries of Information Flow.*** Lior Strahilevitz concludes that "courts are not being terribly explicit or precise about why particular disclosures waive privacy expectations and others do not. Certainly, a simple head-counting approach does not reconcile the precedents. After all, Kubach's disclosure of facts to sixty people did not render them public, but Fisher's disclosure to three people did." Strahilevitz suggests that looking to the number of people who are exposed to a secret is not the right approach. Instead, he uses social network theory.

Social network theory describes how information flows between people. In particular, network theory seeks to assess the probability that information disclosed to one member of a particular group or community will be disseminated to others outside of that realm. According to Strahilevitz, the analysis should not focus on how many people already know a person's secret but how likely the secret is to be widely disseminated beyond the group of people who already know it. Information should be deemed private so long as it remains within a confined group — even if that group is rather large. The law should recognize that a particular person expects information to stay within these boundaries.

Strahilevitz identifies three key factors that affect the likelihood of data staying within a particular group: (1) how interesting the information is (the more interesting, the more likely it is to spread beyond the group); (2) the norms that a particular group has with regard to spreading the kind of information at issue; and (3) the way the group is structured and how information generally flows within and beyond the group. Strahilevtiz agrees with the *Kubach* court's decision that the plaintiff still retained a privacy interest in his HIV-positive status even though 60 others knew about it:

> [An empirical] study of HIV disclosure suggests that information about HIV status is frequently shared with some parts of an individual's social network, while other members, who might know the HIV positive person well and be interested in her health status, remain in the dark. Information about HIV status, therefore, seems not to flow through social networks readily, at least in the case of private figures. . . . Kubach had a reasonable expectation that his disclosure to some people who knew him would not result in the information being revealed to others who knew him, let alone thousands of people in his local community.

Strahilevitz argues that the holding in *Duran* is inconsistent with social network theory:

> According to the court, Duran used her real name when shopping in stores or eating in restaurants, which waived an expectation of privacy in her identity. Under a network theory approach, these acts, combined with her notoriety in Colombia, would not have eliminated her reasonable expectation of privacy in her identity. . . . [When shopping or at a restaurant, at] most, Duran would have come into fleeting contact with other customers or service sector employees. There was nothing interesting about Duran's shopping or eating out.[15]

4. *Closed Communities.* Woodrow Hartzog notes that there are certain closed communities where a strong expectation of confidentiality has developed, such as Alcoholics Anonymous. Closed communities also exist online — indeed, Alcoholics Anonymous has an online group. Hartzog contends: "Members of these closed communities have not disclosed their personal information to the world. Rather, they have revealed their information to other members of the community based on that community's norms and expectations of confidentiality."[16]

Suppose a person shares information with a group of 300 Facebook friends on her profile, which is set to be seen by "friends only." One of that person's friends reveals the information on a publicly accessible media site. In a lawsuit for public disclosure of private facts, the friend argues that the person's

---

[15] Lior Jacob Strahilevitz, *A Social Networks Theory of Privacy*, 72 U. Chi. L. Rev. 919 (2005).
[16] Woodrow Hartzog, *Promises and Privacy: Promissory Estoppel and Confidential Disclosures in Online Communities*, 82 Temple L. Rev. 891 (2009).

information was not private because it was available to 300 individuals on Facebook. How should a court rule on whether the information was private?

5. ***Further Dissemination of Previously Disclosed Information.*** Media entities that further disseminate information already disclosed by another media entity are not liable for public disclosure. *Ritzmann v. Weekly World News*, 614 F. Supp. 1336 (N.D. Tex. 1985) (giving further publicity to information contained in news stories already published is not actionable because the information is no longer private); *Heath v. Playboy Enterprises, Inc.*, 732 F. Supp. 1145 (S.D. Fla. 1990) ("Republication of facts already publicized elsewhere cannot provide a basis for an invasion of privacy claim.").

However, when only partial facts are revealed, the disclosure of more information can give rise to a viable action for public disclosure. For example, in *Michaels v. Internet Entertainment Group, Inc.*, 5 F. Supp. 2d 823 (C.D. Cal. 1998), Bret Michaels, the former lead singer for the rock band Poison, and Pamela Anderson Lee, a celebrity, sought a preliminary injunction to prevent the defendant from making a videotape of the two having sex available on the Internet. The defendant argued that the plaintiffs lacked a privacy interest in the tape because a part of the tape had already been released by a foreign Internet source. The court, however, concluded that "plaintiffs' privacy interest in the unreleased portions of the Tape is undiminished." Further, another videotape depicting Lee having sex with her husband, Tommy Lee, had been widely distributed, and the defendant contended that this negated Lee's privacy interest. The court rejected the defendant's argument: "The Court is not prepared to conclude that public exposure of one sexual encounter forever removes a person's privacy interest in all subsequent and previous sexual encounters." The defendant also contended that Lee lacked a privacy interest because she had previously appeared nude in magazines and on video, but the court concluded that the defendant's "contention unreasonably blurs the line between fiction and reality. Lee is a professional actor. She has played roles involving sex and sexual appeal. The fact that she has performed a role involving sex does not, however, make her real sex life open to the public."

6. ***Obscurity.*** Woodrow Hartzog and Fred Stutzman argue that the law often fails to grasp the concept of obscurity and that the law should better integrate obscurity into its fabric. They contend:

> Perhaps more than anything else, Internet users rely on obscurity for protection of their online information. Obscurity allows Internet users to be genuine by disclosing information that they would not otherwise share in "public." Yet this concept, which is at the very heart of the social web, is largely undeveloped in privacy law. . .[17]

Could locating a publicly available yet obscure piece of information about a person and writing about it in a widely read media outlet constitute a violation of privacy? Suppose a reporter finds information online in a blog that has only a handful of readers. The reporter writes about it on a major news media

---

[17] Woodrow Hartzog & Fred Stutzman, *The Case for Online Obscurity*, 101 Cal. L. Rev. 1, 48 (2013).

website. Is this a violation of privacy? If not, is anything appearing online and accessible to the public no longer able to be deemed private?

(c) The Newsworthiness Test

SIPPLE V. CHRONICLE PUBLISHING CO.

201 Cal. Rptr. 665 (Cal. Ct. App. 1984)

CALDECOTT, J. On September 22, 1975, Sara Jane Moore attempted to assassinate President Gerald R. Ford while the latter was visiting San Francisco, California. Plaintiff Oliver W. Sipple (hereafter appellant or Sipple) who was in the crowd at Union Square, San Francisco, grabbed or struck Moore's arm as the latter was about to fire the gun and shoot at the President. Although no one can be certain whether or not Sipple actually saved the President's life, the assassination attempt did not succeed and Sipple was considered a hero for his selfless action and was subject to significant publicity throughout the nation following the assassination attempt.

Among the many articles concerning the event was a column, written by Herb Caen and published by the San Francisco Chronicle on September 24, 1975. The article read in part as follows: "One of the heroes of the day, Oliver 'Bill' Sipple, the ex-Marine who grabbed Sara Jane Moore's arm just as her gun was fired and thereby may have saved the President's life, was the center of midnight attention at the Red Lantern, a Golden Gate Ave. bar he favors. The Rev. Ray Broshears, head of Helping Hands, and Gay Politico, Harvey Milk, who claim to be among Sipple's close friends, describe themselves as 'proud — maybe this will help break the stereotype.' Sipple is among the workers in Milk's campaign for Supervisor."

Thereafter, the Los Angeles Times and numerous out-of-state newspapers published articles which referring to the primary source, (i.e., the story published in the San Francisco Chronicle) mentioned both the heroic act shown by Sipple and the fact that he was a prominent member of the San Francisco gay community. Some of those articles speculated that President Ford's failure to promptly thank Sipple for his heroic act was a result of Sipple's sexual orientation.[18]

. . . Sipple filed an action against the [newspapers]. The complaint was predicated upon the theory of invasion of privacy and alleged in essence that defendants without authorization and consent published private facts about plaintiff's life by disclosing that plaintiff was homosexual in his personal and private sexual orientation; that said publications were highly offensive to plaintiff inasmuch as his parents, brothers and sisters learned for the first time of his

---

[18] For example, the September 25, 1975, issue of the *Los Angeles Times* wrote inter alia as follows: "A husky ex-marine who was a hero in the attempted assassination of President Ford emerged Wednesday as a prominent figure in the gay community. And questions were raised in the gay community if Oliver (Bill) Sipple, 32, was being shunned by the White House because of his associations. Sipple, who lunged at Sara Jane Moore and deflected her revolver as she fired at the President, conceded that he is a member of the 'court' of Mike Caringi, who was elected 'emperor of San Francisco' by the gay community. A column item in a morning newspaper here strongly implied Wednesday that Sipple is gay. . . . Harvey Milk, a prominent member of this city's large homosexual community and a longtime friend of Sipple, speculated Wednesday that the absence of a phone call or telegram of gratitude from the White House might not be just an oversight."

homosexual orientation; and that as a consequence of disclosure of private facts about his life plaintiff was abandoned by his family, exposed to contempt and ridicule causing him great mental anguish, embarrassment and humiliation. . . .

Appellant's principal contention on appeal is that the trial court prejudicially erred in granting summary judgment in favor of respondents. . . .

Before discussing appellant's contentions on the merits, as an initial matter we set out the legal principles governing the case. It is well settled that there are three elements of a cause of action predicated on tortious invasion of privacy. First, the disclosure of the private facts must be a public disclosure. Second, the facts disclosed must be private facts, and not public ones. Third, the matter made public must be one which would be offensive and objectionable to a reasonable person of ordinary sensibilities. It is likewise recognized, however, that due to the supreme mandate of the constitutional protection of freedom of the press even a tortious invasion of one's privacy is exempt from liability if the publication of private facts is truthful and newsworthy. . . .

When viewed in light of the aforegoing principles, the summary judgment in this case must be upheld on two grounds. First, as appears from the record properly considered for the purposes of summary judgment, the facts disclosed by the articles were not private facts within the meaning of the law. Second, the record likewise reveals on its face that the publications in dispute were newsworthy and thus constituted a protective shield from liability based upon invasion of privacy. . . .

[Regarding the first ground,] the cases explain that there can be no privacy with respect to a matter which is already public or which has previously become part of the "public domain." Moreover, it is equally underlined that there is no liability when the defendant merely gives further publicity to information about the plaintiff which is already public or when the further publicity relates to matters which the plaintiff leaves open to the public eye.

The case at bench falls within the aforestated rules. The undisputed facts reveal that prior to the publication of the newspaper articles in question appellant's homosexual orientation and participation in gay community activities had been known by hundreds of people in a variety of cities, including New York, Dallas, Houston, San Diego, Los Angeles and San Francisco. Thus, appellant's deposition shows that prior to the assassination attempt appellant spent a lot of time in "Tenderloin" and "Castro," the well-known gay sections of San Francisco; that he frequented gay bars and other homosexual gatherings in both San Francisco and other cities; that he marched in gay parades on several occasions; that he supported the campaign of Mike Caringi for the election of "Emperor"; that he participated in the coronation of the "Emperor" and sat at Caringi's table on that occasion; that his friendship with Harvey Milk, another prominent gay, was well-known and publicized in gay newspapers; and that his homosexual association and name had been reported in gay magazines (such as Data Boy, Pacific Coast Times, Male Express, etc.) several times before the publications in question. In fact, appellant quite candidly conceded that he did not make a secret of his being a homosexual and that if anyone would ask, he would frankly admit that he was gay. In short, since appellant's sexual orientation was already in public domain and since the articles in question did no more than to give further publicity to matters which appellant left open to the eye of the public, a vital element of the tort was missing rendering it vulnerable to summary disposal. . . .

[Turning to the second ground — newsworthiness,] our courts have recognized a broad privilege cloaking the truthful publication of all newsworthy matters. . . . [T]he cases and authorities further explain that the paramount test of newsworthiness is whether the matter is of legitimate public interest which in turn must be determined according to the community mores. . . .

In the case at bench the publication of appellant's homosexual orientation which had already been widely known by many people in a number of communities was not so offensive even at the time of the publication as to shock the community notions of decency. Moreover, and perhaps even more to the point, the record shows that the publications were not motivated by a morbid and sensational prying into appellant's private life but rather were prompted by legitimate political considerations, i.e., to dispel the false public opinion that gays were timid, weak and unheroic figures and to raise the equally important political question whether the President of the United States entertained a discriminatory attitude or bias against a minority group such as homosexuals. . . .

Appellant's contention that by saving the President's life he did not intend to enter into the limelight and become a public figure, can be easily answered. In elaborating on involuntary public figures, Restatement Second of Torts section 625D, comment f, sets out in part as follows: "There are other individuals who have not sought publicity or consented to it, but through their own conduct or otherwise have become a legitimate subject of public interest. They have, in other words, become 'news.'"

NOTES & QUESTIONS

1. *The Sad Fate of a Hero.* Sipple passed away in January 1989, alone in a cluttered apartment with half-gallon bottles of bourbon within reach of his bed. A story in the *Los Angeles Times* almost a month after he passed away detailed the sad circumstances of his death and filled in some details of his life. Sipple had been wounded twice in Vietnam, lived on a veteran's disability pension, and, despite his lack of funds and poor health, was remembered by friends as a generous person who would readily give money to charity or to help a derelict.

   The *L.A. Times* also noted that a framed letter hung in the apartment where Sipple had died — it was a letter of "heartfelt appreciation," signed "Jerry Ford," which thanked Sipple for his "selfless actions" in acting quickly and without fear and averting danger to the President and the crowd. The letter was sent three days after Sipple had knocked away the gun of the would-be assassin in San Francisco.

   The *L.A. Times* article also stressed how much Sipple had suffered after the press outed him. It quoted George Sipple, Bill's brother: "His personal life never should have made it back to Detroit" (his hometown). Sipple's parents were shocked by the revelation of their son's sexual orientation; as the *L.A. Times* states: "The estrangement between Sipple and his father was so deep that when his mother died in 1979, his father made it clear that he was not welcome."[19] Sipple remained in San Francisco and did not attend his mother's funeral.

Taking a break from cleaning his brother's apartment, George Sipple noted that his brother was pleased that he left a mark and remembered that his brother once said that long after he died, "somebody will pick up a book and see Oliver Sipple saved President Ford's life."

2. ***Complete Secrecy and Group Privacy.*** The court rejects Sipple's claim in part because Sipple's homosexuality and participation in the gay community were known by hundreds of people in many cities. But Sipple's argument is that he wanted to keep his homosexuality a secret from certain people — namely his parents and siblings. Can Sipple legitimately claim that something known widely to many people can still remain private?

In the view of Ari Ezra Waldman "not all disclosures should be treated equally."[20] Similarly, Scott Skinner-Thompson argues that a complete secrecy requirement precludes claims by the marginalized. For Skinner-Thompson, moreover, *Sipple* illustrates a flaw in the tort, which he argues is applied differently for the privileged and marginalized in society: "[F]or many living at the margins of society who are subjected to high levels of government and private surveillance and transparent living quarters, keeping any information— much less sensitive information—completely secret as the tort purports to require is a practical impossibility."[21]

For Skinner-Thompson, the law should respond by injecting equal protection law into this area to force a relaxation of "the secrecy double standard." By this term, Skinner-Thompson points to the tort's requirements for both (1) secrecy (as in *Sipple*) and (2) widespread publicity or disclosure of the information. The necessary reform of the law requires that "all plaintiffs be able to bring public disclosure claims even if they have shared the information at issue (for example, their HIV status, sexual orientation, or intimate photographs) within certain confines." It also means that "marginalized plaintiffs should be able to state a claim even if the defendant does not publicize to the world the information at issue." A requirement of widespread publicity "should be contextually applied." Should the tort apply differently to particular marginalized communities?

3. ***President Ford's Prejudice.*** In *Sipple*, the newsworthiness of the story did not just turn on exposing the background of a hero who prevented an assassination. The story also exposed President Ford's possible prejudice against homosexuals. Does this fact alone establish that the story was newsworthy?

4. ***Outing.*** There has been extensive debate about the propriety of outing an individual's sexual orientation. Is the fact that a prominent individual is gay newsworthy? John Elwood observes that there are three rationales advanced for outing:

---

[19] Dean Morain, *Sorrow Trailed a Veteran Who Saved a President's Life and Then Was Cast in an Unwanted Spotlight*, L.A. Times, Feb. 13, 1989, at Part 5, 1.

[20] Ari Waldman, *Privacy as Trust* (2018).

[21] Scott Skinner-Thompson, *Privacy's Double Standards*, 93 Wash. L. Rev. 2051 (2018).

According to its advocates, outing serves three basic purposes: (1) to expose the illogic of governmental policies that discriminate against homosexuals and of the hypocrisy of gay public officials who publicly support such policies; (2) to provide positive examples of gays, as role models to other gays and as ambassadors to mainstream America; and (3) to break down the stigma surrounding homosexuality by making it commonplace.

Elwood contends: "Even under the best of circumstances, the relationship between outing a particular figure and effecting a societal change is simply too attenuated to override the outing target's privacy rights." However, "a closeted government official who made disparaging public remarks about homosexuals or who enforced discriminatory programs might be a valid target for outing. Her hypocrisy calls into question her honesty and motivation, and thus information about her sexuality is relevant to the question of her fitness for office."[22] How would this argument apply in the *Sipple* case?

In contrast to Elwood, Kathleen Guzman disagrees with the hypocrisy justification for outing:

. . . [T]his justification presupposes two potentially invalid assumptions. Presuming that the outers are even correct in asserting someone's orientation, one wonders whether there is such a thing as a "gay viewpoint." While abstract generalization may be made regarding the tendency of a group member to sympathize with in-group concerns, it is absurd to attribute to an individual a pre-packaged set of opinions merely because that individual is gay. One's views should no more be determined by sexual orientation than by being Caucasian or agnostic or underweight or female. . . .

Second, what is orientation hypocrisy and at what level of conduct should it be penalized? Hypocrisy is a broad term which can encompass a range of activity: merely keeping same-sex orientation a secret; actively asserting heterosexuality; failing to vote for or affirmatively and publicly support pro-gay legislation; actively opposing similar legislation. The (non)actor whose conduct contravenes the mythical "gay viewpoint" need not necessarily be driven by "hypocrisy," but is equally likely to act through privacy, self-preservation, cowardice, or merely a different belief.[23]

After Sipple's death, Fred Friendly, a journalism professor and former head of CBS News, wrote that journalists did not act fairly in Sipple's case and should not have written about his sexuality.[24] Friendly argued that the right to privacy should prevail unless the "individual's private conduct becomes relevant in assessing his integrity or validity in a public role." Do you agree with this approach? Does it resolve the *Sipple* case?

---

[22] John P. Elwood, Note, *Outing, Privacy, and the First Amendment*, 102 Yale L.J. 747, 748-49, 773-74 (1992).

[23] Kathleen Guzman, *About Outing: Public Discourse, Private Lives*, 73 Wash. U. L.Q. 1531, 1536-37, 1555-56 (1995). For further arguments against outing, see Jean L. Cohen, *Is Privacy a Legal Duty?*, in *Public and Private: Legal, Political, and Philosophical Perspectives* 117, 125 (Maurizio Passerin d'Entreves & Ursula Vogel eds., 2000).

[24] Fred W. Friendly, *Gays, Privacy and a Free Press*, Wash. Post, Apr. 8, 1990, at B7.

5. ***Newsworthiness Tests.*** Courts use at least three newsworthiness tests.[25] First is the "leave it to the press" approach, where courts defer to editorial judgment and do not attempt to distinguish between what is news and what is entertainment. Second, the Restatement looks to the "customs and conventions of the community" and draws a line between the "giving of information to which the public is entitled" and "morbid and sensational prying into private lives for its own sake." A third approach is the "nexus test," which involves the Restatement approach but also requires a "logical nexus (or relationship) . . . between the complaining individual and the matter of legitimate public interest." Which test do you find most appropriate?

6. ***What Is Newsworthy?*** Many of the cases applying the newsworthiness test do so to avoid First Amendment problems. Keep in mind that the newsworthiness test is an element of the tort of public disclosure. Applications of the tort — involving possibly even non-newsworthy facts — can still be subject to an independent First Amendment challenge.

How are courts to determine what is newsworthy? According to the Restatement of Torts § 652D (comment h), courts are to look to the "customs and conventions of the community."

Consider the case of *Diaz v. Oakland Tribune*, 188 Cal. Rptr. 762 (Ct. App. 1983). Diaz was the first woman student body president elected at a community college. The *Oakland Tribune* published the fact that Diaz was transgender. Diaz sued for public disclosure, and the court held that the suit could proceed to the jury, which would determine whether the fact that Diaz was transgender was newsworthy. The court noted: "[W]e find little if any connection between the information disclosed and Diaz's fitness for office. The fact that she is [transgender] does not adversely reflect on her honesty or judgment." Eugene Volokh, who opposes the tort of public disclosure altogether, argues:

> Now I agree with the [*Diaz*] court's factual conclusion; people's gender identity strikes me as irrelevant to their fitness for office. But other voters take a different view. . . . [Being transgender], in their opinion, may say various things about politicians (even student body politicians): It may say that they lack attachment to traditional values, that they are morally corrupt, or even just that they have undergone an unnatural procedure and therefore are somehow tainted by it. These views may be wrong and even immoral, but surely it is not for government agents — whether judges or jurors — to dictate the relevant criteria for people's political choices, and to use the coercive force of law to keep others from informing them of things that they may consider relevant to those choices. I may disagree with what you base your vote on, but I must defend your right to base your vote on it, and the right of others to tell you about it.[26]

If Volokh is right, then what isn't relevant for fitness for office? Do public figures have any claim to privacy, or is everything about them newsworthy?

---

[25] *See* Geoff Dendy, Note, *The Newsworthiness Defense to the Public Disclosure Tort*, 85 Ky. L.J. 147 (1997).

[26] Eugene Volokh, *Freedom of Speech and Information Privacy: The Troubling Implications of a Right to Stop People from Speaking About You*, 52 Stan. L. Rev. 1049, 1090 (2000).

In *Neff v. Time, Inc.*, 406 F. Supp. 858 (W.D. Pa. 1976), a *Sports Illustrated* photographer printed a photograph of John W. Neff, a teacher, with the front zipper of his pants open in *Sports Illustrated*. The photograph was used in a story about Pittsburgh Steelers fans, and the article was entitled: "A Strange Kind of Love." The photograph was taken while Neff was with a group of fans at a football game between the Cleveland Browns and Pittsburgh Steelers. The fans were waving Steeler banners, drinking beer, and appeared slightly intoxicated. When the *Sports Illustrated* photographer approached them and the group found out that the photographer was covering the game for *Sports Illustrated*, the group "hammed it up" while the photographer snapped the pictures. Of the 30 pictures of the group that were taken, a committee of five employees at *Sports Illustrated* selected the photograph of Neff with his fly open for inclusion in the issue. According to the court, "[a]lthough Neff's fly was not open to the point of being revealing, the selection was deliberate and surely in utmost bad taste; subjectively, as to Neff, the published picture could have been embarrassing, humiliating and offensive to his sensibilities." According to Neff, the photograph implied "that he is a 'crazy, drunken slob,' and combined with the title of the article, 'a sexual deviate.'" Neff asserted that the article invaded his right to privacy, caused him reputational injury, subjected him to public ridicule, destroyed his peace of mind, and caused him severe emotional distress. The court, however, rejected Neff's claim:

> . . . It seems to us that art directors and editors should hesitate to deliberately publish a picture which most likely would be offensive and cause embarrassment to the subject when many other pictures of the same variety are available. Notwithstanding, "(t)he courts are not concerned with establishing canons of good taste for the press or the public." . . .

Graham involved a photograph taken of a woman who was in an embarrassing position in public. How does the situation in *Neff* differ from that in *Graham*? *Graham* did not focus much on newsworthiness, but suppose that the case were being decided by the *Neff* court — would the photograph in *Graham* be newsworthy?

7. ***The Privacy of Public Figures.*** To what extent can a public figure's life be private? Consider the Restatement of Torts (Second) § 652D (comment h):

> The extent of the authority to make public private facts is not, however, unlimited. There may be some intimate details of [a celebrity actress's] life, such as sexual relations, which even the actress is entitled to keep to herself. In determining what is a matter of legitimate public interest, account must be taken of the customs and conventions of the community; and in the last analysis what is proper becomes a matter of the community mores. The line is to be drawn when the publicity ceases to be the giving of information to which the public is entitled, and becomes a morbid and sensational prying into private lives for its own sake, with which a reasonable member of the public, with decent standards, would say that he had no concern.

8. ***The Disclosure of Identifying Information.*** In *Barber v. Time, Inc.*, 159 S.W.2d 291 (Mo. 1942), the plaintiff's photograph taken in a hospital was published in a *Time* magazine article about the plaintiff's unusual disease. The

article, "Starving Glutton," described the plaintiff's rare disorder where no matter how much she ate, she continued to lose weight. The photograph showed the plaintiff in her hospital bed. The court held that "[w]hile plaintiff's ailment may have been a matter of some public interest because unusual, certainly the identity of the person who suffered this ailment was not." In other words, the matter about the rare disorder was newsworthy, but the plaintiff's identity was not of public concern.

In contrast, consider *Haynes v. Alfred A. Knopf, Inc.*, 8 F.3d 1222 (7th Cir. 1993). In 1991, Alfred A. Knopf, Inc. published Nicholas Lemann's best-selling historical book entitled *The Promised Land: The Great Black Migration and How It Changed America*. The book chronicled the migration of 5 million African Americans from the rural areas in the South to urban areas in the North from 1940 to 1970. The book focuses centrally around the story of one individual, Ruby Lee Daniels. The book recounts Ruby's troubled marriage to Luther Haynes. Luther had a well-paying factory job but began to drink too much, waste money, and get into bitter fights with Ruby. The book recounts the couple's financial struggles, Luther's squandering of their money, their spiral into poverty, and their difficulties in providing for their children. When the couple was finally able to buy a home, Luther purchased a new car, and as a result, they couldn't meet their house payments and lost the home. Luther would frequently lose jobs and would often fail to come home. Luther then began to have an affair with their neighbor Dorothy Johnson, which was discovered by the children. Ruby and Luther got a divorce.

Subsequently, Luther married Dorothy. He turned his life around and began acting more responsibly. In their new community, nobody knew of Luther's past behavior toward Ruby. As Luther stated: "I know I haven't been no angel, but since almost 30 years ago I have turned my life completely around. I stopped the drinking and all this bad habits and stuff like that. . . . I look good in the eyes of my church members and my community. Now . . . all this is going to go down the drain. And I worked like a son of a gun to build myself up in a good reputation and he has torn it down."

Luther and Dorothy Haynes sued Lemann and his publisher Knopf under the public disclosure tort. Judge Posner, writing for the Seventh Circuit, rejected their claim: "No detail in the book claimed to invade the Hayneses' privacy is not germane to the story that the author wanted to tell, a story not only of legitimate but of transcendent public interest."

Was Luther Haynes's actual name really necessary for telling the story? The court concluded:

> The details of the Hayneses' lives recounted in the book would identify them unmistakably to anyone who has known the Hayneses well for a long time (members of their families, for example), or who knew them before they got married; and no more is required for liability either in defamation law or in privacy law. Lemann would have had to change some, perhaps many, of the details. But then he would no longer have been writing history. He would have been writing fiction. The nonquantitative study of living persons would be abolished as a category of scholarship, to be replaced by the sociological novel. That is a genre with a distinguished history punctuated by famous names, such

as Dickens, Zola, Stowe, Dreiser, Sinclair, Steinbeck, and Wolfe, but we do not think that the law of privacy makes it (or that the First Amendment would permit the law of privacy to make it) the exclusive format for a social history of living persons that tells their story rather than treating them as data points in a statistical study. Reporting the true facts about real people is necessary to "obviate any impression that the problems raised in the [book] are remote or hypothetical."

In *Howard v. Des Moines Register & Tribune Co.*, 870 F.2d 271 (5th Cir. 1989), the identities of victims of involuntary sterilization were disclosed in a report about abuses by a mental institution. The court rejected the argument that the identities were unnecessarily disclosed because they were needed to "strengthen the accuracy of the public perception of the merits of the controversy." In *Ross v. Midwest Communications, Inc.*, 870 F.2d 271 (5th Cir. 1989), the court held that the disclosure of a rape victim's name in an article about the potential innocence of the man convicted of the rape was of "unique importance to the credibility and persuasive force of the story."

9. *The Value of Pseudonyms.* Daniel Solove argues in favor of the approach taken in *Barber,* the case mentioned above regarding a plaintiff's photograph taken in a hospital to accompany an article about the plaintiff's unusual disease. He contends that the use of initials or pseudonyms is a workable compromise between the interests of reporting the news and of protecting privacy: "Journalists generally do not include the names of rape victims or whistleblowers in their stories. On television, the media sometimes obscures the faces of particular people in video footage. With minimal effort, the media can report stories and also protect privacy."[27] In response to arguments about the importance of identifying people to help make the story more verifiable, Solove argues:

> [S]tories of paramount importance have not identified the critical parties; for example, in exposing Watergate, Bob Woodward and Carl Bernstein relied on the well-known pseudonymous source "Deep Throat." Certainly, it affects verifiability when a story does not identify a party. However, when the journalists protect confidential sources, they engage in a balancing determination, sacrificing the public's ability to verity for the importance of protecting confidentiality. Public verifiability is not sacrosanct, but can be outweighed by privacy interests.[28]

10. *Deference to the Media: Who Decides What Is Newsworthy?* Who ought to determine the proper subject for news? Courts? Journalists? The market? Juries? A number of courts defer to the judgment of the press for newsworthiness: "[W]hat is newsworthy is primarily a function of the publisher, not the courts." *Heath v. Playboy Enterprises, Inc.*, 732 F. Supp. 1145, 1149 (S.D. Fla. 1990). If courts are not to second guess the judgment of the press, how are courts to determine newsworthiness? Is anything not newsworthy?

---

[27] Daniel J. Solove, *The Virtues of Knowing Less: Justifying Privacy Protections Against Disclosure*, 53 Duke L.J. 967, 1018-19 (2003).

[28] *Id.* at 1018.

Daniel Solove contends that the deference to the media approach is a poor one. He argues that although the media might be a capable decision maker for assessing public interest in a story, "[w]hat is of interest to most of society is not the same question as what is of legitimate public concern. . . . [Public] interest can stem from a desire for entertainment or sexual pleasure just as much as it can from wanting to learn about the news and current events." Therefore, Solove concludes, "the media should not have a monopoly on determining what is of public concern."[29] In contrast, consider Eugene Volokh, who contends: "Under the First Amendment, it's generally not the government's job to decide what subjects speakers and listeners should concern themselves with."[30]

In today's Internet age with social media and countless media sites of all flavors and philosophies, Amy Gajda observes that judicial deference to the media is currently eroding:

> The result is that courts and other legal actors are beginning to rethink the balance between privacy rights and public interests in free disclosure. The deference that once shielded journalists from editorial control by the government is eroding as courts are showing a new willingness to limit public disclosure of truthful information. Increasingly, personal privacy seems deeply vulnerable and deserving of new, more potent protections, just as the expansive new practices and identity of media are stretching the credibility of journalism's claim to occupy a distinctive and privileged place in democratic life. The combined effect creates a sort of First Amendment bubble, in which constitutional protection for press and news media continually expands to the breaking point, jeopardizing future protection not only at the margins but also for the core.[31]

11. *Is the Newsworthiness Test Necessary or Desirable?* Lior Strahilevitz argues that the newsworthiness test is not the best way to reconcile the public disclosure tort with free speech. He contends that the First Amendment already provides a sufficient constraint on the tort and a newsworthiness test is not needed:

> The fact that the First Amendment may constrain the state's ability to impose damages on those who publish private facts does not mean that the underlying tort causes of action need to look any different. Rather, it simply means that once tort liability is found, the courts should conduct an independent inquiry as to whether imposing liability on that defendant (or class of defendants) will undermine fundamental expressive or self-governance interests. Indeed, such a textured inquiry better coheres with First Amendment doctrine than does the public disclosure tort's binary newsworthiness/non-newsworthiness distinction.[32]

---

[29] Daniel J. Solove, *The Virtues of Knowing Less: Justifying Privacy Protections Against Disclosure*, 53 Duke L.J. 967, 1001, 1006 (2003).

[30] Eugene Volokh, *Freedom of Speech and Information Privacy: The Troubling Implications of a Right to Stop People from Speaking About You*, 52 Stan. L. Rev. 1049, 1089 (2000).

[31] Amy Gajda, *The First Amendment Bubble: How Privacy and Paparazzi Threaten a Free Press* (2015).

[32] Lior Strahilevitz, *Reunifying Privacy Law*, 98 Cal. L. Rev. 2007, 2033 (2010).

If the newsworthiness test is merely designed to protect First Amendment interests, then why not just have the First Amendment provide the protection? Is there a good reason to keep the newsworthiness test?

SHULMAN V. GROUP W PRODUCTIONS, INC.

955 P.2d 469 (Cal. 1998)

[Recall the facts of this case earlier in this chapter. The plaintiffs, Ruth and Wayne Shulman, mother and son, were injured in a car accident. A medical transport and rescue helicopter crew came to their assistance along with a video camera operator, who filmed the plaintiffs' rescue from the car, the flight nurse and medic's medical aid during the rescue, as well as their medical aid in the helicopter en route to the hospital. The flight nurse wore a small microphone that picked up her conversations with Ruth and other rescue workers. The segment was broadcast on a television show called *On Scene: Emergency Response*. Ruth, a paraplegic from the accident, watched the episode in her hospital room in shock. Neither Ruth nor Wayne Shulman consented to the filming or broadcasting. They sued the producers of the show, and their complaint included causes of action for public disclosure of private facts and intrusion upon seclusion. The trial court granted the defendants' motion for summary judgment on all causes of action.

On the intrusion claim, the California Supreme Court held that the activities of the defendants in recording the events in the helicopter constituted a valid cause of action for intrusion upon seclusion. The court's decision on the public disclosure claim is excerpted below.]

WERDEGAR, J. . . . [U]nder California common law the dissemination of truthful, newsworthy material is not actionable as a publication of private facts. If the contents of a broadcast or publication are of legitimate public concern, the plaintiff cannot establish a necessary element of the tort action, the lack of newsworthiness. . . .

Although we speak of the lack of newsworthiness as an element of the private facts tort, newsworthiness is at the same time a constitutional defense to, or privilege against, liability for publication of truthful information. . . . Tort liability, obviously, can extend no further than the First Amendment allows; conversely, we see no reason or authority for fashioning the newsworthiness element of the private facts tort to *preclude* liability where the Constitution would allow it. . . .

Newsworthiness — constitutional or common law — is also difficult to define because it may be used as either a descriptive or a normative term. "Is the term 'newsworthy' a descriptive predicate, intended to refer to the fact there is widespread public interest? Or is it a value predicate, intended to indicate that the publication is a meritorious contribution and that the public's interest is praise-worthy?" A position at either extreme has unpalatable consequences. If "news-worthiness" is completely descriptive — if all coverage that sells papers or boosts ratings is deemed newsworthy — it would seem to swallow the publication of private facts tort, for "it would be difficult to suppose that publishers were in the habit of reporting occurrences of little interest." At the other extreme, if newsworthiness is viewed as a purely normative concept, the courts could become to an unacceptable degree editors of the news and self-appointed guardians of public taste. . . .

Courts balancing these interests in cases similar to this have recognized that, when a person is involuntarily involved in a newsworthy incident, not all aspects of the person's life, and not everything the person says or does, is thereby rendered newsworthy. . . . This principle is illustrated in the decisions holding that, while a particular event was newsworthy, identification of the plaintiff as the person involved, or use of the plaintiff's identifiable image, added nothing of significance to the story and was therefore an unnecessary invasion of privacy. . . .

Consistent with the above, courts have generally protected the privacy of otherwise private individuals involved in events of public interest "by requiring that a logical nexus exist between the complaining individual and the matter of legitimate public interest." . . .

Intensely personal or intimate revelations might not, in a given case, be considered newsworthy, especially where they bear only slight relevance to a topic of legitimate public concern. . . .

Turning now to the case at bar, we consider whether the possibly private facts complained of here — broadly speaking, Ruth's appearance and words during the rescue and evacuation — were of legitimate public interest. If so, summary judgment was properly entered. . . .

We agree at the outset with defendants that the subject matter of the broadcast as a whole was of legitimate public concern. Automobile accidents are by their nature of interest to that great portion of the public that travels frequently by automobile. The rescue and medical treatment of accident victims is also of legitimate concern to much of the public, involving as it does a critical service that any member of the public may someday need. The story of Ruth's difficult extrication from the crushed car, the medical attention given her at the scene, and her evacuation by helicopter was of particular interest because it highlighted some of the challenges facing emergency workers dealing with serious accidents.

The more difficult question is whether Ruth's appearance and words as she was extricated from the overturned car, placed in the helicopter and transported to the hospital were of legitimate public concern. Pursuant to the analysis outlined earlier, we conclude the disputed material was newsworthy as a matter of law. One of the dramatic and interesting aspects of the story as a whole is its focus on flight nurse Carnahan, who appears to be in charge of communications with other emergency workers, the hospital base and Ruth, and who leads the medical assistance to Ruth at the scene. Her work is portrayed as demanding and important and as involving a measure of personal risk (e.g., in crawling under the car to aid Ruth despite warnings that gasoline may be dripping from the car). The broadcast segment makes apparent that this type of emergency care requires not only medical knowledge, concentration and courage, but an ability to talk and listen to severely traumatized patients. One of the challenges Carnahan faces in assisting Ruth is the confusion, pain and fear that Ruth understandably feels in the aftermath of the accident. For that reason the broadcast video depicting Ruth's injured physical state (which was not luridly shown) and audio showing her disorientation and despair were substantially relevant to the segment's newsworthy subject matter.

Plaintiffs argue that showing Ruth's "intimate private, medical facts and her suffering was not *necessary* to enable the public to understand the significance of the accident or the rescue as a public event." The standard, however, is not necessity. That the broadcast *could* have been edited to exclude some of Ruth's words and images and still excite a minimum degree of viewer interest is not determinative. Nor is the possibility that the members of this or another court, or a jury, might find a differently edited broadcast more to their taste or even more interesting. The courts do not, and constitutionally could not, sit as superior editors of the press. . . .

BROWN, J. concurring and dissenting. . . . I respectfully dissent . . . from the conclusion that summary judgment was proper as to plaintiff Ruth Shulman's cause of action for publication of private facts. . . .

. . . The private facts broadcast had little, if any, social value. The public has no legitimate interest in witnessing Ruth's disorientation and despair. Nor does it have any legitimate interest in knowing Ruth's personal and innermost thoughts immediately after sustaining injuries that rendered her a paraplegic and left her hospitalized for months. . . There was nothing voluntary about Ruth's position of public notoriety. She was involuntarily caught up in events of public interest, all the more so because defendants appear to have surreptitiously and unlawfully recorded her private conversations with nurse Laura Carnahan. . . .

NOTES & QUESTIONS

1. *Grief and Newsworthiness.* Reality television shows and "caught on film" docudramas frequently capture people in moments of profound trauma and grief. Is it newsworthy to display footage of grieving relatives after a disaster or personal tragedy occurs?

2. *Post-Mortem Privacy Rights?* Generally, privacy rights are said to expire when the subject of this interest dies. The traditional exception to this doctrine is the right of publicity. Another exception is that courts recognize actions for privacy torts such as public disclosure and intrusion upon seclusion for family members of a decedent in autopsy or death-scene photos. In *Catsouras v. Department of the California Highway Patrol (CHP)*, 104 Cal. Rptr. 3d 352 (2010), 18-year-old Nicole Catsouras "was decapitated in an automobile accident." Police officers took multiple photographs of her corpse. According to allegations in a lawsuit filed by her family, the photos were e-mailed by these police officers to some members of the public.

    The *Catsouras* court found that the decedent's family had a cognizable claim for an invasion of privacy based on the public disclosure tort. The court reasoned that "family members do have their own privacy rights in death images." The court noted that the images were "allegedly disseminated out of sheer morbidity or gossip, as opposed to any official law enforcement purpose or genuine public interest."

    Would it be significant if the Catsouras family had attempted to sue the media and not the police? Would it matter to the outcome of this litigation if the leaked photographs accompanied an article on driving safety?

Bonome v. Kaysen

17 Mass. L. Rptr. 695 (Mass. Supp. 2004)

MUSE, J. Joseph Bonome filed this action alleging invasion of privacy against Susana Kaysen, the author of a memoir at the center of this case, and Random House, Inc., the publisher. . . .

In the early 1990s, Bonome owned and operated a tree surgery and landscaping business primarily in the Cambridge, Massachusetts area. At the time, he was living in New Hampshire and was married with step-children. Kaysen was an author living in Cambridge. She had gained success and notoriety for her book *Girl, Interrupted* which was made into what has been described to be a critically acclaimed film. In 1994, Bonome met Kaysen and the two began having an affair, including a physical relationship. Kaysen pressured Bonome to leave his wife, and Bonome ultimately succumbed to that pressure. Bonome divorced his wife in 1996 and shortly thereafter moved into Kaysen's home, where they continued the relationship.

Within six months or a year into the relationship, Kaysen began to experience severe vaginal pain. She began to regularly see doctors for her problem, but over the course of several years was unable to receive sufficient curative treatment. During this time period, she began working on a new book, which book is the subject of this case. Despite Bonome's inquiries, Kaysen would not reveal the subject of the book to him.

The fact of their relationship was well-known to Bonome's family, friends, and clientele. However, the details of their physical relationship were private. Bonome's parents and three brothers all spent time, including some holidays, with the couple. However, in July 1998, the relationship "ended" when Kaysen asked Bonome to move out, which he did. Despite the breakup, their physical relationship continued for at least three months longer.

In 2001, Random House published the book [*The Camera My Mother Gave Me*]. The book only refers to Bonome as Kaysen's "boyfriend" and alters details about his life — such as where he was from, and his occupation. The book is an autobiographical memoir chronicling the effects of Kaysen's seemingly undiagnosable vaginal pain in a series of ruminations about the condition's effects on many aspects of her life, including her overall physical and emotional state, friendships, and her relationship with her boyfriend. It details her intense pain and discomfort and her many fruitless attempts to obtain an accurate medical diagnosis and effective treatment.

One of the central themes of the book concerns the impact of her chronic pain on the emotional and physical relationship with Kaysen's boyfriend. To that end, the book details, graphically on a few occasions, several sexual encounters between them. It portrays the boyfriend as becoming increasingly frustrated and impatient with Kaysen's condition and her reluctance and/or refusal to engage in physical intimacy. The boyfriend is described as "always bugging [her] for sex" and "whining and pleading" for sex, as well as being ignorant and insensitive to her emotional and physical state. In this vein, it attributes many aggressive and overtly offensive sexual quotes to him. Ultimately, the development of this theme culminates in a scene where the boyfriend is physically forceful in an attempt to engage her in sex. This scene is followed by ruminations about whether the relationship had exceeded the bounds of consensual sexual relations into the realm of coerced non-consensual sex. . . .

After publication of the book, Bonome learned that many local friends and family had read the book and understood the portrayal of the "boyfriend" to be a depiction of him. In addition, Bonome's business clientele included friends of Kaysen who also understood that Bonome was the "boyfriend." As a result of the publication, Bonome has suffered severe personal humiliation, and his reputation has been severely damaged among a substantial percentage of his clients and acquaintances. . . .

General Laws chapter 214 Section 1B provides that: "[a] person shall have a right against unreasonable, substantial or serious interference with his privacy." Section 1B has been interpreted to include the common-law tort of "public disclosure of private facts" as articulated in the Restatement (Second) of Torts. . . .

[T]his case presents an additional challenge in that it pits Kaysen's right of publicity — her own right to disclose intimate facts about herself — directly in conflict Bonome's right to control the dissemination of private information about himself. . . .

Undoubtedly, the information revealed was of an intensely intimate and personal nature. Indeed, commentators and courts have almost universally recognized one's sexual affairs as falling squarely within the sphere of private life. . . .

[O]therwise private information may properly be published when it is sufficiently related to a broader topic of legitimate public concern. In this case, a critical issue is whether the personal information concerning Bonome is in the book for its relevance to issues of legitimate public concern or is merely "morbid and sensational plying into [Bonome's] private [life] for its own sake."After examining the statements concerning the boyfriend and their relevance to the broader themes of the book, it is clear that the details are included to develop and explore those themes. Specifically, the book explores the way in which Kaysen's undiagnosed physical condition impacted her physical and emotional relationship with "her boyfriend." Moreover, it explores the issue of when undesired physical intimacy crosses the line into non-consensual sexual relations in the context of her condition. These broader topics are all matters of legitimate public concern, and it is within this specific context that the explicit and highly personal details of the relationship are discussed. Thus, the defendants had a legitimate and protected interest to publish these facts.

As noted above, there is an additional interest in this case: Kaysen's right to disclose her own intimate affairs. In this case, it is critical that Kaysen was not a disinterested third party telling Bonome's personal story in order to develop the themes in her book. Rather, she is telling *her own* personal story — which inextricably involves Bonome in an intimate way. In this regard, several courts have held that where an autobiographical account related to a matter of legitimate public interest reveals private information concerning a third party, the disclosure is protected so long as there is a sufficient nexus between those private details and the issue of public concern.

Where one's own personal story involves issues of legitimate public concern, it is often difficult, if not impossible, to separate one's intimate and personal experiences from the people with whom those experiences are shared. Thus, it is within the context of Bonome and Kaysen's lives being inextricably bound together by their intimate relationship that the disclosures in this case must be viewed. Because the First Amendment protects Kaysen's ability to contribute *her own* personal experiences to the public discourse on important and legitimate issues of public concern, disclosing Bonome's involvement in those experiences is a necessary incident thereto.

. . . [T]he privilege to disclose private information is limited by the requirement that the disclosure bear the necessary nexus (both logical and proportional) to the issue of legitimate public concern. In this regard, it is of importance that Kaysen did not use Bonome's name in the book. The defendants did not subject Bonome to unnecessary publicity or attention. The realm of people that could identify Bonome as the boyfriend are those close personal friends, family, and business clients that knew of the relationship. This is not to overlook or discount the impact this disclosure may have had on Bonome, or his substantial claim that Kaysen breached a fundamental trust of their relationship. However arguably odious, the defendants did not exercise the right of disclosure in a manner offensive to the balance of those interests. See Restatement (Second) Torts § 652D, comment a ("Publicity . . . means that the matter is made public, by communicating it to the public at large, or to so many persons that the matter must be regarded as substantially certain to become one of public knowledge"). . . .

This court is not unmindful of the injury claimed by Bonome, who alleges to have suffered personal humiliation within his familial circle, as well as with friends and business clientele as a result of the book's publication. Nonetheless, Kaysen's own personal story — insofar as it relates to matters of legitimate public concern — is hers to contribute to the public discourse. This right is protected by the First Amendment. Inasmuch as the book does not exceed the bounds of that constitutional privilege, Bonome's claim for invasion of privacy under G.L.c. 214, § 1B is *DISMISSED.*

NOTES & QUESTIONS

1. ***The Right to Tell One's Story.*** The newsworthiness test examines whether a disclosure is of "legitimate concern to the public." It does not matter who is making the disclosure for the purposes of the test. However, the court suggests that "there is an additional interest in this case: Kaysen's right to disclose her own intimate affairs." The court states that "it is critical that Kaysen was not a disinterested third party telling Bonome's personal story in order to develop the themes in her book. Rather, she is telling *her own* personal story — which inextricably involves Bonome in an intimate way." Does the autobiographical nature of the disclosure change the newsworthiness analysis? Should it?

   Sonja West contends that when autobiographical speech is involved, courts should not look to whether it is of legitimate public interest: "The power to decide what is of consequence in a person's life story should ultimately lie with that person alone. As long as the content and intention of the speech is truly autobiographical, its perceived importance by others should not affect its constitutional protection."[33] Should a person have increased latitude when revealing private information about others when it also involves her own autobiographical details?

Suppose Kaysen told her story to a journalist, who wrote about it in an article. Should the journalist receive less protection for making the disclosure than Kaysen would receive for revealing the same facts?

2. *Blogs, Social Network Websites, and Gossip.* In *Steinbuch v. Cutler*, 463 F. Supp. 2d 1 (D.D.C. 2006), Jessica Cutler, a staff member for a U.S. senator, wrote a blog about her relationships with several men, including a man she was dating who also worked for the senator. In her blog, The Washingtonienne, she recounted in vivid detail their budding romance. Specifically, Cutler described their sexual practices, personal conversations, and other intimate details. Cutler did not identify Steinbuch directly, but she used his real initials and disclosed other personally identifiable information that made it possible for him to be identified. For a few weeks, only a handful of people knew about Cutler's blog. Then Wonkette, a very popular political gossip blog, linked to her blog and tens of thousands began flocking to the site. The story was written about in many major newspapers. Steinbuch sued Cutler for violating his privacy. The case never proceeded to trial because Cutler declared bankruptcy.

One of Cutler's arguments was that the blog was only read by a handful of her friends until Wonkette linked to it. Cutler contended that she never gave widespread publicity to the information — Wonkette did. When information is disclosed on the Internet, but only a few people read it, is disclosure sufficiently widespread for the publicity element to be satisfied?

Cutler also argued that her account of her relationships was newsworthy. According to her motion to dismiss: "Cutler's Blog makes a shocking and disturbing portrayal of casual and even reckless sexual encounters between young, entry-level Capitol Hill staffers like Cutler and more senior staffers like Steinbuch. . . . The interrelationship between youth, beauty, sex, money, and power in Washington has long been a matter of legitimate and sometimes *pressing* public interest." Is Cutler's blog newsworthy? What are the best arguments on each side of the issue?

Daniel Solove notes that there are significant problems when gossip is posted online:

> We may find it increasingly difficult to have a fresh start, a second chance, or a clean slate. We might find it harder to engage in self-exploration if every false step and foolish act is chronicled forever in a permanent record. This record will affect our ability to define our identities, to obtain jobs, to participate in public life, and more. Ironically, the unconstrained flow of information on the Internet might impede our freedom.[34]

---

[33] Sonja West, *The Story of Me: The Underprotection of Autobiographical Speech*, 84 Wash. U. L. Rev. 905, 966 (2006).

[34] Daniel J. Solove, *The Future of Reputation: Gossip, Rumor, and Privacy on the Internet* (2007). For more background about applying the privacy torts to blogs and social network sites, see Patricia Sánchez Abril, *Recasting Privacy Torts in a Spaceless World*, 21 Harv. J.L. & Tech. 1 (2007).

3. *The Breach of Confidentiality Tort.* The breach of confidentiality tort protects against the nonconsensual disclosures of confidential information. To establish liability under the tort, a plaintiff must prove that the defendant owed the plaintiff a duty of confidentiality and that the defendant breached that duty.[35] Unlike the tort of public disclosure, the breach of confidentiality tort does not have the elements of highly offensive, publicity, or the newsworthiness test. In America, the breach of confidentiality tort has been applied to doctors and other professionals. In contrast, in England, which rejects the Warren and Brandeis privacy torts, including the public disclosure tort, has a robust breach of confidentiality tort. As Neil Richards and Daniel Solove observe:

> The law of confidentiality in England also has attributes that the American privacy torts lack. In America, the prevailing belief is that people assume the risk of betrayal when they share secrets with each other. But in England, spouses, ex-spouses, friends, and nearly anyone else can be liable for divulging confidences. As one English court noted: "The fact is that when people kiss and later one of them tells, that second person is almost certainly breaking a confidential arrangement." Confidentiality thus recognizes that nondisclosure expectations emerge not just from norms of individual dignity, but also from norms of relationships, trust, and reliance on promises. American privacy law has never fully embraced privacy within relationships; it typically views information exposed to others as no longer private. Although a tort remedying breach of confidence would emerge later on in American law, it has developed slowly in comparison to the Warren and Brandeis privacy torts.[36]

Should a person accept the risk of betrayal when sharing confidential information with another?

Suppose the breach of confidentiality tort were applied more broadly to situations where friends, spouses, and others disclosed the secrets of others. Andrew McClurg notes that the First Amendment implications of the breach of confidentiality tort are different from those of the public disclosure tort:

> If one accepts the proposition that a party to an intimate relationship impliedly agrees not the breach the other party's confidence by publishing private, embarrassing information about them via an instrument of mass communication, the speech restriction is one that is self-imposed, rather than state-imposed.[37]

How might a broader application of the breach of confidentiality tort impact bloggers like Jessica Cutler who write about their sexual activities with others? Would the tort impair free speech too much? Note that there is no newsworthiness test under the tort, so information of public concern is not

---

[35] For more background about the tort, see Alan B. Vickery, Note, *Breach of Confidence: An Emerging Tort,* 82 Colum. L. Rev. 1426 (1982); G. Michael Harvey, Comment, *Confidentiality: A Measured Response to the Failure of Privacy,* 140 U. Pa. L. Rev. 2385 (1992); Susan M. Gilles, *Promises Betrayed: Breach of Confidence as a Remedy for Invasion of Privacy,* 43 Buff. L. Rev. 1 (1995).

[36] Neil M. Richards & Daniel J. Solove, *Privacy's Other Path: Recovering the Law of Confidentiality,* 96 Geo. L.J. 123 (2007).

[37] Andrew J. McClurg, *Kiss and Tell: Protecting Intimate Relationship Privacy Through Implied Contracts of Confidentiality,* 74 U. Cin. L. Rev. 887, 938 (2006).

protected. On the other hand, as McClurg notes, the breach of confidentiality tort understands that parties have made an implicit contract of confidentiality. Is it a violation of free speech to enforce a person's explicit or implicit promise not to speak about something?

4. ***Reputation-Tracking Technologies.*** Lior Strahilevitz argues that reputation-tracking technologies can yield beneficial results. He points to programs such as "How's My Driving?" (HMD) programs in which some commercial vehicles have stickers with a number to call to complain about bad driving. Insurance company statistics reveal significant reductions in crash costs and accidents (declines of well over 30 percent) following the implementation of HMD programs. Strahilevitz argues that the reason for the effectiveness of HMD programs is that they reduce driver anonymity:

> The problems associated with urban and suburban driving are, by and large, creatures of motorist anonymity. . . . If society were able to monitor its roadways around the clock and to analyze this data immediately to identify and punish problematic motorists, many of the traffic accident deaths that occur every year would be averted.[38]

Strahilevitz points out that various websites such as Amazon.com, Tripadvisor.com, and eBay.com harness user feedback, where people can leave comments about a particular merchant or individual: "Though eBay's reputation system is admittedly imperfect, it has been extraordinarily successful at preventing fraud among auction participants." He proposes that more measures like HMD programs in other contexts might be beneficial. In what other situations would reputation-tracking technologies be useful? What are the potential problems with such technologies? Is there a way to implement these technologies that minimize these problems?

2. FIRST AMENDMENT LIMITATIONS

The language of the First Amendment to the U.S. Constitution provides:

> Congress shall make no law respecting an establishment of religion, or prohibiting the free exercise thereof; or abridging the freedom of speech, or of the press; or the right of the people peaceably to assemble, and to petition the Government for a redress of grievances.

In addition to protecting against criminal laws that punish or ban speech, the First Amendment has been interpreted to also apply to civil actions. Although civil actions are initiated by private parties rather than the government, there is state action in the use of the power of the judicial system to enforce civil penalties for speech.

The First Amendment also has a complex relationship to privacy. In many instances, the First Amendment and privacy are mutually reinforcing. Privacy is often essential to freedom of assembly. The Supreme Court has noted that there is

---

[38] Lior Strahilevitz, *"How's My Driving?" For Everyone (and Everything?)*, 81 N.Y.U. L. Rev. 1699, 1706 (2006).

a "vital relationship between freedom to associate and privacy in one's associations." *NAACP v. Alabama*, 357 U.S. 449 (1958). Privacy is also essential for freedom of speech, as the Supreme Court has recognized the importance of protecting the anonymity of speakers. *See McIntyre v. Ohio Elections Commission*, 514 U.S. 334 (1995).

However, privacy can come into conflict with the First Amendment. The privacy torts exist in an uneasy tension with the First Amendment. Indeed, Warren and Brandeis's article was aimed at the excesses of the press. Recall the authors' strong criticism of the press: "The press is overstepping in every direction the obvious bounds of propriety and of decency. Gossip is no longer the resource of the idle and of the vicious, but has become a trade, which is pursued with industry as well as effrontery."[39]

Although Brandeis was interested in privacy and skeptical of the press's trade in gossip, as a Supreme Court Justice, Brandeis was one of the champions of free speech.[40] Consider Brandeis's concurrence in *Whitney v. California*, 274 U.S. 357, 375 (1927):

> Those who won our independence believed that the final end of the state was to make men free to develop their faculties, and that in its government the deliberative forces should prevail over the arbitrary. They valued liberty both as an end and as a means. They believed liberty to be the secret of happiness and courage to be the secret of liberty. They believed that freedom to think as you will and to speak as you think are means indispensable to the discovery and spread of political truth; that without free speech and assembly discussion would be futile; that with them, discussion affords ordinarily adequate protection against the dissemination of noxious doctrine; that the greatest menace to freedom is an inert people; that public discussion is a political duty; and that this should be a fundamental principle of the American government. They recognized the risks to which all human institutions are subject. But they knew that order cannot be secured merely through fear of punishment for its infraction; that it is hazardous to discourage thought, hope and imagination; that fear breeds repression; that repression breeds hate; that hate menaces stable government; that the path of safety lies in the opportunity to discuss freely supposed grievances and proposed remedies; and that the fitting remedy for evil counsels is good ones. Believing in the power of reason as applied through public discussion, they eschewed silence coerced by law — the argument of force in its worst form. Recognizing the occasional tyrannies of governing majorities, they amended the Constitution so that free speech and assembly should be guaranteed.

Although the privacy torts are litigated by private parties, they employ the machinery of the state (its tort law and legal system) to impose costs on the press for gathering, producing, and disseminating news. The danger is that the threat of lawsuits will chill the press from running certain stories. Further, the threat of

---

[39] Samuel D. Warren & Louis D. Brandeis, *The Right to Privacy*, 4 Harv. L. Rev. 193 (1890).

[40] Neil Richards contends that Brandeis actually changed his views on privacy and free speech: "Although he never repudiated tort privacy, by the end of his life, Brandeis had moved to a position on publicity and free speech that was inconsistent with a broad reading of the tort theory of *The Right to Privacy*." Neil M. Richards, *The Puzzle of Brandeis, Privacy, and Speech*, 63 Vand. L. Rev. 1295, 1298 (2010).

lawsuits alone might chill the press, because even if the press ultimately prevails in such suits, the lawsuits cost money to defend.

The public disclosure tort raises complicated tensions with the First Amendment, for it permits liability for the publication of truthful information. Built into the tort, however, is the newsworthiness test, which a number of courts have stated is required to square the tort with the First Amendment. The newsworthiness test, however, is a limitation *within* the tort. Does the First Amendment provide any additional limitations upon the tort?[41] The cases in this section address this question. In order to understand the cases, some basic background about First Amendment analysis is necessary.

Unprotected Forms of Expression. The Court has held that certain forms of expression receive no First Amendment protection. Such categories include obscenity, *Miller v. California,* 413 U.S. 15 (1973); fighting words, *Chaplinsky v. New Hampshire,* 315 U.S. 568 (1942); and child pornography, *New York v. Ferber,* 458 U.S. 747 (1982).

Strict and Intermediate Scrutiny. Most restrictions on speech are reviewed under either strict or intermediate scrutiny. Under strict scrutiny, a law must be the "least restrictive means" to achieve a "compelling" government interest. *Sable Communications, Inc. v. FCC,* 492 U.S. 115, 116 (1989). Strict scrutiny is very difficult to withstand, and most laws subject to it are struck down. In contrast, under intermediate scrutiny, a law must be narrowly tailored to a "substantial government interest." *United States v. O'Brien,* 391 U.S. 467, 377 (1968).

Content-Based vs. Content-Neutral Regulation. Under First Amendment analysis, the Court first analyzes whether a speech restriction is content-based or content-neutral. A content-based regulation targets particular messages. Content-neutral regulation restricts speech regardless of its message, such as regulating the time, place, or manner of the speech. If a speech restriction is content-based, then strict scrutiny is generally applied. There are some exceptions. For example, the Court has held that the government may single out content if the purpose is to prevent certain secondary effects caused by such speech. In *City of Renton v. Playtime Theatres,* 475 U.S. 41 (1986), the Court did not apply strict scrutiny to an ordinance restricting the location of adult movie theaters because the purpose was to prevent crime — a secondary effect. Content-neutral speech regulation is generally subject to intermediate scrutiny.

In *R.A.V. v. City of St. Paul,* 505 U.S. 377 (1992), the Court held that a content-based regulation of expression that falls in an unprotected category will be subject

---

[41] For more background on the First Amendment and the privacy torts, see Peter B. Edelman, *Free Press v. Privacy: Haunted by the Ghost of Justice Black,* 68 Tex. L. Rev. 1195 (1990); Thomas I. Emerson, *The Right of Privacy and Freedom of Press,* 14 Harv. CR-CL L. Rev. 329 (1979); Edward Bloustein, *The First Amendment and Privacy: The Supreme Court Justice and the Philosopher,* 28 Rutgers L. Rev. 41 (1974); Melville B. Nimmer, *The Right to Speak from Times to Time: First Amendment Theory Applied to Libel and Misapplied to Privacy,* 56 Cal. L. Rev. 935 (1968); Harry Kalven, Jr., *Privacy in Tort Law — Were Warren and Brandeis Wrong?,* 31 Law & Contemp. Probs. 326 (1966); Marc A. Franklin, *A Constitutional Problem in Privacy Protection: Legal Inhibitions on Reporting of Fact,* 16 Stan. L. Rev. 107 (1963; Rodney A. Smolla, *Accounting for the Slow Growth of American Privacy Law,* 27 Nova L. Rev. 289 (2002).

to strict scrutiny. The Court struck down a hate speech law because it regulated the content of "fighting words" — it applied to fighting words based on "race, color, creed, religion, or gender." Unprotected categories of expression, such as fighting words, may be regulated so long as they are not "made the vehicle for content discrimination unrelated to their distinctively proscribable content. Thus, the government may proscribe libel; but it may not make the further content discrimination of proscribing only libel critical of the government." Content-based regulation on an unprotected category of expression is permissible if "based on the very reasons why the particular class of speech . . . is proscribable."

(a) Speech Based on Lawfully Obtained Information

COX BROADCASTING CORP. V. COHN

420 U.S. 469 (1975)

WHITE, J. . . . In August 1971, appellee's 17-year-old daughter was the victim of a rape and did not survive the incident. Six youths were soon indicted for murder and rape. Although there was substantial press coverage of the crime and of subsequent developments, the identity of the victim was not disclosed pending trial, perhaps because of Ga. Code Ann. § 26-9901 (1972),[42] which makes it a misdemeanor to publish or broadcast the name or identity of a rape victim. In April 1972, some eight months later, the six defendants appeared in court. Five pleaded guilty to rape or attempted rape, the charge of murder having been dropped. The guilty pleas were accepted by the court, and the trial of the defendant pleading not guilty was set for a later date.

In the course of the proceedings that day, appellant Wasell, a reporter covering the incident for his employer, learned the name of the victim from an examination of the indictments which were made available for his inspection in the courtroom. That the name of the victim appears in the indictments and that the indictments were public records available for inspection are not disputed. Later that day, Wassell broadcast over the facilities of station WSB-TV, a television station owned by appellant Cox Broadcasting Corp., a news report concerning the court proceedings. The report named the victim of the crime and was repeated the following day.

In May 1972, appellee brought an action for money damages against appellants, relying on § 26-9901 and claiming that his right to privacy had been invaded by the television broadcasts giving the name of his deceased daughter. . . .

Georgia stoutly defends both § 26-9901 and the State's common-law privacy action challenged here. Its claims are not without force, for powerful arguments can be made, and have been made, that however it may be ultimately defined, there

---

[42] "It shall be unlawful for any news media or any other person to print and publish, broadcast, televise, or disseminate through any other medium of public dissemination or cause to be printed and published, broadcast, televised, or disseminated in any newspaper, magazine, periodical or other publication published in this State or through any radio or television broadcast originating in the State the name or identity of any female who may have been raped or upon whom an assault with intent to commit rape may have been made. Any person or corporation violating the provisions of this section shall, upon conviction, be punished as for a misdemeanor." Three other States have similar statutes. . . .

is a zone of privacy surrounding every individual, a zone within which the State may protect him from intrusion by the press, with all its attendant publicity. Indeed, the central thesis of the root article by Warren and Brandeis, *The Right to Privacy*, 4 Harv. L. Rev. 193 (1890), was that the press was overstepping its prerogatives by publishing essentially private information and that there should be a remedy for the alleged abuses.

More compellingly, the century has experienced a strong tide running in favor of the so-called right of privacy. In 1967, we noted that "[it] has been said that a 'right of privacy' has been recognized at common law in 30 States plus the District of Columbia and by statute in four States." *Time, Inc. v. Hill*, 385 U.S. 374, 383 n.7. We there cited the 1964 edition of Prosser's *Law of Torts*. The 1971 edition of that same source states that "[in] one form or another, the right of privacy is by this time recognized and accepted in all but a very few jurisdictions." . . .

These are impressive credentials for a right of privacy, but we should recognize that we do not have at issue here an action for the invasion of privacy involving the appropriation of one's name or photograph, a physical or other tangible intrusion into a private area, or a publication of otherwise private information that is also false although perhaps not defamatory. The version of the privacy tort now before us — termed in Georgia "the tort of public disclosure," — is that in which the plaintiff claims the right to be free from unwanted publicity about his private affairs, which, although wholly true, would be offensive to a person of ordinary sensibilities. Because the gravamen of the claimed injury is the publication of information, whether true or not, the dissemination of which is embarrassing or otherwise painful to an individual, it is here that claims of privacy most directly confront the constitutional freedoms of speech and press. The face-off is apparent, and the appellants urge upon us the broad holding that the press may not be made criminally or civilly liable for publishing information that is neither false nor misleading but absolutely accurate, however damaging it may be to reputation or individual sensibilities. . . .

It is true that in defamation actions, where the protected interest is personal reputation, the prevailing view is that truth is a defense. . . .

The Court has nevertheless carefully left open the question whether the First and Fourteenth Amendments require that truth be recognized as a defense in a defamation action brought by a private person as distinguished from a public official or public figure. . . . In similar fashion, *Time, Inc. v. Hill*, expressly saved the question whether truthful publication of very private matters unrelated to public affairs could be constitutionally proscribed. . . .

Those precedents, as well as other considerations, counsel similar caution here. In this sphere of collision between claims of privacy and those of the free press, the interests on both sides are plainly rooted in the traditions and significant concerns of our society. Rather than address the broader question whether truthful publications may ever be subjected to civil or criminal liability consistently with the First and Fourteenth Amendments, or to put it another way, whether the State may ever define and protect an area of privacy free from unwanted publicity in the press, it is appropriate to focus on the narrower interface between press and privacy that this case presents, namely, whether the State may impose sanctions on the accurate publication of the name of a rape victim obtained from public records — more specifically, from judicial records which are maintained in connection with a public prosecution and which themselves are open to public inspection. We are convinced that the State may not do so.

In the first place, in a society in which each individual has but limited time and resources with which to observe at first hand the operations of his government, he relies necessarily upon the press to bring to him in convenient form the facts of those operations. Great responsibility is accordingly placed upon the news media to report fully and accurately the proceedings of government, and official records and documents open to the public are the basic data of governmental operations. Without the information provided by the press most of us and many of our representatives would be unable to vote intelligently or to register opinions on the administration of government generally. With respect to judicial proceedings in particular, the function of the press serves to guarantee the fairness of trials and to bring to bear the beneficial effects of public scrutiny upon the administration of justice. . . .

. . . By placing the information in the public domain on official court records, the State must be presumed to have concluded that the public interest was thereby being served. Public records by their very nature are of interest to those concerned with the administration of government, and a public benefit is performed by the reporting of the true contents of the records by the media. The freedom of the press to publish that information appears to us to be of critical importance to our type of government in which the citizenry is the final judge of the proper conduct of public business. In preserving that form of government the First and Fourteenth Amendments command nothing less than that the States may not impose sanctions on the publication of truthful information contained in official court records open to public inspection.

We are reluctant to embark on a course that would make public records generally available to the media but forbid their publication if offensive to the sensibilities of the supposed reasonable man. Such a rule would make it very difficult for the media to inform citizens about the public business and yet stay within the law. The rule would invite timidity and self-censorship and very likely lead to the suppression of many items that would otherwise be published and that should be made available to the public. At the very least, the First and Fourteenth Amendments will not allow exposing the press to liability for truthfully publishing information released to the public in official court records. If there are privacy interests to be protected in judicial proceedings, the States must respond by means which avoid public documentation or other exposure of private information. Their political institutions must weigh the interests in privacy with the interests of the public to know and of the press to publish. Once true information is disclosed in public court documents open to public inspection, the press cannot be sanctioned for publishing it. In this instance as in others reliance must rest upon the judgment of those who decide what to publish or broadcast.

NOTES & QUESTIONS

1. *The* **Oklahoma Publishing** *and* **Daily Mail** *Cases.* After *Cox*, the Supreme Court held in *Oklahoma Publishing Co. v. Oklahoma County District Court*, 430 U.S. 308 (1977), that a state court violated the First Amendment by

prohibiting the media from publishing the name or photograph of an 11-year-old boy in a juvenile proceeding which members of the media attended. A few years later, the Court confronted the issue of whether a state could prohibit the press from publishing the name of a juvenile offender. In *Smith v. Daily Mail Publishing Co.*, 443 U.S. 97 (1979), two newspapers published the name and photograph of a 15-year-old who had shot and killed his 14-year-old classmate. The newspapers were indicted for the misdemeanor offense of publishing the name of a juvenile offender without a court order. The Court stated: "At issue is simply the power of a state to punish the truthful publication of an alleged juvenile delinquent's name lawfully obtained by a newspaper. The asserted state interest [to protect the anonymity of juvenile offenders] cannot justify the statute's imposition of criminal sanctions on this type of publication."

2. **Melvin v. Reid.** One of the earliest cases to recognize the tort of public disclosure is *Melvin v. Reid,* 297 P. 91 (Cal. 1931). Gabrielle Darley was a prostitute who was tried for murder but was acquitted. She abandoned her life as a prostitute, married Bernard Melvin, and became a housewife. In 1925, *The Red Kimono,* a motion picture based on her past life, was released. The film used her maiden name of Darley. As a result, some of her friends learned "for the first time of the unsavory incidents of her early life." Gabrielle sued. The California Supreme Court concluded that she had a cause of action, noting the importance of promoting rehabilitation: "Where a person has by his own efforts rehabilitated himself, we, as right-thinking members of society, should permit him to continue in the path of rectitude rather than throw him back into a life of shame or crime. Even the thief on the cross was permitted to repent during the hours of his final agony."

According to Lawrence Friedman, who has examined the history of the case, the facts surrounding Gabrielle's murder trial were sensational. Gabrielle was on trial for murdering her lover, who was also her pimp. Gabrielle had given him money to buy her a wedding ring, but instead he used the money to buy a ring to wed another woman. Gabrielle confronted him in the street with a gun and shot him dead. Gabrielle was charged with murder. Gabrielle was acquitted. But the lurid details surrounding the incident attracted attention:

> Rogers's daughter, Adela Rogers St. John, a writer, covered the trial. Later, she wrote a short story based on the case and called it "The Red Kimono." It used incidents from Gabrielle's life, and it used her actual name. Dorothy Reid bought the story and produced a movie based on it. The film also was called *The Red Kimono.* It was shown in theaters in 1927. The movie identified the heroine as Gabrielle Darley. The next year, Gabrielle, now calling herself Gabrielle Darley Melvin, brought suit against Reid and Reid's motion picture company.

Friedman contends that Gabrielle's claim that she reformed herself was fake:

> There is good evidence that she was, in fact, as phony as a three dollar bill. A journalist in Arizona argues that she was still working as a prostitute and madam

at the time of the trial in a town in Arizona. During her lifetime she had several husbands, but they had the distressing habit of turning up dead.[43]

After Gabrielle won in the California Supreme Court, she moved to dismiss the case in 1933 prior to trial. Evidence suggests that she settled the case, which caused Reid to lose her home in West Hollywood. Today, Reid is considered as an important pioneering woman producer and director. The film, *The Red Kimono*, is available on DVD in a series devoted to "Early Women Filmmakers." Paul Schwartz has noted that the film itself "is a protofeminist account, a morality play, regarding the difficulty faced by a former prostitute in finding a life free of shame notoriety."[44] In this regard, as Friedman also notes, the film makes a point similar to the *Melvin* court.

Are the facts about Gabrielle in *The Red Kimono* newsworthy? Should the interest in allowing people like Gabrielle to start a new life trump people like Reid's right to make her movie or the public's right to know about a person's past? After *Cox Broadcasting,* is *Melvin v. Reid* still good law?

3. ***Information About Past Crimes.*** In *Briscoe v. Reader's Digest*, 483 P.2d 34 (Cal. 1971), a magazine article about hijacking discussed the plaintiff's hijacking of a truck 11 years earlier. Since then, the plaintiff had rehabilitated himself, and many people did not know of his previous crime. Similar to *Melvin v. Reid*, the court held that the article was newsworthy, but that the use of the plaintiff's real name had no relevance to the article.

> We have no doubt that reports of the facts of past crimes are newsworthy. . . . However, identification of the Actor in reports of long past crimes usually serves little independent public purpose. Once legal proceedings have terminated, and a suspect or offender has been released, identification of the individual will not usually aid the administration of justice. Identification will no longer serve to bring forth witnesses or obtain succor for victims. Unless the individual has reattracted the public eye to himself in some independent fashion, the only public "interest" that would usually be served is that of curiosity. . . .
>
> Another factor militating in favor of protecting the individual's privacy here is the state's interest in the integrity of the rehabilitative process. . . .
>
> One of the premises of the rehabilitative process is that the rehabilitated offender can rejoin that great bulk of the community from which he has been ostracized for his anti-social acts. In return for becoming a "new man," he is allowed to melt into the shadows of obscurity. . . .

Eugene Volokh criticizes the *Briscoe* case for not respecting the fact that people are "entitled to adopt a different attitude" about rehabilitation and might want to know about people's criminal pasts so they can 'use extra caution" in dealing with them.[45]

---

[43] Lawrence M. Friedman, *Guarding Life's Dark Secrets: Legal and Social Controls over Reputation, Propriety, and Privacy* 216-18 (2007).

[44] Paul M. Schwartz, *From Victorian Secrets to Cyberspace Shaming*, 76 U. Chi. L. Rev. 1407, 1416 (2009).

[45] Eugene Volokh, *Freedom of Speech and Information Privacy: The Troubling Implications of a Right to Stop People from Speaking About You*, 52 Stan. L. Rev. 1049, 1091-92 (2000). For another critique, see T. Markus Funk, *The Dangers of Hiding Criminal Pasts*, 66 Tenn. L. Rev. 287 (1998).

In *Gates v. Discovery Communications, Inc.*, 101 P.3d 552 (Cal. 2004), the California Supreme Court held that the U.S. Supreme Court's "decision in *Cox* and its subsequent pronouncements . . . have fatally undermined *Briscoe*'s holding that a media defendant may be held liable in tort for recklessly publishing true but not newsworthy facts concerning a rehabilitated former criminal, insofar as that holding applies to facts obtained from public official court records."

To what extent does *Gates* overturn *Melvin* or *Briscoe*? In both cases, the information about them was available in public records. But do *Cox* and its progeny turn on the *availability* of the information in public records or whether the media actually *obtained* the information from public records? In other words, if the information was obtained elsewhere, would plaintiffs in *Melvin* and *Briscoe* still have a cause of action?

4. *The Right to Be Forgotten in the EU and Council of Europe.* In 2014, a Spanish man requested that Google search results stop including links to a 1998 article in a newspaper about an auction for his foreclosed house. The European Union's Court of Justice (CJEU) ruled in favor of the plaintiff. Under what has become known as the "right to be forgotten," search engines are " obliged to remove from the list of results displayed following a search made on the basis of a person's name links to web pages, published by third parties and containing information relating to that person, also in a case where that name or information is not erased beforehand or simultaneously from those web pages, and even, as the case may be, when its publication in itself on those pages is lawful." *Google Spain, S.L., Google Inc. y Agencia Española de Protección de Datos (AEPD)*, European Court of Justice, EU:C:2014:317. This case is excerpted and covered in more detail in Chapter 13.

The CJEU noted that "the removal of links from the list of results could, depending on the information at issue, have effects upon the legitimate interest of internet users potentially interested in having access to that information." Thus, the court stated, "a fair balance should be sought in particular between that interest and the data subject's fundamental [privacy] rights."

The right to be forgotten does not technically require forgetting; the newspapers were not required to delete their articles. Instead, the right merely requires that search engines not show the articles in search results. As Evan Selinger and Woodrow Hartzog note, the use of the word "forgetting" is misleading and that the case really involves obscurity.[46] Another way to think of the CJEU opinion is as involving a right to have certain search results suppressed or delisted.

In 2023, another important European court, the European Court of Human Rights (ECtHR) decided a major "right to be forgotten" case of its own, *Case of Hurbain v. Belgium*, Application no. 57292/16.[47] In *Hurbain*, the ECtHR

---

[46] Evan Selinger & Woodrow Hartzog, *Google Can't Forget You, But It Should Make You Hard to Find,* Wired, May 20, 2014,http://www.wired.com/2014/05/google-cant-forget-you-but-it-should-make-you-hard-to-find/.

[47] The CJEU is the highest court for the 27-member European Union. The European Court of Human Rights is an international court for the Council of Europe, which has 46 member states belonging to it. The role of ECtHR is to interpret the European Convention on Human Rights.

upheld a decision of Belgian court ordering a newspaper to anonymize the electronic version of an article posted on its website. The article concerned an account of a road traffic accident occurring in 1994, involving G., who was under the influence of alcohol behind the wheel. The accident led to the death of two people and injuries to three others. The original article mentioned G.'s full name.

According to the ECtHR, the driver would suffer from a serious harm if the article would have stayed online and continued to identify him. The order of anonymization of this record did not violate the freedom of expression, which is protected by Article 10 of the European Convention. In contrast to the United States, where the Constitution protects the right to free speech but there is no explicit right to privacy, the European Convention protects privacy (Article 8) and speech (Article 10) as co-equal rights. When there is a conflict between privacy and speech, the courts apply a balancing test. Among relevant factors considered by the *Hurbain* Court was the risk of this article creating a "virtual criminal record" for G. It also pointed to the length of time which had elapsed since the accident in 1994, the lack of historical significance for the article, the lack of a role in public life of the person claiming the entitlement to be forgotten, and the relatively low impact on freedom of the press by having an article anonymized but not removed from a digital archive.

In the United States, would the requirement that Google not display information in search results violate the First Amendment? What about an order to a newspaper to anonymize an old news article?

5. *Anti-SLAPP.* When lawsuits implicate a defendant's speech, 30 states and the District of Columbia provide special anti-SLAPP protections. A SLAPP lawsuit — or a "strategic lawsuit against public participation" — is a lawsuit designed to censor or retaliate against a person for their speech. Fearing significant legal defense costs, defendants might retract their speech or stop engaging in new speech about a matter. SLAPP suits can successfully silence people engaging in protected speech even when the suit is without merit because the costs of getting the suit dismissed can still be significant.

Nearly all anti-SLAPP legislation shares important common elements, which include: (1) requirements that the plaintiff demonstrate early that the case has merit; (2) provisions that allow the defendant to seek an expedited hearing; (3) limits on long costly discovery; (4) the right of a prevailing defendant to recover attorney fees and costs.

THE FLORIDA STAR V. B.J.F.

491 U.S. 524 (1989)

MARSHALL, J. Florida Stat. § 794.03 (1987) makes it unlawful to "print, publish, or broadcast . . . in any instrument of mass communication" the name of the victim of a sexual offense. Pursuant to this statute, appellant The Florida Star was found civilly liable for publishing the name of a rape victim which it had obtained from a publicly released police report. The issue presented here is whether this result comports with the First Amendment. We hold that it does not. . . .

The Florida Star is a weekly newspaper which serves the community of Jacksonville, Florida, and which has an average circulation of approximately 18,000 copies. A regular feature of the newspaper is its "Police Reports" section. That section, typically two to three pages in length, contains brief articles describing local criminal incidents under police investigation.

On October 20, 1983, appellee B.J.F.[48] reported to the Duval County, Florida, Sheriff's Department (Department) that she had been robbed and sexually assaulted by an unknown assailant. The Department prepared a report on the incident which identified B.J.F. by her full name. The Department then placed the report in its pressroom. The Department does not restrict access either to the pressroom or to the reports made available therein.

A Florida Star reporter-trainee sent to the pressroom copied the police report verbatim, including B.J.F.'s full name, on a blank duplicate of the Department's forms. A Florida Star reporter then prepared a one-paragraph article about the crime, derived entirely from the trainee's copy of the police report. The article included B.J.F.'s full name. It appeared in the "Robberies" subsection of the "Police Reports" section on October 29, 1983, one of 54 police blotter stories in that day's edition. . . .

In printing B.J.F.'s full name, The Florida Star violated its internal policy of not publishing the names of sexual offense victims.

On September 26, 1984, B.J.F. filed suit in the Circuit Court of Duval County against the Department and The Florida Star, alleging that these parties negligently violated § 794.03. Before trial, the Department settled with B.J.F. for $2,500. The Florida Star moved to dismiss, claiming, inter alia, that imposing civil sanctions on the newspaper pursuant to § 794.03 violated the First Amendment. The trial judge rejected the motion.

At the ensuing daylong trial, B.J.F. testified that she had suffered emotional distress from the publication of her name. She stated that she had heard about the article from fellow workers and acquaintances; that her mother had received several threatening phone calls from a man who stated that he would rape B.J.F. again; and that these events had forced B.J.F. to change her phone number and residence, to seek police protection, and to obtain mental health counseling. In defense, The Florida Star put forth evidence indicating that the newspaper had learned B.J.F.'s name from the incident report released by the Department, and that the newspaper's violation of its internal rule against publishing the names of sexual offense victims was inadvertent.

At the close of B.J.F.'s case, and again at the close of its defense, The Florida Star moved for a directed verdict. On both occasions, the trial judge denied these motions. He ruled from the bench that § 794.03 was constitutional because it reflected a proper balance between the First Amendment and privacy rights, as it applied only to a narrow set of "rather sensitive . . . criminal offenses." . . . The jury awarded B.J.F. $75,000 in compensatory damages and $25,000 in punitive damages. . . .

---

[48] In filing this lawsuit, appellee used her full name in the caption of the case. On appeal, the Florida District Court of Appeal sua sponte revised the caption, stating that it would refer to the appellee by her initials, "in order to preserve [her] privacy interests." Respecting those interests, we, too, refer to appellee by her initials, both in the caption and in our discussion.

Appellant takes the position that this case is indistinguishable from *Cox Broadcasting*. Alternatively, it urges that our decisions . . . can be distilled to yield a broader First Amendment principle that the press may never be punished, civilly or criminally, for publishing the truth. . . .

We conclude that imposing damages on appellant for publishing B.J.F.'s name violates the First Amendment, although not for either of the reasons appellant urges. Despite the strong resemblance this case bears to *Cox Broadcasting*, that case cannot fairly be read as controlling here. The name of the rape victim in that case was obtained from courthouse records that were open to public inspection. . . . Significantly, one of the reasons we gave in *Cox Broadcasting* for invalidating the challenged damages award was the important role the press plays in subjecting trials to public scrutiny and thereby helping guarantee their fairness. That role is not directly compromised where, as here, the information in question comes from a police report prepared and disseminated at a time at which not only had no adversarial criminal proceedings begun, but no suspect had been identified.

Nor need we accept appellant's invitation to hold broadly that truthful publication may never be punished consistent with the First Amendment. Our cases have carefully eschewed reaching this ultimate question, mindful that the future may bring scenarios which prudence counsels our not resolving anticipatorily. . . . We continue to believe that the sensitivity and significance of the interests presented in clashes between First Amendment and privacy rights counsel relying on limited principles that sweep no more broadly than the appropriate context of the instant case.

In our view, this case is appropriately analyzed with reference to such a limited First Amendment principle. It is the one, in fact, which we articulated in *Daily Mail* in our synthesis of prior cases involving attempts to punish truthful publication: "[I]f a newspaper lawfully obtains truthful information about a matter of public significance then state officials may not constitutionally punish publication of the information, absent a need to further a state interest of the highest order." According the press the ample protection provided by that principle is supported by at least three separate considerations, in addition to, of course, the overarching "'public interest, secured by the Constitution, in the dissemination of truth.'" . . .

First, because the *Daily Mail* formulation only protects the publication of information which a newspaper has "lawfully obtain[ed]," the government retains ample means of safeguarding significant interests upon which publication may impinge, including protecting a rape victim's anonymity. . . . Where information is entrusted to the government, a less drastic means than punishing truthful publication almost always exists for guarding against the dissemination of private facts.[49]

A second consideration undergirding the *Daily Mail* principle is the fact that punishing the press for its dissemination of information which is already publicly available is relatively unlikely to advance the interests in the service of which the

---

[49] The *Daily Mail* principle does not settle the issue whether, in cases where information has been acquired unlawfully by a newspaper or by a source, government may ever punish not only the unlawful acquisition, but the ensuing publication as well. This issue was raised but not definitively resolved in *New York Times Co. v. United States*, 403 U.S. 713 (1971), and reserved in *Landmark Communications*, 435 U.S., at 837. We have no occasion to address it here.

State seeks to act. . . . [W]here the government has made certain information publicly available, it is highly anomalous to sanction persons other than the source of its release. . . . As *Daily Mail* observed in its summary of Oklahoma Publishing, "once the truthful information was 'publicly revealed' or 'in the public domain' the court could not constitutionally restrain its dissemination."

A third and final consideration is the "timidity and self-censorship" which may result from allowing the media to be punished for publishing certain truthful information. . . . A contrary rule, depriving protection to those who rely on the government's implied representations of the lawfulness of dissemination, would force upon the media the onerous obligation of sifting through government press releases, reports, and pronouncements to prune out material arguably unlawful for publication. . . .

Applied to the instant case, the *Daily Mail* principle clearly commands reversal. The first inquiry is whether the newspaper "lawfully obtain[ed] truthful information about a matter of public significance." It is undisputed that the news article describing the assault on B.J.F. was accurate. In addition, appellant lawfully obtained B.J.F.'s name. Appellee's argument to the contrary is based on the fact that under Florida law, police reports which reveal the identity of the victim of a sexual offense are not among the matters of "public record" which the public, by law, is entitled to inspect. But the fact that state officials are not required to disclose such reports does not make it unlawful for a newspaper to receive them when furnished by the government. . . . It is, clear, furthermore, that the news article concerned "a matter of public significance," in the sense in which the *Daily Mail* synthesis of prior cases used that term. That is, the article generally, as opposed to the specific identity contained within it, involved a matter of paramount public import: the commission, and investigation, of a violent crime which had been reported to authorities.

The second inquiry is whether imposing liability on appellant pursuant to § 794.03 serves "a need to further a state interest of the highest order." Appellee argues that a rule punishing publication furthers three closely related interests: the privacy of victims of sexual offenses; the physical safety of such victims, who may be targeted for retaliation if their names become known to their assailants; and the goal of encouraging victims of such crimes to report these offenses without fear of exposure.

At a time in which we are daily reminded of the tragic reality of rape, it is undeniable that these are highly significant interests. . . . For three independent reasons, however, imposing liability for publication under the circumstances of this case is too precipitous a means of advancing these interests to convince us that there is a "need" within the meaning of the *Daily Mail* formulation for Florida to take this extreme step.

First is the manner in which appellant obtained the identifying information in question. As we have noted, where the government itself provides information to the media, it is most appropriate to assume that the government had, but failed to utilize, far more limited means of guarding against dissemination than the extreme step of punishing truthful speech. That assumption is richly borne out in this case. B.J.F.'s identity would never have come to light were it not for the erroneous, if inadvertent, inclusion by the Department of her full name in an incident report made available in a pressroom open to the public. Florida's policy against disclosure of rape victims' identities, reflected in § 794.03, was undercut by the Department's failure to abide by this policy. Where, as here, the government has failed to police itself in disseminating information, it is clear under *Cox Broadcasting, Oklahoma Publishing*, and *Landmark Communications* that the imposition of damages against the press for its subsequent publication can hardly be said to be a narrowly tailored means of safeguarding anonymity. . . .

A second problem with Florida's imposition of liability for publication is the broad sweep of the negligence per se standard applied under the civil cause of action implied from § 794.03. Unlike claims based on the common law tort of invasion of privacy, civil actions based on § 794.03 require no case-by-case findings that the disclosure of a fact about a person's private life was one that a reasonable person would find highly offensive. On the contrary, under the per se theory of negligence adopted by the courts below, liability follows automatically from publication. This is so regardless of whether the identity of the victim is already known throughout the community; whether the victim has voluntarily called public attention to the offense; or whether the identity of the victim has otherwise become a reasonable subject of public concern — because, perhaps, questions have arisen whether the victim fabricated an assault by a particular person. Nor is there a scienter requirement of any kind under § 794.03, engendering the perverse result that truthful publications challenged pursuant to this cause of action are less protected by the First Amendment than even the least protected defamatory falsehoods. . . .

Third, and finally, the facial underinclusiveness of § 794.03 raises serious doubts about whether Florida is, in fact, serving, with this statute, the significant interests which appellee invokes in support of affirmance. Section 794.03 prohibits the publication of identifying information only if this information appears in an "instrument of mass communication," a term the statute does not define. Section 794.03 does not prohibit the spread by other means of the identities of victims of sexual offenses. An individual who maliciously spreads word of the identity of a rape victim is thus not covered, despite the fact that the communication of such information to persons who live near, or work with, the victim may have consequences as devastating as the exposure of her name to large numbers of strangers.

When a State attempts the extraordinary measure of punishing truthful publication in the name of privacy, it must demonstrate its commitment to advancing this interest by applying its prohibition evenhandedly, to the smalltime disseminator as well as the media giant. Where important First Amendment interests are at stake, the mass scope of disclosure is not an acceptable surrogate for injury. . . .

Our holding today is limited. We do not hold that truthful publication is automatically constitutionally protected, or that there is no zone of personal privacy within which the State may protect the individual from intrusion by the press, or even that a State may never punish publication of the name of a victim of a sexual offense. We hold only that where a newspaper publishes truthful information which it has lawfully obtained, punishment may lawfully be imposed, if at all, only when narrowly tailored to a state interest of the highest order, and that no such interest is satisfactorily served by imposing liability under § 794.03 to appellant under the facts of this case. . . .

WHITE, J. joined by REHNQUIST, C.J. and O'CONNOR, J. dissenting. . . . *Cox Broadcasting* reversed a damages award entered against a television station, which had obtained a rape victim's name from public records maintained in connection with the judicial proceedings brought against her assailants. While there are similarities, critical aspects of that case make it wholly distinguishable from this one. First, in *Cox Broadcasting*, the victim's name had been disclosed in the hearing where her assailants pleaded guilty; and, as we recognized, judicial records have always been considered public information in this country. . . . Second, unlike the incident report at issue here, which was meant by state law to be withheld from public release, the judicial proceedings at issue in *Cox Broadcasting* were open as a matter of state law. . . .

Cox Broadcasting stands for the proposition that the State cannot make the press its first line of defense in withholding private information from the public — it cannot ask the press to secrete private facts that the State makes no effort to safeguard in the first place. In this case, however, the State has undertaken "means which avoid [but obviously, not altogether prevent] public documentation or other exposure of private information." . . .

More importantly, at issue in *Daily Mail* was the disclosure of the name of the perpetrator of an infamous murder of a 15-year-old student. Surely the rights of those accused of crimes and those who are their victims must differ with respect to privacy concerns. That is, whatever rights alleged criminals have to maintain their anonymity pending an adjudication of guilt — and after *Daily Mail*, those rights would seem to be minimal — the rights of crime victims to stay shielded from public view must be infinitely more substantial. . . .

Consequently, I cannot agree that *Cox Broadcasting*, or *Oklahoma Publishing*, or *Daily Mail* requires — or even substantially supports — the result reached by the Court today. . . .

We are left, then, to wonder whether the . . . "independent reasons" the Court cites for reversing the judgment for B.J.F. support its result.

The first of these reasons relied on by the Court is the fact "appellant gained access to [B.J.F.'s name] through a government news release." "The government's issuance of such a release, without qualification, can only convey to recipients that the government considered dissemination lawful," the Court suggests. So described, this case begins to look like the situation in *Oklahoma Publishing*, where a judge invited reporters into his courtroom, but then tried to prohibit them from reporting on the proceedings they observed. But this case is profoundly different. Here, the "release" of information provided by the government was not, as the Court says, "without qualification." As the Star's own reporter conceded at trial, the crime incident report that inadvertently included B.J.F.'s name was posted in a room that contained signs making it clear that the names of rape victims were not matters of public record, and were not to be published. The Star's reporter indicated that she understood that she "[was not] allowed to take down that information" (i.e., B.J.F.'s name) and that she "[was] not supposed to take the information from the police department." Thus, by her own admission the posting of the incident report did not convey to the Star's reporter the idea that "the government considered dissemination lawful"; the Court's suggestion to the contrary is inapt. . . .

. . . By amending its public records statute to exempt rape victims names from disclosure, and forbidding its officials to release such information, the State has taken virtually every step imaginable to prevent what happened here. This case presents a far cry, then, from *Cox Broadcasting* or *Oklahoma Publishing*, where the State asked the news media not to publish information it had made generally available to the public: here, the State is not asking the media to do the State's job in the first instance. Unfortunately, as this case illustrates, mistakes happen: even when States take measures to "avoid" disclosure, sometimes rape victims' names are found out. As I see it, it is not too much to ask the press, in instances such as this, to respect simple standards of decency and refrain from publishing a victims' name, address, and/or phone number. . . .

. . . By holding that only "a state interest of the highest order" permits the State to penalize the publication of truthful information, and by holding that protecting a rape victim's right to privacy is not among those state interests of the highest order, the Court accepts appellant's invitation to obliterate one of the most noteworthy legal inventions of the 20th century: the tort of the publication of private facts. Even if the Court's opinion does not say as much today, such obliteration will follow inevitably from the Court's conclusion here. . . .

NOTES & QUESTIONS

1. *The Government's Responsibility for Leaking Information.* What more could the state have done to protect the information? Florida made it a crime to disseminate the information. The state recognized that the police might make a mistake in certain cases and accidentally fail to redact a rape victim's name from the report. To protect against this, signs were put up outside the room notifying the press not to record a rape victim's name that was inadvertently left on the report. The Court did not dispute that the government could refuse to divulge the rape victim's name. If the government is not required to divulge the name, what is the problem with the government making it available and then punishing its further disclosure?

2. *The Future of the Public Disclosure Tort After* **Florida Star.** What effect does *Florida Star* have on the public disclosure tort? Rodney Smolla writes that the public disclosure tort exists "more 'in the books' than in practice."[50] Commentators describe the tort as "alive, but on life support"[51] and as "a phantom tort."[52] According to Jacqueline Rolfs: "Given the narrow class of information that fulfills the *Florida Star* requirements, the tort can no longer be

---

[50] Rodney A. Smolla, *Privacy and the First Amendment Right to Gather News*, 67 Geo. Wash. L. Rev. 1097 (1999).

[51] Richard S. Murphy, *Property Rights in Personal Information: An Economic Defense of Privacy*, 84 Geo. L.J. 2381, 2388 (1996). *But see* John A. Jurata, Jr., *Comment, The Tort That Refuses to Go Away: The Subtle Reemergence of Public Disclosure of Private Facts*, 36 San Diego L. Rev. 489 (1999).

[52] Phillip E. DeLaTorre, *Resurrecting a Sunken Ship: An Analysis of Current Judicial Attitudes Toward Public Disclosure Claims*, 38 Sw. L.J. 1151, 1184 (1985).

an effective tool for protecting individual privacy."[53] Peter Edelman contends: "The Court paid lip service to the possibility that a private fact plaintiff may recover in some cases, but its decisions leave little hope for vindication of such a plaintiff's rights."[54] Do you agree with these characterizations?

Consider Daniel Solove:

> Many have read *Florida Star* as a broad indication that restrictions on the disclosure of true information are unconstitutional. Nevertheless, this case can be read very narrowly. The Court suggested that the Florida statute was far too broad. The statute applied "regardless of whether the identity of the victim is already known throughout the community; whether the victim has voluntarily called public attention to the offense; or whether the identity of the victim [had] otherwise become a reasonable subject of public concern." The law focused only on the nature of the information, rather than on whether each particular use of a rape victim's name in a specific context would be of public or private concern. *Florida Star* can be construed to suggest that a law adopting a less categorical approach—by addressing the use of the identifying data more contextually—might not be subject to strict scrutiny under the First Amendment.[55]

Under this analysis, how could the Florida statute be rewritten to pass constitutional muster?

3. *Pseudonymous Litigation*. Note that the plaintiff in the Florida Star case is named with a pseudonym — B.J.F. In a major analysis of when parties in civil cases may proceed pseudonymously, Eugene Volokh finds the law "to be deeply unsettled."[56] This area is more important than ever, moreover, "because court records are more visible than ever, including to casual Internet searches." Volokh observes that cases are "sharply split on whether to allow pseudonymity in nearly every category of cases." These include cases involving potential disclosure of people's sensitive personal information that run a risk of "social stigma."

Volokh finds that the relevant factors to be assessed in deciding on permitting pseudonymity are also vague and include "the bases upon which disclosure is feared to sought to be avoided, and the substantiality of these bases" and "the magnitude of the public interest in maintaining the confidentiality of the litigant's identity." Are these factors the right ones to consider? Should other factors be considered?

4. *Free Speech and Privacy: Weighing the Values.* Eugene Volokh argues that both normatively and doctrinally, free speech considerations outweigh privacy:

> . . . [T]he speech vs. privacy and speech vs. speech tensions are not tensions between constitutional rights on both sides. The Constitution presumptively

---

[53] Jacqueline K. Rolfs, The Florida Star v. B.J.F.: *The Beginning of the End for the Tort of Public Disclosure*, 1990 Wis. L. Rev. 1107, 1128.

[54] Peter B. Edelman, *Free Press v. Privacy: Haunted by the Ghost of Justice Black*, 68 Tex. L. Rev. 1195, 1207 (1990).

[55] Solove, *Virtues of Knowing Less, supra.*

[56] Eugene Volokh, *The Law of Pseudonymous Litigation*, 73 Hastings L.J. 1353 (2022).

prohibits government restrictions on speech and perhaps some government revelation of personal information, but it says nothing about interference with
speech or revelation of personal information by nongovernmental speakers. . .

[I]s it constitutional for the government to suppress certain kinds of speech
in order to protect dignity, prevent disrespectful behavior, prevent emotional
distress, or to protect a supposed civil right not to be talked about? Under current
constitutional doctrine, the answer seems to be no. . . . Even offensive,
outrageous, disrespectful, and dignity-assaulting speech is constitutionally
protected.

. . . [A] good deal of speech that reveals information about people, including
speech that some describe as being of merely "private concern," is actually of
eminently legitimate interest. Some of it is directly relevant to the formation of
general social and political opinions; most of it is of interest to people deciding
how to behave in their daily lives, whether daily business or daily personal lives
— whom to approach to do business, whom to trust with their money, and the
like.[57]

In contrast to Volokh, Daniel Solove argues that privacy fares quite well
when balanced against free speech. Solove argues that "speech of private
concern does not strongly further the interests justifying free speech. If society
wants to promote the interests justifying free speech, a vigorous protection of
speech at the expense of privacy can, in fact, impair these interests." Free
speech is often justified as essential for individual autonomy, but Solove
contends that "[t]here is no clear reason why the autonomy of speakers or
listeners should prevail over that of the harmed individuals." Regarding the
theory that free speech is valued because it promotes democratic self-
governance, Solove argues:

[S]peech of private concern often does not promote democratic self-
governance. For example, it is difficult to justify how the sale from one
company to another of mailing lists about people's hobbies and incomes
promotes democratic self-governance. Additionally, the reporting of one's
personal secrets often does not illuminate the sphere of politics. . . .

Privacy encourages uninhibited speech by enabling individuals to direct
frank communication to those people they trust and who will not cause them
harm because of what they say. . . . [P]rivacy protections do not just inhibit free
speech; they can promote it as well.

Solove argues that the value of speech of private concern is significantly less
than that of public concern: "Privacy regulations that promote speech should
not simply be viewed in terms of their speech-restrictive elements; they should
be understood holistically, in terms of their overall purpose in the protection of

---

[57] Eugene Volokh, *Freedom of Speech and Information Privacy: The Troubling Implications of a Right to Stop People from Speaking About You,* 52 Stan. L. Rev. 1049, 1089, 1092-93, 1107, 1112-15 (2000). For other free speech critiques of privacy protections, see Thomas I. Emerson, *The System of Freedom of Expression* (1970); Solveig Singleton, *Privacy Versus the First Amendment: A Skeptical Approach,* 11 Fordham Intell. Prop. Media & Ent. L.J. 97 (2000); Harry Kalven, Jr., *Privacy in Tort Law — Were Warren and Brandeis Wrong?,* 31 Law & Contemp. Probs. 326 (1966); Diane L. Zimmerman, *Requiem for a Heavyweight: A Farewell to Warren and Brandeis's Privacy Tort,* 68 Cornell L. Rev. 291 (1983).

free speech. We protect free speech to promote certain ends. Volokh loses sight of the ends of the First Amendment by focusing too heavily on the means."[58]

5. *The Value of Gossip.* Diane Zimmerman questions the very existence of the public disclosure tort. She argues that the tort should be "scuttled" as inconsistent with the First Amendment. According to Zimmerman, the "idle gossip" Warren and Brandeis complained about is highly valuable speech, entitled to no less protection than any other form of speech:

> . . . [F]rom the perspective of the anthropologist and sociologist, gossip is a basic form of information exchange that teaches about other lifestyles and attitudes, and through which community values are changed or reinforced. This description is a far cry from that of Warren and Brandeis, which characterized gossip as a trivializing influence that destroys "robustness of thought and delicacy of feeling" and serves the interests primarily of the "prurient" and the "indolent."
>
> Gossip thus appears to be a normal and necessary part of life for all but the rare hermit among us. Perceived in this way, gossip contributes directly to the first amendment "marketplace of ideas," and the comparative weight assigned to an interest in its limitation merits careful consideration.[59]

Do you agree with Zimmerman about the high value of gossip? Does the value of gossip outweigh the harms it causes?

6. *Contracts, Promises, and the First Amendment.* Does the enforcement of a contract of confidentiality against a media entity trigger First Amendment scrutiny? In *Cohen v. Cowles Media Co.*, 501 U.S. 663 (1991), a journalist had promised a source confidentiality but nevertheless published the source's name. The source sued and obtained a promissory estoppel damage award. According to the Court, *Florida Star* did not control because "generally applicable laws do not offend the First Amendment simply because their enforcement against the press has incidental effects on its ability to gather and report the news." Why is a suit under contract or promissory estoppel different from a suit under tort, such as public disclosure of private facts?

After *Cohen,* the courts apply two dramatically different rules when it comes to free speech and civil liability. As Daniel Solove and Neil Richards explain:

> For a panoply of torts for harms caused by speech, the well-settled rule is that the First Amendment provides full protection. There are, however, many instances where the Supreme Court applies virtually no First Amendment scrutiny when civil liability implicates speech. In particular, many lawsuits involving the enforcement of contracts or property rights do not trigger any significant First Amendment scrutiny. Thus, there are two radically different ways that the First Amendment addresses civil liability involving speech — either full First Amendment protection or virtually none at all. . . .

---

[58] Daniel J. Solove, *The Virtues of Knowing Less: Justifying Privacy Protections Against Disclosure*, 53 Duke L.J. 967, 988-98 (2003).

[59] Diane L. Zimmerman, *Requiem for a Heavyweight: A Farewell to Warren and Brandeis's Privacy Tort*, 68 Cornell L. Rev. 291, 333-34, 340 (1983). Katherine Strandburg contends that society does not exalt unfettered gossip and that it is regulated by norms of restraint (which she calls "willpower norms"). Katherine J. Strandburg, *Privacy, Rationality, and Temptation: A Theory of Willpower Norms*, 57 Rutgers L. Rev. 1235 (2005).

Solove and Richards point out that contract and tort are often not distinct categories but bleed into one another. Certain torts, such as the breach of confidentiality tort, are premised on notions of implied contractual duties. They propose a new way to determine which First Amendment rule should apply to certain forms of civil liability:

> We suggest that when government power is used to dictate the terms of civil duties not to speak (what we call the "duty-defining power"), the special dangers of this power warrant application of the First Amendment. In contrast, when private parties create the content of speech-restrictive rules, the First Amendment should not apply.[60]

Should a distinction be made in free speech protection for various forms of civil liability? Does focusing on government power serve as a coherent way to make the distinction? If not, what approach would work better?

(b) Speech Based on Unlawfully Obtained Information

BARTNICKI V. VOPPER
532 U.S. 514 (2001)

STEVENS, J. These cases raise an important question concerning what degree of protection, if any, the First Amendment provides to speech that discloses the contents of an illegally intercepted communication. That question is both novel and narrow. Despite the fact that federal law has prohibited such disclosures since 1934, this is the first time that we have confronted such an issue. . . .

During 1992 and most of 1993, the Pennsylvania State Education Association, a union representing the teachers at the Wyoming Valley West High School, engaged in collective-bargaining negotiations with the school board. Petitioner Kane, then the president of the local union, testified that the negotiations were "'contentious'" and received "a lot of media attention." In May 1993, petitioner Bartnicki, who was acting as the union's "chief negotiator," used the cellular phone in her car to call Kane and engage in a lengthy conversation about the status of the negotiations. An unidentified person intercepted and recorded that call.

In their conversation, Kane and Bartnicki discussed the timing of a proposed strike, difficulties created by public comment on the negotiations, and the need for a dramatic response to the board's intransigence. At one point, Kane said: "'If they're not gonna move for three percent, we're gonna have to go to their, their homes. . . . To blow off their front porches, we'll have to do some work on some of those guys. (PAUSES). Really, uh, really and truthfully because this is, you know, this is bad news. (UNDECIPHERABLE).'"

In the early fall of 1993, the parties accepted a non-binding arbitration proposal that was generally favorable to the teachers. In connection with news reports about the settlement, respondent Vopper, a radio commentator who had been critical of the union in the past, played a tape of the intercepted conversation on his public

---

[60] Daniel J. Solove & Neil M. Richards, *Rethinking Free Speech and Civil Liability,* 109 Colum. L. Rev. 1650, 1651-52, 1686 (2009).

affairs talk show. Another station also broadcast the tape, and local newspapers published its contents. After filing suit against Vopper and other representatives of the media, Bartnicki and Kane (hereinafter petitioners) learned through discovery that Vopper had obtained the tape from Jack Yocum, the head of a local taxpayers' organization that had opposed the union's demands throughout the negotiations. Yocum, who was added as a defendant, testified that he had found the tape in his mailbox shortly after the interception and recognized the voices of Bartnicki and Kane. Yocum played the tape for some members of the school board, and later delivered the tape itself to Vopper. . . .

In their amended complaint, petitioners alleged that their telephone conversation had been surreptitiously intercepted by an unknown person using an electronic device, that Yocum had obtained a tape of that conversation, and that he intentionally disclosed it to Vopper, as well as other individuals and media representatives. Thereafter, Vopper and other members of the media repeatedly published the contents of that conversation. The amended complaint alleged that each of the defendants "knew or had reason to know" that the recording of the private telephone conversation had been obtained by means of an illegal interception. Relying on both federal and Pennsylvania statutory provisions, petitioners sought actual damages, statutory damages, punitive damages, and attorney's fees and costs. . . .

[Title 18 U.S.C. § 2511(1)(c) provides that any person who "intentionally discloses, or endeavors to disclose, to any other person the contents of any wire, oral, or electronic communication, knowing or having reason to know that the information was obtained through the interception of a wire, oral, or electronic communication in violation of this subsection; . . . shall be punished. . . ." The Pennsylvania Act contains a similar provision.]

. . . First, respondents played no part in the illegal interception. Rather, they found out about the interception only after it occurred, and in fact never learned the identity of the person or persons who made the interception. Second, their access to the information on the tapes was obtained lawfully, even though the information itself was intercepted unlawfully by someone else. Third, the subject matter of the conversation was a matter of public concern. If the statements about the labor negotiations had been made in a public arena — during a bargaining session, for example — they would have been newsworthy. This would also be true if a third party had inadvertently overheard Bartnicki making the same statements to Kane when the two thought they were alone.

We agree with petitioners that § 2511(1)(c), as well as its Pennsylvania analog, is in fact a content-neutral law of general applicability. . . . The statute does not distinguish based on the content of the intercepted conversations, nor is it justified by reference to the content of those conversations. Rather, the communications at issue are singled out by virtue of the fact that they were illegally intercepted — by virtue of the source, rather than the subject matter.

On the other hand, the naked prohibition against disclosures is fairly characterized as a regulation of pure speech. . . .

As a general matter, "state action to punish the publication of truthful information seldom can satisfy constitutional standards." *Smith v. Daily Mail Publishing Co.*, 443 U.S. 97, 102 (1979). More specifically, this Court has repeatedly held that "if a newspaper lawfully obtains truthful information about a matter of public significance then state officials may not constitutionally punish publication of the information, absent a need . . . of the highest order." *Id.*, at 103; *see also Florida Star v. B.J.F.*; *Landmark Communications, Inc. v. Virginia.* . . .

. . . [T]he issue here is this: "Where the punished publisher of information has obtained the information in question in a manner lawful in itself but from a source who has obtained it unlawfully, may the government punish the ensuing publication of that information based on the defect in a chain?" . . .

The Government identifies two interests served by the statute — first, the interest in removing an incentive for parties to intercept private conversations, and second, the interest in minimizing the harm to persons whose conversations have been illegally intercepted. . . .

The normal method of deterring unlawful conduct is to impose an appropriate punishment on the person who engages in it. If the sanctions that presently attach to a violation of § 2511(1)(a) do not provide sufficient deterrence, perhaps those sanctions should be made more severe. But it would be quite remarkable to hold that speech by a law-abiding possessor of information can be suppressed in order to deter conduct by a non-law-abiding third party. . . .

The Government's second argument, however, is considerably stronger. Privacy of communication is an important interest, and Title III's restrictions are intended to protect that interest, thereby "encouraging the uninhibited exchange of ideas and information among private parties. . . ." Moreover, the fear of public disclosure of private conversations might well have a chilling effect on private speech. . . .

Accordingly, it seems to us that there are important interests to be considered on both sides of the constitutional calculus. . . .

In this case, privacy concerns give way when balanced against the interest in publishing matters of public importance. . . .

We think it clear that parallel reasoning requires the conclusion that a stranger's illegal conduct does not suffice to remove the First Amendment shield from speech about a matter of public concern. The months of negotiations over the proper level of compensation for teachers at the Wyoming Valley West High School were unquestionably a matter of public concern, and respondents were clearly engaged in debate about that concern. . . .

BREYER, J. joined by O'CONNOR, J. concurring. As the Court recognizes, the question before us—a question of immunity from statutorily imposed civil liability—implicates competing constitutional concerns. The statutes directly interfere with free expression in that they prevent the media from publishing information. At the same time, they help to protect personal privacy—an interest here that includes not only the "right to be let alone." Given these competing interests "on both sides of the equation, the key question becomes one of proper fit." . . .

As a general matter, despite the statutes' direct restrictions on speech, the Federal Constitution must tolerate laws of this kind because of the importance of these privacy and speech-related objectives. . . . Rather than broadly forbid this kind of legislative enactment, the Constitution demands legislative efforts to tailor the laws in order reasonably to reconcile media freedom with personal, speech-related privacy.

Nonetheless, looked at more specifically, the statutes, as applied in these circumstances, do not reasonably reconcile the competing constitutional objectives. Rather, they disproportionately interfere with media freedom. For one thing, the broadcasters here engaged in no unlawful activity other than the ultimate publication of the information another had previously obtained. They "neither encouraged nor participated directly or indirectly in the interception.". . . .

For another thing, the speakers had little or no *legitimate* interest in maintaining the privacy of the particular conversation. That conversation involved a suggestion about "blow[ing] off . . . front porches" and "do[ing] some work on some of those guys," thereby raising a significant concern for the safety of others. Where publication of private information constitutes a wrongful act, the law recognizes a privilege allowing the reporting of threats to public safety. . . .

Further, the speakers themselves, the president of a teacher's union and the union's chief negotiator, were "limited public figures," for they voluntarily engaged in a public controversy. They thereby subjected themselves to somewhat greater public scrutiny and had a lesser interest in privacy than an individual engaged in purely private affairs. . . .

Here, the speakers' legitimate privacy expectations are unusually low, and the public interest in defeating those expectations is unusually high. Given these circumstances, along with the lawful nature of respondents' behavior, the statutes' enforcement would disproportionately harm media freedom.

REHNQUIST, C.J., joined by SCALIA and THOMAS, JJ., dissenting. Technology now permits millions of important and confidential conversations to occur through a vast system of electronic networks. These advances, however, raise significant privacy concerns. We are placed in the uncomfortable position of not knowing who might have access to our personal and business e-mails, our medical and financial records, or our cordless and cellular telephone conversations. In an attempt to prevent some of the most egregious violations of privacy, the United States, the District of Columbia, and 40 States have enacted laws prohibiting the intentional interception and knowing disclosure of electronic communications. The Court holds that all of these statutes violate the First Amendment insofar as the illegally intercepted conversation touches upon a matter of "public concern," an amorphous concept that the Court does not even attempt to define. But the Court's decision diminishes, rather than enhances, the purposes of the First Amendment: chilling the speech of the millions of Americans who rely upon electronic technology to communicate each day. . . .

The Court correctly observes that these are "content-neutral law[s] of general applicability" which serve recognized interests of the "highest order": "the interest in individual privacy and . . . in fostering private speech." It nonetheless subjects these laws to the strict scrutiny normally reserved for governmental attempts to censor different viewpoints or ideas. There is scant support, either in precedent or in reason, for the Court's tacit application of strict scrutiny.

A content-neutral regulation will be sustained if

> "'it furthers an important or substantial governmental interest; if the governmental interest is unrelated to the suppression of free expression; and if the incidental restriction on alleged First Amendment freedoms is no greater than is essential to

the furtherance of that interest.'" *Turner Broadcasting System, Inc. v. FCC*, 512 U.S. 622, 662 (1994). . . .

The Court's attempt to avoid these precedents by reliance upon the *Daily Mail* string of newspaper cases is unpersuasive. In these cases, we held that statutes prohibiting the media from publishing certain truthful information — the name of a rape victim, *Florida Star v. B. J. F.*; *Cox Broadcasting Corp. v. Cohn*, the confidential proceedings before a state judicial review commission, *Landmark Communications, Inc. v. Virginia*, and the name of a juvenile defendant, *Daily Mail* — violated the First Amendment. In so doing, we stated that "if a newspaper lawfully obtains truthful information about a matter of public significance then state officials may not constitutionally punish publication of the information, absent a need to further a state interest of the highest order." *Daily Mail*. Neither this *Daily Mail* principle nor any other aspect of these cases, however, justifies the Court's imposition of strict scrutiny here. . . .

These laws are content neutral; they only regulate information that was illegally obtained; they do not restrict republication of what is already in the public domain; they impose no special burdens upon the media; they have a scienter requirement to provide fair warning; and they promote the privacy and free speech of those using cellular telephones. It is hard to imagine a more narrowly tailored prohibition of the disclosure of illegally intercepted communications, and it distorts our precedents to review these statutes under the often fatal standard of strict scrutiny. These laws therefore should be upheld if they further a substantial governmental interest unrelated to the suppression of free speech, and they do. . .

The "dry up the market" theory, which posits that it is possible to deter an illegal act that is difficult to police by preventing the wrongdoer from enjoying the fruits of the crime, is neither novel nor implausible. It is a time-tested theory that undergirds numerous laws, such as the prohibition of the knowing possession of stolen goods. We ourselves adopted the exclusionary rule based upon similar reasoning, believing that it would "deter unreasonable searches," by removing an officer's "incentive to disregard [the Fourth Amendment]."

The same logic applies here and demonstrates that the incidental restriction on alleged First Amendment freedoms is no greater than essential to further the interest of protecting the privacy of individual communications. Were there no prohibition on disclosure, an unlawful eavesdropper who wanted to disclose the conversation could anonymously launder the interception through a third party and thereby avoid detection. Indeed, demand for illegally obtained private information would only increase if it could be disclosed without repercussion. The law against interceptions, which the Court agrees is valid, would be utterly ineffectual without these antidisclosure provisions. . . .

These statutes undeniably protect this venerable right of privacy. Concomitantly, they further the First Amendment rights of the parties to the conversation. . . . The chilling effect of the Court's decision upon these private conversations will surely be great. . . .

Although public persons may have forgone the right to live their lives screened from public scrutiny in some areas, it does not and should not follow that they also have abandoned their right to have a private conversation without fear of it being intentionally intercepted and knowingly disclosed. . . .

NOTES & QUESTIONS

1. *Privacy and Free Speech.* The concurrence and dissent both recognize that the statutory provisions of federal wiretap law serve to protect, rather than merely infringe, First Amendment values. How should the Court analyze statutes that restrict some speech in order to promote more speech?

2. *The Effect of* **Bartnicki** *on the Public Disclosure Tort.* According to Rodney Smolla, "*Bartnicki* accepted the premise that the conflict posed between speech and privacy is a conflict between two rights of constitutional stature. By this important measure, all nine Justices in *Bartnicki* were in agreement." Smolla reads *Bartnicki* to be "inviting the importation into First Amendment jurisprudence of the 'newsworthiness' analysis as it has developed so far in common-law cases."[61] The Court has yet to confront whether the tort of public disclosure is constitutional. As Daniel Solove observes:

> In numerous cases, the Court has articulated a public and private concern distinction, and it has applied the First Amendment to curtail restrictions on speech of public concern without answering questions about limiting speech of private concern. . . . The Court appears to view the public and private concern distinction as having significance because it has used this distinction to limit the application of heightened scrutiny to restrictions on speech of public concern.[62]

Eugene Volokh takes issue with this conclusion:

> Though the Court has often said in dictum that political speech or public-issue speech is on the "highest rung" of constitutional protection, it has never held that there's any general exception for speech on matters of "private concern." Political speech, scientific speech, art, entertainment, consumer product reviews, and speech on matters of private concern are thus all doctrinally entitled to the same level of high constitutional protection, restrictable only through laws that pass strict scrutiny.[63]

Consider Neil Richards:

> The hallmark of modern American First Amendment jurisprudence is that hurt feelings alone cannot justify the suppression of truthful information or opinion. And under the modern, post-*New York Times v. Sullivan* First Amendment regulation of speech (even by tort) on the grounds that it causes emotional injury is highly disfavored. It should thus be unsurprising that in a series of Supreme Court cases in which psychological privacy harms have been balanced against free press rights, the First Amendment has always prevailed. . . .

---

[61] Rodney A. Smolla, *Information as Contraband: The First Amendment and Liability for Trafficking in Speech*, 96 Nw. U. L. Rev. 1099, 1150, 1153 (2002).

[62] Solove, *Virtues of Knowing Less, supra*, at 987.

[63] Eugene Volokh, *Freedom of Speech and Information Privacy: The Troubling Implications of a Right to Stop People from Speaking About You*, 52 Stan. L. Rev. 1049, 1089, 1092-95 (2000). For other free speech critiques of privacy protections, see Thomas I. Emerson, *The System of Freedom of Expression* (1970); Solveig Singleton, *Privacy Versus the First Amendment: A Skeptical Approach*, 11 Fordham Intell. Prop. Media & Ent. L.J. 97 (2000); Harry Kalven, Jr., *Privacy in Tort Law — Were Warren and Brandeis Wrong?*, 31 Law & Contemp. Probs. 326 (1966); Diane L. Zimmerman, *Requiem for a Heavyweight: A Farewell to Warren and Brandeis's Privacy Tort*, 68 Cornell L. Rev. 291 (1983).

In extraordinary cases, perhaps involving sexually-themed disclosures such as sex tapes, tort privacy can survive a direct clash with the First Amendment protections given to the press. A few such cases impose liability for psychological injuries over free press challenges. But such cases are likely to remain outliers, and appropriately so. . . .[64]

(c) Harassment, Threats, and Abusive Speech

Imaged-Based Sexual Abuse. A growing societal problem is image-based sexual abuse (IBSA), which refers to the nonconsensual disclosure of a sexually explicit image or video of a person. IBSA was originally called "revenge porn" or "nonconsensual pornography," but these terms were dropped for several reasons, as one commentator explains:

> The term "revenge porn" focuses too much on the motivations of perpetrators at the expense of the harms to victims.
> Nor does 'revenge porn' cover the sharing of images created without consent and then shared, whether they are recordings of a sexual assault, or upskirt images, or from voyeurs.
> Second, the term image-based sexual abuse is also preferable because it emphasizes what these practices are — abusive. The non-consensual creation and/or distribution of private, sexual images is a serious harm often resulting in considerable mental and physical injuries.[65]

To what extent can victims use the privacy torts and other laws discussed in this chapter to obtain a remedy? Which torts would be most suitable? How strong a case would a plaintiff have under these torts? One practical difficulty is that defendants often lack much money to pay if a plaintiff prevails, and thus lawyers do not want to take these cases on a contingent fee basis.

The federal cyber stalking statute has been invoked to pursue defendants. *See* 18 U.S.C. § 2261A. For example, in *United States v. Petrovic*, 701 F.3d 849 (8th Cir. 2012), a defendant was convicted of cyber stalking because he posted revenge porn of his ex-wife online and then tried to extort money from her to remove it. In *United States v. Shepard*, 2012 WL 113027 (D. Ariz. Jan. 13, 2012), a defendant was convicted of cyber stalking for posting his ex-girlfriend's nude photos online in porn advertisements. However, according to Danielle Citron, the federal cyber stalking statute has rarely been invoked.[66]

A majority of states have criminalized IBSA. In 2004, New Jersey adopted the first criminal invasion of privacy statute prohibiting the disclosure of someone's sexually explicit images without that person's consent. *See* N.J. Stat. Ann. § 2C:14-9. Under New Jersey law, a person commits criminal invasion of privacy if, "knowing that he is not licensed or privileged to do so, he discloses any photograph, film, videotape, recording or any other reproduction of the image of another person whose intimate parts are exposed or who is engaged in an act of

---

[64] Neil M. Richards, *The Puzzle of Brandeis, Privacy, and Speech,* 63 Vand. L. Rev. 1295, 1345-47 (2010).

[65] Clare McGlynn and Erika Rackley, *Not 'Revenge Porn,' but Abuse: Let's Call It Image-Based Sexual Abuse,* Inherently Human (Feb. 15, 2016), https://inherentlyhuman.wordpress.com/2016/02/15/not-revenge-porn-but-abuse-lets-call-it-image-based-sexual-abuse/.

[66] *See* Danielle Keats Citron, *Hate Crimes in Cyberspace* (2014).

sexual penetration or sexual contact, unless that person has consented to such disclosure." The crime carries a prison sentence of between three and five years and monetary penalties of up to $30,000.

IBSA laws in other states vary in their effectiveness and scope. For example, California's law requires that the defendant must have the intent to cause the victim substantial emotional distress and does not cover images that victims take of themselves. Mary Anne Franks contends that IBSA laws should not require an intent to cause harm:

> [T]he law should not be limited to offenders who intend to cause their victims harm or distress. Nonconsensual pornography, while sometimes a form of harassment, is always an invasion of privacy. . . . [T]he vast majority of perpetrators do not intend to harm their victims. . . .
>
> [T]he insistence that nonconsensual pornography laws must include a motive requirement originated with the American Civil Liberties Union (ACLU) and was later echoed by the Media Coalition and the Motion Picture Association of America. These groups have unfortunately been successful in convincing some legislators that such requirements are necessary for laws to comport with the First Amendment. This is despite the fact that there is no constitutional basis for characterizing nonconsensual pornography as harassment rather than privacy, and no basis for claiming that privacy laws must include motive requirements in order to survive constitutional scrutiny. In fact, . . . motive requirements create constitutional vulnerabilities. Cyberbullying laws in North Carolina and New York have recently been declared unconstitutional on the grounds that phrases such as harass, torment, and embarrass are unconstitutionally vague. . .
>
> "Intent to harass" requirements, despite the phrasing, are not intent requirements at all, in the sense of mens rea, but are in fact motive requirements. While, as explained above, the requisite mens rea for each element of a criminal law should be clearly stated, criminal laws are not required to include—and indeed the majority do not include—motive requirements. "Intent to harass" requirements result in arbitrary distinctions between perpetrators motivated by personal desire to harm and those motivated by other reasons. Imposing such motive requirements ignores the reality that many perpetrators act not with an intent to distress but out of a desire to entertain, to make money, or to achieve notoriety.[67]

Should this kind of behavior be criminalized? Some contend that civil lawsuits are the more appropriate way to address the problem. On the other hand, consider the following argument by Mary Anne Franks, a law professor who has helped states draft IBSA laws, writing with Citron:

> At a fundamental level, nonconsensual pornography is an extreme invasion of privacy, one that causes serious and often irreversible harm to a person's physical and emotional well-being, damage to their reputations, and can even threaten their financial security. As modern societies, we impose criminal punishments for far

---

[67] Mary Anne Franks, *"Revenge Porn" Reform: A View from the Front Lines*, 69 Florida L. Rev. 1251 (2017).

less. We punish theft, drug possession and destruction of property. So why don't we punish revenge porn?[68]

Do nonconsensual pornography laws violate the First Amendment? Consider Citron's argument:

> Maintaining the confidentiality of someone's sexually explicit images has little impact on a poster's expression of ideas. Revenge porn does not promote civic character or educate us about cultural, religious, or political issues. On the other hand, the nonconsensual disclosure of a person's nude images would assuredly chill private expression. Without any expectation of privacy, victims would not share their naked images. With an expectation of privacy, victims would be more inclined to engage in communications of a sexual nature. Such sharing may enhance intimacy among couples and the willingness to be forthright in other aspects of relationships.[69]

Some have challenged these laws as not being sufficiently narrow and clear and thus raising concerns of overbreadth and vagueness. In defense of these statutes, Citron has argued that they can avoid these problems if they make clear that (1) the "images do not concern matters of public importance"; (2) the defendant shared the revenge porn intentionally; and (3) the defendant knew that sharing the revenge porn would violate the victim's reasonable expectation of privacy or reasonable expectation that the image or video would remain confidential.[70] Would these requirements cure overbreadth and vagueness concerns?

IBSA often does not fall into unprotected categories of speech such as obscenity or true threats. Does this mean that it cannot be criminalized?

Lee Rowland, a lawyer with the ACLU, argues that "revenge porn laws tend to criminalize the sharing of nude images that people lawfully own."[71] Rowland also raises concerns that such laws could potentially criminalize the activities of many teenagers. Free speech proponents also raise concerns of a slippery slope if revenge porn is a crime. What if all violations of the public disclosure of private facts tort were criminalized?

In contrast, consider Citron and Franks:

> First Amendment doctrine holds that not all forms of speech regulation are subject to strict scrutiny. Certain categories of speech can be regulated due to their propensity to bring about serious harms and only slight contributions to First Amendment values. They include true threats, speech integral to criminal conduct, defamation, obscenity, and imminent and likely incitement of violence. Courts also have employed "less rigorous" scrutiny in upholding the constitutionality of penalties for nonconsensual disclosures of private communications, such as sex

---

[68] Mary Anne Franks & Danielle Citron, *It's Simple: Criminalize Revenge Porn, or Let Men Punish Women They Don't Like*, The Guardian, Apr. 17, 2014, http://www.theguardian.com/commentisfree/2014/apr/17/revenge-porn-must-be-criminalized-laws.

[69] Citron, *Hate Crimes in Cyberspace, supra.*

[70] Danielle Citron, *How to Make Revenge Porn a Crime* Slate, Nov. 7, 2013, http://www.slate.com/articles/news_and_politics/jurisprudence/2013/11/making_revenge_porn_a_c rime_without_trampling_free_speech.html..

[71] Liz Halloran, *Race to Stop 'Revenge Porn' Raises Free Speech Worries*, NPR, Mar. 6, 2014, http://www.npr.org/blogs/itsallpolitics/2014/03/06/286388840/race-to-stop-revenge-porn-raises-free-speech-worries.

tapes, on the ground that such communications are not matters of public concern. . . .

In *Bartnicki v. Vopper*, for instance, an unidentified person intercepted and recorded a cell phone call between the president of a local teacher's union and the union's chief negotiator. The conversation concerned the negotiations between the union and the school board. . . . A radio commentator, who received a copy of the intercepted call in his mailbox, broadcasted it on his talk show. The question was whether the radio commentator could be penalized under the Wiretap Act for publishing the recorded cell phone conversation. . . .

The Court struck down the penalties assessed against the radio commentator as unconstitutional because the private communications concerned negotiations over the proper level of compensation for teachers that were "unquestionably a matter of public concern." As the Court underscored, *Bartnicki* did not involve the nonconsensual publication of "trade secrets or domestic gossip or other information of purely private concern." . . .

Following that reasoning, courts have upheld civil penalties under the federal Wiretap Act where the unwanted disclosures of private communications involved "purely private matters."[72]

Are images and videos different from other things? Could merely writing about the private sexual activities of another person be criminalized?

First Amendment Limits on Criminalizing Online Threats and Harassment. In *Counterman v. Colorado,* 600 U.S. __ (2023), C.W., a local musician, had received hundreds of messages from Billy Counterman, a stalker whom she had never met. Many of his messages were scary and threatening. Some of the messages suggested that Counterman might be watching C.W. Although C.W. repeatedly blocked Counterman on Facebook, he would create new Facebook accounts and continue to send her messages. C.W. stopped her public singing performances and felt unsafe in her daily activities.

Counterman was convicted under a law that criminalized one who "[r]epeatedly . . . makes any form of communication with another person" in "a manner that would cause a reasonable person to suffer serious emotional distress and does cause that person . . . to suffer serious emotional distress." Colo. Rev. Stat. § 18–3–602(1)(c).

The Supreme Court held that for a state to punish these messages, it had to prove that the defendant had some subjective understanding of the threatening nature of his statements. For the Court, at least "a mental state of recklessness" is required and the state must "show that the defendant consciously disregarded a substantial risk that his communications would be viewed as threatening violence." The Court reasoned:

"True threats" of violence is another historically unprotected category of communications. The "true" in that term distinguishes what is at issue from jests, "hyperbole," or other statements that when taken in context do not convey a real possibility that violence will follow (say, "I am going to kill you for showing up late").

---

[72] Danielle Keats Citron & Mary Anne Franks, *Criminalizing Revenge Porn,* 49 Wake Forest L. Rev. 345 (2014).

Yet the First Amendment may still demand a subjective mental-state requirement shielding some true threats from liability. The reason relates to what is often called a chilling effect. Prohibitions on speech have the potential to chill, or deter, speech outside their boundaries. A speaker may be unsure about the side of a line on which his speech falls. Or he may worry that the legal system will err, andcount speech that is permissible as instead not. Or he may simply be concerned about the expense of becoming entangled in the legal system. The result is "self-censorship" of speech that could not be proscribed—a "cautious and restrictive exercise" of First Amendment freedoms.

In dissent, Justice Barrett argued:

The nature of a true threat points to an objective test for determining the scope of First Amendment protection: Neither its "social value" nor its potential for "injury" depends on the speaker's subjective intent. *Chaplinsky*, 315 U. S., at 572. They can relate, of course—a speaker who does not intend to threaten is less likely to utter a statement that could be taken that way. But the Constitution ultimately declines to protect true threats for objective reasons, not subjective ones. . . .

Many States have long had statutes like Colorado's on the books. Before we took this case, the vast majority of Courts of Appeals and state high courts had upheld these statutes as constitutional. So objective tests are effectively the status quo today, yet Counterman still struggles to identify past prosecutions that came close to infringing on protected speech.

In a sharp critique of this decision, Mary Anne Franks faults *Counterman* for failing to adequately protect the victim of "a relentless, six-year stalking campaign by a man determined to insert himself into a woman's life without her consent." According to Franks: "The court ignores the reality that many stalkers fervently believe that their actions are or should be welcomed by their victims; indeed, the court's holding means that the more delusional the stalker, the more the stalking is protected."[73]

Copyright and Image-Based Sexual Abuse. If victims took the photos or videos themselves, they could bring civil copyright claims against the people who posted them. A person who creates the photo or video has common law copyright in the material, and this branch of intellectual property law provides some protections.

Note, however, that the Digital Millenium Copyright Act (DMCA) provides strong protections for copyright that are not available in the context of IBSA. In particular, the DMCA creates a "notice and take-down" regime. It sets up a regime for ISPs to be protected for copyright infringement, if they respond to reports of infringement by copyright owners and remove the offending material.

Amanda Levendowski notes, however, that there are limits to this approach. She writes, "Copyright is not a panacea for revenge porn. Victims must be willing to invest time to submit takedown notices and, if that fails, money into hiring an attorney to proceed with litigation."[74] Another problem is that websites that traffic exclusively in IBSA create a "whack-a-mole" problem in which infringing

---

[73] Mary Anne Franks, *The Supreme Court Just Legalized Stalking*, Slate (July 6, 2023).
[74] Amanda Levendowski, *Using Copyright to Combat Revenge Porn*, 3 N.Y.U. J. Intell. Prop. & Ent. L. 422, 446 (2014).

material may quickly appear elsewhere. Moreover, the offending material may be posted outside of the United States, which makes enforcement highly difficult.

First Amendment Limits on Civil Liability for Threats and Doxing. Beyond criminal statutes, civil liability is another recourse for victims of online threats and harassment. One form of this threatening speech is "doxing" — posting personal information about an individual, such as a person's home address or identifying information about their cars. Victims fear that they might be tracked down and harmed or killed.

In *Planned Parenthood v. American Coalition of Life Activists*, 290 F.3d 1058 (9th Cir. 2002) (en banc), the American Coalition of Life Activists (ACLA), an antiabortion advocacy group, provided a series of dossiers it assembled on doctors, clinic employees, politicians, judges, and other abortion rights supporters to Neal Horsley, an antiabortion activist, who posted the information on his website entitled the "Nuremberg Files." The "Nuremberg Files" dossiers included doctors' names, photos, Social Security numbers, home addresses, descriptions of their cars, and information about their families. The website marked the names of doctors who had been killed with a black line through them and the names of wounded doctors shaded in gray. The website did not contain any explicit threats against the doctors. The website caused the doctors great fear, and several protected themselves by wearing bulletproof vests, closing all the curtains to the windows of their homes, and even asking for the protection of the U.S. Marshals. Some of the doctors sued ACLA alleging a variety of causes of action including the Freedom of Access to Clinic Entrances Act of 1994 (FACE), 18 U.S.C. § 248.

A jury awarded the doctors $107 million in actual and punitive damages. The Ninth Circuit, en banc, affirmed the actual damages and reversed on punitive damages. The court held that the "Nuremberg Files" (in combination with "wanted" posters of various doctors) constituted a "true threat" to the doctors' lives under FACE, and such true threats were not protected under the First Amendment. Although speech advocating violence is protected, speech "directed to inciting or producing imminent lawless action" is not. "Violence is not a protected value. Nor is a *true threat* of violence *with intent to intimidate*. . . . ACLA was not staking out a position of debate but of threatened demise." According to a dissent by Judge Kozinski: "The Nuremberg Files website is clearly an expression of a political point of view. . . . [S]peech, including the intimidating message, does not constitute a direct threat because there is no evidence other than the speech itself that the speakers intend to resort to physical violence if their threat is not heeded." Would the doctors have a cause of action for public disclosure of private facts? Would the First Amendment prohibit liability on this basis?

In 2023, former President Donald Trump posted former President Obama's home address online. Soon thereafter, a man was arrested nearby the Obama house with guns and bombs. Trump did not explicitly urge people to do anything to Obama. Suppose Obama were to sue Trump for doxing. Would Obama likely prevail? If not, should the law permit plaintiffs to recover for doxing that does not involve an express threat?

Restricting Speech to Protect Speech: Cyber Civil Rights. Danielle Citron argues that online attacks, especially those against women, can have the effect of silencing them. In one incident, a group of anonymous people engaged in extensive online harassment of blogger Kathy Sierra. They threatened to rape and strangle her and posted doctored photos of her with a noose near her neck. She stopped blogging and canceled public speaking appearances out of fear. Citron argues:

> One of free speech's most important functions is promoting individual autonomy. This view urges that people be free to choose their own path. Free speech facilitates self-mastery, allowing people to author their own narratives. . . .
>
> Restraining a mob's most destructive assaults is essential to defending the expressive autonomy and equality of its victims. Preventing mobs from driving vulnerable people offline would "advance the reasons why we protect free speech in the first place," even though it would inevitably chill some speech of online mobs. Free from mob attacks, victims might continue to blog, join online discussions, and generally express themselves on public issues. Protecting them from grotesque defamation, threats, invasions of privacy, and technological attacks would allow them to be candid about their ideas.
>
> Although online mobs express themselves and their autonomy through their assaults, their actions also implicate their victims' autonomy and ability to participate in political and social discourse. Self-expression should receive no protection if its sole purpose is to extinguish the self-expression of another. . . . Rarely is that more true than when one group of voices consciously exploits the Internet's aggregating power to silence others and its disaggregative power to escape social responsibility for the group's actions.

Citron argues that civil rights law should apply in this context:

> Online assaults motivated by race discrimination that interfere with an individual's ability to make a living can support civil and criminal actions. Title 42 U.S.C. § 1981 guarantees members of racial minorities "the same right in every State . . . to make and enforce contracts . . . as is enjoyed by white citizens . . . ." A plaintiff must show that the defendant intended to discriminate on the basis of race and that the discrimination concerned the "making and enforcing" of contracts. Courts have upheld § 1981 damages in cases where masked mob members used tactics of intimidation to prevent members of racial minorities from "making a living" in their chosen field. Section 1981 remedies "purely private" acts of racial discrimination and thus does not require state action.
>
> Similarly, 18 U.S.C. § 245(b)(2)(C), a provision of the Civil Rights Act of 1968, criminalizes "force or threat[s] of force" designed to intimidate or interfere with a person's private employment due to that person's race, religion, or national origin. . . .
>
> Gender discrimination that interferes with a person's ability to make a living can be pursued under Title VII of the Civil Rights Act of 1964, which sanctions those who intimidate, threaten, or coerce, or attempt to intimidate, threaten, or coerce someone with the purpose of interfering with employment opportunities due to their gender. The Attorney General can file civil suits for injunctive relief. . . .
>
> Because the Internet fuses our public and private lives and is a workplace for many, online attacks on vulnerable individuals often interfere with their equal right to pursue work. For instance, women who stop blogging in the face of an online mob's attack lose advertising revenue and opportunities for advancement. . . .
>
> Online mob attacks also implicate state laws penalizing those who harass or stalk another by communicating words, images, or language through electronic

mail or the Internet, directed to a specific person, which would cause a reasonable person substantial emotional distress or fear of bodily harm. Some states explicitly criminalize posting messages with the intent to urge or incite others to harass a particular individual.[75]

Is the "sole purpose" of those who engage in online attacks of others to silence them? How can we draw the line between harassment triggering civil rights laws and mere crude speech, which is common online? To what extent should individuals be responsible for the actions of the mob? Suppose each individual said one or two nasty things, but collectively, the impact was severe. How should the law handle such an instance? Should the First Amendment look not just to the extent to which the law is restricting speech but also to the extent to which the law's restrictions are promoting speech?

C. DISSEMINATION OF FALSE INFORMATION

1. DEFAMATION

(a) Introduction

At the most practical level, an understanding of defamation law is essential to understanding some of the aspects and issues related to the privacy torts. While the privacy torts are a relatively recent invention, a remedy for defamation extends far back in history. Since ancient times, one's reputation and character have been viewed as indispensable to one's ability to engage in public life. Accordingly, the importance of permitting people to protect their reputations has given rise to the law of defamation.[76]

Defamation goes way back to pre-Norman times. "Defamation" (*diffamatus*) was a technical term in church law. It signified a reputation bad enough to be put on trial in ecclesiastical court. Money awards for defamation were a way to prevent people from engaging in duels. Defamation law also served as a popular tool of the monarchy to prosecute its critics.[77]

According to modern defamation law:

To create liability for defamation there must be:

(a) a false and defamatory statement concerning another;
(b) an unprivileged publication to a third party;
(c) fault amounting at least to negligence on the part of the publisher; and
(d) either actionability of the statement irrespective of special harm or the existence of special harm caused by the publication. Restatement (Second) of Torts § 558.

---

[75] Danielle Keats Citron, *Cyber Civil Rights,* 89 B.U. L. Rev. 61, 92-93, 97-98 (2009); *see also* Danielle Keats Citron, *Law's Expressive Value in Combating Cyber Gender Harassment,* 108 Mich. L. Rev. 373 (2009).

[76] For an excellent discussion of the rationales behind defamation law, see Robert C. Post, *The Social Foundations of Defamation Law: Reputation and the Constitution,* 74 Cal. L. Rev. 691 (1986).

[77] *See generally* Theodore F.T. Plucknett, *A Concise History of the Common Law* 484-87 (5th ed. 1956).

A "defamatory" statement "tends so to harm the reputation of another as to lower him in the estimation of the community or to deter third persons from associating or dealing with him." Restatement § 559.

A defamatory statement must also be "false." Therefore, a true statement that harms the reputation of another cannot give rise to liability for defamation.

"Publication" means that a defamatory statement is communicated "intentionally or by a negligent act to one other than the person defamed." Restatement § 577. If a person intentionally and unreasonably fails to remove defamatory matter that she knows is under her control, then that person is subject to liability for its continued publication. *See* Restatement § 577. Further "one who repeats or otherwise republishes defamatory matter is subject to liability as if he had originally published it." Restatement § 578.

One who distributes, transmits, or broadcasts on television or radio defamatory material is also liable if she knows or would have reason to know of its defamatory character. *See* Restatement § 581.

Libel vs. Slander. There are two forms of defamation: libel, which consists of written defamatory statements, and slander, which consists of spoken defamatory statements. According to the Restatement:

> (1) Libel consists of the publication of defamatory matter by written or printed words, by its embodiment in physical form or by any other form of communication that has the potentially harmful qualities characteristic of written or printed words.
> (2) Slander consists of the publication of defamatory matter by spoken words, transitory gestures or by any form of communication other than those stated in Subsection (1). Restatement § 568.

As is demonstrated by the above definitions, the Restatement takes a rather broad view of what constitutes libel.

The classification of certain types of statements as either libel or slander has proven difficult. One example is a statement made over the radio or on television. According to the Restatement, all broadcasting is libel, see Restatement § 568A, but some states take a contrary view.

The distinction between libel and slander is important for the purposes of proving harm. To establish libel, a plaintiff does not need to show "special harm" (i.e., a particular harm or injury); damages are presumed. In contrast, for slander, a plaintiff must show actual pecuniary harm, with the exception of four types of slander known as "slander per se" for which damages are presumed. Slander per se consists of defamatory statements imputing to another (1) a criminal offense; (2) a loathsome disease; (3) a matter incompatible with one's business, trade, profession, or office; or (4) serious sexual misconduct. *See* Restatement §§ 570-574. The distinction between libel and slander is less important today, since, in the cases you will read below, the Supreme Court curtailed the availability of presumed damages in defamation law.

Why is libel treated more severely than slander? As then Judge Cardozo put it:

> The schism in the law of defamation between the older wrong of slander and the newer one of libel is not the product of mere accident. It has its genesis in evils

which the years have not erased. Many things that are defamatory may be said with impunity through the medium of speech. Not so, however, when speech is caught upon the wing and transmuted into print. What gives the sting to writing is its permanence in form. The spoken word dissolves, but the written one abides and perpetuates the scandal. *Ostrowe v. Lee*, 175 N.E. 505, 506 (N.Y. Ct. App. 1931).

Defamation and Privacy. It might strike you that defamation does not have much to do with privacy. After all, defamation involves false information about individuals, whereas privacy seems to be about true information. This, however, is a limited view of privacy. Privacy involves more than finding out true things about individuals. If privacy is understood as an individual's ability to have some control over the self-image she projects to society, then the ability to prevent the spread of false information about oneself is essential for this sort of control. Indeed, one of the cornerstone principles of privacy law is the ability to correct errors in one's records.

(b) Defamation, the Internet, and the CDA Section 230

The Internet presents interesting problems for the application of defamation law and the privacy torts because the Internet enables the widespread publication of information by any individual. Typically, it was through the news media that defamatory or private information about individuals was communicated. As a result, it would be viable to sue such entities, since they would be able to pay any judgment a plaintiff might obtain. With the Internet, however, suppose an individual posts defamatory information about another person on her website. Most likely, that individual isn't wealthy enough to be sued. Further, information is sometimes posted anonymously. As a result of this difficulty, plaintiffs have attempted to advance theories upon which Internet Service Providers (ISPs) would be liable.

In defamation law, in addition to the one who makes a libelous statement, other parties who disseminate the libelous statement can also be found liable. Repeating or publishing the libelous statements of others can give rise to "publisher" liability. A newspaper is an example of a publisher because it exercises editorial control over its content. Merely disseminating a libelous statement can give rise to "distributor" liability. In contrast to a publisher, a distributor cannot be found liable unless it is found to be at fault — if it knew or had reason to know about the defamatory statement. Bookstores and libraries are examples of distributors. When a person posts a statement on an ISP's electronic bulletin board or other online forum, is the ISP a "publisher," "distributor," or neither?

The first two courts to reach this issue reached contrary conclusions. In *Cubby, Inc. v. CompuServe, Inc.*, 776 F. Supp. 135 (S.D.N.Y. 1991), CompuServe, an Internet Service Provider, was held not liable for the statements because it didn't have knowledge or reason to know of the statements. The court held that CompuServe was a distributor rather than a publisher: "CompuServe has no more editorial control over such a publication than does a public library, book store, or newsstand, and it would be no more feasible for CompuServe to examine every publication it carries for potentially defamatory statements than it would be for any other distributor to do so."

In *Stratton Oakmont, Inc. v. Prodigy Services Co.*, 23 Media L. Rep. 1794 (N.Y. Sup. 1995), the plaintiff brought a defamation action against Prodigy, the operator of the computer network. An unidentified user posted allegedly defamatory statements on one of Prodigy's electronic bulletin boards. The plaintiffs contended that Prodigy should be considered the "publisher" of the statements. Under Prodigy's stated policy, it was a family-oriented computer network and would screen posts for offensive content. The court concluded that Prodigy was liable as a publisher because "Prodigy held itself out to the public and its members as controlling the content of its computer bulletin boards."

In response to *Stratton Oakmont,* Congress passed Section 230 of the Communications Decency Act (CDA) of 1996. Its header reads, "Protection for 'Good Samaritan' Blocking and Screening of Offensive Material." Section 230 provides in relevant part:

> No provider or user of an interactive computer service shall be treated as the publisher or speaker of any information provided by another information content provider." 47 U.S.C. § 230(c)(1).

Jeff Kosseff has titled his book about this provision, *The Twenty-Six Words that Created the Internet.*[78] He notes how the most popular websites in the United States primarily depend on user provided content. In Kosseff's judgment, Section 230 has permitted these third-party content-based services to flourish. At the same time, however, Kosseff ends his book by conceding that "his once absolute enthusiasm for Section 230 waned a bit during the two years in which I researched this book." But he concludes: "Still, I believe that Section 230 has produced, overall, more benefits than harms for U.S. society."

There is also more to Section 230 than those 26 words. First, Section 230's provision of immunity is accompanied by language intended to encourage internet services to engage in moderation. Its goal is to promote private blocking and screening of offensive material. Immediately after the famous 26 words of 47 U.S.C. § 230(c)(1), 230(c)(2) provides:

> No provider or user of an interactive computer service shall be held liable on account of—
> (A) any action voluntarily taken in good faith to restrict access to or availability of material that the provider or user considers to be obscene, lewd, lascivious, filthy, excessively violent, harassing, or otherwise objectionable, whether or not such material is constitutionally protected; or
> (B) any action taken to enable or make available to information content providers or others the technical means to restrict access to material described in paragraph (1).

This language is important; it points to Section 230 as being a law that seeks to encourage removal by private platforms of content that is problematic.

It is also important to note that other sections of the CDA create significant carve-outs for Section 230's grant of immunity. For example, Section 230 has no

---

[78] Jeff Kosseff, *The Twenty-Six Words that Created the Internet* (2019).

effect on any other federal criminal statutes such as laws criminalizing obscenity or sexual exploitation of children. The statute states that it does not limit "any law pertaining to intellectual property." It also has no effect on federal electronics communication privacy laws.

Finally, Congress enacted the Allow States and Victims to Fight Online Sex Trafficking Act (FOSTA) in 2018. This statute added a section to Section 230 to limit immunity for online services that have knowingly hosted third-party content that promotes or facilitates sex trafficking.

ZERAN V. AMERICA ONLINE, INC.

129 F.3d 327 (4th Cir. 1997)

WILKINSON, C.J. . . . On April 25, 1995, an unidentified person posted a message on an [America Online (AOL)] bulletin board advertising "Naughty Oklahoma T-Shirts." The posting described the sale of shirts featuring offensive and tasteless slogans related to the April 19, 1995, bombing of the Alfred P. Murrah Federal Building in Oklahoma City. Those interested in purchasing the shirts were instructed to call "Ken" at [Kenneth] Zeran's home phone number in Seattle, Washington. As a result of this anonymously perpetrated prank, Zeran received a high volume of calls, comprised primarily of angry and derogatory messages, but also including death threats. Zeran could not change his phone number because he relied on its availability to the public in running his business out of his home. Later that day, Zeran called AOL and informed a company representative of his predicament. The employee assured Zeran that the posting would be removed from AOL's bulletin board but explained that as a matter of policy AOL would not post a retraction. The parties dispute the date that AOL removed this original posting from its bulletin board.

On April 26, the next day, an unknown person posted another message advertising additional shirts with new tasteless slogans related to the Oklahoma City bombing. Again, interested buyers were told to call Zeran's phone number, to ask for "Ken," and to "please call back if busy" due to high demand. The angry, threatening phone calls intensified. Over the next four days, an unidentified party continued to post messages on AOL's bulletin board, advertising additional items including bumper stickers and key chains with still more offensive slogans. During this time period, Zeran called AOL repeatedly and was told by company representatives that the individual account from which the messages were posted would soon be closed. Zeran also reported his case to Seattle FBI agents. By April 30, Zeran was receiving an abusive phone call approximately every two minutes.

Meanwhile, an announcer for Oklahoma City radio station KRXO received a copy of the first AOL posting. On May 1, the announcer related the message's contents on the air, attributed them to "Ken" at Zeran's phone number, and urged the listening audience to call the number. After this radio broadcast, Zeran was inundated with death threats and other violent calls from Oklahoma City residents. Over the next few days, Zeran talked to both KRXO and AOL representatives. He also spoke to his local police, who subsequently surveilled his home to protect his safety. By May 14, after an Oklahoma City newspaper published a story exposing the shirt advertisements as a hoax and after KRXO made an on-air apology, the number of calls to Zeran's residence finally subsided to fifteen per day.

Zeran first filed suit on January 4, 1996, against radio station KRXO in the United States District Court for the Western District of Oklahoma. On April 23, 1996, he filed this separate suit against AOL in the same court. Zeran did not bring any action against the party who posted the offensive messages.[79] . . . AOL answered Zeran's complaint and interposed [the Communications Decency Act,] 47 U.S.C. § 230 as an affirmative defense. AOL then moved for judgment on the pleadings pursuant to Fed. R. Civ. P. 12(c). The district court granted AOL's motion, and Zeran filed this appeal.

Because § 230 was successfully advanced by AOL in the district court as a defense to Zeran's claims, we shall briefly examine its operation here. Zeran seeks to hold AOL liable for defamatory speech initiated by a third party. He argued to the district court that once he notified AOL of the unidentified third party's hoax, AOL had a duty to remove the defamatory posting promptly, to notify its subscribers of the message's false nature, and to effectively screen future defamatory material. Section 230 entered this litigation as an affirmative defense pled by AOL. The company claimed that Congress immunized interactive computer service providers from claims based on information posted by a third party.

The relevant portion of § 230 states: "No provider or user of an interactive computer service shall be treated as the publisher or speaker of any information provided by another information content provider." 47 U.S.C. § 230(c)(1). By its plain language, § 230 creates a federal immunity to any cause of action that would make service providers liable for information originating with a third-party user of the service. Specifically, § 230 precludes courts from entertaining claims that would place a computer service provider in a publisher's role. Thus, lawsuits seeking to hold a service provider liable for its exercise of a publisher's traditional editorial functions — such as deciding whether to publish, withdraw, postpone or alter content — are barred.

The purpose of this statutory immunity is not difficult to discern. Congress recognized the threat that tort-based lawsuits pose to freedom of speech in the new and burgeoning Internet medium. The imposition of tort liability on service providers for the communications of others represented, for Congress, simply another form of intrusive government regulation of speech. . . .

. . . Interactive computer services have millions of users. The amount of information communicated via interactive computer services is therefore staggering. The specter of tort liability in an area of such prolific speech would have an obvious chilling effect. It would be impossible for service providers to screen each of their millions of postings for possible problems. Faced with potential liability for each message republished by their services, interactive computer service providers might choose to severely restrict the number and type of messages posted. Congress considered the weight of the speech interests

---

[79] Zeran maintains that AOL made it impossible to identify the original party by failing to maintain adequate records of its users. The issue of AOL's recordkeeping practices, however, is not presented by this appeal.

implicated and chose to immunize service providers to avoid any such restrictive effect.

Another important purpose of § 230 was to encourage service providers to self-regulate the dissemination of offensive material over their services. In this respect, § 230 responded to a New York state court decision, *Stratton Oakmont, Inc. v. Prodigy Servs. Co.* . . .

Congress enacted § 230 to remove the disincentives to self-regulation created by the *Stratton Oakmont* decision. Under that court's holding, computer service providers who regulated the dissemination of offensive material on their services risked subjecting themselves to liability, because such regulation cast the service provider in the role of a publisher. Fearing that the specter of liability would therefore deter service providers from blocking and screening offensive material, Congress enacted § 230's broad immunity "to remove disincentives for the development and utilization of blocking and filtering technologies that empower parents to restrict their children's access to objectionable or inappropriate online material." 47 U.S.C. § 230(b)(4). In line with this purpose, § 230 forbids the imposition of publisher liability on a service provider for the exercise of its editorial and self-regulatory functions.

Zeran argues, however, that the § 230 immunity eliminates only publisher liability, leaving distributor liability intact. Publishers can be held liable for defamatory statements contained in their works even absent proof that they had specific knowledge of the statement's inclusion. According to Zeran, interactive computer service providers like AOL are normally considered instead to be distributors, like traditional news vendors or book sellers. Distributors cannot be held liable for defamatory statements contained in the materials they distribute unless it is proven at a minimum that they have actual knowledge of the defamatory statements upon which liability is predicated. Zeran contends that he provided AOL with sufficient notice of the defamatory statements appearing on the company's bulletin board. This notice is significant, says Zeran, because AOL could be held liable as a distributor only if it acquired knowledge of the defamatory statements' existence.

Because of the difference between these two forms of liability, Zeran contends that the term "distributor" carries a legally distinct meaning from the term "publisher." Accordingly, he asserts that Congress' use of only the term "publisher" in § 230 indicates a purpose to immunize service providers only from publisher liability. He argues that distributors are left unprotected by § 230 and, therefore, his suit should be permitted to proceed against AOL. We disagree. Assuming arguendo that Zeran has satisfied the requirements for imposition of distributor liability, this theory of liability is merely a subset, or a species, of publisher liability, and is therefore also foreclosed by § 230. . . .

AOL falls squarely within this traditional definition of a publisher and, therefore, is clearly protected by § 230's immunity. . . .

Zeran simply attaches too much importance to the presence of the distinct notice element in distributor liability. The simple fact of notice surely cannot transform one from an original publisher to a distributor in the eyes of the law. . .

If computer service providers were subject to distributor liability, they would face potential liability each time they receive notice of a potentially defamatory statement — from any party, concerning any message. Each notification would require a careful yet rapid investigation of the circumstances surrounding the posted information, a legal judgment concerning the information's defamatory character, and an on-the-spot editorial decision whether to risk liability by allowing the continued publication of that information. Although this might be feasible for the traditional print publisher, the sheer number of postings on interactive computer services would create an impossible burden in the Internet context. Because service providers would be subject to liability only for the publication of information, and not for its removal, they would have a natural incentive simply to remove messages upon notification, whether the contents were defamatory or not. Thus, like strict liability, liability upon notice has a chilling effect on the freedom of Internet speech. . . .

More generally, notice-based liability for interactive computer service providers would provide third parties with a no-cost means to create the basis for future lawsuits. Whenever one was displeased with the speech of another party conducted over an interactive computer service, the offended party could simply "notify" the relevant service provider, claiming the information to be legally defamatory. In light of the vast amount of speech communicated through interactive computer services, these notices could produce an impossible burden for service providers, who would be faced with ceaseless choices of suppressing controversial speech or sustaining prohibitive liability. Because the probable effects of distributor liability on the vigor of Internet speech and on service provider self-regulation are directly contrary to § 230's statutory purposes, we will not assume that Congress intended to leave liability upon notice intact. . . .

NOTES & QUESTIONS

1. *Critiques of* **Zeran.** Consider the following argument against *Zeran* from *Barrett v. Rosenthal*, 5 Cal. Rptr. 3d 416 (Cal. Ct. App. 2003):

   . . . [W]e . . . think it debatable whether notice liability would actually have an unduly chilling effect on cyberspeech. Neither the record before us nor any other information brought to our attention provides an answer to that question. Moreover, the speculative conclusion of the *Zeran* court that exposing Internet intermediaries to knowledge-based liability would significantly chill online speech is disputed by the speculations of other authorities. . . .

   It is also asserted that by ignoring how difficult it is for a plaintiff to prevail on a defamation claim or receive significant money damages, the *Zeran* court overstated the danger such claims present to Internet intermediaries, and therefore also exaggerated the danger they would engage in excessive self-censorship.

   The California Supreme Court reversed the court of appeals in *Barrett v. Rosenthal*, 146 P.3d 510 (Cal. 2006):

   We reject the argument that the difficulty of prevailing on a defamation claim mitigates the deterrent effect of potential liability. Defamation law is complex, requiring consideration of multiple factors. These include whether the statement at issue is true or false, factual or figurative, privileged or unprivileged, whether the matter is of public or private concern, and whether the plaintiff is a public or private figure. Any investigation of a potentially defamatory Internet posting is thus a daunting and expensive challenge. For that reason, we have observed that even when a defamation claim is "clearly nonmeritorious," the threat of liability "ultimately chills the free exercise of expression."

Nor are we convinced by the observation that a "distributor" faces no liability without notice. Distributors are liable not merely upon receiving notice from a third party, but also if they independently "knew or had reason to know" of the defamatory statement. Thus, as the *Zeran* court pointed out, this aspect of distributor liability would discourage active monitoring of Internet postings. It could also motivate providers to insulate themselves from receiving complaints. Such responses would frustrate the goal of self-regulation.

The third practical implication noted in *Zeran* is no less compelling, and went unaddressed by the Court of Appeal. Notice-based liability for service providers would allow complaining parties to impose substantial burdens on the freedom of Internet speech by lodging complaints whenever they were displeased by an online posting. . . .

Which opinion has the better argument as to the meaning and purpose of § 230? Consider Daniel Solove:

Unfortunately, courts are interpreting Section 230 so broadly as to provide too much immunity, eliminating the incentive to foster a balance between speech and privacy. The way courts are using Section 230 exalts free speech to the detriment of privacy and reputation. As a result, a host of websites have arisen that encourage others to post gossip and rumors as well as to engage in online shaming. These websites thrive under Section 230's broad immunity.[80]

Solove contends that a notice and take-down system is preferable to a broader immunity that eliminates distributor liability. What are the benefits and problems of a notice and take-down regime? In copyright law, "one who distributes a device with the object of promoting its use to infringe copyright, as shown by clear expression or other affirmative steps taken to foster infringement, is liable for the resulting acts of infringement by third parties." *MGM Studios, Inc. v. Grokster, Ltd.*, 545 U.S. 913 (2005). Examine the pros and cons of such a rule for defamation or privacy tort liability.

2. ***CDA Section 230 and the Privacy Torts.*** Note that the CDA Section 230 is not limited to defamation law. The immunity applies broadly to prevent any "provider or user of an interactive computer service" from being "treated as the publisher or speaker of any information provided by another information content provider." This "information" can be true information, including private details about a person's life or a nude photo in violation of the public disclosure of private facts tort.

However, when it comes to the tort of appropriation (and its sister tort, the right of publicity), the applicability of Section 230 is more complicated. In *Hepp v. Facebook*, 14 F.4th 204 (3d Cir. 2021), a photograph of TV newscaster Karen Hepp was used "in online advertisements for erectile dysfunction and dating websites" without her permission. Hepp sued Facebook, which had permitted Hepp's image to be used in an advertisement for a dating app. Facebook argued that it was immune under Section 230, but the Third Circuit

---

[80] Daniel J. Solove, *The Future of Reputation: Gossip, Rumor, and Privacy on the Internet* 159 (2007).

concluded that the right of publicity was a kind of intellectual property right and encompassed by the exception for intellectual property under Section 230. In contrast, the Ninth Circuit decided that Section 230's intellectual property exception applies only to "federal intellectual property." *Perfect 10, Inc. v. CCBill LLC,* 488 F.3d 1102 (9th Cir. 2007).

3. ***Excluding Websites that Encourage Harmful Speech from Section 230.*** Danielle Citron and Benjamin Wittes argue that § 230 should be revised to exclude from immunity a site that "purposefully encourages cyber stalking, nonconsensual pornography, sex trafficking, child sexual exploitation, or that principally hosts such material."[81] In their view, "Extending immunity to Bad Samaritans undermines section 230's purpose by eliminating incentives for better behavior by those in the best position to minimize harm." Would this change avoid some of the concerns raised by supporters of § 230 immunity?

4. ***Who Is the Content Provider?*** In *Batzel v. Smith*, 333 F.3d 1018 (9th Cir. 2003), a handyman (Robert Smith) who worked at Ellen Batzel's home e-mailed Ton Cremers, the director of security at a museum in Amsterdam, who maintained an e-mail listserv about looted art. Smith said that several of Batzel's paintings were stolen from the Jews by the Nazis during World War II. Cremers made a few small changes to the text of Smith's e-mail and sent it out to his listserv. The paintings were not looted art from the Nazis, and Batzel sued both Smith and Cremers. The court concluded that since Cremers was not the originator of the information, he was immune under § 230:

> Obviously, Cremers did not create Smith's e-mail. Smith composed the e-mail entirely on his own. . . . [T]he exclusion of "publisher" liability necessarily precludes liability for exercising the usual prerogative of publishers to choose among proffered material and to edit the material published while retaining its basic form and message.
>
> Because Cremers did no more than select and make minor alterations to Smith's e-mail, Cremers cannot be considered the content provider of Smith's e-mail for purposes of § 230. . . .
>
> We therefore hold that a service provider or user is immune from liability under § 230(c)(1) when a third person or entity that created or developed the information in question furnished it to the provider or user under circumstances in which a reasonable person in the position of the service provider or user would conclude that the information was provided for publication on the Internet or other "interactive computer service."

In dissent, Judge Gould wrote:

> Congress wanted to ensure that excessive government regulation did not slow America's expansion into the exciting new frontier of the Internet. But Congress did not want this new frontier to be like the Old West: a lawless zone governed by retribution and mob justice. The CDA does not license anarchy. A person's decision to disseminate the rankest rumor or most blatant falsehood should not escape legal redress merely because the person chose to disseminate it through the Internet rather than through some other medium. . . . In this case, I would

---

[81] Danielle Keats Citron & Benjamin Wittes, *The Internet Will Not Break: Denying Bad Samaritans Section 230 Immunity*, 86 Fordham L. Rev. 401 (2017).

hold that Cremers is *not* entitled to CDA immunity because Cremers actively selected Smith's e-mail message for publication.

Batzel demonstrates the difficulties in certain situations of determining whether a person is providing content or is merely disseminating the content of another. If a person is deemed the content provider, then § 230 immunity does not apply, as § 230 is designed to immunize a person from being liable for disseminating the content of others. In *Batzel,* is Cremers the content provider because he decided to forward the e-mail? Or is Smith the content provider because he wrote the e-mail?

Suppose Cremers has a blog about stolen art. Smith is interested in spreading the rumor about the stolen art on Cremers's blog. Consider the following situations and examine whether Cremers would have § 230 immunity under the majority's rule and also under Judge Gould's:

(a) Cremers's blog allows anybody to post comments. Smith posts a comment about the rumor on Cremers's blog. Batzel wants Cremers to delete the comment, but Cremers refuses to do so.

(b) Cremers has a comment moderation system on his blog where he must approve comments before they are published on his blog. Smith posts the stolen art comment and Cremers approves it, whereupon it is published on the blog.

(c) Smith e-mails Cremers and tells him about the stolen art rumor. Instead of posting the e-mail itself, Cremers writes a blog post about the rumor in his own words and posts it.

(d) Smith calls Cremers and tells him the rumor about the stolen art. Cremers writes a post about the rumor.

Is there any meaningful difference between the above situations and the way that Cremers disseminated Smith's e-mail to the listserv? Should Cremers's liability be different in any of the above situations?

5. *Wikipedia.* Wikipedia is an online encyclopedia that anybody can edit. It has millions of entries and is widely used and cited. What are the legal consequences when a Wikipedia entry is defamatory?

A notable case occurred in 2005 involving John Seigenthaler, a former assistant to Attorney General Bobby Kennedy during the Kennedy Administration. His Wikipedia entry falsely accused him of being involved in President John F. Kennedy's assassination. In an article in *USA Today,* Seigenthaler wrote:

I have no idea whose sick mind conceived the false, malicious "biography" that appeared under my name for 132 days on Wikipedia, the popular, online, free encyclopedia whose authors are unknown and virtually untraceable.[82]

Eventually, the anonymous person who wrote the defamatory statement was identified, and he apologized. If Seigenthaler sued Wikipedia for defamation,

---

[82] John Seigenthaler, *A False Wikipedia "Biography,"* USA Today, Nov. 29, 2005.

would § 230 provide Wikipedia with immunity? Consider the views of Ken Myers on this topic:

> The Wikipedia community is self-consciously inclusive, designating all of its contributors as "Wikipedians." Presumably, this inclusiveness fosters the cooperative atmosphere critical to Wikipedia's success. However, if *all* members of the Wikipedia community — that is, all contributors — are considered part of the Wikipedia "entity," then it would, by definition and by operation of the third prong, not be eligible for § 230(c)(1) immunity because Wikipedia would be the site's only contributor — there could be no "[]other information content provider." . . .
>
> Wikipedia would argue that, for purposes of § 230(f)(3), only employees of the Wikimedia Foundation should be considered as part of the Wikipedia "entity." However, "the fact that work is performed gratuitously does not relieve a principal of liability."[83]

To the extent that websites like Wikipedia create hierarchies of users, with some having greater editorial powers, does this alter immunity for the actions of the users at the top of the hierarchy?

(c) First Amendment Limitations

NEW YORK TIMES CO. V. SULLIVAN

376 U.S. 254 (1964)

[L.B. Sullivan, one of the three elected Commissioners of Montgomery, Alabama, sued four African-American clergymen and the *New York Times* for libel. Sullivan claimed that a full-page advertisement in the *New York Times* on March 29, 1960, entitled "Heed Their Rising Voices" defamed him. The advertisement discussed the civil rights movement and the wave of terror against the nonviolent protest. It was signed by various clergymen in Southern cities, including the four clergymen named in the lawsuit.

Two paragraphs of the ten in the advertisement were the basis of Sullivan's libel claim.

> . . . In Montgomery, Alabama, after students sang "My Country, 'Tis of Thee" on the State Capitol steps, their leaders were expelled from school, and truckloads of police armed with shotguns and tear-gas ringed the Alabama State College Campus. When the entire student body protested to state authorities by refusing to re-register, their dining hall was padlocked in an attempt to starve them into submission. . . .
>
> Again and again the Southern violators have answered Dr. King's peaceful protests with intimidation and violence. They have bombed his home almost killing his wife and child. They have assaulted his person. They have arrested him seven times — for "speeding," "loitering" and similar "offenses." And now they have charged him with "perjury" — a felony under which they could imprison him for ten years. . . .

---

[83] Ken S. Myers, *Wikimmunity: Fitting the Communications Decency Act to Wikipedia*, 20 Harv. J.L. & Tech. 163, 188-90 (2006).

Although Sullivan was never mentioned by name, he claimed that the word "police" implicated him because he supervised the police department. Although Sullivan made no effort to prove he suffered actual pecuniary loss as a result of the alleged libel, a Montgomery County jury awarded Sullivan damages of $500,000, the full amount claimed against all the petitioners, and the Supreme Court of Alabama affirmed.]

BRENNAN, J. . . . Under Alabama law as applied in this case, a publication is "libelous per se" if the words "tend to injure a person . . . in his reputation" or to "bring (him) into public contempt"; the trial court stated that the standard was met if the words are such as to "injure him in his public office, or impute misconduct to him in his office, or want of official integrity, or want of fidelity to a public trust. . . ." The jury must find that the words were published "of and concerning" the plaintiff, but where the plaintiff is a public official his place in the governmental hierarchy is sufficient evidence to support a finding that his reputation has been affected by statements that reflect upon the agency of which he is in charge. Once "libel per se" has been established, the defendant has no defense as to stated facts unless he can persuade the jury that they were true in all their particulars. His privilege of "fair comment" for expressions of opinion depends on the truth of the facts upon which the comment is based. Unless he can discharge the burden of proving truth, general damages are presumed, and may be awarded without proof of pecuniary injury. A showing of actual malice is apparently a prerequisite to recovery of punitive damages, and the defendant may in any event forestall a punitive award by a retraction meeting the statutory requirements. Good motives and belief in truth do not negate an inference of malice, but are relevant only in mitigation of punitive damages if the jury chooses to accord them weight.

The question before us is whether this rule of liability, as applied to an action brought by a public official against critics of his official conduct, abridges the freedom of speech and of the press that is guaranteed by the First and Fourteenth Amendments.

Respondent relies heavily, as did the Alabama courts, on statements of this Court to the effect that the Constitution does not protect libelous publications. . . . Like insurrection, contempt, advocacy of unlawful acts, breach of the peace, obscenity, solicitation of legal business, and the various other formulae for the repression of expression that have been challenged in this Court, libel can claim no talismanic immunity from constitutional limitations. It must be measured by standards that satisfy the First Amendment.

The general proposition that freedom of expression upon public questions is secured by the First Amendment has long been settled by our decisions. . . .

. . . [W]e consider this case against the background of a profound national commitment to the principle that debate on public issues should be uninhibited, robust, and wide-open, and that it may well include vehement, caustic, and sometimes unpleasantly sharp attacks on government and public officials. The present advertisement, as an expression of grievance and protest on one of the major public issues of our time, would seem clearly to qualify for the constitutional protection. The question is whether it forfeits that protection by the falsity of some of its factual statements and by its alleged defamation of respondent.

Authoritative interpretations of the First Amendment guarantees have consistently refused to recognize an exception for any test of truth — whether administered by judges, juries, or administrative officials — and especially one that puts the burden of proving truth on the speaker. The constitutional protection does not turn upon "the truth, popularity, or social utility of the ideas and beliefs which are offered." . . .

That erroneous statement is inevitable in free debate, and that it must be protected if the freedoms of expression are to have the "breathing space" that they "need to survive." . . .

A rule compelling the critic of official conduct to guarantee the truth of all his factual assertions — and to do so on pain of libel judgments virtually unlimited in amount — leads to a comparable "self-censorship." . . . Under such a rule, would-be critics of official conduct may be deterred from voicing their criticism, even though it is believed to be true and even though it is in fact true, because of doubt whether it can be proved in court or fear of the expense of having to do so. They tend to make only statements which "steer far wider of the unlawful zone." The rule thus dampens the vigor and limits the variety of public debate. It is inconsistent with the First and Fourteenth Amendments.

The constitutional guarantees require, we think, a federal rule that prohibits a public official from recovering damages for a defamatory falsehood relating to his official conduct unless he proves that the statement was made with "actual malice" — that is, with knowledge that it was false or with reckless disregard of whether it was false or not. . . .

We hold today that the Constitution delimits a State's power to award damages for libel in actions brought by public officials against critics of their official conduct. Since this is such an action, the rule requiring proof of actual malice is applicable. While Alabama law apparently requires proof of actual malice for an award of punitive damages, where general damages are concerned malice is "presumed." Such a presumption is inconsistent with the federal rule. Since the trial judge did not instruct the jury to differentiate between general and punitive damages, it may be that the verdict was wholly an award of one or the other. But it is impossible to know, in view of the general verdict returned. Because of this uncertainty, the judgment must be reversed and the case remanded. . . .

NOTES & QUESTIONS

1. *Should Defamation Have Survived?* Justices Black, Douglas, and Goldberg would have gone further, eliminating all defamation liability for public officials. In other words, public officials could not sue for defamation even if the defamatory statement were made with actual malice. As Justice Goldberg explained, the right to criticize public officials is unconditional and "should not depend upon a probing by the jury of the motivation of the citizen or press." Should the court have barred all defamation actions by public officials?

   More broadly, should the court have held that all defamation law is unconstitutional? Consider Justice Holmes's dissent in *Abrams v. United States*, 250 U.S. 616, 630 (1919):

But when men have realized that time has upset many fighting faiths, they may come to believe even more than they believe the very foundations of their own conduct that the ultimate good desired is better reached by free trade in ideas — that the best test of truth is the power of the thought to get itself accepted in the competition of the market, and that truth is the only ground upon which their wishes safely can be carried out. That at any rate is the theory of our Constitution.

If Holmes is right, and the marketplace of ideas will result in the truth eventually winning out, then is defamation law even necessary?[84]

2. *Actual Malice.* The actual malice standard is a subjective one. As Randall Bezanson describes it:

The actual malice inquiry is avowedly focused on the subjective state of mind of the publisher at the time of publication. It asks only whether falsity was calculated or whether the publisher's decision was sufficiently indifferent to likely falsity that the publication decision should not be respected under the First Amendment. Actual malice, in short, reveals a frame of mind, an animating intention for the publication, that belies any significant publisher concern for the audience or for the function being performed in the selection and presentation of information, or news. . . .

In practice, actual malice is very difficult for plaintiffs to establish. Bezanson observes:

In making actual malice determinations, state courts attempt to determine the speaker's subjective state of mind by two primary means. First, courts examine the speaker's observable conduct at the time of the speech act, viewing such outward manifestations as a potential insight into the speaker's state of mind. . . . The second means by which courts attempt to determine the speaker's state of mind is through the personal testimony of the speaker. State courts grant considerable weight to the speaker's own reflective statements concerning his or her belief as to the truth of the speech at the time the speech judgment was made.[85]

3. *Public Figures.* Subsequently, the Court extended the approach in *New York Times* to persons who were not public officials but who were "public figures" — people "involved in issues in which the public has a justified and important interest." *Curtis Publishing Co. v. Butts*, 388 U.S. 130 (1967).

GERTZ V. ROBERT WELCH, INC.

418 U.S. 323 (1974)

[In 1968, Nuccio, a Chicago policeman, shot and killed Nelson, a youth. Nuccio was prosecuted and convicted for murder in the second degree. The Nelson

---

[84] For more background about *New York Times v. Sullivan*, see Anthony Lewis, *Make No Law: The Sullivan Case and the First Amendment* (1991).

[85] Randall P. Bezanson, *The Developing Law of Editorial Judgment*, 78 Neb. L. Rev. 754, 774-75, 763-64 (1999).

family retained attorney Elmer Gertz to represent them in civil litigation against Nuccio.

Robert Welch, Inc. published *American Opinion*, a monthly magazine representing the views of the John Birch Society. The magazine had been warning of a national conspiracy to discredit local police forces and create a national police force as a step toward establishing a Communist dictatorship. In 1969, the magazine published an article about the murder trial of Officer Nuccio, alleging that he was framed as part of the Communist campaign against the police. Among other things, the article portrayed Gertz as the mastermind of the frame-up. It stated that Gertz was a "Leninist" and a "Communist-fronter," that Gertz belonged to Marxist and Socialist organizations, and that Gertz had a criminal record. All of these statements were false. Gertz sued for libel and won a jury verdict of $50,000. The district court, however, decided that the *New York Times* standard should apply and entered judgment for Robert Welch, Inc.]

POWELL, J. . . . The principal issue in this case is whether a newspaper or broadcaster that publishes defamatory falsehoods about an individual who is neither a public official nor a public figure may claim a constitutional privilege against liability for the injury inflicted by those statements. . . .

The legitimate state interest underlying the law of libel is the compensation of individuals for the harm inflicted on them by defamatory falsehood. We would not lightly require the State to abandon this purpose, for, as Mr. Justice Stewart has reminded us, the individual's right to the protection of his own good name

> reflects no more than our basic concept of the essential dignity and worth of every human being — a concept at the root of any decent system of ordered liberty. The protection of private personality, like the protection of life itself, is left primarily to the individual States under the Ninth and Tenth Amendments. But this does not mean that the right is entitled to any less recognition by this Court as a basic of our constitutional system. *Rosenblatt v. Baer*, 383 U.S. 75, 92 (1966) (concurring opinion). . . .

. . . [W]e have no difficulty in distinguishing among defamation plaintiffs. The first remedy of any victim of defamation is self-help — using available opportunities to contradict the lie or correct the error and thereby to minimize its adverse impact on reputation. Public officials and public figures usually enjoy significantly greater access to the channels of effective communication and hence have a more realistic opportunity to counteract false statements then private individuals normally enjoy. Private individuals are therefore more vulnerable to injury, and the state interest in protecting them is correspondingly greater.

More important than the likelihood that private individuals will lack effective opportunities for rebuttal, there is a compelling normative consideration underlying the distinction between public and private defamation plaintiffs. An individual who decides to seek governmental office must accept certain necessary consequences of that involvement in public affairs. He runs the risk of closer public scrutiny than might otherwise be the case. And society's interest in the officers of government is not strictly limited to the formal discharge of official duties. As the Court pointed out in *Garrison v. Louisiana*, the public's interest extends to "anything which might touch on an official's fitness for office. . . . Few personal attributes are more germane to fitness for office than dishonesty, malfeasance, or improper motivation, even though these characteristics may also affect the official's private character."

Those classed as public figures stand in a similar position. Hypothetically, it may be possible for someone to become a public figure through no purposeful action of his own, but the instances of truly involuntary public figures must be exceedingly rare. For the most part those who attain this status have assumed roles of especial prominence in the affairs of society. Some occupy positions of such persuasive power and influence that they are deemed public figures for all purposes. More commonly, those classed as public figures have thrust themselves to the forefront of particular public controversies in order to influence the resolution of the issues involved. In either event, they invite attention and comment.

Even if the foregoing generalities do not obtain in every instance, the communications media are entitled to act on the assumption that public officials and public figures have voluntarily exposed themselves to increased risk of injury from defamatory falsehood concerning them. No such assumption is justified with respect to a private individual. He has not accepted public office or assumed an "influential role in ordering society." He has relinquished no part of his interest in the protection of his own good name, and consequently he has a more compelling call on the courts for redress of injury inflicted by defamatory falsehood. Thus, private individuals are not only more vulnerable to injury than public officials and public figures; they are also more deserving of recovery.

For these reasons we conclude that the States should retain substantial latitude in their efforts to enforce a legal remedy for defamatory falsehood injurious to the reputation of a private individual. The extension of the *New York Times* test . . . would abridge this legitimate state interest to a degree that we find unacceptable. . . .

We hold that, so long as they do not impose liability without fault, the States may define for themselves the appropriate standard of liability for a publisher or broadcaster of defamatory falsehood injurious to a private individual. . . .

. . . Under the traditional rules pertaining to actions for libel, the existence of injury is presumed from the fact of publication. Juries may award substantial sums as compensation for supposed damage to reputation without any proof that such harm actually occurred. The largely uncontrolled discretion of juries to award damages where there is no loss unnecessarily compounds the potential of any system of liability for defamatory falsehood to inhibit the vigorous exercise of First Amendment freedoms. Additionally, the doctrine of presumed damages invites juries to punish unpopular opinion rather than to compensate individuals for injury sustained by the publication of a false fact. More to the point, the States have no substantial interest in securing for plaintiffs such as this petitioner gratuitous awards of money damages far in excess of any actual injury. . . .

. . . It is necessary to restrict defamation plaintiffs who do not prove knowledge of falsity or reckless disregard for the truth to compensation for actual injury. . . . Suffice it to say that actual injury is not limited to out-of-pocket loss. Indeed, the more customary types of actual harm inflicted by defamatory falsehood include impairment of reputation and standing in the community, personal humiliation, and mental anguish and suffering. . . .

We also find no justification for allowing awards of punitive damages against publishers and broadcasters held liable under state-defined standards of liability for defamation. In most jurisdictions jury discretion over the amounts awarded is limited only by the gentle rule that they not be excessive. Consequently, juries assess punitive damages in wholly unpredictable amounts bearing no necessary relation to the actual harm caused. And they remain free to use their discretion selectively to punish expressions of unpopular views. Like the doctrine of presumed damages, jury discretion to award punitive damages unnecessarily exacerbates the danger of media self-censorship, but, unlike the former rule, punitive damages are wholly irrelevant to the state interest that justifies a negligence standard for private defamation actions. They are not compensation for injury. Instead, they are private fines levied by civil juries to punish reprehensible conduct and to deter its future occurrence. In short, the private defamation plaintiff who establishes liability under a less demanding standard than that stated by *New York Times* may recover only such damages as are sufficient to compensate him for actual injury.

Notwithstanding our refusal to extend the *New York Times* privilege to defamation of private individuals, respondent contends that we should affirm the judgment below on the ground that petitioner is either a public official or a public figure. . . .

. . . In some instances an individual may achieve such pervasive fame or notoriety that he becomes a public figure for all purposes and in all contexts. More commonly, an individual voluntarily injects himself or is drawn into a particular public controversy and thereby becomes a public figure for a limited range of issues. In either case such persons assume special prominence in the resolution of public questions.

Petitioner has long been active in community and professional affairs. He has served as an officer of local civic groups and of various professional organizations, and he has published several books and articles on legal subjects. Although petitioner was consequently well known in some circles, he had achieved no general fame or notoriety in the community. None of the prospective jurors called at the trial had ever heard of petitioner prior to this litigation, and respondent offered no proof that this response was atypical of the local population. We would not lightly assume that a citizen's participation in community and professional affairs rendered him a public figure for all purposes. Absent clear evidence of general fame or notoriety in the community, and pervasive involvement in the affairs of society, an individual should not be deemed a public personality for all aspects of his life. It is preferable to reduce the public-figure question to a more meaningful context by looking to the nature and extent of an individual's participation in the particular controversy giving rise to the defamation.

In this context it is plain that petitioner was not a public figure. He played a minimal role at the coroner's inquest, and his participation related solely to his representation of a private client. He took no part in the criminal prosecution of Officer Nuccio. Moreover, he never discussed either the criminal or civil litigation with the press and was never quoted as having done so. He plainly did not thrust himself into the vortex of this public issue, nor did he engage the public's attention in an attempt to influence its outcome. We are persuaded that the trial court did not err in refusing to characterize petitioner as a public figure for the purpose of this litigation. . . .

NOTES & QUESTIONS

1. *Public vs. Private Figures.* What distinguishes a public from a private figure? In *Time, Inc. v. Firestone*, 424 U.S. 448 (1976), Mary Alice Firestone and her husband had a messy divorce. The court issued a judgment granting the divorce, stating that according to the testimony of the husband, the wife's "extramarital escapades . . . were bizarre and of an amatory nature which would have made Dr. Freud's hair curl. Other testimony . . . would indicate that [the husband] was guilty of bounding from one bedpartner to another with the erotic zest of a satyr. The court is inclined to discount much of this testimony as unreliable." *Time* magazine published the following article in its "Milestones" section the following week:

> DIVORCED. By Russell A. Firestone Jr., 41, heir to the tire fortune: Mary Alice Sullivan Firestone, 32, his third wife; a onetime Palm Beach schoolteacher; on grounds of extreme cruelty and adultery; after six years of marriage, one son; in West Palm Beach, Fla. The 17-month intermittent trial produced enough testimony of extramarital adventures on both sides, said the judge, "to make Dr. Freud's hair curl."

Mary Firestone sued for libel. When the case ended up in the U.S. Supreme Court, the issue was whether Firestone was a public or private figure. According to the Court:

> Petitioner contends that because the Firestone divorce was characterized by the Florida Supreme Court as a "cause celebre," it must have been a public controversy and respondent must be considered a public figure. But in so doing petitioner seeks to equate "public controversy" with all controversies of interest to the public. . . .
>
> Dissolution of a marriage through judicial proceedings is not the sort of "public controversy" referred to in *Gertz*, even though the marital difficulties of extremely wealthy individuals may be of interest to some portion of the reading public. Nor did respondent freely choose to publicize issues as to the propriety of her married life. She was compelled to go to court by the State in order to obtain legal release from the bonds of matrimony. We have said that in such an instance "(r)esort to the judicial process . . . is no more voluntary in a realistic sense than that of the defendant called upon to defend his interests in court." . . . She assumed no "special prominence in the resolution of public questions." *Gertz*, 418 U.S., at 351. We hold respondent was not a "public figure" for the purpose of determining the constitutional protection afforded petitioner's report of the factual and legal basis for her divorce.

In *Atlanta Journal-Constitution v. Jewell*, 555 S.E.2d 175 (Ga. Ct. App. 2001), Richard Jewell, a security guard in Olympic Park during the 1996 Olympics in Atlanta, spotted a suspicious unattended package and helped to evacuate the area. The package contained a bomb, and Jewell was initially recognized as a hero for helping prevent the terrorist attack. The FBI, however, believed that Jewell might have planted the bomb to make himself into a hero, and the FBI's suspicions of Jewell were leaked to the press. The *Atlanta Journal-Constitution* published an article entitled "FBI Suspects 'Hero' Guard May Have Planted Bomb." The FBI investigation eventually cleared Jewell. However, during the interim, Jewell's life was turned upside down, and he could not seek employment or even go out in public without being mobbed by reporters. Jewell sued the *Journal-Constitution* for defamation. The court held that Jewell was a voluntary limited-purpose public figure:

> In *Silvester v. American Broadcasting Cos.*, 839 F.2d 1491 (11th Cir. 1988), the Eleventh Circuit adopted a three-prong test to determine whether a person is a limited-purpose public figure. Under this test, the court must isolate the public controversy, examine the plaintiff's involvement in the controversy, and determine whether the alleged defamation was germane to the plaintiff's participation in the controversy. Whether a person is a public figure, general or limited, is a question of law for the court to resolve. . . .
>
> Jewell's actions show that he voluntarily assumed a position of influence in the controversy. Jewell granted ten interviews and one photo shoot in the three days between the bombing and the reopening of the park, mostly to prominent members of the national press. . . .
>
> Jewell was initially drawn into the controversy unwillingly and thereafter assumed a prominent position as to its outcome. Jewell did not reject any role in the public controversy debate, was a prominent figure in the coverage of the controversy, and, whatever his reticence regarding his media appearances, encountered them voluntarily. . . .
>
> Certainly, the information reported regarding Jewell's character was germane to Jewell's participation in the controversy over the Olympic Park's safety. A public figure's talents, education, experience, and motives are relevant to the public's decision to listen to him. The articles and the challenged statements within them dealt with Jewell's status as a suspect in the bombing and his law enforcement background. . . .
>
> Whether he liked it or not, Jewell became a central figure in the specific public controversy with respect to which he was allegedly defamed: the controversy over park safety. . . .

2. ***Matters of Private Concern: The* Dun & Bradstreet *Case.*** After *Gertz*, a plurality of the Court examined whether the *Gertz* rule would apply when, in contrast to the situation in *Gertz*, the alleged defamatory statements did not involve a matter of public concern. In *Dun & Bradstreet, Inc. v. Greenmoss Builders, Inc.*, 472 U.S. 749 (1985), Dun & Bradstreet, a credit reporting agency, provided an erroneous report about the financial condition of Greenmoss Builders. Upon learning of the defamatory report, the president of Greenmoss called Dun & Bradstreet and asked for a correction and a list of all those to whom Dun & Bradstreet had sent the report. Dun & Bradstreet corrected the report but did not inform Greenmoss of the list of recipients of the report. Greenmoss sued for defamation, winning $50,000 in compensatory or presumed damages and $300,000 in punitive damages. The Court held that this did not involve a matter of public concern and that therefore the *Gertz* rule should not apply:

The First Amendment interest . . . is less important than the one weighed in Gertz. We have long recognized that not all speech is of equal First Amendment importance. It is speech on "'matters of public concern'" that is "at the heart of the First Amendment's protection." . . .

In contrast, speech on matters of purely private concern is of less First Amendment concern. As a number of state courts, including the court below, have recognized, the role of the Constitution in regulating state libel law is far more limited when the concerns that activated *New York Times* and *Gertz* are absent. . . .

While such speech is not totally unprotected by the First Amendment, its protections are less stringent. In *Gertz*, we found that the state interest in awarding presumed and punitive damages was not "substantial" in view of their effect on speech at the core of First Amendment concern. . . . In light of the reduced constitutional value of speech involving no matters of public concern, we hold that the state interest adequately supports awards of presumed and punitive damages — even absent a showing of "actual malice." . . .

2. FALSE LIGHT

(a) Introduction

PUBLICITY PLACING PERSON IN FALSE LIGHT

Restatement (Second) of Torts § 652E

One who gives publicity to a matter concerning another that places the other before the public in a false light is subject to liability to the other for invasion of his privacy, if

(a) the false light in which the other was placed would be highly offensive to a reasonable person, and

(b) the actor had knowledge of or acted in reckless disregard as to the falsity of the publicized matter and the false light in which the other would be placed.

NOTES & QUESTIONS

1. *False Light vs. Defamation.* False light is similar in many respects to defamation. Both torts protect against material false statements. However, defamation requires some form of reputational injury (although, once shown, one can collect for emotional distress). False light, on the other hand, can compensate exclusively for emotional distress.

   According to the Restatement: "It is enough that he is given unreasonable and highly objectionable publicity that attributes to him characteristics, conduct or beliefs that are false, and so is placed before the public in a false position. When this is the case and the matter attributed to the plaintiff is not defamatory, the rule here stated affords a different remedy, not available in an action for defamation." Comment (b). Since false light does not require reputational harm, a plaintiff can recover for false light that even improves her reputation.[86] While defamation concerns one's status in the community, false light concerns one's peace of mind. As Bryan Lasswell explains, the "false light tort, to the extent distinct from the tort of defamation . . . rests on an awareness that people who are made to seem pathetic or ridiculous may be shunned, and not just people who are thought to be dishonest or incompetent or immoral."[87]

Another difference between false light and defamation is that false light requires a wider communication of the information. False light requires "publicity," which must be made to the public at large. Defamation requires "publication," which means that the communication merely requires communication to another person.

Can you think of a hypothetical of a false light claim that also is not defamatory? The challenge is that the scenario would need to involve something that is highly offensive yet not injurious to one's reputation.

3. ***Damages for False Light and Defamation.*** In *Braun v. Flynt*, 726 F.2d 245 (5th Cir. 1984), Jeannie Braun worked at an amusement park and performed a routine with "Ralph the Diving Pig." The pig dove into the pool and was fed by Braun from a milk bottle. One of Larry Flynt's publications, *Chic*, a pornographic magazine, obtained a photograph of Braun's act. The picture appeared in a section of the magazine called "Chic Thrills," implying that something kinky was going on. When Braun saw the photograph, she was mortified. She could not return to work and suffered from depression. She sued Flynt for defamation and false light. A jury awarded her actual and punitive damages for both causes of action. Flynt appealed, arguing among other things that liability was barred by the First Amendment. The court, applying the *Gertz* rule, concluded that Braun was not a public figure and that the First Amendment did not bar her recovery. However, the court concluded that she could not recover damages for both false light and defamation. Accordingly, the case was remanded for a new trial on damages.

3. ***Forms of False Light.*** An illustration of the type of misleading statement that can give rise to a false light action is when a mostly true story is somewhat embellished. *See Varnish v. Best Medium Publishing Co.*, 405 F.2d 608 (2d Cir. 1968) (viable false light action for false facts about the relationship between husband and wife who killed herself and their three children). Another example of a false light claim is when one's photograph is used out of context. *See, e.g., Thompson v. Close-up, Inc.*, 98 N.Y.S.2d 300 (1950) (article on drug dealing using the plaintiff's photo); *Holmes v. Curtis Publishing Co.*, 303 F. Supp. 522 (D.S.C. 1969) (use of plaintiff's photo with caption that plaintiff was a high-stakes gambler); *Morrell v. Forbes, Inc.*, 603 F. Supp. 1305 (D. Mass. 1985) (photo used in connection with article about organized crime).

---

[86] *See, e.g.*, Nathan E. Ray, *Let There Be False Light: Resisting the Growing Trend Against an Important Tort*, 84 Minn. L. Rev. 713, 735 (2000).

[87] Bryan R. Lasswell, *In Defense of False Light: Why False Light Must Remain a Viable Cause of Action*, 34 S. Tex. L. Rev. 149, 176 (1993).

(b) First Amendment Limitations

TIME, INC. V. HILL
385 U.S. 374 (1967)

[In 1952, the Hill family was held prisoner in their home for 19 hours by three escaped convicts. The family escaped unharmed and were treated courteously by the convicts. The convicts were later killed by police during their apprehension. The story made the front page news. The Hill family tried hard to remain out of the spotlight. Nevertheless, the Hill family's experience was written about in a novel by Joseph Hayes called *The Desperate Hours*. In contrast to the actual events, the book depicted the convicts beating the father and son and making a verbal sexual insult to the daughter. A Broadway play and a movie were made based on the book. In 1955, *Life* magazine published an article entitled "True Crime Inspires Tense Play." The article stated that "Americans all over the country read about the desperate ordeal of the James Hill family" and "read about it in Joseph Hayes's novel, *The Desperate Hours*, inspired by the family's experience." The article then stated: "Now they can see the story re-enacted in Hayes's Broadway play based on the book." Pictures accompanying the article displayed scenes from the play depicting the son being beaten and the daughter biting the hand of a convict. The *Life* magazine photographs were taken in the Hills' former home, where they had been held hostage. The Hills sued under §§ 50-51 of the New York Civil Rights Law, contending that the *Life* article gave the false impression that the play accurately depicted the Hills' experience. A jury awarded the Hills $50,000 compensatory and $25,000 punitive damages.]

BRENNAN, J. . . . In *New York Times Co. v. Sullivan*, we held that the Constitution delimits a State's power to award damages for libel in actions brought by public officials against critics of their official conduct. Factual error, content defamatory of official reputation, or both, are insufficient for an award of damages for false statements unless actual malice — knowledge that the statements are false or in reckless disregard of the truth — is alleged and proved. . . .

. . . We hold that the constitutional protections for speech and press preclude the application of the New York statute to redress false reports of matters of public interest in the absence of proof that the defendant published the report with knowledge of its falsity or in reckless disregard of the truth.

The guarantees for speech and press are not the preserve of political expression or comment upon public affairs, essential as those are to healthy government. One need only pick up any newspaper or magazine to comprehend the vast range of published matter which exposes persons to public view, both private citizens and public officials. Exposure of the self to others in varying degrees is a concomitant of life in a civilized community. The risk of this exposure is an essential incident of life in a society which places a primary value on freedom of speech and of press. "Freedom of discussion, if it would fulfill its historic function in this nation, must embrace all issues about which information is needed or appropriate to enable the members of society to cope with the exigencies of their period." . . . We have no doubt that the subject of the Life article, the opening of a new play linked to an actual incident, is a matter of public interest. "The line between the informing and the entertaining is too elusive for the protection of . . . (freedom of the press)." Erroneous statement is no less inevitable in such a case than in the case of comment upon public affairs, and in both, if innocent or merely negligent, ". . . it must be protected if the freedoms of expression are to have the 'breathing space' that they 'need . . . to survive' . . . ." *New York Times Co. v. Sullivan.* . . . We create a grave risk of serious impairment of the indispensable service of a free press in a free society if we saddle the press with the impossible burden of verifying to a certainty the facts associated in news articles with a person's name, picture or portrait, particularly as related to nondefamatory matter. Even negligence would be a most elusive standard, especially when the content of the speech itself affords no warning of prospective harm to another through falsity. A negligence test would place on the press the intolerable burden of guessing how a jury might assess the reasonableness of steps taken by it to verify the accuracy of every reference to a name, picture or portrait.

In this context, sanctions against either innocent or negligent misstatement would present a grave hazard of discouraging the press from exercising the constitutional guarantees. Those guarantees are not for the benefit of the press so much as for the benefit of all of us. A broadly defined freedom of the press assures the maintenance of our political system and an open society. Fear of large verdicts in damage suits for innocent or merely negligent misstatement, even fear of the expense involved in their defense, must inevitably cause publishers to "steer . . . wider of the unlawful zone," *New York Times Co. v. Sullivan*, and thus "create the danger that the legitimate utterance will be penalized."

But the constitutional guarantees can tolerate sanctions against calculated falsehood without significant impairment of their essential function. We held in *New York Times* that calculated falsehood enjoyed no immunity in the case of alleged defamation of a public official concerning his official conduct. Similarly, calculated falsehood should enjoy no immunity in the situation here presented us. . . .

Turning to the facts of the present case, the proofs reasonably would support either a jury finding of innocent or merely negligent misstatement by Life, or a finding that Life portrayed the play as a reenactment of the Hill family's experience reckless of the truth or with actual knowledge that the portrayal was false. . . . [The jury instructions were thus defective because they did not instruct the jury that liability could only be found against *Life* if *Life* acted in reckless disregard for the truth or with actual knowledge that the play was false.]

The judgment of the Court of Appeals is set aside and the case is remanded for further proceedings not inconsistent with this opinion. . . .

NOTES & QUESTIONS

1. *An Inside Look at* **Time, Inc. v. Hill.** In *Newsworthy*, Samantha Barbas provides interesting background about the case: "The sudden reappearance of the hostage incident in their lives traumatized [the Hills] by forcing them to relive it, remember it, and think about it." In his professional life, James Hill, the father, "became an object of spectacle and curiosity." As for Elizabeth, the

publicity following the incident had already caused her to become depressed, but after the *Life* magazine article, her "mental state plummeted." Elizabeth Hill committed suicide in August 1971. Originally, the Court voted 6-3 in favor of the Hills, with Chief Justice Earl Warren assigning the majority opinion to Justice Abe Fortas. But after an initial and then a revised draft of Fortas opinion were circulated among the Justices, Justice Hugo Black pushed to have a rehearing of the case, and he ultimately convinced a majority of the Court to join him in finding for *Time*.[88]

2. *Nixon at the Supreme Court.* Before the Supreme Court, the Hills were represented by Richard Nixon, the future President, then in private practice. In a memoir, Leonard Garment, a long-time Nixon advisor and his co-counsel on *Time v. Hill*, noted that this was Nixon's first argument in any appellate court; Nixon "sounded like a polished professional of the bar — his footing confident, his language lawyer-like, his organization clear."[89]

3. **Hill** *After* **Gertz.** *Hill* was decided after *New York Times v. Sullivan* but before *Gertz*. *Gertz* established that private figures do not have to prove actual malice. Do false light actions involving private figures also have to prove actual malice? The Restatement codifies the actual malice standard as an element of false light, but it notes in a comment that if "*Time v. Hill* is modified along the lines of *Gertz v. Robert Welch*, then the reckless-disregard rule would apparently apply if the plaintiff is a public official or public figure and the negligence rule will apply to other plaintiffs." Restatement (Second) of Torts § 652E comment d. Courts are split on the issue. *See Braun v. Flynt*, 726 F.2d 245 (5th Cir. 1984) (applying *Gertz*); *Dietz v. Wometco West Michigan TV*, 407 N.W.2d 649 (Mich. App. 1987) (applying *Gertz*); *Dodrill v. Arkansas Democrat*, 590 S.W.2d 840 (Ark. 1979) (applying *New York Times*); *Schifano v. Greene County Greyhound Park, Inc.*, 624 So. 2d 178 (Ala. 1993) (applying *New York Times*).

3. INFLICTION OF EMOTIONAL DISTRESS

Another tort remedy for the dissemination of false or misleading information is the tort of infliction of emotional distress. This tort may also serve as a remedy to the disclosure of true information. As defined by the Restatement (Second) of Torts § 46, the tort requires:

> One who by extreme and outrageous conduct intentionally or recklessly causes severe emotional distress to another is subject to liability for such emotional distress, and if bodily harm to the other results from it, for such bodily harm.

The tort has some significant limitations as a remedy for privacy infringements. First, it requires "extreme and outrageous conduct," which is conduct significantly outside the bounds of propriety. This is quite a high bar for a

---

[88] Samantha Barbas, *Newsworthy: The Supreme Court Battle Over Privacy and Press Freedom* 2 (2017).

[89] Leonard Garment, *Crazy Rhythm: From Brooklyn and Jazz to Nixon's White House, Watergate, and Beyond* (1997).

plaintiff to leap over. Second, it requires "severe emotional distress," and many privacy violations may not be viewed by courts as causing such a high level of psychological turmoil. For example, in *DeGregario v. CBS*, 473 N.Y.S.2d 922 (N.Y. Sup. Ct. 1984), a news segment called "Couples in New York" included video of two construction workers, a male and a female, holding hands. Each was married or engaged to another person. After the video was shot, the workers asked the television crew not to include them in the segment, but they were included anyway. The court rejected their infliction of emotional distress claim because "broadcasting a film depicting unnamed couples engaging in romantic conduct on a public street . . . in a news report about romance cannot be said to be unusual conduct transcending the norms tolerated by a decent society."

In a similar fashion to the privacy torts, the tort of infliction of emotional distress is subject to First Amendment restrictions. In *Hustler Magazine v. Falwell*, 485 U.S. 46 (1988), an issue of *Hustler* magazine featured a parody using nationally known minister Jerry Falwell's name and photo. The parody, entitled "Jerry Falwell Talks About His First Time," was patterned after a series of ads for a brand of liquor which interviewed celebrities about their "first times" trying the liquor (but playing on the sexual double meaning). In a similar layout, *Hustler*'s parody interview with Falwell had him drunk and engaging in incest with his mother. In small print, the parody contained the disclaimer, "ad parody — not to be taken seriously." Falwell sued for, among other things, intentional infliction of emotional distress. This issue made it to the U.S. Supreme Court, where the Court confronted the task of defining whether the First Amendment limitations that applied to defamation and false light should also be applied to intentional infliction of emotional distress.

The Supreme Court held that "public figures and public officials may not recover for the tort of intentional infliction of emotional distress by reason of publications such as the one here at issue without showing in addition that the publication contains a false statement of fact which was made with "actual malice," *i.e.*, with knowledge that the statement was false or with reckless disregard as to whether or not it was true." The Court reasoned that "such a standard is necessary to give adequate 'breathing space' to the freedoms protected by the First Amendment." The critical factual finding behind the *Hustler* decision was a decision of the jury when the case had gone to trial. As the Supreme Court explained, the jury had decided "the Hustler ad parody could not 'reasonably be understood as describing actual facts about [respondent] or actual events in which [he] participated.'" And for the *Hustler* Court, the ad parody was like a historic series of political cartoons and satires, such as an "early cartoon portraying George Washington as an ass."

Parody also need not have a disclaimer to be protected speech. If a reasonable reader would not think that there was a statement of fact, there can be no intentional infliction of emotional distress. Moreover, as lawyers for the *Onion*, a leading satirical website, observed in an amicus brief, "The reasonable-reader test gauges whether a statement can reasonably be interpreted as stating actual facts, thereby ensuring that neither the least humorous nor the most credulous audience dictates the boundaries of protected speech."[90] The brief added, "Parodists intentionally inhabit the rhetorical form of their target in order to exaggerate or implode it—and by doing so demonstrate the target's illogic or absurdity."

The *Hustler* Court focused on public figures and public officials, imposing the *New York Times* standard requiring proof of actual malice. What should the standard be for private figures? The standard in *Gertz*?

In *Snyder v. Phelps,* 562 U.S. 443 (2011), the Supreme Court answered that the standard should turn on whether the speech involves a matter of public or private concern. Fred Phelps founded the Westboro Baptist Church, which believes that "God hates and punishes the United States for its tolerance of homosexuality, particularly in America's military." One church activity is to picket soldiers' funerals. Among the funerals they picketed was that of Marine Lance Corporal Matthew Snyder, who was killed in Iraq. During the funeral, which was held in a church, Westboro Baptist parishioners picketed outside at several locations and held signs that stated, among other things, that "God Hates the USA/Thank God for 9/11," "Thank God for IEDs," and "Thank God for Dead Soldiers. One of the locations was about 1,000 feet from the church where the funeral took place. The picketers did not go to the cemetery and were not visible or audible in the church. According to the Court, the "funeral procession passed within 200 to 300 feet of the picket site. Although Snyder testified that he could see the tops of the picket signs as he drove to the funeral, he did not see what was written on the signs until later that night, while watching a news broadcast covering the event." A jury concluded that Westboro was liable for intentional infliction of emotional distress and intrusion upon seclusion. The jury awarded Snyder $2.9 million in compensatory damages and $8 million in punitive damages.

The Supreme Court set aside the verdict. According to the Court, "Westboro's speech was at a public place on a matter of public concern, that speech is entitled to 'special protection' under the First Amendment. Such speech cannot be restricted simply because it is upsetting or arouses contempt." The Court reasoned: "While these messages may fall short of refined social or political commentary, the issues they highlight—the political and moral conduct of the United States and its citizens, the fate of our Nation, homosexuality in the military, and scandals involving the Catholic clergy—are matters of public import." For speech of private concern, the Court noted that "First Amendment protections are often less rigorous. That is because restricting speech on purely private matters does not implicate the same constitutional concerns as limiting speech on matters of public interest."

The Court also concluded that Westboro could not be held liable for intrusion upon seclusion because "Westboro stayed well away from the memorial service. Snyder could see no more than the tops of the signs when driving to the funeral. And there is no indication that the picketing in any way interfered with the funeral service itself." Although not discussed by the Court, it is unclear how the elements of intrusion upon seclusion could have been met given that the picketing was not visible or audible during the funeral and the picketers were not present at the church or cemetery. The claim should likely have been dismissed before reaching the jury.

---

[90] Brief of The Onion as Amicus Curiae in Support of Petitioner, Novak v. Parma, On Petition for a Writ of Certiorari to the United States Court of Appeals for the Sixth Circuit (Oct. 2022).

In a dissent, Justice Alito argued that "the First Amendment ensures that Westboro practitioners had ample ways to express their views without 'intentionally inflict[ing] severe emotional injury on private persons at a time of intense emotional sensitivity by launching vicious verbal attacks that make no contribution to public debate.'" Justice Alito noted that instead of making "general comments," Westboro "addressed the Snyder family directly" by saying:

> "God blessed you, Mr. and Mrs. Snyder, with a resource and his name was Matthew. He was an arrow in your quiver! In thanks to God for the comfort the child could bring you, you had a DUTY to prepare that child to serve the LORD his GOD — PERIOD! You did JUST THE OPPOSITE — you raised him for the devil. . . .
>
> "Albert and Julie RIPPED that body apart and taught Matthew to defy his Creator, to divorce, and to commit adultery. They taught him how to support the largest pedophile machine in the history of the entire world, the Roman Catholic monstrosity. Every dime they gave the Roman Catholic monster they condemned their own souls. They also, in supporting satanic Catholicism, taught Matthew to be an idolater. . . ."

Justice Alito argued that although "commentary on the Catholic Church or the United States military constitutes speech on matters of public concern, speech regarding Matthew Snyder's purely private conduct does not."

Writing about the case, Jeffrey Shulman argues that the actual malice standard is ill-suited for intentional infliction of emotional distress:

> The literal application of the actual malice standard offers no protection to the plaintiff claiming emotional injury from rhetorically hyperbolic speech. The victim of a libel can show that the statement was false. The victim of rhetorical hyperbole can prove or disprove nothing that will bring judicial redress. This may be the cost of doing business in the public arena, but why should the private plaintiff be left defenseless against emotionally injurious speech that serves no valid communicative purpose?[91]

D. APPROPRIATION OF NAME OR LIKENESS

1. INTRODUCTION

APPROPRIATION OF NAME OR LIKENESS
Restatement (Second) of Torts § 652C

One who appropriates to his own use or benefit the name or likeness of another is subject to liability to the other for invasion of his privacy.

---

[91] Jeffrey Shulman, *Free Speech at What Cost?* Snyder v. Phelps *and Speech-Based Tort Liability*, 2010 Cardozo L. Rev. De Novo 312, 315.

NOTES & QUESTIONS

1. ***The Development of the Appropriation Tort.*** The tort of appropriation protects "the interest of the individual in the exclusive use of his own identity, in so far as it is represented by his name or likeness, and in so far as the use may be of benefit to him or to others." Restatement § 652C, comment (a). To be liable for appropriation, "the defendant must have appropriated to his own use or benefit the reputation, prestige, social or commercial standing, public interest or other values of the plaintiff's name or likeness." *Id.*, comment (c).

   Recall from section A that two of the first cases to address the creation of new causes of action in response to the Warren and Brandeis article — *Roberson* and *Pavesich* — both involved appropriation claims.

   One of the most widely discussed state appropriation tort formulations is that of New York. New York's statute, passed in response to *Roberson*, which refused to recognize the tort in the common law, provides criminal and civil remedies for appropriation. Pursuant to New York Civil Rights Law § 50:

   > A person, firm or corporation that uses for advertising purposes, or for the purposes of trade, the name, portrait or picture of any living person without having first obtained the written consent of such person, or if a minor of his or her parent or guardian, is guilty of a misdemeanor.

   New York Civil Rights Law § 51 provides a civil remedy:

   > Any person whose name, portrait, picture or voice is used within this state for advertising purposes or for the purposes of trade without the written consent first obtained . . . may maintain an equitable action in the supreme court of this state against the person, firm or corporation so using his name, portrait, picture or voice, to prevent and restrain the use thereof; and may also sue and recover damages for any injuries sustained by reason of such use. . . .

   California has a similar statute, which provides: "Any person who knowingly uses another's name, photograph or likeness, in any manner, for purposes of advertising . . . or for purposes of solicitation of purchases of products . . . without . . . prior consent . . . shall be liable for any damages." Cal. Civ. Code § 3344. In many states, the tort of appropriation is recognized through the common law and is not statutory in nature.

2. ***Appropriation and the Right of Publicity.*** The original rationale for the tort of appropriation was privacy-based, as a protection of one's dignity against the exploitation of her identity. However, another rationale for the tort has emerged, one that is property-based. Many courts and commentators refer to this alternative rationale as the "right of publicity."[92] The "right of publicity" was first referred to as such in *Haelan Laboratories v. Topps Chewing Gum, Inc.*, 202 F.2d 866 (2d Cir. 1953), where Judge Jerome Frank held that New

---

[92] J. Thomas McCarthy, *The Rights of Publicity and Privacy* (2d ed. 2011); Melville B. Nimmer, *The Right of Publicity*, 19 Law & Contemp. Probs. 203 (1954); Sheldon Halpern, *The Right of Publicity: Maturation of an Independent Right Protecting the Associative Value of Personality*, 46 Hastings L.J. 853 (1995); Oliver R. Goodenough, *Go Fish: Evaluating the Restatement's Formulation of the Law of Publicity*, 47 S.C. L. Rev. 709 (1996).

York recognized a common law tort of "publicity" distinct from §§ 50-51's remedy for appropriation:

> We think that, in addition to and independent of that right of privacy (which in New York derives from statute), a man has a right in the publicity value of his photograph, i.e., the right to grant the exclusive privilege of publishing his picture, and that such a grant may validly be made "in gross," i.e., without an accompanying transfer of a business or of anything else. Whether it be labeled a "property" right is immaterial; for here, as often elsewhere, the tag "property" simply symbolizes the fact that courts enforce a claim which has pecuniary worth.
>
> This right might be called a "right of publicity." For it is common knowledge that many prominent persons (especially actors and ball-players), far from having their feelings bruised through public exposure of their likenesses, would feel sorely deprived if they no longer received money for authorizing advertisements, popularizing their countenances, displayed in newspapers, magazines, busses, trains and subways.

Subsequently, courts held that the publicity tort was subsumed under § 51 and was not a common law cause of action. *See Welch v. Group W Productions, Inc.*, 525 N.Y.S.2d 466, 468 n.1 (N.Y. Sup. Ct. 1987) ("In New York State the so-called 'right of publicity' is merely an aspect of the right of privacy and is not an independent common-law right.").

How is the "right of publicity" distinct from the privacy interests involved in appropriation? As one court describes the distinction:

> The privacy-based action is designed for individuals who have not placed themselves in the public eye. It shields such people from the embarrassment of having their faces plastered on billboards and cereal boxes without their permission. The interests protected are dignity and peace of mind, and damages are measured in terms of emotional distress. By contrast, a right of publicity action is designed for individuals who have placed themselves in the public eye. It secures for them the exclusive right to exploit the commercial value that attaches to their identities by virtue of their celebrity. The right to publicity protects that value as property, and its infringement is a commercial, rather than a personal tort. Damages stem not from embarrassment but from the unauthorized use of the plaintiffs' property. *Jim Henson Productions, Inc. v. John T. Brady & Associates, Inc.*, 687 F. Supp. 185, 188-89 (S.D.N.Y. 1994).

Thomas McCarthy articulates the distinction most succinctly: "Simplistically put, while the appropriation branch of the right of privacy is invaded by an injury to the psyche, the right of publicity is infringed by an injury to the pocket book."[93]

The Restatement (Third) of the Law of Unfair Competition § 46 provides for a distinct tort of "publicity":

> *Appropriation of the Commercial Value of a Person's Identity: The Right of Publicity.* One who appropriates the commercial value of a person's identity by using without consent the person's name, likeness, or other indicia of identity for purposes of trade is subject to liability for [monetary and injunctive] relief.

---

[93] J. Thomas McCarthy, *The Rights of Publicity and Privacy* § 5:63 (2d ed. 2011).

The commentary to the Restatement § 46 contrasts the "publicity" right in § 46 with the "appropriation tort" in the Restatement of Torts: "The 'appropriation' tort as described by Prosser and the Restatement, Second, of Torts, subsumes harm to both personal and commercial interests caused by an unauthorized exploitation of the plaintiff's identity." Restatement (Third) of the Law of Unfair Competition § 46, comment (b). A number of jurisdictions recognize a distinct tort of "publicity."

Although there is now a separate "right of publicity" to protect property interests, the tort of appropriation has shifted towards being a property protection similar to the right of publicity. William Prosser, in his 1960 article describing the torts spawned by Warren and Brandeis's article, did not recognize a distinct tort of publicity; it was merely a part of the appropriation tort. Likewise, the Restatement (Second) of Torts did not recognize a distinct tort of publicity. However, according to the Restatement, it appears that the central interest protected by appropriation is property rather than privacy: "Although the protection of [a person's] personal feelings against mental distress is an important factor leading to a recognition of the [appropriation tort], the right created by it is in the nature of a property right. . . ." Restatement (Second) of Torts § 652C, comment (a). A number of jurisdictions follow this approach. *See Ainsworth v. Century Supply Co.*, 693 N.E.2d 510 (Ill. App. 1998); *Candlebat v. Flanagan*, 487 So. 2d 207 (Miss. 1986). According to Jonathan Kahn:

> While publicity is grounded in property rights, appropriation of identity involves the personal right to privacy. Publicity rights implicate monetary interests. In contrast, privacy rights protect and vindicate less tangible personal interests in dignity and integrity of the self. However, both rights are clearly linked and find their common origin in American law around the turn of this century. Yet over the years, the privacy-based tort of appropriation has receded into the background as its flashier cousin, publicity, has risen to prominence. Such is perhaps to be expected in a world where seemingly everything has been turned into a saleable commodity.[94]

Is privacy or property the central interest of appropriation? Or does the tort adequately redress both interests?

2. NAME OR LIKENESS

CARSON V. HERE'S JOHNNY PORTABLE TOILETS, INC.

698 F.2d 831 (6th Cir. 1983)

BROWN, J. . . . Appellant, John W. Carson (Carson), is the host and star of "The Tonight Show," a well-known television program broadcast five nights a week by the National Broadcasting Company. . . . From the time he began hosting "The

[94] Jonathan Kahn, *Bringing Dignity Back to Light: Publicity Rights and the Eclipse of the Tort of Appropriation of Identity*, 17 Cardozo Arts & Ent. L.J. 213, 213-14 (1999); *see also* Jonathan Kahn, *What's in a Name? Law's Identity Under the Tort of Appropriation*, 74 Temp. L. Rev. 263 (2001).

Tonight Show" in 1962, he has been introduced [by Ed McMahon] on the show each night with the phrase "Here's Johnny." . . . The phrase "Here's Johnny" is generally associated with Carson by a substantial segment of the television viewing public. In 1967, Carson first authorized use of this phrase by an outside business venture, permitting it to be used by a chain of restaurants called "Here's Johnny Restaurants." . . .

. . . The phrase "Here's Johnny" has never been registered by appellants as a trademark or service mark.

Appellee, Here's Johnny Portable Toilets, Inc., is a Michigan corporation engaged in the business of renting and selling "Here's Johnny" portable toilets. Appellee's founder was aware at the time he formed the corporation that "Here's Johnny" was the introductory slogan for Carson on "The Tonight Show." He indicated that he coupled the phrase with a second one, "The World's Foremost Commodian," to make "a good play on a phrase."

[Carson brought an action for, among other things, invasion of privacy and the right to publicity.] . . .

We do not believe that Carson's claim that his right of privacy has been invaded is supported by the law or the facts. Apparently, the gist of this claim is that Carson is embarrassed by and considers it odious to be associated with the appellee's product. Clearly, the association does not appeal to Carson's sense of humor. But the facts here presented do not, it appears to us, amount to an invasion of any of the interests protected by the right of privacy. . . .

The right of publicity has developed to protect the commercial interest of celebrities in their identities. The theory of the right is that a celebrity's identity can be valuable in the promotion of products, and the celebrity has an interest that may be protected from the unauthorized commercial exploitation of that identity. . . .

The district court dismissed appellants' claim based on the right of publicity because appellee does not use Carson's name or likeness. . . . We believe that, on the contrary, the district court's conception of the right of publicity is too narrow. The right of publicity, as we have stated, is that a celebrity has a protected pecuniary interest in the commercial exploitation of his identity. If the celebrity's identity is commercially exploited, there has been an invasion of his right whether or not his "name or likeness" is used. Carson's identity may be exploited even if his name, John W. Carson, or his picture is not used. . . .

In this case, Earl Braxton, president and owner of Here's Johnny Portable Toilets, Inc., admitted that he knew that the phrase "Here's Johnny" had been used for years to introduce Carson. Moreover, in the opening statement in the district court, appellee's counsel stated:

> Now, we've stipulated in this case that the public tends to associate the words "Johnny Carson," the words "Here's Johnny" with plaintiff, John Carson and, Mr. Braxton, in his deposition, admitted that he knew that and probably absent that identification, he would not have chosen it.

That the "Here's Johnny" name was selected by Braxton because of its identification with Carson was the clear inference from Braxton's testimony irrespective of such admission in the opening statement.

We therefore conclude that, applying the correct legal standards, appellants are entitled to judgment. The proof showed without question that appellee had appropriated Carson's identity in connection with its corporate name and its product. . . .

. . . It is not fatal to appellant's claim that appellee did not use his "name." Indeed, there would have been no violation of his right of publicity even if appellee had used his name, such as "J. William Carson Portable Toilet" or the "John William Carson Portable Toilet" or the "J. W. Carson Portable Toilet." The reason is that, though literally using appellant's "name," the appellee would not have appropriated Carson's identity as a celebrity. Here there was an appropriation of Carson's identity without using his "name." . . .

KENNEDY, J. dissenting. . . . The majority's extension of the right of publicity to include phrases or other things which are merely associated with the individual permits a popular entertainer or public figure, by associating himself or herself with a common phrase, to remove those words from the public domain. . . .

. . . [T]he majority is awarding Johnny Carson a windfall, rather than vindicating his economic interests, by protecting the phrase "Here's Johnny" which is merely associated with him. In *Zacchini*, the Supreme Court stated that a mechanism to vindicate an individual's economic rights is indicated where the appropriated thing is "the product of . . . [the individual's] own talents and energy, the end result of much time, effort and expense." There is nothing in the record to suggest that "Here's Johnny" has any nexus to Johnny Carson other than being the introduction to his personal appearances. The phrase is not part of an identity that he created. In its content "Here's Johnny" is a very simple and common introduction. The content of the phrase neither originated with Johnny Carson nor is it confined to the world of entertainment. The phrase is not said by Johnny Carson, but said of him. Its association with him is derived, in large part, by the context in which it is said — generally by Ed McMahon in a drawn out and distinctive voice after the theme music to "The Tonight Show" is played, and immediately prior to Johnny Carson's own entrance. Appellee's use of the content "Here's Johnny," in light of its value as a double entendre, written on its product and corporate name, and therefore outside of the context in which it is associated with Johnny Carson, does little to rob Johnny Carson of something which is unique to him or a product of his own efforts. . . .

Protection under the right of publicity confers a monopoly on the protected individual that is potentially broader, offers fewer protections and potentially competes with federal statutory monopolies. As an essential part of three federal monopoly rights, copyright, trademark and patents, notice to the public is required in the form of filing with the appropriate governmental office and use of an appropriate mark. This apprises members of the public of the nature and extent of what is being removed from the public domain and subject to claims of infringement. The right of publicity provides limited notice to the public of the extent of the monopoly right to be asserted, if one is to be asserted at all. As the right of privacy is expanded beyond protections of name, likeness and actual performances, which provide relatively objective notice to the public of the extent of an individual's rights, to more subjective attributes such as achievements and identifying characteristics, the public's ability to be on notice of a common law monopoly right, if one is even asserted by a given famous individual, is severely diminished. Protecting phrases and other things merely associated with an individual provides virtually no notice to the public at all of what is claimed to be protected. By ensuring the invocation of the adjudicative process whenever the commercial use of a phrase or other associated thing is considered to have been wrongfully appropriated, the public is left to act at their peril. The result is a chilling effect on commercial innovation and opportunity.

Also unlike the federal statutory monopolies, this common law monopoly right offers no protections against the monopoly existing for an indefinite time or even in perpetuity. . . .

NOTES & QUESTIONS

1. ***Privacy or Property?*** In *Carson*, Johnny Carson made two claims. First, he contended that a privacy interest was violated because his identity was being associated with toilets, which he found quite unflattering. The court appears to reject this claim. Carson's other claim is that a property interest was violated by his valuable identity being stolen and used for the commercial purposes of another. What do you think was the real reason Carson brought this suit? To vindicate his privacy interest, his property interest, or both? Suppose Carson were not famous and his name had little value. Would he be likely to succeed under the reasoning of the court?

2. ***Post-Mortem Publicity Rights.*** Despite losing the case before the Sixth Circuit in 1987, Earl Braxton, the defendant in the *Carson* case, did not give up his dream. Johnny Carson died in 2005, and in 2006 Braxton sought to trademark the phrase "Here's Johnny." A trademark is a form of intellectual property that identifies the source of a product or service. The Trademark and Trial Appeal Board held that the relevant states in question recognized post-mortem rights of publicity and that these rights had passed to Carson's estate. Thus, the *Carson* decision still prevents Braxton from use of the phrase, "Here's Johnny."

    Concerning post-mortem rights, the overwhelming majority of states in the United States have also recognized a postmortem dimension to the publicity right. The publicity right can be inherited, sold in whole or in part, and otherwise licensed after the subject's death. The question of whether or not these interests were exploited during a party's life is irrelevant. A survey of the duration of the postmortem right in the United States found periods ranging from a potentially unlimited period to 100 years to 20 years.[95]

    In California, the legislature has even extended the applicable statute *backward* in time to protect the interests of those who died as long as 70 years before the state first legislatively acknowledged this right. Publicity rights are also a routine subject in negotiations with prominent individuals and, in the case of deceased celebrities, with their estates.

3. ***What Constitutes "Name or Likeness"?*** The appropriation tort has been extended far beyond a person's actual name and likeness. Courts have held that the use of well-known nicknames can give rise to an appropriation action. In

---

[95] J. Thomas McCarthy, 2 *The Rights of Publicity and Privacy* 435-37, 445-46 (2009).

Hirsch v. S.C. Johnson & Son, Inc., 280 N.W.2d 129 (Wis. 1979), the Supreme Court of Wisconsin found that an unauthorized commercial use of Elroy Hirsch's (a famous football player) nickname "Crazylegs" raised triable issues regarding violation of the appropriation tort. S.C. Johnson had used "Crazylegs" as the product name for a shaving gel for women. The court rejected the argument that an appropriation claim by Hirsch was not possible because Crazylegs was his nickname, not his actual name. It stated that to overcome the lower court's rejection of the cause of action, "[a]ll that is required is that the name clearly identify the wronged person." It also declared that "[t]he question whether Crazylegs identifies Elroy Hirsch, however, is one of fact to be determined by the jury on remand. . . ."

Courts have also held that certain drawings depicting one's profession but otherwise with no distinctive facial characteristics can still give rise to an appropriation claim. In *Ali v. Playgirl, Inc.*, 447 F. Supp. 723 (S.D.N.Y. 1978), Muhammad Ali, former heavyweight boxing champion, sued *Playgirl* magazine for appropriation when the magazine published a drawing of a nude African-American male sitting on a stool in a corner of a boxing ring with hands taped. The drawing did not mention Ali's name and was entitled "Mystery Man," but accompanying text identified the man in the drawing as "The Greatest." Because "The Greatest" was Ali's nickname, the picture was sufficiently identifiable as Ali to constitute his likeness. The court emphasized the offensive nature of the full frontal nude of Ali; the fact that the portrait was clearly one of Ali; and that the publication was for "purposes of trade" within New York Civil Rights Law § 51. It stated, "the picture is a dramatization, an illustration falling somewhere between representational art and cartoon, and is accompanied by a plainly fictional and allegedly libelous bit of doggerel."

Appropriation has even been extended to identifying characteristics. In *Motschenbacher v. R.J. Reynolds Tobacco Co.*, 498 F.2d 821 (9th Cir. 1974), a famous race car driver alleged that a photograph of his distinctive racing car, which did not include a likeness of himself or use his name, was nevertheless an appropriation of his name or likeness. The court agreed. The photograph did use a "likeness" of the plaintiff because the "distinctive decorations" on his car "were not only peculiar to the plaintiff's cars but they caused some persons to think the car in question was plaintiff's and to infer that the person driving the car was the plaintiff."

Further, appropriation can also extend to use of a look-alike model. In *Onassis v. Christian Dior*, 472 N.Y.S. 2d 254 (N.Y. Supp. 1984), Jacqueline Kennedy Onassis won an injunction against use of a look-alike model in an advertisement. The *Onassis* court found a cause of action under the New York Civil Rights Law § 51, so long as the advertisement created an illusion that the plaintiff herself had appeared in the advertisement.

Courts have also recognized appropriation liability for the imitation of one's voice. In *Midler v. Ford Motor Co.*, 849 F.2d 460 (9th Cir. 1988), the Ninth Circuit held that singer Bette Midler had a viable cause of action for appropriation for the use of a singer to imitate her voice in a commercial. When a voice is a sufficient indication of the celebrity's identity, appropriation protects against a company hiring someone to imitate it for commercial purposes without the celebrity's consent.

In a later sound-alike case, the Ninth Circuit found for Tom Waits, a singer with a distinctive sound. *Waits v. Frito Lay*, 978 F. 2d 1093 (9th Cir. 1992). The court noted that Waits had "a distinctive gravelly singing voice, described by one fan as 'like how you'd sound if you drank a quart of bourbon, smoked a pack of cigarettes and swallowed a pack of razor blades. . . . Late at night. After not sleeping for three days.' " The *Waits* court upheld a jury verdict that found the celebrity plaintiff had a voice that was distinctive, widely known, and deliberately imitated by a defendant for a commercial purpose. The Ninth Circuit added that even if Tom Waits was not as well known as Bette Midler, "'[w]ell-known' is a relative term, and differences in the extent of celebrity are adequately reflected in the amount of damages recoverable."

4. ***Property Rights and the Manufacturing of Identity.*** One of the predominant rationales for the right of publicity is that the celebrity, through her labor, creates her persona. But, with regard to celebrities, does this rationale always hold true? According to Michael Madow, the identity of a celebrity is "the product of a complex social process in which the 'labor' of the celebrity is but one ingredient, and not always the main one."[96] In a similar argument, Rosemary Coombe observes: "Star images are authored by studios, the mass media, public relations agencies, fan clubs, gossip columnists, photographers, hairdressers, body-building coaches, athletic trainers, teachers, screenwriters, ghostwriters, directors, lawyers, and doctors."[97] Why should we afford celebrities property rights in their names and likenesses when frequently a celebrity's persona is manufactured by others?

Madow also argues that individuals and groups participating actively in the process of generating and circulating meanings that constitute "culture." Thus, "against-the-grain readings" of mainstream cultural products are possible. As an example, Madow points to the example of a card showing "John Wayne, wearing cowboy hat and bright red lipstick, above the caption, 'It's such a bitch being butch.' " Wayne's children, among others, objected to the card. Madow comments:

> What it comes down to, then, is that the power to license is the power to suppress. When the law gives a celebrity a right of publicity, it does more than funnel additional income her way. It gives her (or her assignee) a substantial measure of power over the production and circulation of meaning and identity in our society: power, if she so chooses, to suppress readings or appropriations of her persona that depart from, challenge, or subvert the meaning she prefers; power to deny to others the use of her persona in the construction and communication of alternative or oppositional identities and social relations; power, ultimately, to limit the expressive and communicative opportunities of

---

[96] Michael T. Madow, *Private Ownership of Public Image: Popular Culture and Publicity Rights*, 81 Cal. L. Rev. 127, 195 (1993).

[97] Rosemary J. Coombe, *The Cultural Life of Intellectual Properties: Authorship, Appropriation, and the Law* 94 (1998).

the rest of us. The result is a potentially significant narrowing of the space available for alternative cultural and dialogic practice.

5. *Are Privacy and Property Rights Mutually Exclusive?* According to Robert Post, the right of publicity views one's personality as "commodified," as an object separate from oneself that can be valued by the market. In his view, Warren and Brandeis's right to privacy, in contrast, "attaches personality firmly to the actual identity of a living individual." The right of publicity protects personality as detachable from individuals, as a commodity that can be bought and sold (and can persist after the death of the individual). The right to privacy, in contrast, protects personality as constitutive of the individual. Post suggests that perhaps we need both property rights and privacy rights to protect our personalities: "Personality can so effortlessly be legally embodied by either property or privacy rights precisely because it embraces both these aspects."[98]

6. *Narrowing the Right to Publicity.* According to Jennifer Rothman, cases have too widely expanded the right to publicity beyond its roots "in personal liberty and dignity, and the prevention of economic, reputational, and emotional harms to individuals."[99] Regarding the new restrictions on this right, Rothman states, "Use of person's actual name, likeness or voice should be actionable, but when the use is more attenuated, such as simply evoking a person's identity or looking similar to the person, then an additional hurdle should have to be met before there can be liability." Such a hurdle would include "a likelihood of confusion as to sponsorship or endorsement."

3. FOR ONE'S OWN USE OR BENEFIT

The Restatement of Torts recognizes appropriation of another's name or likeness when it is used for the appropriator's "own use or benefit." Consider the Restatement § 652C comment (b):

The common form of invasion of privacy under the rule here stated is the appropriation and use of the plaintiff's name or likeness to advertise the defendant's business or product, or for some similar commercial purpose. Apart from statute, however, the rule stated is not limited to commercial appropriation. It applies also when the defendant makes use of the plaintiff's name or likeness for his own purposes and benefit, even though the use is not a commercial one, and even though the benefit sought to be obtained is not a pecuniary one. Statutes in some states have, however, limited the liability to commercial uses of the name or likeness.

What does "use or benefit" mean? In many jurisdictions, appropriation occurs only when the use or benefit is commercial in nature — i.e., used to promote or endorse a service or product.

[98] Robert C. Post, *Rereading Warren and Brandeis: Privacy, Property, and Appropriation*, 41 Case W. Res. L. Rev. 647 (1991).

[99] Jennifer Rothman, *The Right of Publicity: Privacy Reimagined for a Public World* (2018).

RAYMEN V. UNITED SENIOR ASSOCIATION, INC.

409 F. Supp. 2d 15 (D.D.C. 2006)

WALTON, J. On March 9, 2005, the plaintiffs filed this action seeking to prevent the defendants from further using their images in an advertising campaign which challenged various public policy positions taken by the American Association of Retired Persons ("AARP") regarding Social Security reform and the military. Currently before the Court are the defendants' motions to dismiss, and the plaintiffs' opposition thereto. . . .

On March 3, 2004, the plaintiffs were among 300 citizens of Multnomah County, Oregon who were married pursuant to a newly established right to same-sex marriage in that county. While at City Hall awaiting their opportunity to marry, the plaintiffs, Steve Hansen and Richard Raymen, kissed. A photographer from a Portland, Oregon newspaper, the *Tribune,* captured the kiss in a photograph he took. The photograph was subsequently published in both the *Tribune* newspaper on March 4, 2004, and later on the *Tribune*'s website. At some later point in time, the *Tribune*'s website photograph was used without permission as part of an advertisement created by defendant Mark Montini. The advertising campaign was created for a nonprofit organization, United Senior Association, Inc., which does business under the name USA Next. The advertisement, which features the photograph of the plaintiffs kissing, was part of a campaign by USA Next challenging various public policy positions purportedly taken by the AARP. Specifically, the advertisement contains two pictures. The first is a picture of an American soldier, who presumably is in Iraq, with a red "X" superimposed over it, and the second is the photograph of the plaintiffs with a green checkmark superimposed over it. The caption under the advertisement reads: "The Real AARP Agenda," suggesting that the AARP opposes the United States military efforts abroad and supports the gay lifestyle. This advertisement ran on the website of *The American Spectator* magazine from February 15, 2005, to February 21, 2005.

According to the plaintiffs, the purpose of the advertising campaign was "to incite viewer passions against the AARP because of its alleged support of equal marriage rights for same-sex couples and its alleged lack of support of American troops." Moreover, the plaintiffs opine that the "advertisement also conveys the message that the plaintiffs . . . are against American troops . . . and are unpatriotic." The plaintiffs contend that the advertisement attracted media attention, which then caused an even wider distribution of the advertisement throughout the media. The plaintiffs assert that because of the advertisement, they "have suffered embarrassment, extreme emotional distress, and the invasion of their privacy." In addition, the plaintiffs represent that as a result of the false and misleading inference "communicated by the [a]dvertisement about [the] plaintiffs, their reputations as patriotic American citizens has been severely damaged." . . .

"'One who appropriates to his own use or benefit the name or likeness of another is subject to liability to the other for invasion of his privacy.'" *Martinez v. Democrat-Herald Publ'g Co., Inc.,* 669 P.2d 818, 820 (1983) (quoting Restatement (Second) of Torts § 652C (1976)). Under § 652C of the Restatement, plaintiffs can recover "damages when their names, pictures or other likenesses have been used without their consent to advertise a defendant's product, to accompany an article sold, to add luster to the name of a corporation or for some other business purpose." However, there is no actionable appropriation of a person's likeness claim "when a person's picture is used to illustrate a noncommercial, newsworthy article." . . . Whether a communication is commercial or noncommercial is a question of law. . . .

The photograph of the plaintiffs was used as part of USA Next's advertising campaign, which sought, at least in part, to engender opposition to AARP's policy position on social security reform. Presumably, the advertisement sought to vilify the AARP by conveying a message concerning AARP's alleged views on two hot button policy issues — support of same-sex marriage and opposition to the military. While the advertisement itself lacked any substantive discussion of these issues, it did convey AARP's purported position on both subjects. And someone who viewed the advertisement online could then access the USA Next's webpages which described the organization and its position on Social Security reform. Clearly the issues of same-sex marriage and support for the military are issues of public concern and both have been widely discussed in the media. In fact, the plaintiffs contend in their complaint that the purpose of the advertisement was to influence Congress.

The plaintiffs' argument that the advertisement is commercial in nature because it sought contributions and promoted USA Next's lobbying services, is unpersuasive. First, nothing in the advertisement itself seeks donations. Rather, only after using the advertisement (by clicking on it) to access the webpages were viewers exposed to the information about USA Next and the solicitation for financial contributions. This Court cannot conclude that this detached solicitation elevates the advertisement itself to a level where it can be deemed commercial in nature. . . .

NOTES & QUESTIONS

1. *The Fuzzy Line Between Commercial and Non-Commercial Uses.* In *Raymen,* the image of the plaintiffs kissing was used not as a positive endorsement but as a way to spark outrage in their readers and spur them to donate. Isn't this using their image for financial gain? On the other hand, the plaintiffs' anger at the use of their photograph stems from their outrage over the defendants' message. The defendant could argue that the image of the plaintiffs was a popular iconic image representing gay marriage. Should the plaintiffs be able to control that image whenever they dislike the viewpoints of those that use it?

2. *Girls Gone Wild.* In *Lane v. MRA Holdings, LLC,* 242 F. Supp. 2d 1205 (M.D. Fla. 2002), the plaintiff was approached by a crew who produced the Girls Gone Wild video series, which featured clips of women stripping at various parties and events, such as spring break or Mardi Gras. The plaintiff claimed that the crew promised that the footage would be for their personal use only, but it was used in a Girls Gone Wild video. Among many claims, the plaintiff argued that the makers of Girls Gone Wild appropriated her likeness. The court, however, rejected her appropriation claim:

As a matter of law, this Court finds that Lane's image and likeness were not used to directly promote a product or service. In coming to this conclusion, this Court relies upon Section 47 of the Restatement (Third) of Unfair Competition which defines "the purposes of trade" as follows:

> The names, likeness, and other indicia of a person's identity are used "for the purposes of trade" . . . if they are used in advertising the user's goods or services, or are placed on merchandise marketed by the user, or are used in connection with services rendered by the user. However, use "for the purpose of trade" does not ordinarily include the use of a person's identity in news reporting, commentary, entertainment, works of fiction or nonfiction, or in advertising incidental to such uses. . . .

In this case, it is irrefutable that the *Girls Gone Wild* video is an expressive work created solely for entertainment purposes. Similarly, it is also irrefutable that while Lane's image and likeness were used to sell copies of *Girls Gone Wild,* her image and likeness were never associated with a product or service unrelated to that work. Indeed, in both the video and its commercial advertisements, Lane is never shown endorsing or promoting a product, but rather, as part of an expressive work in which she voluntarily participated. Consequently, in accordance with Section 47 of the Restatement, the use of Lane's image or likeness in *Girls Gone Wild,* and in the marketing of that video cannot give rise to liability. . . .

The court's definition of commercial use in this case appears to be a use for "endorsing or promoting a product." Is this too limited a definition of commercial use? Would selling posters of a celebrity constitute a commercial use according to the *Lane* court?

4. CONNECTION TO MATTERS OF PUBLIC INTEREST

Unlike the tort of public disclosure, the lack of newsworthiness is not an element of the appropriation tort. However, appropriation protects against the "commercial" exploitation of one's name or likeness, not the use of one's name or likeness for news, art, literature, parody, satire, history, and biography. Otherwise, a newspaper would have to obtain the consent of every person it wrote about or photographed for use in a story. People could prevent others from writing their biographies or from criticizing them, making a parody of them, or using their names in a work of literature. In New York, for example, one's name or likeness must be used for "advertising purposes or for the uses of trade." N.Y. Civ. Rights L. §§ 50-51. Although not employing the same language, other states adopt a similar approach, requiring that the use of one's name or likeness be for "commercial" purposes. Some courts refer to this as a "First Amendment privilege" to use one's name or likeness in matters of legitimate public concern.

The quintessential instance where the use of one's name or likeness is newsworthy and not "commercial" is in connection with the reporting of the news. In *Time Inc. v. Sand Creek Partners*, 825 F. Supp. 210 (S.D. Ind. 1993), country singer Lyle Lovett and actress Julia Roberts were photographed together at a Lovett concert immediately prior to their marriage. Roberts was in her wedding gown. A photographer for *People* magazine snapped several rolls of film, but they were confiscated by security. The magazine's publisher sued to get the photos back, but Lovett claimed that they were his, because he had a property interest in his name or likeness. The court sided with the magazine:

> Lovett and Roberts are widely known celebrities and in that sense are public figures and, in addition, their appearance on stage before thousands of people on the day of their highly-publicized but theretofore unannounced and private wedding ceremony, with Roberts still wearing her wedding dress, was a newsworthy event of widespread public interest.

Beyond news, uses that are "commercial" or "for advertising or trade purposes" generally do not encompass works of fiction or nonfiction or artistic expression. In *Rosemont Enterprises, Inc. v. Random House, Inc.*, 294 N.Y.S.2d 122 (1968), the defendants published an unauthorized biography of the reclusive Howard Hughes. The court concluded that the biography "falls within those 'reports of newsworthy people or events'" and is therefore not subject to liability for appropriation. A sculpture of supermodel Cheryl Tiegs was not appropriation because "[w]orks of art, including sculptures, convey ideas, just as do literature, movies or theater." *Simeonov v. Tiegs*, 602 N.Y.S.2d 1014 (Civ. Ct. 1993). The use of a person's identity in a work of fiction generally cannot give rise to an appropriation action. *See, e.g., Maritote v. Desilu Productions, Inc.*, 345 F.2d 418 (7th Cir. 1965); *Loft v. Fuller*, 408 So. 2d 619 (Fla. Ct. App. 1981).

However, in New York and other states, the right of the media to use one's name or likeness for news purposes is not absolute. There must exist a "legitimate connection between the use of plaintiff's name and picture and the matter of public interest sought to be portrayed." *Delan by Delan v. CBS, Inc.*, 458 N.Y.S.2d 608 (N.Y. Ct. App. 1983). As another court articulated the test:

> A picture illustrating an article on a matter of public interest is not considered used for the purpose of trade or advertising within the prohibition of the statute unless it has no real relationship to the article, or unless the article is an advertisement in disguise. It makes no difference whether the article appears in a newspaper; a magazine; a newsreel; on television; in a motion picture; or in a book. The test of permissible use is not the currency of the publication in which the picture appears but whether it is illustrative of a matter of public interest. *Dallesandro v. Henry Holt & Co.*, 106 N.Y.S.2d 805 (1957).

This test has become known as the "real relationship" test. *See, e.g., Haskell v. Stauffer Communications, Inc.*, 990 P.2d 163 (Kan. App. 1999); *Lane v. Random House*, 985 F. Supp. 141 (D.D.C. 1995).

FINGER V. OMNI PUBLICATIONS INTERNATIONAL, LTD.
566 N.E.2d 141 (N.Y. Ct. App. 1990)

ALEXANDER, J. Plaintiffs Joseph and Ida Finger commenced this action on behalf of themselves and their six children against defendant Omni Publications International, Ltd. seeking damages for the publication, without their consent, of a photograph of plaintiffs in conjunction with an article in Omni magazine discussing a research project relating to caffeine-aided fertilization. . . .

. . . The June 1988 issue of Omni magazine included in its "Continuum" segment an article entitled "Caffeine and Fast Sperm," in which it was indicated that based on research conducted at the University of Pennsylvania School of Medicine, in vitro fertilization rates may be enhanced by exposing sperm to high concentrations of caffeine.

A photograph of plaintiffs depicting two adults surrounded by six attractive and apparently healthy children accompanied the article. The caption beneath the photograph read "Want a big family? Maybe your sperm needs a cup of Java in the morning. Tests reveal that caffeine-spritzed sperm swim faster, which may increase the chances for in vitro fertilization." Neither the article nor the caption mentioned plaintiffs' names or indicated in any fashion that the adult plaintiffs used caffeine or that the children were produced through in vitro fertilization.

Plaintiffs commenced this action alleging only violations of Civil Rights Law §§ 50 and 51. Defendant moved to dismiss the complaint, arguing that its use of the photograph in conjunction with the article did not violate Civil Rights Law §§ 50 and 51 because the picture was not used for trade or advertising but to illustrate a related news article on fertility. Defendant contended that because fertility is a topic of legitimate public interest, its use of the picture fit within the "newsworthiness exception" to the prohibitions of Civil Rights Law § 50. . . .

Plaintiffs contend that defendant violated Civil Rights Law §§ 50 and 51 by using their photograph without their consent "for advertising purposes or for the purposes of trade." . . .

Although the statute does not define "purposes of trade" or "advertising," courts have consistently refused to construe these terms as encompassing publications concerning newsworthy events or matters of public interest. Additionally, it is also well settled that "'[a] picture illustrating an article on a matter of public interest is not considered used for the purpose of trade or advertising within the prohibition of the statute . . . unless it has no real relationship to the article . . . or unless the article is an advertisement in disguise.'"

Plaintiffs do not contest the existence of this "newsworthiness exception" and concede that the discussion of in vitro fertilization and the use of caffeine to enhance sperm velocity and motility are newsworthy topics. They contend, however, that their photograph bears "no real relationship" to the article, that none of plaintiffs' children were conceived by in vitro fertilization or any other artificial means, and that they never participated in the caffeine-enhanced reproductive research conducted at the University of Pennsylvania.

Consequently, according to plaintiffs, there was no "real relationship" between their photograph and the article, and any relationship that may exist is too tenuous to be considered a relationship at all. They argue that there are no "external and objective" criteria . . . that would indicate that plaintiffs have any real or legitimate connection with the subject of caffeine-enhanced in vitro fertilization. . . .

Plaintiffs misperceive the "newsworthy" theme of the article, which is fertility or increased fertility. Indeed, the article, in its opening sentences, observes that caffeine "can increase a man's fertility by boosting the performance of his sperm" and further indicates that "those who are looking for a fertility tonic shouldn't head for the nearest coffee pot" because the concentrations of caffeine used in the experiment "were so high [as to] be toxic."

The theme of fertility is reasonably reflected both in the caption beneath the picture, "Want a big family?", and the images used — six healthy and attractive children with their parents to whom each child bears a striking resemblance. Clearly then, there is a "real relationship" between the fertility theme of the article and the large family depicted in the photograph. That the article also discusses in vitro fertilization as being enhanced by "caffeine-spritzed sperm" does no more than discuss a specific aspect of fertilization and does not detract from the relationship between the photograph and the article.

As we have noted, the "newsworthiness exception" should be liberally applied. . . . [Q]uestions of "newsworthiness" are better left to reasonable editorial judgment and discretion; judicial intervention should occur only in those instances where there is "no real relationship" between a photograph and an article or where the article is an "advertisement in disguise." . . .

NOTES & QUESTIONS

1. *Levels of Generality in Applying the Real Relationship Test.* Do you agree with the court's approach to the relationship between the photograph and the article? Does the court properly view the topic of the article broadly as about fertility in general? The Fingers' argument, however, is not that the picture has no relation to the subject matter of the article; rather, they contend that they have nothing to do with the article's specific topic. Is this relevant to the court?

2. *What Injuries Does the Appropriation Tort Redress?* What type of interest are the Fingers attempting to protect? Why doesn't the appropriation tort protect that interest?

5. FIRST AMENDMENT LIMITATIONS

ZACCHINI V. SCRIPPS-HOWARD BROADCASTING CO.

433 U.S. 562 (1977)

WHITE, J. Petitioner, Hugo Zacchini, is an entertainer. He performs a "human cannonball" act in which he is shot from a cannon into a net some 200 feet away. Each performance occupies some 15 seconds. In August and September 1972, petitioner was engaged to perform his act on a regular basis at the Geauga County Fair in Burton, Ohio. He performed in a fenced area, surrounded by grandstands, at the fair grounds. Members of the public attending the fair were not charged a separate admission fee to observe his act.

On August 30, a freelance reporter for Scripps-Howard Broadcasting Co., the operator of a television broadcasting station and respondent in this case, attended the fair. He carried a small movie camera. Petitioner noticed the reporter and asked him not to film the performance. The reporter did not do so on that day; but on the instructions of the producer of respondent's daily newscast, he returned the following day and videotaped the entire act. This film clip approximately 15 seconds in length, was shown on the 11 o'clock news program that night, together with favorable commentary.

Petitioner then brought this action for damages, alleging that he is "engaged in the entertainment business," that the act he performs is one "invented by his father and . . . performed only by his family for the last fifty years," that respondent "showed and commercialized the film of his act without his consent," and that such conduct was an "unlawful appropriation of plaintiff's professional property." Respondent answered and moved for summary judgment, which was granted by the trial court.

[The Ohio Supreme Court held that the broadcast was protected by the First Amendment because the press "must be accorded broad latitude in its choice of how much it presents of each story or incident, and of the emphasis to be given to such presentation." The United States Supreme Court granted certiorari to determine whether the First Amendment immunized the media broadcaster from damages under Ohio's "right of publicity" (appropriation tort).]

. . . The Ohio Supreme Court relied heavily on *Time, Inc. v. Hill*, 385 U.S. 374 (1967), but that case does not mandate a media privilege to televise a performer's entire act without his consent. Involved in *Time, Inc. v. Hill* was a claim under the New York "Right of Privacy" statute that Life Magazine, in the course of reviewing a new play, had connected the play with a long-past incident involving petitioner and his family and had falsely described their experience and conduct at that time. The complaint sought damages for humiliation and suffering flowing from these nondefamatory falsehoods that allegedly invaded Hill's privacy. The Court held, however, that the opening of a new play linked to an actual incident was a matter of public interest and that Hill could not recover without showing that the Life report was knowingly false or was published with reckless disregard for the truth the same rigorous standard that had been applied in *New York Times Co. v. Sullivan*.

Time, Inc. v. Hill, which was hotly contested and decided by a divided Court, involved an entirely different tort from the "right of publicity" recognized by the Ohio Supreme Court. As the opinion reveals in *Time, Inc. v. Hill*, the Court was steeped in the literature of privacy law and was aware of the developing distinctions and nuances in this branch of the law. . . . The Court was aware that it was adjudicating a "false light" privacy case involving a matter of public interest, not a case involving "intrusion," "appropriation" of a name or likeness for the purposes of trade, or "private details" about a non-newsworthy person or event. It is also abundantly clear that *Time, Inc. v. Hill* did not involve a performer, a person with a name having commercial value, or any claim to a "right of publicity." This discrete kind of "appropriation" case was plainly identified in the literature cited by the Court and had been adjudicated in the reported cases.

The differences between these two torts are important. First, the State's interests in providing a cause of action in each instance are different. "The interest protected" in permitting recovery for placing the plaintiff in a false light "is clearly that of reputation, with the same overtones of mental distress as in defamation." By contrast, the State's interest in permitting a "right of publicity" is in protecting the proprietary interest of the individual in his act in part to encourage such entertainment. As we later note, the State's interest is closely analogous to the goals of patent and copyright law, focusing on the right of the individual to reap the reward of his endeavors and having little to do with protecting feelings or reputation. Second, the two torts differ in the degree to which they intrude on dissemination of information to the public. In "false light" cases the only way to protect the interests involved is to attempt to minimize publication of the damaging matter, while in "right of publicity" cases the only question is who gets to do the publishing. An entertainer such as petitioner usually has no objection to the widespread publication of his act as long as he gets the commercial benefit of such publication. Indeed, in the present case petitioner did not seek to enjoin the broadcast of his act; he simply sought compensation for the broadcast in the form of damages. . . .

. . . *Time, Inc. v. Hill*, *New York Times*, *Metromedia*, *Gertz*, and *Firestone* all involved the reporting of events; in none of them was there an attempt to broadcast or publish an entire act for which the performer ordinarily gets paid. It is evident, and there is no claim here to the contrary, that petitioner's state-law right of publicity would not serve to prevent respondent from reporting the newsworthy facts about petitioner's act. Wherever the line in particular situations is to be drawn between media reports that are protected and those that are not, we are quite sure that the First and Fourteenth Amendments do not immunize the media when they broadcast a performer's entire act without his consent. The Constitution no more prevents a State from requiring respondent to compensate petitioner for broadcasting his act on television than it would privilege respondent to film and broadcast a copyrighted dramatic work without liability to the copyright owner, or to film and broadcast a prize fight, or a baseball game, where the promoters or the participants had other plans for publicizing the event. . . .

The broadcast of a film of petitioner's entire act poses a substantial threat to the economic value of that performance. . . . The effect of a public broadcast of the performance is similar to preventing petitioner from charging an admission fee. The rationale for (protecting the right of publicity) is the straightforward one of preventing unjust enrichment by the theft of good will. . . .

There is no doubt that entertainment, as well as news, enjoys First Amendment protection. It is also true that entertainment itself can be important news. But it is important to note that neither the public nor respondent will be deprived of the benefit of petitioner's performance as long as his commercial stake in his act is appropriately recognized. Petitioner does not seek to enjoin the broadcast of his performance; he simply wants to be paid for it. . . .

We conclude that although the State of Ohio may as a matter of its own law privilege the press in the circumstances of this case, the First and Fourteenth Amendments do not require it to do so. . . .

NOTES & QUESTIONS

1. *Different First Amendment Treatment.* Why does the *Zacchini* Court conclude that the First Amendment impacts the torts of appropriation and publicity differently than the other privacy torts? Do you agree with the distinction the Court makes?

2. *Newsworthiness.* Is Zacchini's human cannonball act newsworthy? The media frequently provides news about entertainment, such as sports and movies. If the

act is newsworthy, then why shouldn't the First Amendment protect the broadcast of it? If Zacchini suffered an accident while performing his cannonball act, would a broadcast of it be newsworthy? Would this accident justify broadcast of the entire act?

In a case involving commercial use of a charcoal drawing of the Three Stooges, *Comedy III Productions, Inc. v. Gary Saderup, Inc.*, 25 Cal. 4th 387 (2001), the California Supreme Court found that use of the image on a t-shirt implicated the First Amendment: "First Amendment doctrine does not disfavor nontraditional media of expression." The *Comedy III* court identified a need to balance the right of publicity against the First Amendment. Its key test was whether a work represented a "transformative" use of the celebrity's identity. According to the California Supreme Court, one way to identify a transformative use of a celebrity image was whether the work is "primarily the defendant's own expression rather than the celebrity's likeness." Another inquiry was whether "the marketability and economic value of the challenged work derive primarily from the fame of the celebrity depicted."

In *DeHavilland v. FX Networks*, a California Appellate Court built on the *Comedy III* approach in a case involving a television show involving Olivia de Haviland, a famous movie star from Hollywood's Golden Age, in a peripheral role. De Havilland objected to her portrayal on numerous legal grounds. The resulting case looked at the First Amendment protections for a television series use of a "celebrity likeness."

DE HAVILLAND V. FX NETWORKS, LLC

21 Cal.App.5th 845 (Cal. App. 2018)

EGERTON, J. Authors write books. Filmmakers make films. Playwrights craft plays. And television writers, directors, and producers create television shows and put them on the air—or, in these modern times, online. The First Amendment protects these expressive works and the free speech rights of their creators. Some of these works are fiction. Some are factual. And some are a combination of fact and fiction. That these creative works generate income for their creators does not diminish their constitutional protection. The First Amendment does not require authors, filmmakers, playwrights, and television producers to provide their creations to the public at no charge.

Books, films, plays, and television shows often portray real people. Some are famous and some are just ordinary folks. Whether a person portrayed in one of these expressive works is a world-renowned film star—"a living legend"—or a person no one knows, she or he does not own history. Nor does she or he have the legal right to control, dictate, approve, disapprove, or veto the creator's portrayal of actual people.

In this case, actress Olivia de Havilland sues FX Networks, LLC, and Pacific 2.1 Entertainment Group, Inc. (collectively FX), the creators and producers of the television miniseries *Feud: Bette and Joan* (Feud). In the docudrama about film stars Bette Davis and Joan Crawford, an actress plays de Havilland, a close friend of Davis. De Havilland alleges causes of action for violation of the statutory right of publicity and the common law tort of misappropriation. De Havilland grounds her claims on her assertion—which FX does not dispute—that she "did not give [her] permission to the creators of 'Feud' to use [her] name, identity[,] or image in any manner." De Havilland also sues for false light invasion of privacy based on FX's portrayal in the docudrama of a fictitious interview and the de Havilland character's reference to her sister as a "bitch" when in fact the term she used was "dragon lady." De Havilland seeks to enjoin the distribution and broadcast of the television program and to recover money damages. . . .

In March 2017, FX began airing its eight-part docudrama, *Feud: Bette and Joan*. The docudrama portrays the rivalry between actresses Joan Crawford and Bette Davis. The central theme of the program is that powerful men in Hollywood pressured and manipulated women in the industry into very public feuds with one another to advance the economic interests of those men and the institutions they headed. A secondary theme—as timely now as it was in the 1960s—is the poor treatment by Hollywood of actresses as they age.

Academy-Award-winning actress Catherine Zeta-Jones portrays de Havilland in the docudrama. The de Havilland role is a limited one, consuming fewer than 17 minutes of the 392-minute, eight-episode miniseries. The role consists essentially of two parts: (1) a fictitious interview in which Zeta-Jones—often accompanied by Academy-Award-winning actress Kathy Bates playing actress Joan Blondell—talks to an interviewer (a young man named "Adam") about Hollywood, its treatment of women, and the Crawford/Davis rivalry; and (2) scenes in which Zeta-Jones interacts with Academy-Award-winning actress Susan Sarandon playing Bette Davis. These scenes portray the close friendship between Davis and de Havilland. As played by Zeta-Jones, the de Havilland character is portrayed as beautiful, glamorous, self-assured, and considerably ahead of her time in her views on the importance of equality and respect for women in Hollywood. *Feud* was nominated for 18 Emmy awards. . . .

As noted, de Havilland alleges causes of action for violation of the statutory right of publicity, Civil Code section 3344, and for the common law tort of misappropriation. Section 3344, subdivision (a) provides, in part, "Any person who knowingly uses another's name, voice, signature, photograph, or likeness, in any manner, on or in *products, merchandise, or goods*, or for purposes of advertising or selling, or soliciting purchases of, *products, merchandise, goods, or services*, without such person's prior consent, . . . shall be liable for any damages sustained by the person or persons injured as a result thereof." (Italics added.) Misappropriation is one of the four branches of the privacy tort identified by Dean William Prosser.

De Havilland's statutory claim raises a preliminary question of whether the portrayal of a real person in a television program (or a book, play, or film) constitutes the "use" of that person's name or "likeness" "on or in" a product, merchandise, or good. Books, films, and television shows are "things" but are they "merchandise" or "products"? Many of the cases in this area involve products and merchandise such as T-shirts and lithographs (*Comedy III*), greeting cards, and video games, or advertisements for products and merchandise.

We need not decide this question, however, because *Feud* is constitutionally protected in any event. . . .

Assuming for argument's sake that a television program is a "product, merchandise, or good" and that Zeta-Jones's portrayal of de Havilland constitutes a "use" of de Havilland's name or likeness within the scope of both the right of publicity statute and the misappropriation tort, we come to FX's First Amendment defense. . . .

Feud is as constitutionally protected as was the film in *Sarver, The Hurt Locker*. As with that expressive work, *Feud* "is speech that is fully protected by the First Amendment, which safeguards the storytellers and artists who take the raw materials of life—including the stories of real individuals, ordinary or extraordinary—and transform them into art, be it articles, books, movies, or plays." (*Sarver, supra*).

That *Feud*'s creators did not purchase or otherwise procure de Havilland's "rights" to her name or likeness does not change this analysis. Producers of films and television programs may enter into agreements with individuals portrayed in those works for a variety of reasons, including access to the person's recollections or "story" the producers would not otherwise have, or a desire to avoid litigation for a reasonable fee. But the First Amendment simply does not require such acquisition agreements. The creators of *The People v. O.J. Simpson: American Crime Story* can portray Trial Judge Lance Ito without acquiring his rights. *Fruitvale Station*'s writer and director Ryan Coogler can portray Bay Area Rapid Transit officer Johannes Mehserle without acquiring his rights. HBO can portray Sarah Palin in *Game Change* (HBO 2013) without acquiring her rights. There are myriad additional examples.

De Havilland also contends the fictitious interview "is structured as an endorsement of [*Feud*]." The miniseries itself does not support this contention. Nothing Zeta-Jones says or does as de Havilland in the docudrama suggests—much less constitutes—an "endorsement" of the work by de Havilland. De Havilland's argument seems to be that, whenever a filmmaker includes a character based on a real person, that inclusion implies an "endorsement" of the film or program by that real person. We have found no case authority to support this novel argument.

Nor does the use of de Havilland's name—along with photographs of Zeta-Jones—in social media promotion for the miniseries support de Havilland's claims for violation of her right of publicity. Constitutional protection for an expressive work such as *Feud* "'extends to the truthful use of a public figure's name and likeness in advertising [that] is merely an adjunct of the protected publication and promotes only the protected publication.'" (*Montana v. San Jose Mercury News, Inc.* (1995) 34 Cal.App.4th 790, 797) (1st Amend. protected posters that reproduced newspaper stories and photographs of famous quarterback "for two distinct reasons: first, because the posters themselves report newsworthy items of public interest, and second, because a newspaper has a constitutional right to promote itself by reproducing its originally protected articles or photographs"). . .

The parties spend considerable time discussing the "transformative" test set forth in *Comedy III*. There, a company that owns the rights under Civil Code section 990 to The Three Stooges (all three are deceased) sued an artist who had made a charcoal drawing of The Three Stooges, put it on T-shirts and lithographs, and sold those items. The Supreme Court noted the statute imposes liability on a person who uses a deceased personality's name or likeness "either (1) 'on or in' a product, *or* (2) in 'advertising or selling' a product." (*Comedy III*) The T-shirts and lithographs were, the court said, "tangible personal property," "consisting of fabric and ink" and "paper and ink." (*Ibid*.) The court found the artist's drawing was an "expressive work[ ] and not an advertisement for or endorsement of a product." (*Id*.) But, the court continued, "[A] celebrity's heirs and assigns have a legitimate protectible interest in exploiting the value to be obtained from *merchandising* the celebrity's image." (*Id.* italics added.)

To resolve this "difficult issue" (*Comedy III*), the court borrowed a concept from copyright law: " 'whether and to what extent the new work [the product bearing the deceased personality's likeness] is "transformative." ' " (*Id*.)

Comedy III's "transformative" test makes sense when applied to products and merchandise—"tangible personal property," in the Supreme Court's words. Lower courts have struggled mightily, however, to figure out how to apply it to expressive works such as films, plays, and television programs.

. . . The fictitious, "imagined" interview in which Zeta-Jones talks about Hollywood's treatment of women and the Crawford/Davis rivalry is a far cry from T-shirts depicting a representational, pedestrian, uncreative drawing of The Three Stooges. The de Havilland role, performed by Zeta-Jones, constitutes about 4.2 percent of *Feud*. The docudrama tells the story, in nearly eight hours, of the competition between Hollywood's leading ladies of the day, Bette Davis and Joan Crawford, for film roles, attention, awards, and acclaim. The miniseries tells many stories within the story as well: Jack Warner's demeaning and dismissive treatment of director Robert Aldrich; Crawford's and Davis's struggles with their personal relationships: husbands, partners, and children; the obstacles faced by capable women like Aldrich's assistant Pauline Jameson who want to direct motion pictures; and the refusal of powerful men in the entertainment business to take women seriously, even when their movies make money.

In the words of the *Comedy III* Court, Zeta-Jones's "celebrity likeness [of de Havilland] is one of the 'raw materials' from which [the] original work [*Feud*] is synthesized." (*Comedy III, supra*) Applying *Comedy III*'s "useful subsidiary inquiry" here, we conclude as a matter of law that *Feud*'s "marketability and economic value" does not "derive primarily from [de Havilland's] fame" but rather "comes principally from . . . the creativity, skill, and reputation" of *Feud*'s creators and actors. Ryan Murphy is a successful screenwriter, director, and producer who counts among his credits the television series *Glee* and the Emmy-award-winning miniseries *The People v. O.J. Simpson: American Crime Story*. Accomplished writers contributed to the script. Highly-regarded and award-winning actors including Susan Sarandon, Jessica Lange, Catherine Zeta-Jones, Stanley Tucci, Alfred Molina, Judy Davis, and Kathy Bates performed in *Feud*. In short, *Feud* constitutes "significant expression"—a story of two Hollywood legends—of which the de Havilland character is but a small part. While viewers may have "tuned in" to see these actors and watch this Hollywood tale, there is no evidence that de Havilland as a character was a significant draw.

NOTES & QUESTIONS

1. **De Havilland: *The Holding.*** Overturning the judgment of the trial court, the *De Havilland* case found that the miniseries *Feud* did not violate the rights of publicity of Olivia de Havilland. Due to the First Amendment, there was no need for the creators and producers of the miniseries to purchase the rights to this celebrity's name and likeness. Most importantly, the marketability and economic value of the show derived principally from the creativity and skill of the show's creators and actors. How would you reconcile this decision with *Zacchini*? Can you think of circumstances in which a docudrama based on real-life characters would violate the right of publicity?

2. ***The Rolling Stones*, Some Girls, *and* Comedy III.** De Havilland draws upon the influential "transformative" test of *Comedy III*. Consider the use of this test in assessing the legality of the original artwork for Some Girls (1978), an album from the Rolling Stones. This artwork was based on a catalogue for Valmor Products; the cover for *Some Girls* replaced the original illustrations for wigs with images of the members of the Rolling Stones as well as of female and male celebrities. George Harrison did not object to the use of his photograph, but among those threatening legal action were Lucille Ball, Farrah Fawcett, Raquel Welch, and the Estate of Marilyn Monroe. The Stones had not received permission to use the images of these noted figures, and redesigned the cover and removed these photographs. The cover artwork as originally designed can be viewed on Wikepedia and elsewhere.[100]

   Do you think the original artwork was sufficiently transformative under *Comedy III* to insulate the Rolling Stones from a right of publicity claim from the celebrities who objected to the unauthorized use of their images? Which of the *Comedy III* factors would be most important in reaching your judgment?

3. ***False Light and Defamation Claims.*** The *de Havilland* court also rejected the false light and defamation claims before it. It found that the portrayal of de Havilland was "as a wise, witty, sometimes playful woman." *Feud* did not place her in a "highly offensive light." In fact, the court found that with possibly one exception, "*Feud*'s portrayal [of de Havilland] is the most favorable of any character in the docudrama."

   Moreover, regarding defamation, the court held that for a fictional work the required showing was not simply that something was false. It stated, "[F]iction is by definition untrue. It is imagined, made-up. Put more starkly, it is false." For a fictional work where a defamatory portrayal was merely *implied*, moreover, the court held that the plaintiff had to show that the defendant deliberately cast her words in an equivocal fashion to insinuate a defamatory import, or acted in reckless disregard of how its words would be interpreted by the average person. De Havilland did not demonstrate that she could prove that *Feud*'s creators met this "actual malice" test for defamation.

4. ***Four Rights and Not One?*** For Robert Post and Jennifer Rothman, the right of publicity seeks to vindicate four torts and not one, and each of these four

---

[100] https://en.wikipedia.org/wiki/Some_Girls#/media/File:Some_Girls.png

interests requires its own First Amendment analysis.[101] The four kinds of right of publicity are a right of performance, right of commercial value, right of control, and right of dignity. *Zachinni* is a right of performance case. It is a "claim designed to authorize persons who create performances to protect these performances from misappropriation." For Rothman and Post, *Zacchini* was correctly decided. The underlying performance was "a discrete set of acts in space and time," and without a legal right to it, a reward for these endeavors would not be protected adequately.

The next interest is the right of commercial value of a person's identity. For Post and Rothman, a plaintiff making this claim should be required to show that her identity is widely recognized and invested with significant market value, and that the defendant's contested use would cause confusion, diminishment of value, or unfair appropriation. The *Carson* case is a diminishment case.

As for the right of control, it is a property-like interest in prohibiting use of one's identity. Post and Rothman view it as necessarily subject to "various limitations and defenses" and associate it with the European development of data protection interests, such as the "right to be forgotten."

Finally, the right of dignity focuses on the integrity of personality. Tom Waits' lawsuit against the use of a sound-alike voice in a Doritos commercial "focused in part on the public shame and emotional distress he experienced due to the violation of his strict policy against appearing or singing in any advertisements." Post and Rothman call for a "highly offensive" requirement to be grafted onto this branch of the right of publicity.

Turning then to the First Amendment, the two authors argue that the failure to separate out the different kinds of interests in the right of publicity has led to chaos in constitutional analysis. Regarding the right of performance, there is a need for limitations on this interest similar to those in the "fair use" defense in copyright. The right of commercial value should also be subject to fair use defenses. As for the confusion subpart of this branch, it should be limited to situations in which "a speaker has seriously and perhaps explicitly misled the public as to a plaintiff's participation in, or sponsorship of, the allegedly infringing use."

The third branch of publicity is the right of control. Here, Post and Rothman argue that this interest if "expansive, like that accepted in Europe in the context of the 'right to be forgotten,' would likely be unconstitutional in the United States." It would not pass constitutional muster to limit public discourse based on otherwise public information. Finally, as to the right of dignity, highly offensive speech acts that do not speak to a matter of public concern should be actionable without violating the First Amendment.

Are these different categories helpful in organizing the right of publicity cases in this Chapter? What significant problems still remain in this area of doctrine?

---

[101] Robert Post & Jennifer Rothman, *The First Amendment and the Right(s) of Publicity*, 130 Yale L.J. 86 (2020).

E. PRIVACY PROTECTIONS FOR ANONYMITY AND RECEIPT OF IDEAS

When it comes to the privacy torts, the First Amendment typically has clashed with privacy. But in other contexts, the First Amendment is used as a way to protect privacy. Anonymous speakers have invoked First Amendment rights to protect themselves from being identified. The First Amendment has been used by those who want to explore ideas without being monitored. And the First Amendment is invoked by journalists seeking to protect themselves from being compelled to reveal their anonymous sources.

1. ANONYMITY

One of the most major such contexts is anonymity. Anonymity (or the use of pseudonyms) involves people's ability to conduct activities without being identified. People may want to speak anonymously because their speech might be unpopular or might be disliked by an employer or others who might retaliate against them. People may also want to read or surf the Internet anonymously because they are concerned about negative reactions toward their intellectual interests. Anonymity promotes freedom to speak or read without fear of reprisal or ostracism. However, when people can engage in anonymous activities, they might cause significant harm to other people and escape from being held accountable because their identities are not known. In a paradoxical way, people might use the cloak of anonymity to violate the privacy of others by revealing their private information.

When should the government be able to remove the cloak of anonymity on a person? When should a private party be able to do so? And to what extent can the government restrict anonymity to prevent fraud, crime, or other problems?

(a) Anonymous Speech

TALLEY V. STATE OF CALIFORNIA

362 U.S. 60 (1960)

BLACK, J. The question presented here is whether the provisions of a Los Angeles City ordinance restricting the distribution of handbills "abridge the freedom of speech and of the press secured against state invasion by the Fourteenth Amendment of the Constitution." The ordinance, § 28.06 of the Municipal Code of the City of Los Angeles, provides:

> No person shall distribute any hand-bill in any place under any circumstances, which does not have printed on the cover, or the face thereof, the name and address of the following:
>
> > (a) The person who printed, wrote, compiled or manufactured the same.

(b) The person who caused the same to be distributed; provided, however, that in the case of a fictitious person or club, in addition to such fictitious name, the true names and addresses of the owners, managers or agents of the person sponsoring said hand-bill shall also appear thereon.

The petitioner was arrested and tried in a Los Angeles Municipal Court for violating this ordinance. . . .

Anonymous pamphlets, leaflets, brochures and even books have played an important role in the progress of mankind. Persecuted groups and sects from time to time throughout history have been able to criticize oppressive practices and laws either anonymously or not at all. The obnoxious press licensing law of England, which was also enforced on the Colonies was due in part to the knowledge that exposure of the names of printers, writers and distributors would lessen the circulation of literature critical of the government. The old seditious libel cases in England show the lengths to which government had to go to find out who was responsible for books that were obnoxious to the rulers. John Lilburne was whipped, pilloried and fined for refusing to answer questions designed to get evidence to convict him or someone else for the secret distribution of books in England. Two Puritan Ministers, John Penry and John Udal, were sentenced to death on charges that they were responsible for writing, printing or publishing books. Before the Revolutionary War colonial patriots frequently had to conceal their authorship or distribution of literature that easily could have brought down on them prosecutions by English-controlled courts. Along about that time the Letters of Junius were written and the identity of their author is unknown to this day. Even the Federalist Papers, written in favor of the adoption of our Constitution, were published under fictitious names. It is plain that anonymity has sometimes been assumed for the most constructive purposes.

We have recently had occasion to hold in two cases that there are times and circumstances when States may not compel members of groups engaged in the dissemination of ideas to be publicly identified. *Bates v. City of Little Rock*, 361 U.S. 516; *N.A.A.C.P. v. State of Alabama*, 357 U.S. 449. The reason for those holdings was that identification and fear of reprisal might deter perfectly peaceful discussions of public matters of importance. This broad Los Angeles ordinance is subject to the same infirmity. We hold that it, like the Griffin, Georgia, ordinance, is void on its face. . . .

MCINTYRE V. OHIO ELECTIONS COMMISSION

514 U.S. 334 (1995)

STEVENS, J. . . . On April 27, 1988, Margaret McIntyre distributed leaflets to persons attending a public meeting at the Blendon Middle School in Westerville, Ohio. At this meeting, the superintendent of schools planned to discuss an imminent referendum on a proposed school tax levy. The leaflets expressed Mrs. McIntyre's opposition to the levy. There is no suggestion that the text of her message was false, misleading, or libelous. She had composed and printed it on her home computer and had paid a professional printer to make additional copies. Some of the handbills identified her as the author; others merely purported to express the views of "CONCERNED PARENTS AND TAX PAYERS." Except for the help provided by her son and a friend, who placed some of the leaflets on car windshields in the school parking lot, Mrs. McIntyre acted independently.

While Mrs. McIntyre distributed her handbills, an official of the school district, who supported the tax proposal, advised her that the unsigned leaflets did not conform to the Ohio election laws. Undeterred, Mrs. McIntyre appeared at another meeting on the next evening and handed out more of the handbills.

The proposed school levy was defeated at the next two elections, but it finally passed on its third try in November 1988. Five months later, the same school official filed a complaint with the Ohio Elections Commission charging that Mrs. McIntyre's distribution of unsigned leaflets violated § 3599.09(A) of the Ohio Code [which prohibited the distribution of political literature without the name and address of the person or organization responsible for the distribution]. The commission agreed and imposed a fine of $100. . . .

Ohio maintains that the statute under review is a reasonable regulation of the electoral process. . . .

"Anonymous pamphlets, leaflets, brochures and even books have played an important role in the progress of mankind." *Talley v. California.* Great works of literature have frequently been produced by authors writing under assumed names.[102] Despite readers' curiosity and the public's interest in identifying the creator of a work of art, an author generally is free to decide whether or not to disclose his or her true identity. The decision in favor of anonymity may be motivated by fear of economic or official retaliation, by concern about social ostracism, or merely by a desire to preserve as much of one's privacy as possible. Whatever the motivation may be, at least in the field of literary endeavor, the interest in having anonymous works enter the marketplace of ideas unquestionably outweighs any public interest in requiring disclosure as a condition of entry. Accordingly, an author's decision to remain anonymous, like other decisions concerning omissions or additions to the content of a publication, is an aspect of the freedom of speech protected by the First Amendment.

. . . On occasion, quite apart from any threat of persecution, an advocate may believe her ideas will be more persuasive if her readers are unaware of her identity. Anonymity thereby provides a way for a writer who may be personally unpopular to ensure that readers will not prejudge her message simply because they do not like its proponent. Thus, even in the field of political rhetoric, where "the identity of the speaker is an important component of many attempts to persuade," the most effective advocates have sometimes opted for anonymity. The specific holding in *Talley* related to advocacy of an economic boycott, but the Court's reasoning embraced a respected tradition of anonymity in the advocacy of political causes.[103]

---

[102] American names such as Mark Twain (Samuel Langhorne Clemens) and O. Henry (William Sydney Porter) come readily to mind. Benjamin Franklin employed numerous different pseudonyms. Distinguished French authors such as Voltaire (François Marie Arouet) and George Sand (Amandine Aurore Lucie Dupin), and British authors such as George Eliot (Mary Ann Evans), Charles Lamb (sometimes wrote as "Elia"), and Charles Dickens (sometimes wrote as "Boz"), also published under assumed names. . . .

[103] That tradition is most famously embodied in the Federalist Papers, authored by James Madison, Alexander Hamilton, and John Jay, but signed "Publius." Publius' opponents, the Anti-Federalists, also tended to publish under pseudonyms. . . .

This tradition is perhaps best exemplified by the secret ballot, the hard-won right to vote one's conscience without fear of retaliation. . . .

. . . [Section] 3599.09(A) of the Ohio Code does not control the mechanics of the electoral process. It is a regulation of pure speech. Moreover, even though this provision applies evenhandedly to advocates of differing viewpoints, it is a direct regulation of the content of speech. . . .

When a law burdens core political speech, we apply "exacting scrutiny," and we uphold the restriction only if it is narrowly tailored to serve an overriding state interest. . . .

Nevertheless, the State argues that, even under the strictest standard of review, the disclosure requirement in § 3599.09(A) is justified by two important and legitimate state interests. Ohio judges its interest in preventing fraudulent and libelous statements and its interest in providing the electorate with relevant information to be sufficiently compelling to justify the anonymous speech ban. These two interests necessarily overlap to some extent, but it is useful to discuss them separately.

Insofar as the interest in informing the electorate means nothing more than the provision of additional information that may either buttress or undermine the argument in a document, we think the identity of the speaker is no different from other components of the document's content that the author is free to include or exclude. . . . The simple interest in providing voters with additional relevant information does not justify a state requirement that a writer make statements or disclosures she would otherwise omit. Moreover, in the case of a handbill written by a private citizen who is not known to the recipient, the name and address of the author add little, if anything, to the reader's ability to evaluate the document's message. . . .

Under our Constitution, anonymous pamphleteering is not a pernicious, fraudulent practice, but an honorable tradition of advocacy and of dissent. Anonymity is a shield from the tyranny of the majority. It thus exemplifies the purpose behind the Bill of Rights, and of the First Amendment in particular: to protect unpopular individuals from retaliation — and their ideas from suppression — at the hand of an intolerant society. . . .

SCALIA, J. joined by REHNQUIST, C.J. dissenting. . . . The Court's unprecedented protection for anonymous speech does not even have the virtue of establishing a clear (albeit erroneous) rule of law. . . . It may take decades to work out the shape of this newly expanded right-to-speak-incognito, even in the elections field. And in other areas, of course, a whole new boutique of wonderful First Amendment litigation opens its doors. Must a parade permit, for example, be issued to a group that refuses to provide its identity, or that agrees to do so only under assurance that the identity will not be made public? Must a municipally owned theater that is leased for private productions book anonymously sponsored presentations? Must a government periodical that has a "letters to the editor" column disavow the policy that most newspapers have against the publication of anonymous letters? Must a public university that makes its facilities available for a speech by Louis Farrakhan or David Duke refuse to disclose the on-campus or off-campus group that has sponsored or paid for the speech? Must a municipal "public-access" cable channel permit anonymous (and masked) performers? The

silliness that follows upon a generalized right to anonymous speech has no end. . .
.

. . . [A] person who is required to put his name to a document is much less likely to lie than one who can lie anonymously. . . Thus, people will be more likely to observe a signing requirement than a naked "no falsity" requirement; and, having observed that requirement, will then be significantly less likely to lie in what they have signed. . . .

NOTES & QUESTIONS

1. ***Why Is Anonymity in Speaking Protected by the First Amendment?*** *Talley* and *McIntyre* conclude that anonymous speech is protected under the First Amendment but do so based on different rationales. What are those rationales? Which rationale seems most persuasive to you?

2. ***Anonymity of Petitions.*** In *Doe v. Reed*, 130 S. Ct. 1886 (2010), the State of Washington passed a law that provided rights to same-sex domestic partners. A group of petitioners, called "Protect Marriage Washington," collected signatures to put a referendum on the ballot to nullify the law. The group collected more than 137,000 signatures, a sufficient amount to put the referendum (R-71) on the ballot. Several groups sought to obtain copies of the petition and the names and addresses of the people who signed it. The groups indicated they planned to post the names online. Protect Marriage Washington and several signers sought to enjoin the release of the petitions as a violation of the First Amendment. The Supreme Court held that because the plaintiffs sought to bar the state from making all referendum petitions available to the public, the plaintiffs were challenging the disclosure facially rather than as applied. The Court held that the plaintiffs' First Amendment interests were implicated but that their facial challenge to the disclosure was outweighed by the state's interest in "preserving the integrity of the electoral process." The state's interest encompassed fraud prevention and "promoting transparency and accountability in the electoral process."

   The Court left open whether the plaintiffs would prevail on a separate "as applied" challenge to the disclosure. The plaintiffs' facial challenge involved the disclosure requirement generally, without proof of specific harm to specific plaintiffs. In contrast, an "as applied" challenge would require specific plaintiffs to prove they were chilled in their speech.

3. ***Anonymity in Cyberspace and "John Doe" Lawsuits.*** E-mail and the Internet enable people to communicate anonymously with ease. People can send e-mail or post messages to electronic bulletin boards under pseudonyms. However, this anonymity is quite fragile, and in some cases illusory. Websites log the IP address of the computers of visitors of the site, and these IP addresses can be traced back to a person. An individual's Internet Service Provider (ISP) has information linking IP addresses to particular account holders. Under federal wiretap law, an ISP must disclose information identifying a particular user to the government pursuant to a subpoena. However, no subpoena is required for private parties. An ISP "may disclose a record or other information pertaining

to a subscriber . . . to any person other than a governmental entity." 18 U.S.C. § 2703(c)(1)(A).

In what is known as a "John Doe" lawsuit, plaintiffs can sue to find out the identity of an anonymous or pseudonymous speaker in order to pursue a defamation or privacy action. Plaintiffs bring a lawsuit against anonymous speakers (the John Does) and then seek civil subpoenas or court orders to compel ISPs to reveal the identities of these speakers. Courts must consider the First Amendment rights of the speakers when determining whether plaintiffs are entitled to discover the identities of speakers people allege have defamed them or invaded their privacy.[104] What standard should courts use to make this determination? The case below addresses this issue.

DOE V. CAHILL

884 A.2d 451 (Del. 2005)

STEELE, C.J. . . . On November 2, 2004, the plaintiffs below, Patrick and Julia Cahill, both residents of Smyrna, Delaware, filed suit against four John Doe defendants asserting defamation and invasion of privacy claims. This appeal involves only one of the John Doe defendants, John Doe No. 1 below and "Doe" in this opinion. Using the alias "Proud Citizen," Doe posted two statements on an internet website sponsored by the Delaware State News called the "Smyrna/Clayton Issues Blog" concerning Cahill's performance as a City Councilman of Smyrna. The "Guidelines" at the top of the blog stated "[t]his is your hometown forum for opinions about public issues." The first of Doe's statements, posted on September 18, 2004, said:

> If only Councilman Cahill was able to display the same leadership skills, energy and enthusiasm toward the revitalization and growth of the fine town of Smyrna as Mayor Schaeffer has demonstrated! While Mayor Schaeffer has made great strides toward improving the livelihood of Smyrna's citizens, Cahill has devoted all of his energy to being a divisive impediment to any kind of cooperative movement. *Anyone who has spent any amount of time with Cahill would be keenly aware of such character flaws, not to mention an obvious mental deterioration.* Cahill is a prime example of failed leadership — his eventual ousting is exactly what Smyrna needs in order to move forward and establish a community that is able to thrive on its own economic stability and common pride in its town.

The next day, Doe posted another statement:

> *Gahill* [sic] *is as paranoid* as everyone in the town thinks he is. The mayor needs support from his citizens and protections from unfounded attacks. . . .

Pursuant to Superior Court Rule 30, the Cahills sought and obtained leave of the Superior Court to conduct a pre-service deposition of the owner of the internet blog, Independent Newspapers. After obtaining the IP addresses associated with the blog postings from the blog's owner, the Cahills learned that Comcast Corporation owned Doe's IP address. An IP address is an electronic number that

---

[104] Lyrissa Barnett Lidsky, *Silencing John Doe: Defamation and Discourse in Cyberspace*, 49 Duke L.J. 855 (2000).

specifically identifies a particular computer using the internet. IP addresses are often owned by internet service providers who then assign them to subscribers when they use the internet. These addresses are unique and assigned to only one ISP subscriber at a time. Thus, if the ISP knows the time and the date that postings were made from a specific IP address, it can determine the identity of its subscriber.

Armed with Doe's IP address, the Cahills obtained a court order requiring Comcast to disclose Doe's identity. As required by Federal Statute,[105] when Comcast received the discovery request, it notified Doe. On January 4, 2005, Doe filed an "Emergency Motion for a Protective Order" seeking to prevent the Cahills from obtaining his identity from Comcast. . . .

It is clear that speech over the internet is entitled to First Amendment protection. This protection extends to anonymous internet speech. Anonymous internet speech in blogs or chat rooms in some instances can become the modern equivalent of political pamphleteering. . . .

It also is clear that the First Amendment does not protect defamatory speech. . . . Certain classes of speech, including defamatory and libelous speech, are entitled to no Constitutional protection. . . . Accordingly, we must adopt a standard that appropriately balances one person's right to speak anonymously against another person's right to protect his reputation. . . .

In this case, this Court is called upon to adopt a standard for trial courts to apply when faced with a public figure plaintiff's discovery request that seeks to unmask the identity of an anonymous defendant who has posted allegedly defamatory material on the internet. Before this Court is an entire spectrum of "standards" that could be required, ranging (in ascending order) from a good faith basis to assert a claim, to pleading sufficient facts to survive a motion to dismiss, to a showing of *prima facie* evidence sufficient to withstand a motion for summary judgment, and beyond that, hurdles even more stringent. . . . [W]e hold that a defamation plaintiff must satisfy a "summary judgment" standard before obtaining the identity of an anonymous defendant.

We are concerned that setting the standard too low will chill potential posters from exercising their First Amendment right to speak anonymously. The possibility of losing anonymity in a future lawsuit could intimidate anonymous posters into self-censoring their comments or simply not commenting at all. A defamation plaintiff, particularly a public figure, obtains a very important form of relief by unmasking the identity of his anonymous critics. The revelation of identity of an anonymous speaker "may subject [that speaker] to ostracism for expressing unpopular ideas, invite retaliation from those who oppose her ideas or from those whom she criticizes, or simply give unwanted exposure to her mental processes." Plaintiffs can often initially plead sufficient facts to meet the good faith test applied by the Superior Court, even if the defamation claim is not very strong, or worse, if they do not intend to pursue the defamation action to a final decision. After obtaining the identity of an anonymous critic through the compulsory discovery process, a defamation plaintiff who either loses on the merits or fails to pursue a lawsuit is still free to engage in extra-judicial self-help remedies; more bluntly, the plaintiff can simply seek revenge or retribution.

---

[105] 47 U.S.C. 551(c)(2) requires a court order to a cable ISP and notice to the ISP subscriber before an ISP can disclose the identity of its subscriber to a third party.

Indeed, there is reason to believe that many defamation plaintiffs bring suit merely to unmask the identities of anonymous critics. As one commentator has noted, "[t]he sudden surge in John Doe suits stems from the fact that many defamation actions are not really about money." "The goals of this new breed of libel action are largely symbolic, the primary goal being to silence John Doe and others like him." This "sue first, ask questions later" approach, coupled with a standard only minimally protective of the anonymity of defendants, will discourage debate on important issues of public concern as more and more anonymous posters censor their online statements in response to the likelihood of being unmasked. . . .

Long-settled doctrine governs this Court's review of dismissals under Rule 12(b)(6). Under that doctrine, the threshold for the showing a plaintiff must make to survive a motion to dismiss is low. Delaware is a notice pleading jurisdiction. Thus, for a complaint to survive a motion to dismiss, it need only give "general notice of the claim asserted." A court can dismiss for failure to state a claim on which relief can be granted only if "it appears with reasonable certainty that the plaintiff could not prove any set of facts that would entitle him to relief." On a motion to dismiss, a court's review is limited to the well-pleaded allegations in the complaint. An allegation, "though vague or lacking in detail" can still be well-pleaded so long as it puts the opposing party on notice of the claim brought against it. Finally, in ruling on a motion to dismiss under Rule 12(b)(6), a trial court must draw all reasonable factual inferences in favor of the party opposing the motion. . . .

We conclude that the summary judgment standard is the appropriate test by which to strike the balance between a defamation plaintiff's right to protect his reputation and a defendant's right to exercise free speech anonymously. We accordingly hold that before a defamation plaintiff can obtain the identity of an anonymous defendant through the compulsory discovery process he must support his defamation claim with facts sufficient to defeat a summary judgment motion. . . .

[T]o obtain discovery of an anonymous defendant's identity under the summary judgment standard, a defamation plaintiff "must submit sufficient evidence to establish a *prima facie* case for each essential element of the claim in question." In other words, the defamation plaintiff, as the party bearing the burden of proof at trial, must introduce evidence creating a genuine issue of material fact for all elements of a defamation claim *within the plaintiff's control. . . .*

[W]e are mindful that public figures in a defamation case must prove that the defendant made the statements with actual malice. Without discovery of the defendant's identity, satisfying this element may be difficult, if not impossible. Consequently, we do NOT hold that the public figure defamation plaintiff is required to produce evidence on this element of the claim. . . .

Having adopted a summary judgment standard, we now apply it to the facts of this case. . . .

In deciding whether or not a statement is defamatory we determine, "*first,* whether alleged defamatory statements are expressions of fact or protected expressions of opinion; and [*second*], whether the challenged statements are capable of a defamatory meaning." . . .

Applying a good faith standard, the trial judge concluded, "it is enough to meet the 'good faith' standard that the Cahills articulate a legitimate basis for claiming defamation in the context of their particular circumstances." He continued "[g]iven that Mr. Cahill is a married man, [Doe's] statement referring to him as "Gahill" might reasonably be interpreted as indicating that Mr. Cahill has engaged in an extra-marital same-sex affair. Such a statement may form the basis of an actionable defamation claim." We disagree. Using a "G" instead of a "C" as the first letter of Cahill's name is just as likely to be a typographical error as an intended misguided insult. Under the summary judgment standard, no reasonable person would interpret this statement to indicate that Cahill had an extra-marital same-sex affair.
. . .

We agree that the context in which the statements were made is probative, but reach the opposite conclusion. Given the context, no reasonable person could have interpreted these statements as being anything other than opinion. . . .

NOTES & QUESTIONS

1. *Postscript.* The anonymous speaker in *Doe v. Cahill* turned out to be Mayor Schaeffer's 25-year-old stepdaughter. Her identity was revealed inadvertently in discovery. The Schaeffers and Cahills were next-door neighbors, and they had feuded since 2003. Until the mayor's stepdaughter was unmasked, he had denied that anybody in his household made the statements against Cahill. Subsequently, Cahill settled his defamation lawsuit against Schaeffer's stepdaughter.

   After the Delaware Supreme Court decision was issued, Patrick and Julia Cahill were arrested following a shouting match with the Schaeffers. The Cahills were charged with terroristic threatening, harassment, and disorderly conduct. They were subsequently acquitted of these charges, but Patrick Cahill was convicted of violating a police order to avoid contacting the Schaeffers. He was fined $100 and sentenced to a year of probation.

2. *The Standard for Unmasking an Anonymous Speaker.* Courts have established different standards for a plaintiff to find out the identity of an anonymous speaker. The most common include:

   • *The Motion to Dismiss Standard.* The plaintiff must establish that the case would survive a motion to dismiss. *See Columbia Insurance Co. v. Seescandy.com*, 185 F.R.D. 573 (N.D. Cal. 1999).

   • *The Prima Facie Case Standard.* The plaintiff must produce evidence showing a prima facie case on all elements and must demonstrate that revealing the identity of the anonymous speaker will not severely harm the speaker's free speech or privacy rights and will be "necessary to enable plaintiff to protect against or remedy serious wrongs." *Highfields Capital Mgmt., LP v. Doe*, 385 F. Supp. 2d 969 (N.D. Cal. 2005); *Dendrite Int'l v. Doe No. 3*, 775 A.2d 756 (N.J. Super. App. Div. 2001).

- *The Summary Judgment Standard.* The plaintiff must prove the case could survive a motion for summary judgment. *See Doe v. Cahill, supra.*

- *The Variable Standard.* This standard varies depending upon the nature of the speech, with commercial speech being protected by a much lower standard than non-commercial speech. *See In re Anonymous Online Speakers*, 611 F.3d 653 (9th Cir. 2010) (known as the "*Quixtar*" case).

What are the pros and cons of each approach?

3. ***The Identities of Third Parties to the Litigation.*** In *Doe v. 2TheMart.com, Inc.* 140 F. Supp. 2d 1088 (W.D. Wash. 2001), shareholders of 2TheMart.com, Inc. brought a derivative class action against the corporation. The company, in preparing its defense, subpoenaed the identity of 23 anonymous speakers who posted messages on an online message board. These postings were very critical of 2TheMart. One of the anonymous speakers challenged the subpoena. The court concluded:

> The Court will consider four factors in determining whether the subpoena should issue. These are whether: (1) the subpoena seeking the information was issued in good faith and not for any improper purpose, (2) the information sought relates to a core claim or defense, (3) the identifying information is directly and materially relevant to that claim or defense, and (4) information sufficient to establish or to disprove that claim or defense is unavailable from any other source. . . .
>
> Only when the identifying information is needed to advance core claims or defenses can it be sufficiently material to compromise First Amendment rights. If the information relates only to a secondary claim or to one of numerous affirmative defenses, then the primary substance of the case can go forward without disturbing the First Amendment rights of the anonymous Internet users.
>
> The information sought by TMRT does not relate to a core defense. Here, the information relates to only one of twenty-seven affirmative defenses raised by the defendant, the defense that "no act or omission of any of the Defendants was the cause in fact or the proximate cause of any injury or damage to the plaintiffs." . . .
>
> [Moreover,] TMRT has failed to demonstrate that the identity of the Internet users is directly and materially relevant to a core defense. These Internet users are not parties to the case and have not been named as defendants as to any claim, cross-claim or third-party claim. . . .

Should the standard for unmasking non-parties to the litigation be stricter than that for parties to a case?

4. ***Can Being Anonymous Online Be Criminalized?*** In *ACLU v. Miller*, 977 F. Supp. 1228 (N.D. Ga. 1997), plaintiffs challenged a law that criminalized falsely identifying oneself in online communications. The court held that the law ran afoul of the First Amendment:

> Defendants allege that the statute's purpose is fraud prevention, which the Court agrees is a compelling state interest. However, the statute is not narrowly tailored to achieve that end and instead sweeps innocent, protected speech

within its scope. Specifically, by its plain language the criminal prohibition applies regardless of whether a speaker has any intent to deceive or whether deception actually occurs. Therefore, it could apply to a wide range of transmissions which "falsely identify" the sender, but are not "fraudulent" within the specific meaning of the criminal code. . . .

5. ***The WHOIS Database.*** Currently, the Internet Corporation for Assigned Names and Numbers (ICANN) Registrar Accreditation Agreement (RAA) requires that the identity and addresses of domain name holders be publicly disclosed, as well as the identities, addresses, e-mail addresses, and telephone numbers for technical and administrative contacts. Domain names are the names assigned to particular websites (e.g., cnn.com). In other words, an individual who wants to create her own website must publicly disclose personal information and cannot remain anonymous. The registration scheme extends to anyone who owns a domain name, including commercial services and publishers of political newsletters.

Dawn Nunziato observes that the ICANN identification policy was enacted "[a]t the behest of interested intellectual property owners, who were concerned about their ability to police infringing content on the Internet." She argues:

> Because of the important role anonymous speech serves within expressive forums — which in turn are integral to democratic governments — ICANN should, in reevaluating its policies to accord meaningful protection for freedom of expression, revise its policy requiring domain name holders publicly to disclose their names and addresses. While protecting anonymous Internet speech is clearly an important component of free speech within the United States, it is even more important for ICANN to protect the identity of speakers from countries that are more inclined to retaliate against speakers based on the ideas they express.

Nunziato suggests that ICANN should still collect registrants' names and addresses, but only make public their e-mail addresses. Only upon a "heightened showing by a rights holder" should ICANN release a registrant's name and address.[106]

6. ***Anonymity vs. Pseudonymity.*** Tal Zarsky argues that anonymity "come[s] at a high price to society" because "[i]n an anonymous society where locations, interactions, and transactions are hidden behind a veil of anonymity, the lack of accountability will spread to all areas of conduct, interfering with the formation of business and other relationships and allowing individuals to act without inhibitions." Zarsky contends that "traceable pseudonymity" is preferable because it "allows us to interact with consistent personalities" yet protects our "physical identity" and because it provides "accountability with partial anonymity."[107] What are the relative benefits and costs of traceable pseudonymity versus anonymity?

---

[106] Dawn C. Nunziato, *Freedom of Expression, Democratic Norms, and Internet Governance,* 52 Emory L.J. 187, 202, 257, 259 (2003).

[107] Tal Z. Zarsky, *Thinking Outside the Box: Considering Transparency, Anonymity, and Pseudonymity as Overall Solutions to the Problems of Information Privacy in the Internet Society,* 58 U. Miami L. Rev. 991, 1028, 1032, 1044 (2004).

(b) Reporter's Privilege

Another instance where anonymity plays an important role in promoting First Amendment rights is anonymity of sources who share information with journalists. One of the most famous anonymous sources was Deep Throat, the source that revealed information about the Watergate burglary and cover-up by the Nixon Administration to Bob Woodward and Carl Bernstein, reporters at *The Washington Post*. Their reporting ultimately lead to President Nixon's resig-nation.

In criminal and civil cases, there are often demands on journalists to reveal the identity of an anonymous source. Journalists have sought protection from divulging the information in what is called "reporter's privilege," "journalist privilege," or "journalist-source privilege."

First Amendment and Federal Recognition of Reporter's Privilege. In *Branzburg v. Hayes*, 408 U.S. 665 (1972), the Supreme Court held that there is no First Amendment reporter's privilege against grand jury requests for evidence. However, at the conclusion of the opinion, the Court noted that:

> [N]ews gathering is not without its First Amendment protections, and grand jury investigations if instituted or conducted other than in good faith, would pose wholly different issues for resolution under the First Amendment. . . . Grand juries are subject to judicial control and subpoenas to motions to quash. We do not expect courts will forget that grand juries must operate within the limits of the First Amendment as well as the Fifth.

Justice Powell, the swing vote in the 5-4 majority, wrote a concurrence to note that the "Court does not hold that newsmen, subpoenaed to testify before a grand jury, are without constitutional rights with respect to the gathering of news or in safeguarding their sources. . . . In short, the courts will be available to newsmen under circumstances where legitimate First Amendment interests require protection." Powell wrote that privilege claims should be assessed "by the striking of a proper balance between freedom of the press and the obligation of all citizens to give relevant testimony with respect to criminal conduct. The balance of these vital constitutional and societal interests on a case-by-case basis accords with the tried and traditional way of adjudicating such questions."

Following *Branzburg*, many federal circuit courts have recognized a qualified reporter's privilege. The reporter's privilege has fared much better in civil cases than in criminal ones.

State Recognition of Reporter's Privilege. In the states, the reporter's privilege has been recognized, with sources in state constitutions, state statutes, and common law. Forty-nine states and the District of Columbia have recognized it.[108] In most states, there is a qualified reporter's privilege, which can be overridden if the government establishes that it has no alternative way to obtain the information and that there is a compelling interest to do so. About 13 states have an absolute privilege, which cannot be overridden.

---

[108] Geoffrey R. Stone, *We Need a Federal Journalist-Source Privilege NOW*, Huffington Post (Feb. 21, 2007), http://www.huffingtonpost.com/geoffrey-r-stone/we-need-a-federal-journal_b_41747.html.

Currently, there is no reporter's privilege recognized under the Federal Rules of Evidence. In calling for such a privilege Geoffrey Stone argues that at "the hands of unrestrained federal prosecutors, journalists have taken a serious battering." He contends:

> A strong and effective journalist-source privilege is essential to a robust and independent press and to a well-functioning democratic society. It is in society's interest to encourage those who possess information of significant public value to convey it to the public, but without a journalist-source privilege, such communication will often be chilled because sources fear retribution, embarrassment or just plain getting "involved."[109]

Do you think that such a privilege should exist? Would sources with important information about companies come forward if they risked potential losing their jobs? Would sources come forward with information about the government if they risked criminal prosecution? On the other hand, if sources remain anonymous, would that allow them to divulge information and escape punishment?

2. PRIVACY OF READING AND INTELLECTUAL EXPLORATION

Privacy is also central to the exploration of ideas. Neil Richards contends that the First Amendment protects what he calls "intellectual privacy." According to Richards:

> Intellectual privacy is the ability, whether protected by law or social circumstances, to develop ideas and beliefs away from the unwanted gaze or interference of others. Surveillance or interference can warp the integrity of our freedom of thought and can skew the way we think, with clear repercussions for the content of our subsequent speech or writing.[110]

To what extent does the First Amendment protect a person's right to privacy in reading, Web-surfing, and exploration of ideas?

STANLEY V. GEORGIA

394 U.S. 557 (1969)

MARSHALL, J. . . . An investigation of appellant's alleged bookmaking activities led to the issuance of a search warrant for appellant's home. Under authority of this warrant, federal and state agents secured entrance. They found very little evidence of bookmaking activity, but while looking through a desk drawer in an upstairs bedroom, one of the federal agents, accompanied by a state officer, found three reels of eight-millimeter film. Using a projector and screen found in an upstairs living room, they viewed the films. The state officer concluded that they were obscene and seized them. Since a further examination of the bedroom indicated that appellant occupied it, he was charged with possession of obscene matter and placed under arrest. He was later indicted for "knowingly hav(ing)

---

[109] *Id.*

[110] Neil M. Richards, *Intellectual Privacy,* 87 Tex. L. Rev. 387, 389 (2008).

possession of . . . obscene matter" in violation of Georgia law. Appellant was tried before a jury and convicted. . . .

Appellant argues here . . . that the Georgia obscenity statute, insofar as it punishes mere private possession of obscene matter, violates the First Amendment. . . . [W]e agree that the mere private possession of obscene matter cannot constitutionally be made a crime. . . .

It is true that *Roth* does declare, seemingly without qualification, that obscenity is not protected by the First Amendment. That statement has been repeated in various forms in subsequent cases. However, neither *Roth* nor any subsequent decision of this Court dealt with the precise problem involved in the present case. Roth was convicted of mailing obscene circulars and advertising, and an obscene book, in violation of a federal obscenity statute. . . . None of the statements cited by the Court in *Roth* for the proposition that "this Court has always assumed that obscenity is not protected by the freedoms of speech and press" were made in the context of a statute punishing mere private possession of obscene material; the cases cited deal for the most part with use of the mails to distribute objectionable material or with some form of public distribution or dissemination. Moreover, none of this Court's decisions subsequent to *Roth* involved prosecution for private possession of obscene materials. Those cases dealt with the power of the State and Federal Governments to prohibit or regulate certain public actions taken or intended to be taken with respect to obscene matter. . . .

In this context, we do not believe that this case can be decided simply by citing *Roth*. . . .

It is now well established that the Constitution protects the right to receive information and ideas. "This freedom (of speech and press) . . . necessarily protects the right to receive. . . ." This right to receive information and ideas, regardless of their social worth, is fundamental to our free society. Moreover, in the context of this case — a prosecution for mere possession of printed or filmed matter in the privacy of a person's own home — that right takes on an added dimension. . . .

These are the rights that appellant is asserting in the case before us. He is asserting the right to read or observe what he pleases — the right to satisfy his intellectual and emotional needs in the privacy of his own home. He is asserting the right to be free from state inquiry into the contents of his library. Georgia contends that appellant does not have these rights, that there are certain types of materials that the individual may not read or even possess. Georgia justifies this assertion by arguing that the films in the present case are obscene. But we think that mere categorization of these films as "obscene" is insufficient justification for such a drastic invasion of personal liberties guaranteed by the First and Fourteenth Amendments. Whatever may be the justifications for other statutes regulating obscenity, we do not think they reach into the privacy of one's own home. If the First Amendment means anything, it means that a State has no business telling a man, sitting alone in his own house, what books he may read or what films he may watch. Our whole constitutional heritage rebels at the thought of giving government the power to control men's minds. . . .

We hold that the First and Fourteenth Amendments prohibit making mere private possession of obscene material a crime. *Roth* and the cases following that decision are not impaired by today's holding. As we have said, the States retain broad power to regulate obscenity; that power simply does not extend to mere possession by the individual in the privacy of his own home. Accordingly, the judgment of the court below is reversed and the case is remanded for proceedings not inconsistent with this opinion.

NOTES & QUESTIONS

1. *Possession of Obscenity Outside the Home.* Stanley possessed obscene material that Georgia could constitutionally outlaw because the First Amendment does not protect obscenity. According to the Court, states can ban obscene films outside the home. Thus, were Stanley to step outside the door with his films, a police officer could arrest him. Should Stanley's location inside his home make any difference? Suppose Stanley possessed and used illegal narcotics in his home. Does the state have any business telling a person, sitting alone in her home, what substances she may or may not ingest?

2. *The Limits of* **Stanley.** In *Osborne v. Ohio,* 495 U.S. 103 (1990), the Court held that the rule in *Stanley* does not apply to the possession of child pornography in the home:

   > In *Stanley,* Georgia primarily sought to proscribe the private possession of obscenity because it was concerned that obscenity would poison the minds of its viewers. We responded that "[w]hatever the power of the state to control public dissemination of ideas inimical to the public morality, it cannot constitutionally premise legislation on the desirability of controlling a person's private thoughts." The difference here is obvious: The State does not rely on a paternalistic interest in regulating Osborne's mind. Rather, Ohio has enacted § 2907.323(A)(3) in order to protect the victims of child pornography; it hopes to destroy a market for the exploitative use of children.

3. *The First Amendment and Postal Mail.* In *Lamont v. Postmaster General of the United States,* 381 U.S. 301 (1965), a 1962 federal statute required that all mail (except sealed letters) that originates or is prepared in a foreign country and is determined by the Secretary of the Treasury to be "communist political propaganda" be detained at the post office. The addressee would be notified of the matter, and the mail would be delivered to the addressee only upon her request. The Court struck down the statute on First Amendment grounds:

   > We rest on the narrow ground that the addressee in order to receive his mail must request in writing that it be delivered. This amounts in our judgment to an unconstitutional abridgment of the addressee's First Amendment rights. The addressee carries an affirmative obligation which we do not think the Government may impose on him. This requirement is almost certain to have a deterrent effect, especially as respects those who have sensitive positions. Their livelihood may be dependent on a security clearance. Public officials like schoolteachers who have no tenure, might think they would invite disaster if they read what the Federal Government says contains the seeds of treason. Apart from them, any addressee is likely to feel some inhibition in sending for literature which federal officials have condemned as "communist political propaganda." The regime of this Act is at war with the "uninhibited, robust, and wide-open debate and discussion" that are contemplated by the First Amendment.

4. ***Anonymous Reading and Receiving of Ideas.*** In *Tattered Cover, Inc. v. City of Thornton,* 44 P.3d 1044 (Colo. 2002), law enforcement officials (local City of Thornton police and a federal DEA agent) suspected that a methamphetamine lab was being operated out of a trailer home. On searching through some garbage from the trailer, an officer discovered evidence of drug operations and a mailing envelope from the Tattered Cover bookstore addressed to one of the suspects (Suspect A). There was an invoice and order number corresponding to the books shipped in the envelope, but no evidence about what those books were. Subsequently, a search warrant was obtained for the trailer home. In the bedroom, the police discovered a methamphetamine laboratory and drugs. Although there were a number of suspects, the police believed that Suspect A occupied the bedroom. Among the items seized from the bedroom were two books: *Advanced Techniques of Clandestine Psychedelic and Amphetamine Manufacture,* by Uncle Fester, and *The Construction and Operation of Clandestine Drug Laboratories,* by Jack B. Nimble.

The officers believed that these books were the ones mailed to Suspect A in the mailing envelope from the Tattered Cover found in the trash. The officers served The Tattered Cover with a DEA administrative subpoena, but Tattered Cover refused to comply, citing concern for its customers' privacy and First Amendment rights. The City then obtained a search warrant to search the bookstore's records. The Tattered Cover sued to enjoin the officers from executing the warrant.

The Colorado Supreme Court held that Colorado's First Amendment protects "the right to receive information and ideas." According to the court, "Everyone must be permitted to discover and consider the full range of expression and ideas available in our 'marketplace of ideas.' " The court further reasoned:

> Bookstores are places where a citizen can explore ideas, receive information, and discover myriad perspectives on every topic imaginable. When a person buys a book at a bookstore, he engages in activity protected by the First Amendment because he is exercising his right to read and receive ideas and information. Any governmental action that interferes with the willingness of customers to purchase books, or booksellers to sell books, thus implicates First Amendment concerns. . . .
>
> The need to protect anonymity in the context of the First Amendment has particular applicability to book-buying activity. . . . The right to engage in expressive activities anonymously, without government intrusion or observation, is critical to the protection of the First Amendment rights of book buyers and sellers, precisely because of the chilling effects of such disclosures. Search warrants directed to bookstores, demanding information about the reading history of customers, intrude upon the First Amendment rights of customers and bookstores because compelled disclosure of book-buying records threatens to destroy the anonymity upon which many customers depend. . . .

In contrast to the U.S. Supreme Court, which held in *Zurcher v. Stanford Daily,* 436 U.S. 547 (1978) that First Amendment concerns of government searches of expressive material can be satisfied by the government obtaining a search warrant, the Colorado Supreme Court concluded the state's First Amendment "requires a more substantial justification from the government," which must "demonstrate a sufficiently compelling need for the specific customer purchase record sought from the innocent, third-party bookstore."

In applying this standard, the court noted that the government desired the evidence about the books to link Suspect A to the master bedroom where the lab was located along with the books. The court, however, concluded that physical evidence and witnesses could have been used to establish this fact.

The City also argued that proof that Suspect A purchased the books would link him to the crime. But the court rejected this argument:

> The dangers, both to Suspect A and to the book-buying public, of permitting the government to access the information it seeks, and to use this proof of purchase as evidence of Suspect A's guilt, are grave. Assuming that Suspect A purchased the books in question, he may have done so for any of a number of reasons, many of which are in no way linked to his commission of any crime. He might have bought them for a friend or roommate, unaware that they would subsequently be placed in the vicinity of an illegal drug lab. He might have been curious about the process of making drugs, without having any intention to act on what he read.

Do you agree with the decision in *Tattered Cover* that, in addition to the right to speak anonymously, there is also a right to read anonymously? Does such a right follow logically from the Supreme Court's freedom of association and anonymity cases?

Consider the following argument by Julie Cohen:

> For the most part, First Amendment jurisprudence has defined readers' rights only incidentally. Historically, both courts and commentators have been more concerned with protecting speakers than with protecting readers. . . .
>
> Logically, that zone of protection should encompass the entire series of intellectual transactions through which [speakers] formed the opinions they ultimately chose to express. Any less protection would chill inquiry, and as a result, public discourse, concerning politically and socially controversial issues — precisely those areas where vigorous public debate is most needed, and most sacrosanct.[111]

How far can the rationale of *Tattered Cover* be extended? Suppose the police obtained a search warrant for one's home and sought to seize a person's diary? Would such a seizure be subject to strict scrutiny? What about the search of one's computer, which can reveal anonymous speech as well as one's online reading activities? Isn't the government's questioning of various witnesses to whom a person spoke also likely to interfere with that person's expressive activities? Why are books different (or are they)?

---

[111] Julie E. Cohen, *A Right to Read Anonymously: A Closer Look at "Copyright Management" in Cyberspace*, 28 Conn. L. Rev. 981 (1996); *see also* Marc Jonathan Blitz, *Constitutional Safeguards for Silent Experiments in Living Libraries, the Right to Read, and a First Amendment Theory for an Unaccompanied Right to Receive Information*, 74 U. Mo. Kan. City L. Rev. 799, 881-82 (2006).

INDEX